(1987-
Lot Ed.)

Publications of
The Colonial Society of Massachusetts
Volume 63

# Seventeenth-Century

# New England

A CONFERENCE HELD BY

The Colonial Society of Massachusetts

JUNE 18 AND 19, 1982

The Colonial Society of Massachusetts

BOSTON · 1984

*Distributed by The University Press of Virginia*

VOLUME EDITORS

*David D. Hall*
*David Grayson Allen*

Philip Chadwick Foster Smith
*Associate Editor*
*The Colonial Society of Massachusetts*

# Contents

# Illustrations

# Foreword

FOR more than a decade, the Colonial Society of Massachusetts has sponsored periodic conferences devoted to the illumination of specific areas of life and living during the colonial era of America. Each conference, in turn, has resulted in one or more volumes published by the Society and subsequently distributed by the University Press of Virginia. Thus, the series to date has explored in considerable detail the intricacies of American colonial architecture, furniture, medicine, music, prints and printmakers, and seafaring. To these is now added *Seventeenth-Century New England*. Others volumes concerning colonial law and music are forthcoming in the not-too-distant future.

A brainchild of the late Walter Muir Whitehill, for many years the Society's principal shaker, mover, and motive spirit, these conferences and their attendant volumes have filled numerous gaps in the existing literature and have tapped the knowledge, the fruits of continuing research, and the current thinking of many a preeminent scholar in the various fields they have addressed. Each conference and volume, however, has borne the mark not only of Walter Muir Whitehill and his successor as the Society's Editor of Publications, Frederick S. Allis, Jr., but also of the individual conference organizers, who have labored diligently as well to gather, organize, scrutinize, and prepare the papers for publication.

As the Society's Associate Editor deputed to undertake the overall production responsibility for the present work, I must commend the energy and dedication of Messrs. David Grayson Allen and David D. Hall. The "two Davids," as they have become known to Fritz Allis and me, have constantly striven for excellence and have had no small part in the editing process as a result. We are both in their debt for their monumental labors, and I, especially, thank them both for their patient assistance over the past eighteen months.

*Seventeenth-Century New England* is an unusual volume, as I am sure its readers will agree. That it is, is entirely due to the doggedness of these two scholars and to their colleagues who have thoughtfully kindled lamps in many an obscure corner of our colonial legacy.

PHILIP CHADWICK FOSTER SMITH
Associate Editor

*Bath, Maine*
*September 1984*

# Introduction

GREAT anniversaries summon us to commemorate the past. The 350th anniversary of the founding of Massachusetts also called for something more. It challenged us to think anew about the meaning of the seventeenth century, a complex period that found the American colonists still recognizably English, yet somehow set apart from European culture and society.

This task of reappraisal was central to "New England Begins," a major exhibition at the Boston Museum of Fine Arts.[1] "New England Begins" celebrated a New England that did not correspond to stock wisdom or standard images. The glories of the exhibition were the abundance of portraits, furniture, and silver that in their glowing colors and elaborated forms silently rebuked old and still persistent notions that the Puritanism of the colonists or the harshness of a frontier settlement had stifled the artistic impulse. To the contrary, "New England Begins" was a convincing demonstration of high standards and sophistication—of continuity, not of change or deprivation. Here were works of art that flowed from an aesthetic originating in Catholic Italy. Here, too, were other forms of culture embodying a deep, almost instinctive, conservatism, as in the Latin broadsides from Harvard College commencements or maps portraying how the colonists imposed themselves upon the wilderness. The theme of "New England Begins" was undoubtedly the transfer of culture from Europe to America.

It was no accident that this was the theme of the exhibition or that its scope was so encompassing. From the moment of its inception, the planning of "New England Begins" was entrusted to an interdisci-

1. "New England Begins" opened on 5 May 1982 and closed on 22 August. The rebuilding program at the Museum of Fine Arts was a principal reason why the exhibition did not coincide exactly with the 350th anniversary (1980).

plinary group chaired by the Curator of American Decorative Arts, Jonathan L. Fairbanks, and including members of his staff, as well as historians from other institutions in the Boston area. Early on, this group sensed that the issues being raised would merit more attention than the exhibition by itself would offer. The Colonial Society of Massachusetts agreed to be the sponsor of a conference addressed to such issues and entrusted the planning to David D. Hall and David Grayson Allen, both of whom were also engaged with the development of the exhibition. *Seventeenth-Century New England* contains all the essays that were presented at this conference, which met in Boston on 18 and 19 June 1982. The essays are grouped here, as they were for the conference itself, into two broad categories: Economy and Society and Religion and Mentality.

To its organizers the conference seemed to coincide with a new phase of New England studies. The 1960's and early 1970's had witnessed an influx of ideas and energies that cumulatively transformed the social history of colonial New England. Much of this influx was in the form of local studies of a single town. A cluster of books deserve to be mentioned as inaugurating this transformation: histories of seventeenth-century Sudbury and Boston by Sumner C. Powell and Darrett Rutman, and, in 1970, the *annus mirabilis* of such local studies, histories of Andover and Dedham by Philip Greven and Kenneth Lockridge.[2]

Several lines of influence would converge in these local histories and their successors. One was certainly the methods of historical demography as they had been popularized by the British historian Peter Laslett in *The World We Have Lost*. Laslett himself acknowledged the primacy of French historical demography, and some Americans went directly to that work. Various of the social sciences were influential in suggesting that history must rest upon quantifiable data that was used to test hypotheses and to construct models. Some older kinds of history, and especially intellectual or religious history, seemed

2. Sumner C. Powell, *Puritan Village: The Formation of a New England Town* (Middletown, Conn., 1963); Darrett B. Rutman, *Winthrop's Boston: Portrait of a Puritan Town* (Chapel Hill, N.C., 1965); Philip J. Greven, *Four Generations: Population, Land, and Family in Colonial Andover, Massachusetts* (Ithaca, N.Y., 1970); Kenneth A. Lockridge, *A New England Town: The First Hundred Years* (New York, 1970).

quite lacking in this regard. From France came yet another strand of thinking, the emphasis associated with the *Annales* school on peasants in the setting of rural society. Local history as practiced by British historians provided something of a counterpart to an ideal type of peasant communalism, for English towns and villages appeared immensely different one from another. There were general patterns, to be sure, but these patterns were unevenly dominant depending on such factors as soil type and distances to market. Out of English social history came, therefore, the concept of localism. In general, the French and British points of view served to suggest that change came slowly in rural society.

These overlapping strands of influence were crucial to the conference and the exhibition. Consider, for example, the twin themes of continuity and cultural transfer. Scarcely twenty years ago historians of colonial America were emphasizing the disruptive consequences of immigration to the New World. The thrust of their argument was that a series of circumstances—the uprooting from an ordered web of relationships, the actual voyage to America, and most importantly, the "disorder" resulting from frustrated expectations—had functioned to Americanize the colonists, making them a people accustomed to disorder and fluidity, and America a society that lacked stable institutions. The history of the family seemed paradigmatic of this process; by comparison with Europe, the structure of the colonial family—so it was argued—became looser and less hierarchical as authority shifted from fathers to sons.[3]

This understanding of the seventeenth century would rapidly collapse as historians rediscovered the stability of New World institutions. The most stable institution of all now seemed to be the seventeenth-century New England family, with the town not far behind. By comparison with Europe, the demographers were demonstrating that the colonists lived longer and raised more children to adulthood. As for continuity, these families had practiced an inheritance system that functioned to preserve enough land—the essential form of economic security—in the hands of successive generations. "Familial

3. Oscar Handlin, "The Significance of the Seventeenth Century," in *Seventeenth-Century America*, ed. James M. Smith (Chapel Hill, N.C., 1959), 3–12.

continuity" and the social norm of consensus made the seventeenth-century New England town seem highly "traditional," so much so, indeed, that some historians began to liken them to "peasant" communities. The old assumption that Americans "have been a permanently uprooted and mobile people from the beginning," yielded to an emphasis on stability and order.[4] And in place of the assumption that Americans began anew, improvising in response to the wilderness, appeared the story of the persistence of "English ways" in architecture, crops, and field systems. Moreover, the localism of English landed society would carry over to the colonies; these distinct units of culture were transported across the Atlantic in the minds of people who, in exchanging Europe for America, intended (consciously or not) to recreate familiar ways of doing things.[5] Instead of reading the social history of post-Revolutionary America back into colonial times, historians were locating early New England within the context of European rural life.

Some of this revisionism has not stood the test of time, and certain lines of inquiry have proved less fruitful than anticipated. That the emphasis upon stability was overstated would become evident from a careful reappraisal of mobility rates in England and New England.[6] Historians in the 1950's had erred in regarding English society as extremely stable and hierarchical. Ironically, historians of the New England town were committing the same mistake. To characterize these towns as "peasant" societies was useful insofar as the term drew attention to an ethos of communal solidarity and to the nexus of land ownership, inheritance patterns, and family structure. Otherwise the term had little relevance to a society in which land was owned in freehold and where most adult males participated vigorously (or could, if they wished) in wider political, economic, and religious systems. In Bernard Bailyn's afterword to the essays in *Seventeenth-*

4. Greven, *Four Generations*, 268–269; Lockridge, *A New England Town*, 19–20.

5. The most self-conscious adaptation of "localism" to New England history is David Grayson Allen, *In English Ways: The Movement of Societies and the Transferal of English Local Law and Custom to Massachusetts Bay in the Seventeenth Century* (Chapel Hill, N.C., 1981).

6. W. R. Prest, "Stability and Change in Old and New England: Clayworth and Dedham," *Journal of Interdisciplinary History*, 6 (1976), 359–374.

*Century New England*, he notes that none of them employ the word "frontier." Nor do any invoke "peasant" culture or society.[7] Instead these essays suggest adaptation and flexibility in response to market forces. Another difference between these essays and New England studies of some fifteen years ago is their silence on demography and family structure. We have learned much about these topics, yet the data remains inconsistent, incomplete, or curiously without broad meaning. The editors have therefore preferred other topics. There remains the question of when and with what consequences the colonists were drawn into a market economy. For England itself, the transition may have occurred long before the founding of the colonies.[8] Some of the emigrants—certainly the fishermen who formed transient communities along the coast, but also many of the merchants and even, possibly, the farmers who emigrated from particular areas of England—were entrepreneurial in spirit.

The opening series of essays in *Seventeenth-Century New England* explain the interplay of environment and culture, of land, labor, and capital. Karen Ordahl Kupperman addresses a factor that has long deserved more adequate attention, the climate of early New England. Describing the weather that the colonists experienced, she also tells a story of long held expectations, reluctant adaptation, and realities that darkened the mood of the colonists in the closing decades of the century. Joan Thirsk describes experiments in agriculture and cropping among English farmers from about 1640 to 1750. Her essay reinforces the conclusion, long held by agricultural historians, that pre-industrial farmers lived in a dynamic world and were responsive to new crops, markets, and opportunities created by general economic changes. David Grayson Allen reviews the similarities between seventeenth-century England and New England before exploring local life in four Connecticut towns where the replication of English regional patterns was wider and more striking than has been found in comparable Massachusetts communities. Allen also analyzes several

---

7. John W. Adams, "Consensus, Community, and Exoticism," *Journal of Interdisciplinary History*, 12 (1981), 253–265.

8. As Alan Macfarlane speculates in *The Origins of English Individualism* (Oxford, 1978).

dimensions of New England localism and the degrees to which "English ways" persisted throughout the region's early history. Daniel Vickers' study of Essex County fishermen illustrates the cultural gap between the "worldly fishing periphery of New England [and] its settled Puritan core." According to Vickers, the mainland colonists found it necessary for their economic survival to coexist with non-Puritan outsiders who, like other fishermen scattered along the Atlantic coast, lived in rough-and-tumble communities of their own.

The final essay in this section brings the vantage point of the historical geographer to bear upon the history of settlement in the Northwest Atlantic. Cole Harris describes a process of elimination and recombination in culture and economy as Europeans moved into the wilderness or set about harvesting the abundance of the sea. New relationships among land, labor, and capital, and selective pressures of the environment made it impossible, he argues, to recreate the "complex texture" of European society. His essay is a tale of change, but also of continuities.

The question of Puritanism and its significance is as inescapable as the question of continuity or change. Even more so than in the social history of early New England, the conference coincided with a shift in direction. To place this shift in perspective, we must return to the town studies and especially to Darrett Rutman's *Winthrop's Boston*. Rutman was reacting to the work of Perry Miller, who in two magisterial books, *The New England Mind: the Seventeenth Century* and *The New England Mind: From Colony to Province*, had described Puritanism as a complex intellectual system. But from Rutman's point of view Miller had failed to demonstrate that the pronouncements of the ministry expressed in any way the thinking of ordinary citizens. A telling fact for Rutman was the diminishing number of Bostonians who were church members. In place of intellectual and institutional coherence—which was what Rutman took Puritanism to mean—he described a community that was "fragmented almost from the very beginning," one that improvised a church order and contradicted in practice its ideals of peace and order.[9]

9. Rutman, *Winthrop's Boston*, viii.

Suddenly it seemed as though Puritanism was not a powerful factor in the making of New England. In an important study of the merchants who engaged in international trade, Bernard Bailyn had previously argued that this group resented the social norms of the magistrates and ministers, preferring flexibility and the values of the marketplace to any *a priori* or communal ethics. As the merchants rose, Puritanism waned.[1] Was decline and fragmentation the story of New England Puritanism? Even in the agrarian community of Sudbury, the minister was unable to preserve peace when disputes broke out in the 1650's over the division of the town commons. Farmers seemed more concerned with land and family security than with salvation. When social historians happened to refer to Puritanism, they had in mind not a highly elaborated theological system but an ethic of communal harmony and attitudes toward childrearing, neither of which was unique to the colonists.

The importance of Puritanism was called into question, finally, by new work on popular belief in early modern Europe. As Keith Thomas demonstrated in *Religion and the Decline of Magic*, ordinary people in seventeenth-century England resorted to all sorts of beliefs that did not square with Protestant Christianity. Indeed these were beliefs that helped such people to meet spiritual and psychological needs that Protestants ignored or tried to force in other channels. *Religion and the Decline of Magic* seemed to differentiate popular religion from the religion of orthodox and zealous Protestants, and in doing so, opened the way to suggestions that many of the colonists preferred occult or "magical" beliefs to the tenets of the ministers.[2]

Separately from this turmoil, literary historians and historians of religion were revising Miller's portrait of New England Puritanism. According to more recent studies, the sermons of the ministers were less concerned with issues of free will and God's sovereignty than with experiential piety. An emphasis on conversion, and, more broadly, on religion as *experience*, emerged in Edmund S. Morgan's *Visible*

---

1. Bernard Bailyn, *The New England Merchants in the Seventeenth Century* (Cambridge, Mass., 1955).

2. Keith Thomas, *Religion and the Decline of Magic* (London, 1971).

*Saints: The History of a Puritan Idea* and in several other books.[3] Patterns of experience became the basis for institutionalized procedures, for Morgan demonstrated that the colonists' familiarity with conversion underlay their conception of church membership. Another theme that Miller had neglected was the colonists' expectation that Christ's kingdom would soon be reestablished. Apocalyptic expectations had surrounded and sustained the migration to New England and the emergence of Congregationalism. Could this apocalypticism be described as "popular religion"? In effect, religion was becoming more inclusive, a matter of ritual, experience, and prophecy as well as of the covenantal relationship between God's will and man's. As several of these essays demonstrate, religious motifs in this broad sense penetrated far into the culture of the colonists.

The conference thus took place at a time when the history of New England Puritanism and the history of New England society seemed no longer as divergent. The essays on religion and mentality all take up the task of finding bridges. Lillian B. Miller's essay on the portrait in seventeenth-century New England takes as its point of the departure the false stereotype that Puritanism was hostile to the art of the portrait. She demonstrates that portrait painting in New England incorporated motifs common to many English portraits of the Tudor-Stuart period; the colonial artist may have been responsive to Puritanism, but he also worked within a broader tradition. Inquiring into the nature of lay Puritanism, Steven Foster describes the emergence of a "militance" in late sixteenth- and early seventeenth-century England that had important consequences on both sides of the Atlantic. Foster challenges the story of "declension," pointing out that in late seventeenth-century New England the ministers implemented new strategies that were effective in sustaining lay commitment. As Foster views it, popular Puritanism was closely linked with the Puritanism of the ministry.

David D. Hall describes a lore of portents and prodigies that was credible to many Europeans and Americans in the seventeenth cen-

---

3. Edmund S. Morgan, *Visible Saints: The History of a Puritan Idea* (New York, 1963); Charles Hambrick-Stowe, *The Practice of Piety: Puritan Devotional Disciplines in Seventeenth-Century New England* (Chapel Hill, N.C., 1982).

tury. This lore was surely "popular," as the printing history of such stories indicates, and it circulated in New England via story telling. Yet the ministry was as much involved as were the plain people to whom they preached their sermons. Hall concludes that Puritanism was far more tolerant of folk belief than most historians have assumed, and, like Foster, he disputes the distinction of the religion of the ministers from the religion of the people. Robert St. George takes up the meaning of speech among the colonists, and finds it richly significant. Speech was threatening to these people, and in explicating its dangers, St. George uncovers structures of belief, as in the significance of gender, that owed little or nothing to Puritanism per se. These two essays tell of collective beliefs, a folklore if you will, that was endemic in late medieval culture. In this regard the colonists seem remarkably traditional in their mentality, even though as Puritans they were breaking with the past.

These concluding essays underscore the persistence and power of deeply rooted habits and beliefs. The essays in *Seventeenth-Century New England* acknowledge change and innovation while placing their main emphasis upon continuity. In arguing for a popular Puritanism, several of these essays help dispell the spectre of a social history without religion; they also make it plain that culture in New England was enriched or inherited from several directions. Many questions remain unanswered. Historians of material culture have mapped several different regions of production within New England. Are these regions meaningfully discrete in other respects? Authority became decentralized in early New England with the rise of the town. Yet most (if not all) of these towns remained parts of some larger whole. What were the patterns that linked these scores of semi-isolated communities? In what ways was rural society in New England responsive to a marketplace that stretched across to Europe? And was there a transition point within the century, a moment when the agrarian economy entered a new phase or when the mechanisms of consensus faltered?

We leave to the curious reader the task of adding to this list of queries and the pleasure of finding answers to them in the pages of *Seventeenth-Century New England*. It has been a singularly comfortable experience to share with the Editor of Publications for the Colonial Society, Frederick S. Allis, and the Associate Editor, Philip Chadwick Foster Smith, the preparation of this book for publication. We are grateful to Fritz Allis and Sinclair Hitchings for undertaking, with patience and skill, all of the housekeeping tasks associated with the conference of 18 and 19 June 1982. These essays contain little direct trace of the audience to which they were initially presented. Yet in the best tradition of the Colonial Society comments from the floor were informed and argumentative. To all those who, by participating in the discussions, helped enrich our understanding of the past, we offer a final word of thanks.

DAVID D. HALL
DAVID GRAYSON ALLEN

# SEVENTEENTH-CENTURY
# NEW ENGLAND

◆◦ KAREN ORDAHL KUPPERMAN ◦◆

# Climate and Mastery of the Wilderness in Seventeenth-Century New England

Of all the preconceptions English people brought with them to New England, perhaps none was so important or so mistaken as that about the American climate. Colonists came with the common sense idea that climate would be constant in any given latitude around the world. New England, whose latitude is the low forties, was expected to have the climate of Spain or southern France. The debilitating effect of excessive summer heat on English character was the promoters' main fear in the early years. What they found, of course, was that New England was in fact very hot in summer but that it was also extremely cold, much colder than England, in winter. Colonists were forced to make sense of their actual experience of America's climate, explaining why New England deviated from the "normal" European climate, as well as trying to understand what would grow and how life should be constituted here.

The physical challenge may have been made more severe by the fact that much of the northern hemisphere, probably including northern North America, was in the grip of the Little Ice Age, during which the growing season was shortened by as much as three weeks to a month in northern England and Scotland, and some areas in Europe went out of cultivation altogether. The coldest period of the

Karen Ordahl Kupperman is Associate Professor of History at the University of Connecticut.

Research for this article was supported by a Mellon Faculty Fellowship at Harvard University and by a grant from the University of Connecticut Research Foundation. The author wishes to thank David B. Quinn and Harry S. Stout for their very helpful suggestions.

3

Little Ice Age was from 1550 to 1700. Greatest winter cold and least summer warmth occurred in the 1590's, the first decade of the seventeenth century, the 1640's and the 1690's, and, especially in these decades, there were times of famine in northern England and in Scandinavia. The Thames froze for extended periods four times in the sixteenth, eight in the seventeenth, and six in the eighteenth centuries, something which had rarely happened before.[1]

This paper offers a reconstruction of the seventeenth-century New England climate from letters, diaries, and histories, and an analysis of how colonists perceived and explained weather phenomena.[2] There were several major shifts in weather patterns in the course of the century. The first determinable pattern was established during the 1630's and 1640's, the first decades of Massachusetts Bay's settlement. Another held sway during the 1650's, 1660's, and 1670's, and a third during the final decades. Because colonists saw weather phenomena, like all other natural events, as providential and therefore meaningful, these shifts contributed to changes in their self-perceptions and feelings about their mission in the New World.

Early English experience of winter cold in New England was dramatic. In 1607, when the London Virginia Company planted the colony of Jamestown, the western merchants' Virginia Company founded a colony at Sagadahoc in Maine. Partly because of the death

1. H. H. Lamb, *Climate: Present, Past, and Future*, 2 vols. (London, 1972, 1977), II, 463; and his *The Changing Climate* (London, 1966), 11, 65, 144; John Gribbin and H. H. Lamb, "Climatic Change in Historical Times," in John Gribbin, ed., *Climatic Change* (Cambridge, 1978), 70–71; Martin L. Parry, *Climatic Change, Agriculture, and Settlement* (Hamden, Conn., 1978), 38–39, 66, 163–168; Andrew B. Appleby, *Famine in Tudor and Stuart England* (Stanford, Calif., 1978); and "Epidemics and Famine in the Little Ice Age," *Journal of Interdisciplinary History*, X (1979–1980), 645; John D. Post, "Climatic Change and Historical Explanation," ibid., 296; Gustav Utterstrom, "Climatic Fluctuations and Population Problems in Early Modern History," *Scandinavian Economic History Review*, III (1955), 3–47. Professor Lamb sees evidence of severe weather in Asia during the seventeenth century. For a somewhat different interpretation of the evidence for the Little Ice Age, see Emmanuel LeRoy Ladurie, *Times of Feast, Times of Famine: A History of Climate Since the Year 1000*, trans. Barbara Bray (New York, 1971).

2. There apparently were no thermometers in New England in the seventeenth century, so this reconstruction relies on colonists' statements and evidence about the weather. All dates have been converted into New Style by the addition of 10 days, so readers can judge such weather events as first and last snowfall or frost by modern standards.

of its major sponsor, Lord Chief Justice John Popham, and other reversals, but also because of the severe winter, "fit to freeze the heart of a Plantation," that colony lasted less than a year. The winter of 1607–1608 was one of the landmark severe winters of the seventeenth century, when the Thames froze solid. After this failure New England was "esteemed as a cold, barren, mountainous, rocky Desert," and interest in colonization there was retarded.[3]

The Plymouth colonists wrote little about their early experience of the weather. They complained about the first winter, but this was apparently one in which the late November-early December weather was hard and the rest of the winter mild and rainy.[4] The summer of 1623 saw a long and nearly disastrous drought, which was ended by a day of prayer and humiliation.[5] William Wood of Massachusetts Bay repeated Indian lore that every ten years there is no real winter; to confirm this he pointed to the winter of 1620–1621, "no Winter in comparison," and the winter of 1629–1630, which he said was "a

3. Sir Ferdinando Gorges, *A briefe Relation of the Discovery and Plantation of New England*, 1622, reprinted in James Phinney Baxter, ed., *Sir Ferdinando Gorges and His Province of Maine*, 3 vols. (New York, 1967 [orig. publ. 1890]), I, 206–207; and *A Briefe Narration of the Originall Undertakings of the Advancement of Plantations Into the Parts of America*, 1658, ibid., II, 16–17; Raleigh Gilbert, quoted in Samuel Purchas, *Hakluytus Posthumus or Purchas His Pilgrimes*, 20 vols. (Glasgow, 1906 [orig. publ. 1625]), XIX, 296; Charles Edward Banks, "New Documents Relating to the Popham Expedition, 1607," American Antiquarian Society, *Proceedings*, XXXIX (1929), 318, 321, 324, 327, 330, 334; William Strachey, *The Historie of Travell into Virginea Britannia*, Louis B. Wright and Virginia Freund, eds. (London, 1953), 173; John Smith, *The Generall Historie of Virginia, New-England, and the Summer Isles*, in Edward Arber and A. G. Bradley, eds., *The Travels and Works of Captain John Smith*, 2 vols. (Edinburgh, 1910), II, 696; and Rev. William Hubbard, *A General History of New England from the Discovery to 1680*, 2d ed. (Boston, 1848), 37. See also Richard A. Preston, *Gorges of Plymouth Fort* (Toronto, 1953), 141–150; David M. Ludlum, *Early American Winters, 1604–1820* (Boston, 1966), 6; and Douglas R. McManis, *European Impressions of the New England Coast, 1497–1620*, University of Chicago Department of Geography, Research Paper No. 139 (Chicago, 1972), 106–108, 137.

4. William Bradford, *Of Plymouth Plantation, 1620–1647*, ed. Samuel Eliot Morison (New York, 1953), 70–71; Bradford and Edward Winslow, *A Relation or Journall of the English Plantation setled at Plimoth in New England* (London, 1622), 8–21, 25–30, 62, hereafter referred to by its common name, *Mourt's Relation*; Nathaniel Morton, *New Englands Memoriall* (Cambridge, Mass., 1669), 17–21; and William Wood, *New Englands Prospect* (London, 1634), 4.

5. Bradford, *Of Plymouth Plantation*, ed. Morison, 131–132; Edward Winslow, *Good Newes from New-England* (London, 1624), 48–50; and Morton, *New Englands Memoriall*, 37–39.

very milde season, little Frost, and lesse Snow, but cleare serene weather."[6] Wood came in the vanguard of the Great Migration. The main body faced a much harder winter in 1630–1631. The weather was gentle until the beginning of the new year, when it turned violently cold, and remained so through January and February. The frost broke on 20 February and both Wood and Winthrop recorded that it had done so on that exact date for many years. Therefore, Wood argued, the winter, though sharp, was not too long to bear.[7] The cold, wet spring and summer of 1632 were followed by an extremely cold winter, with an "extremity of . . . snow and frost." The summer of 1633 was hot and dry.[8] The mild but very snowy winter of 1633–1634 was followed by another hot summer in which a September hurricane spoiled the maize harvest. Winter in 1634–1635 came early and carried with it much snow and frost. In November of 1634 Winthrop recorded that no courts can be expected to meet in the three winter months, and many times during that winter people were forced to stay away from lectures because they could not travel.[9]

The winter of 1635 opened with a great hurricane in late August, which was so devastating that William Bradford wrote that "signs and marks of it will remain this hundred years," and dearth resulted from its harm to the harvest.[1] November and December were re-

6. Wood, *New Englands Prospect*, 4. Ludlum, *Early American Winters*, 12, identifies the second of these as the winter of 1629–1630.

7. Wood, *New Englands Prospect*; John Winthrop, *Winthrop's Journal: History of New England, 1630–1649*, ed. James Kendall Hosmer, 2 vols. (New York, 1908), I, 55–58; Hubbard, *General History of New England*, 136, 138; and Thomas Hutchinson, *The History of the Colony and Province of Massachusetts-Bay*, ed. Lawrence Shaw Mayo, 3 vols. (Cambridge, Mass., 1936 [orig. publ. 1765]), I, 22.

8. Winthrop, *History of New England*, ed. Hosmer, 95, 98; Edward Johnson, *Wonder-Working Providence of Sion's Saviour in New-England* (Andover, Mass., 1867 [orig. publ. 1654]), 55, 57–58; Hubbard, *General History of New England*, 194; and "The Early Records of Charlestown," in Alexander Young, ed., *Chronicles of the First Planters of Massachusetts Bay, 1623–1636* (New York, 1970 [orig. publ. 1846]), 385–386.

9. Winthrop, *History of New England*, ed. Hosmer, 114, 119, 137–138, 143, 146; and John Winthrop to John Winthrop, Jr., 12 December 1634, in Everett Emerson, ed., *Letters from New England: The Massachusetts Bay Colony, 1629–1638* (Amherst, Mass., 1976), 135; Johnson, *Wonder-Working Providence*, 57–58; and Hubbard, *General History of New England*, 197–198, 239; John Hull, "Diary," in American Antiquarian Society, *Transactions and Collections*, III (1857), 169.

1. Bradford, *Of Plymouth Plantation*, ed. Morison, 279–280; Winthrop, *History of*

corded as extremely cold and snowy. In the following April, Winthrop said the people who had moved into Connecticut had lost most of their cattle and were in "great straits for want of provisions."[2] June of 1637 was so hot that newcomers died of the heat, and Winthrop was forced to travel at night.[3] This hot summer was followed by the very hard winter of 1637–1638, in which the snow lay up to three feet deep from mid-November until early April. In January, the bay was frozen except for a small channel. Winthrop wrote to his son that in Connecticut "they were shutt up with snowe above a month since: and we at Boston were almost readye to breake up for want of wood."[4] The spring of 1638 was so cold that the seed rotted in the ground and had to be replanted several times, but then a warm season provided a good harvest.[5] An earthquake in June was thought by many to be responsible for an extremely rainy and stormy fall in 1638 and, according to Bradford, for several successive cool, wet summers, though May of 1639 was very hot and dry.[6] The period of 1639–1640 was another extremely sharp winter in New England "with very bitter blasts."[7]

The winter of 1640–1641 was cold and snowy, but it was far surpassed by the "intollerable peircing winter" of 1641–1642, of which Thomas Gorges wrote, "the like was never known by Inglish or Indian. It is incredible to relate the extremity of the weather. Fouls & fish lay frozen Flotinge thicke on the waters in the sea." John Win-

New England, ed. Hosmer, I, 155–157; Anthony Thacher to Peter Thacher, September 1635, in Emerson, ed., Letters from New England, 169; Richard Mather to William Rathband and Mr. T, 25 June 1636, ibid., 205; Hubbard, General History of New England, 162, 198–201, 239; John Josselyn, An Account of Two Voyages to New England, 2d ed., 1675, in Massachusetts Historical Society, Collections, 3d Ser., III (Boston, 1833), 380; Samuel Danforth, An Almanack (Cambridge, Mass., 1649); and Morton, New Englands Memoriall, 94–95.

2. Winthrop, History of New England, ed. Hosmer, I, 165, 167, 178; Hubbard, General History of New England, 306, 308.

3. Winthrop, History of New England, ed. Hosmer, I, 223.

4. Ibid., 258, 269; John Winthrop to John Winthrop, Jr., 22 January 1638, Winthrop Papers, 5 vols. (Boston, 1929–1947), IV, 10.

5. Winthrop, History of New England, ed. Hosmer, I, 270.

6. Ibid., 270–272, 278–279, 291, 306–307, Bradford, Of Plymouth Plantation, ed. Morison, 303; Danforth, Almanack, 1649; Josselyn, Two Voyages to New England, 227.

7. Johnson, Wonder-Working Providence, 137; John Josselyn, New-Englands Rarities Discovered (London, 1672), 109; and his Two Voyages to New England, 82.

throp also reported the winter cold was unprecedented in the Indians' experience, and he stressed that not only was Massachusetts Bay frozen out "to sea so far as one could well discern" and so thick that "horses and carts went over in many places where ships have sailed," but Chesapeake Bay, too, was similarly ice-covered. The snow in New England was very deep. The summers of the early 1640's also brought their distresses, for these hard winters were followed by the short, cold, wet summers which Bradford thought were caused by the earthquake of 1638. Thomas Gorges in Maine wrote of scarcity there in the spring of 1642, and by the following year scarcity was also being felt in Massachusetts, where dearth was compounded by hordes of corn-devouring pigeons.[8] The winter of 1642–1643 was the snowiest yet, but mild, and it was followed by the mild and dry winter of 1643–1644, which brought its own problems in the form of house fires.[9] Except for a late cold snowy period, the winter of 1644–1645 was also mild and dry until February, but the mildness and freedom from snow were paid for in the form of summer drought in 1644 and 1645.[1]

The season of 1645–1646 was another landmark hard winter, "the earliest and sharpest winter we had since our arrival in the country," according to Winthrop. As in 1642, he stressed that the extraordinary cold was felt to the south as well. "At New Haven a ship bound for England was forced to be cut out of the ice three miles. And in Virginia the ships were frozen up six weeks." John Winthrop, Jr., reported that the Connecticut River was frozen above Windsor.[2] The sudden onset of spring caused great floods, and the summer crops were attacked by swarms of caterpillars, which Winthrop thought were a quasi-meteo-

8. Thomas Gorges, *The Letters of Thomas Gorges, Deputy Governor of the Province of Maine, 1640–1643*, ed. Robert E. Moody (Portland, Maine, 1978), 49, 58, 92, 98, 100–101, 110; Winthrop, *History of New England*, ed. Hosmer, II, 45, 54–55, 57, 81–82, 90–92; Danforth, *Almanack*, 1649; Josselyn, *Two Voyages to New England*, 383; and Johnson, *Wonder-Working Providence*, 170.

9. Winthrop, *History of New England*, ed. Hosmer, II, 158.

1. Ibid., 220, 224; and W. DeLoss Love, Jr., *The Fast and Thanksgiving Days of New England* (Boston, 1895), 178, 319.

2. Winthrop, *History of New England*, ed. Hosmer, II, 263; John Winthrop, Jr., "Overland to Connecticut in 1645: A Travel Diary," trans. William R. Carlton, *New England Quarterly*, X (1937), 497, 501–505; and Hubbard, *General History of New England*, 322.

rological phenomenon, as they had fallen, according to "divers good observers," in a "great thunder shower."[3] The mild winter of 1646–1647 was followed by a summer drought severe enough to produce scarcity the following summer and an embargo on exports of grain until the harvest of 1648. In March of 1648 the Massachusetts Bay General Court decreed a day of humiliation in order to ward off another punishing summer. Winthrop attributed scarcity of corn in the summer of 1648 mostly to excessive exports, though he noted that corn was also scarce in Europe that year, indicating the possibility of a more widespread climatic effect. We know little about the weather in the rest of the 1640's, except that January of 1649 was unseasonably cold.[4]

By 1650, then, New England colonists were well aware of the extreme physical challenge posed by the harsh and turbulent New England climate. Cold had contributed to the failure of one colony, that at Sagadahoc, and the sources record much suffering, both from cold and famine, as a result of the extreme weather of the 1630's and especially of the 1640's. The American climate also presented an extreme intellectual challenge, one which colonists were quick to take up. The problem, simply stated, is that New England should not have been so cold. London is north of fifty degrees of latitude; New England lies between forty and forty-five degrees. Common sense told settlers that New England, being closer to the sun, by which they meant nearer the equator, must be warmer, winter and summer, than England. When they were forced to face conclusive evidence that New England was actually colder in winter than England, the possibility loomed that America was fundamentally defective.

Early reports reflected extreme confusion, some colonists affirming that New England was warmer winter and summer than England,

3. Winthrop, *History of New England*, ed. Hosmer, II, 264, 277; Danforth, *Almanack*, 1649; Johnson, *Wonder-Working Providence*, 214; "Rev. John Eliot's Records of the First Church in Roxbury, Massachusetts," *New England Historical and Genealogical Register*, XXXIII (1879), 65.

4. Winthrop, *History of New England*, ed. Hosmer, II, 341; Nathaniel B. Shurtleff, ed., *Records of the Governor and Company of the Massachusetts Bay in New England*, 6 vols. in 5 (Boston, 1853–1854), II, 229–230, 240; Eliot, "Roxbury Church Records," 65, 237; and Thomas Olcott to John Winthrop, Jr., 8 January 1649, *Winthrop Papers*, V, 301.

others saying it was colder in all seasons. Bartholomew Gosnold thought the problem was that the seasons were displaced, with spring and fall both beginning later than in Europe.[5] Everyone was puzzled, as was, for example, Edward Winslow of Plymouth in 1624:

Then for the temperature of the air, in almost three years' experience I can scarce distinguish New England from Old England, in respect of heat and cold, frost, snow, rain, winds, &c. Some object, because our Plantation lieth in the latitude of 42 degrees, it must needs be much hotter. I confess I cannot give the reason of the contrary; only experience teacheth us, that if it do exceed England, it is so little as must require better judgments to discern it. And for the winter, I rather think (if there be difference) it is both sharper and longer in New England than Old.

Winslow thought it might have been lack of the comforts of home which made colonists feel colder than they should.[6] Confusion continued into the 1630's and 1640's, and the stumbling block remained the latitude of New England as compared to Europe. John Smith wrote that New England was at the mean for heat and cold, because it lies near forty-five degrees, midway between the pole and the equator. Thomas Morton similarly said New England was at the "golden meane" and "doth participate of heate and cold indifferently." He affirmed that though it was ten degrees south of England, its climate was similar to England's. The appeal of the old assumptions can be seen in the fact that later in the same book Morton said New England was warmer in winter than some parts of France and neerer the Sunne." In 1630 John Winthrop wrote home that the climate of New England was "very like our own," and he allayed fears of excessive heat by noting that only two days had been hotter

5. Bartholomew Gosnold, "Master Bartholomew Gosnold's Letter to his Father," in Purchas, *Purchas His Pilgrimes*, XVIII, 300–302; Edward Hayes, *A Treatise, containing important inducements for the planting in these parts, and finding a passage that way to the South Sea and China*, in John Brereton, *A Briefe and true Relation of the Discoverie of the North part of Virginia*, 2d ed. (London, 1602), 15; James Rosier, *A True Relation of the most prosperous voyage made by Captaine George Waymouth* (London, 1605), sig. E2; and John Smith, *A Description of New England*, 1616, in Arber and Bradley, eds., *Travels and Works*, I, 198.

6. Winslow, *Good Newes*, 62. See also *Mourt's Relation*, 62; Sir Ferdinando Gorges, *Briefe Relation*, in Baxter, ed., *Gorges and His Province*, 209; and Christopher Levett, *A Voyage into New England* (London, 1624), 23, 26.

than in England. By 1634 he said the winters were "sharp and long," and the summers "more fervent in heat" than England's. As late as 1641 Thomas Gorges was still puzzled about the discrepancy between Maine's latitude and the climate he experienced there.[7]

By the 1630's and increasingly in the 1640's, though, it was becoming important that a realistic picture of the American climate be available so that practical plans could be made and realizable expectations generated. By the early 1630's, fear of the debilitating effect of excessive heat had been replaced by fear of extreme cold: "It may be objected that it is too cold a Countrey for our English men."[8] Francis Higginson, who was an enthusiastic promoter of New England and its healthfulness, nevertheless affirmed that this part of America was both colder and hotter than England, and he put the two months' winter snow cover on his list of the discommodities of the country. William Wood wrote in detail of the heat of the summer, which was so great that he felt colonists should come in the fall, as well as the winter's cold, of which he told many stories. But he also assured his readers that he preferred New England's climate to the "Summer Winters and Winter Summers of England."[9] In the 1640's, Thomas Gorges wrote home of the dread with which his colonists anticipated the coming winter, and told his uncle at home, "you must looke uppon us as prisoners from the end of 9ber till the beginning of Aprille." In 1642, Thomas Lechford wrote of the extremes of both summer and winter, but especially of the cold, and went so far as to say that

7. John Smith, *Advertisements For the unexperienced Planters of New-England, or any where*, in Arber and Bradley, eds., *Travels and Works*, II, 938; Thomas Morton, *New English Canaan*, in Peter Force, compiler, *Tracts and Other Papers*, 4 vols. (Gloucester, Mass., 1963 [orig. publ. 1836]), II, 14, 62; John Winthrop to John Winthrop, Jr., 23 July 1630, in Emerson, ed., *Letters from New England*, 50–51; and to Sir Nathaniel Rich, 22 May 1634, ibid., 116; Hubbard, *General History of New England*, 20; and Gorges, *Letters of Thomas Gorges*, ed. Moody, 47. The American climate and its interpretation in the early period is discussed for all the colonies in Karen Ordahl Kupperman, "The Puzzle of the American Climate in the Early Colonial Period," *American Historical Review*, LXXXIX (1982), 1262–1289.

8. Wood, *New Englands Prospect*, 4.

9. Ibid., 3–8; Francis Higginson, *New Englands Plantation*, 1630, in Force, compiler, *Tracts*, I, 10–12.

America was thought to be "not habitable" sixty leagues to the north.[1]

The immediate practical question was, what did this all mean for the future of these English colonies? How would plans have to be changed, and what practical steps would have to be taken? Early colonists agreed that movement would be somewhat restricted in winter, as Thomas Gorges' image of the colonists as winter prisoners shows dramatically. Gorges warned his uncle not to expect the mills to operate, and both Winthrop and Gorges said the court system did not meet during the winter months. Moreover, cattle would require winter feeding and perhaps even shelter, making them expensive on early colonial farms.[2]

Even while colonists were still puzzling over the reasons for the European/American difference, however, they were looking ahead with an experimental air to the problems the climate posed for them. They asserted that English people could live well in America. As John Smith pointed out, "the French in Canada, the Russians, Swethlanders, Polanders, Germans, and our neighbour Hollanders, are much colder and farre more Northward; [and] for all that, rich Countreyes and live well." John White reminded his readers of the greater snow and cold of Germany, implying a rebuke to those who excessively feared the cold of New England. Surely English people were as tough and flexible as other Europeans![3]

Colonists pointed to the abundance of wood, in contrast to England's shortage, and said New Englanders could have "Christmas

---

1. Gorges, *Letters of Thomas Gorges*, Moody ed., 87, 114; Thomas Lechford, *Plain Dealing: or, Newes from New-England* (London, 1642), 114; Edmund Browne to Sir Simonds D'Ewes, 7 September 1638, in Emerson, ed., *Letters from New England*, 228. See also Josselyn, *Two Voyages to New England*, 247–249; Morton, *New Englands Memoriall*, 13; and Edward Ward, *A Trip to New England* (London, 1699), 48–49.

2. Gorges, *Letters of Thomas Gorges*, ed. Moody, 100–101, 112, 114; Winthrop, *History of New England*, ed. Hosmer, I, 138; and his letter to Sir Nathaniel Rich, in Emerson, ed., *Letters from New England*, 116; and Smith, *Advertisements For the unexperienced Planters of New-England, or any where*, in Arber and Bradley, eds., *Travels and Works*, II, 949.

3. Smith, *Advertisements For the unexperienced Planters of New-England, or any where*, in Arber and Bradley, eds., *Travels and Works*, II, 952–953; and John White, *The Planters Plea*, 1630, in Force, compiler, *Tracts*, II, 16.

fires all winter."[4] John Eliot said both the heat and cold were tolerable, even by the weakest, in their warm houses.[5] Though few went so far as John Smith in his ridicule of the "silly" people, "infirmed bodies or tender educats," who complained about the cold, many early colonists wrote fervently of the healthfulness of the country. Of all parts of America, they believed New England was closest in environment to England, and therefore most suited to English constitutions. Agreement between climate and the individual constitution was considered the single most important underlying condition of good health. Therefore, the very cold of New England recommended it, for, as William Hubbard put it, "the salubriousness of the air in this country depends much upon the winter's frost."[6]

What was required was to work hard, build sound houses, and realize the opportunities presented by the country. As Hubbard assured his readers, though agriculture was impossible for six months of the year, November to April, the fruitfulness of the hot summer abundantly made up for the cold winter.[7]

4. Philip Vincent, *A True Relation of the Late Battel fought in New England, between the English, and the Salvages* (London, 1637), 19; Higginson, *New Englands Plantation*, in Force, compiler, *Tracts*, I, 11; White, *Planters Plea*, ibid., II, 16; Smith, *Advertisements For the unexperienced Planters of New-England, or any where*, in Arber and Bradley, eds., *Travels and Works*, II, 952–953.

5. John Eliot to Sir Simonds D'Ewes, 18 September 1633, in Emerson, ed., *Letters from New England*, 106. In fact, because of poor construction and wide flues in their chimneys, the colonists' houses were cold; Charles F. Carroll, *The Timber Economy of Colonial New England* (Providence, R.I., 1974), 65.

6. Hubbard, *General History of New England*, 20–21; Smith, *Advertisements For the unexperienced Planters of New-England, or any where*, in Arber and Bradley, eds., *Travels and Works*, II, 952; Brereton, *Briefe and true Relation*, 11; Rosier, *True Relation*, sig. E2; Higginson, *New Englands Plantation*, in Force, compiler, *Tracts*, I, 9; White, *Planters Plea*, ibid., II, 13; *Letters of Thomas Gorges*, ed. Moody, 47, 110; Thomas Welde to his former parishioners at Tarling [Terling], June–July 1632, in Emerson, ed., *Letters from New England*, 96; Thomas Graves, "A Letter sent from New-England by Master Graves, Engineer, now there resident," 1630, in Young, ed., *Chronicles of Massachusetts Bay Planters*, 265–266; and Wood, *New Englands Prospect*, 5–6. See Wood's description of what the heat of Virginia was doing to the constitutions of English settlers there, ibid., 8–9. On beliefs about the effect of climate on the human constitution, see Sir William Vaughan, *The Newlanders Cure* (London, 1630), 6; Clarence Glacken, *Traces on the Rhodian Shore: Nature and Culture in Western Thought from Ancient Times to the End of the Eighteenth Century* (Berkeley, Calif., 1967), 12, 449–450; and John K. Wright, *The Geographical Lore of the Time of the Crusades* (New York, 1925), 180.

7. Hubbard, *General History of New England*, 20–21.

The primary task was organization of agriculture. It is in this area that the experimental spirit shows itself most clearly. Maize was the first grain in the colonies, and continued to be an important staple even after English grains were well established. There was some controversy over the healthfulness of Indian corn, as it was called, and some people did not like the taste, but it helped get them over the early difficult period, and many people were lavish in its praise.[8] Gerard's *Herball* of 1636 said maize was much less nourishing than English grains, that it produced a very hard and dry bread, which was constipating. This allegation was answered by John Parkinson, who said in his *Theatricum Botanicum* of 1640 that maize was indeed nourishing and pointed to the nations of Indians and Christians which fed on it and thrived. John Winthrop, Jr., attempted the definitive answer in a communication to the Royal Society in 1662 in which he wrote that Europeans in America continued to grow and eat maize even though wheat and other grains were by that time plentiful: "It is now found by much Experience, that it is wholesome and pleasant for Food of which great Variety may be made out of it."[9]

The real issue was whether Indian corn was not better suited to the climate and soil of New England than English grains. The Plymouth colonists reported poor success with English corn in the early years and stressed that maize was their chief grain, as did the Massachusetts Bay settlers in the first decades. They pointed to the dryness of the New England summer as compared to England and argued that maize, which requires heat and dryness to mature, was naturally suited to the climate. Edward Winslow even wrote that New England could never produce Indian corn as abundantly as Virginia did, because of the grain's great requirement for heat.[1] John Winthrop,

8. See White, *Planters Plea*, in Force, compiler, *Tracts*, II, 13; and Johnson, *Wonder-Working Providence*, 84, for criticism of the taste of maize. John Winthrop noted in 1630 that a cow and a goat were said to have died of eating Indian corn. *History of New England*, ed. Hosmer, I, 54.

9. John Gerard, *The Herball or Generall Historie of Plantes*, enlarged and amended by Thomas Johnson (London, 1636), 82; John Parkinson, *Theatrum Botanicum: the Theater of Plants. Or, An Herball of Large Extent* (London, 1640), 1138–1139; John Winthrop, Jr., "Of Maiz," ed. Fulmer Mood, *New England Quarterly*, X (1937), 125.

1. Winslow, *Good Newes*, 62–63; *Mourt's Relation*, 60–61; Wood, *New Englands*

Jr., argued that maize was protected against all the possible extremes of the New England weather, as the thick husks wrapping the kernels protected them from too much moisture and from too early frosts in September.[2]

Colonists stressed the tremendous yield of corn and its great variety of uses. Letters home in the early years again and again referred to the wholesomeness of the puddings and bread made with this "very precious grain." John Winthrop, Jr.'s communication to the Royal Society gave detailed directions for making beer from cornbread. There was also the sense, implicit in the letters of men such as Thomas Graves, the "Engineer" sent by the Massachusetts Bay Company before the main body of settlers, that New England's economy would have to be built on its natural products, especially fruits and grains, and that an open and experimental attitude was therefore required. Edward Johnson praised the great yield of maize, which in the early years was their "chiefest Corne," and indignantly went on: "and let no man make a jest at Pumpkins, for with this fruit the Lord was pleased to feed his people to their good content."[3]

However wholesome and plentiful the native products of New England were, promoters knew prospective settlers needed confidence that English plants would grow there. Not only would this assure any colonists they would not be cut off from the familiar diet and routines of home, but it would also quiet fears about the alien quality of the new land. Every party that came to New England, even those which were here only a few weeks, respected the instructions of their backers to plant and experiment with English seeds.

---

*Prospect,* 7; Johnson, *Wonder-Working Providence,* 57; Josselyn, *Two Voyages to New England,* 249; Gerard, *Herball,* 82.

2. Winthrop, "Of Maiz," 125–126.

3. On the wholesomeness, usefulness, and great increase of maize, see ibid., 131–132; Winslow, *Good Newes,* 62–63; *Mourt's Relation,* 41, 64; Higginson, *New Englands Plantation,* in Force, compiler, *Tracts,* I, 6–7; John Winthrop to Margaret Winthrop, 29 November 1630, in Emerson, ed., *Letters from New England,* 61; Welde to his former parishioners at Tarling, ibid., 227; Edmund Browne to Sir Simonds D'Ewes, ibid., 232; and Josselyn, *New Englands Rarities Discovered,* 52–53. On the need to look at the natural products, see Graves, "Letter sent from New-England" in Young, ed., *Chronicles of Massachusetts Bay Planters,* 265; White, *Planters Plea,* in Force, compiler, *Tracts,* II, 13; and Johnson, *Wonder-Working Providence,* 56.

Bartholomew Gosnold's expedition of 1602 planted wheat, barley, oats, and peas or pulses, and found they grew six to nine inches in fourteen days.[4] Martin Pring reported success with the same crops in 1603, even though they were "late sowne," which he said gave "certaine testimonie of the goodnesse of the Climate and of the Soyle." The native grasses also gave him hope of growing oats, hemp, flax, and rape-seed.[5] George Waymouth's company in 1605 planted garden seeds, peas, and barley, which grew eight inches in sixteen days and one-half inch daily thereafter. This experiment was highlighted in a marginal note: "Corne sowed."[6] Years later Samuel Maverick saw evidence of the failed Sagadahoc colony's attempts to grow English seeds in the roots and garden herbs growing by some old walls on the site.[7]

Plymouth colony reported early failures with English grains; they tried peas and barley first, neither of which did well, apparently because of hot, dry weather. By 1624 they reported that though "the chiefest grain is the Indian mays, or Guinea wheat," they believed English grains would do even better once they had cattle to till the ground. Wheat, rye, barley, peas, and oats were specifically mentioned.[8] The Massachusetts Bay colonists similarly experimented with English grains and other plants while relying on maize in the early years. Many wrote home in the first two decades of the fruitfulness of the new colony and their success in growing familiar grains and in raising animals, which were said to grow bigger and healthier in this environment. Thomas Morton said the herbs in America were more masculine than the same species in England and others said the environment increased female fecundity. William Wood attributed the

4. Gabriel Archer, *The Relation of Captaine Gosnols Voyage to the North part of Virginia*, in Purchas, *Purchas His Pilgrimes*, XVIII, 308; and Brereton, *Briefe and true Relation*, 6–7.

5. Martin Pring, *A Voyage set out from the Citie of Bristoll*, in Purchas, *Purchas His Pilgrimes*, XVIII, 327.

6. Rosier, *True Relation*, sig. B2.

7. Samuel Maverick, *A Briefe Discription of New England*, circa 1660 (Boston, 1885), 7.

8. *Mourt's Relation*, 60–61; Winslow, *Good Newes*, 62–63. See also John Smith, *New Englands Trials*, 1620, in Arber and Bradley, eds., *Travels and Works*, I, 264; and Gorges, *Briefe Relation*, in Baxter, ed., *Gorges and His Province of Maine*, I, 229, for an example of contemporary thinking on the subject.

great number of twins born in New England to the healthfulness of the climate and its agreement with English constitutions. Others noted that American animals were more apt to have multiple births.[9]

Experimentation continued at an accelerating pace. The Massachusetts Bay Company arranged to send wheat, barley, and rye for planting to the vanguard party of colonists. These were to be followed by fruit stones and other seeds and even "Tame turkeys."[1] Planters asked, as did Edward Trelawney of his brother Robert, for many kinds of seeds and "any other things that you may conceive may conduce to the furtherance and future benefit of the plantation, for I would let no probable thing slip, but without trial, which is the true settling and furthering of a plantation to future posterity."[2] By the end of the first decade there seems to have been general agreement that barley, oats, and rye did well in New England, though the evidence on wheat was still inconclusive. John Josselyn said summer wheat often changed into rye.[3] Many of the same people also said

9. Morton, *New English Canaan*, in Force, compiler, *Tracts*, II, 46, and Book II generally; White, *Planters Plea*, 13–14; Higginson, *New Englands Plantation*, I, 8; Wood, *New Englands Prospect*, 9–11, 21; Vincent, *True Relation*, 19; John Underhill, *Newes from America* (London, 1638), 21; Graves, "Letter sent from New-England," in Young, ed., *Chronicles of Massachusetts Bay Planters*, 265; and Welde to his former parishioners at Tarling, in Emerson, ed., *Letters from New England*, 96. One dissenter from this picture of abundance and fecundity was Thomas Gorges in Maine, who said that cows gave only half as much milk in America as they did in England. Gorges, *Letters of Thomas Gorges*, ed. Moody, 101–102.

1. Massachusetts Bay Company, "The Company's First General Letter of Instructions to Endicott and his Council," 1629, in Young, ed., *Chronicles of Massachusetts Bay Planters*, 156; and *Records of Massachusetts Bay*, I, 24–25. Turkeys had been brought from Mexico to Europe in the second decade of the sixteenth century and were plentiful in Norfolk by the end of the century. *The Agrarian History of England and Wales*, IV, *1500–1640*, ed. Joan Thirsk (Cambridge, 1967), 194.

2. Edward Trelawney to Robert Trelawney, 10 October 1635, in Emerson, ed., *Letters from New England*, 175.

3. Josselyn, *Two Voyages to New England*, 336; and *New Englands Rarities Discovered*, 89–91; Wood, *New Englands Prospect*, 13–14; Graves, "Letter sent from New-England," in Young, ed., *Chronicles of Massachusetts Bay Planters*, 265; Samuel Clarke, *A True, and Faithful Account of the Four Chiefest Plantations of the English in America* (London, 1670), typed MS, Widener Library, Harvard University, 27; Hubbard, *General History of New England*, 671–672; William Hammond to Sir Simonds D'Ewes, 26 September 1633, in Emerson, ed., *Letters from New England*, 112; John Winthrop to Sir Nathaniel Rich, ibid., 116; Higginson, *New Englands Plantation*, in Force, compiler, *Tracts*, I, 7. Thomas Lechford agreed that oats and rye thrived, but said barley did

that garden herbs, fruits, and peas and beans thrived here. The emphasis throughout was on testing and examining. Edward Johnson, for instance, wrote of the joy of the people, when rye was first grown in 1633, "to see the land would beare it."[4] The importance of these experiments can be seen in the case of John Pratt, who was hauled before the General Court in 1635. Pratt had written a letter to England critical of the prospects of Massachusetts Bay and saying that English grains did not prosper there. He was acquitted only when he dictated a long letter of apology, explaining his mistaken thinking. He said he had now seen in his own fields that rye and oats prospered, but he still had doubts about whether other English grains would flourish to the same height of perfection as in the country of which he and they were native.[5]

Experience also taught that some adjustments would be necessary. William Wood suggested that wheat and rye would do better if winter-sown, so the snow could keep them warm through the winter, but this practice was found to render the crop too vulnerable to extreme winter temperatures and was abandoned until after the onset of wheat blight in the middle of the century. Since the blast or blight appeared in mid-summer, winter wheat had a better chance of resisting it than that sown in spring.[6] Samuel Clough's *New-England Almanack* for 1703 mentioned July as the month when mildew threatens English grains. In practice throughout the century and beyond, a two-tier farming pattern continued, with English corn and maize equally occupying the farmer's attention. The 1723 *Almanack* of Nathaniel Whittemore headed July's page with a poem on the English harvest and the September entry with one on the Indian. Above all, the two types of farming, with their very different climatological

---

poorly. *Plain Dealing*, 109. See Howard S. Russell, *A Long, Deep Furrow: Three Centuries of Farming in New England* (Hanover, N.H., 1976), 39–45, for a complete discussion of early planting.

4. *Wonder-Working Providence*, 62. He may have been mistaken about the grain; see Russell, *Long, Deep Furrow*, 40–41.

5. *Massachusetts Bay Records*, I, 358–359.

6. Wood, *New Englands Prospect*, 7; Hubbard, *General History of New England*, 23; Darrett Rutman, *Husbandmen of Plymouth: Farms and Villages in the Old Colony, 1620–1692* (Boston, 1967), 50–52.

demands, offered insurance to the farmer and the economy in general that there would be a sufficient harvest.[7]

By the end of the 1640's, then, the truth about New England's climate had been assimilated, and people were adjusting their expectations and practices to it. The European/American difference had been accepted and to some extent accounted for, and colonists were prepared to admit that New England was both colder and hotter than England. But this does not mean that they saw this difference as permanent or fundamental. Many colonists believed that European technology would have such a profound impact on America that it would completely change the environment, including the weather.

Early modern English people believed that human beings are responsible for the environment, and that this responsibility entails taking an active role in perfecting and shaping it. Raw, unfinished nature was not beautiful and only accidentally bountiful. John Brereton's party had been so overcome by the "beautie and delicacie" of the land that he said it was "as if Nature would shew her selfe above her power, artificiall." John Smith answered charges that other parts of the world in the same latitude were superior by pointing out that: "They are beautified by the long labour and diligence of industrious people and Art. This is onely as God made it, when he created the worlde." He argued that as settlers moved inland and as the land was "cultured, planted and manured by men of industrie, judgement, and experience," it would soon equal any in the world. The "artificiall" impact of human beings on the environment is both more powerful and more salutary than nature left to itself. Nature requires the effect of people's labor, and all places are better for "humane culture."[8]

7. Russell, *Long, Deep Furrow*, 134–136. See Thomas Minor, *The Diary of Thomas Minor of Stonington, Connecticut, 1653–1684*, Sidney H. Miner and George D. Stanton, Jr., eds. (New London, Conn., 1899) for the annual round of planting and harvesting, including the fall and spring sowing.

8. Brereton, *Briefe and true Relation*, 7–8; Smith, *Description of New England*, in Arber and Bradley, eds., *Travels and Works*, I, 197; Hubbard, *General History of New England*, 671; Vincent, *True Relation*, sig. B; Graves, "Letter sent from New England," in Young, ed., *Chronicles of Massachusetts Bay Planters*, 265; Charles Webster, *The Great Instauration: Science, Medicine and Reform, 1626–1660* (London, 1975), 2, 8, 16; and Cecelia Tichi, *New World, New Earth: Environmental Reform in American Literature from the Puritans through Whitman* (New Haven, Conn., 1979), 54–62.

In New England this meant, most especially, hope for an improved climate. Philip Vincent asserted that New England would be as temperate as northern Spain and southern France, in the same latitudes, "if managed by industrious hands." John Mason and Richard Whitbourne argued that habitation by Europeans would make even Newfoundland warmer. Whitbourne wrote that cutting down the woods would let in the sun's beams, which would not only make the country warmer, winter and summer, but would lengthen the growing season. Mason asserted that lands not "manured" are "more naturally cold," and, furthermore, the smoke and heat of peoples' fires in towns "much qualifieth the coldnesse of the Aire."[9] Some people in the early decades believed the American climate was already changing as a result of cultivation by Europeans. William Wood thought he saw evidence as early as 1634 that rainfall patterns were changing, and he argued that New England's weather was as England's had formerly been. He reported Indian testimony that the weather was better since the arrival of the English: "the times and seasons being much altered in seven or eight yeares, freer from lightning and thunder, long droughts, suddaine and tempestuous dashes of raine, and lamentable cold Winters." In 1654 Edward Johnson wrote that cutting down the woods and breaking up the land for agriculture had caused a marked change in "the very nature of the seasons, moderating the Winters cold of late very much." Elsewhere he also argued that the summers were becoming more temperate.[1]

---

9. Vincent, *True Relation*, sig. A4; Richard Whitbourne, *A Discourse and Discovery of New-found-land* (London, 1620), 57; John Mason, *A Briefe Discourse of the New-found. land.* (Edinburgh, 1620), sig. B2v.

1. Wood, *New Englands Prospect*, 7–9, 84; Johnson, *Wonder-Working Providence*, 55, 120, 171; Hubbard, *General History of New England*, 20. For a vivid description of Johnson's technological vision, see Tichi, *New World, New Earth*, 54–62, and Alan Heimert, "Puritanism, the Wilderness, and the Frontier," *New England Quarterly*, XXVI (1953), 368–369. On the actual effect of agriculture and forest clearance on local climate, see Lamb, *Climate: Present, Past and Future*, I, 7, 50; Crispin Tickell, *Climatic Change and World Affairs* (Cambridge, Mass., 1977), 26; John E. Oliver, *Climate and Man's Environment: An Introduction to Applied Climatology* (New York, 1973), 164–168; and Alexander T. Wilson, "Isotope Evidence from Past Climatic and Environmental Change," *Journal of Interdisciplinary History*, X (1979–1980), 810–812; William Cronon, *Changes in the Land: Indians, Colonists and the Ecology of New England* (New York, 1983).

Colonists' belief in the transforming power of European technology was crucial to their perception of the American environment and their place in it. As it happened, experience was for a time strongly confirmatory of this presumption. The harsh 1630's and harsher 1640's were followed by the more temperate and controlled 1650's and 1660's. Much of the 1670's was also moderate. For people accustomed to believing that their agricultural methods were part of God's plan to complete nature, and that their lives were lived in accordance with God's wishes, this improvement must have been powerful reinforcement. The short-term experience set the settlers up for a profound disillusionment in the 1680's and 1690's just at the time when their other concerns were also creating anxiety and doubt.

No evidence has come to light about the early 1650's. In the winter of 1654–1655, the bay was frozen for one month; the rest of the winter was normal. February of 1656 was cold, and the rest of the winter "normal." John Hull said the winters of 1656–1657 and 1657–1658 were very mild, with little snow.[2] Planting was delayed by a wet spring in 1658. William Hubbard said that 30 April was the coldest day of the year and reported that two men had been frozen in Maine. Though the early harvest was good, the late was spoiled by rain so heavy that cattle in Massachusetts were threatened.[3] The winter of 1658–1659 was stormy and cold in patches, but it was followed by a good summer and harvest despite a cold and rainy April. The winter of 1659–1660 was snowy, and the bay was frozen by the end of December. March was cold, but without much frost, and the worst storm of the winter occurred in mid-April. The winter of 1660–1661 was a mild one with little snow or frost. There was a cold, wet spring with floods in Connecticut and a bad hailstorm in June, but the summer of 1661 was hot and good for agriculture. The winter of 1661–1662 was very snowy, but it was followed by a "very great drought" in the early summer. The harvest was saved, though. The

---

2. John Hull, "Diary," American Antiquarian Society, *Transactions and Collections,* III (1857), 177, 179, 183. Ludlum, *Early American Winters,* 15, says the winter of 1656–1657 was severe, but gives no citation.

3. Hull, "Diary," 184; Hubbard, *General History of New England,* 647, 654; Samuel Danforth, "Records of the First Church in Roxbury, Massachusetts," *New England Historical and Genealogical Register,* XXXIV (1880), 87.

winter of 1662–1663 began mild but saw a deep snow cover from January to March.[4]

The summer of 1663 saw the wheat blight or blast on crops throughout New England. John Hull attributed it to the series of cold, wet springs and the drought of the preceding year. He said many acres were not worth the reaping. Wheat blast reappeared in the summer of 1664 and there was drought at the end of the summer, but the Indian corn harvest was good.[5] The winters of 1663–1664 and 1664–1665 were mild, though there was a cold period beginning in late February 1665. The springs were cold in 1664 and 1665 with no buds on the trees until 11 May in the latter year. The cold winter of 1665–1666 was followed by a cold, wet spring with great floods. The apple trees leafed on 21 May. The summer was hot and dry. The summers of 1665 and 1666 again saw devastating blast or mildew on wheat; other grains were all right except that some were affected by drought in 1666.[6] The winter of 1666–1667 was cold and very snowy. Spring was early, with the apple trees leafing on 22 April, and the winter of 1667–1668 was mild, with little frost or snow. The apple trees bloomed on 28 April, but a frost in early June damaged corn and fruit. John Hull said the winter of 1668–1669 was "very temperate," but other sources note great snows. Simon Bradstreet of New London said that grain was very scarce for years because of the blast. Spring was promising, but in the following summer many children died of flux and vomiting, which was attributed to the wet season continuing through late August. The rest of the summer was then hot and dry, and the blast continued to attack the wheat crop. The winter of 1669–1670 was very snowy, "sharp and tedious."

4. Hull, "Diary," 175–178, 190, 197, 199, 200–203, 206, 207; Thomas Minor, *Diary*, 54; Michael Wigglesworth, "God's Controversy with New England," Massachusetts Historical Society, *Proceedings*, 1st Ser., XII (1871–1873), 83; Danforth, "Roxbury Church Records," 87–88.

5. Hull, "Diary," 208–210, 213; Hubbard, *General History of New England*, 642; Morton, *New Englands Memorial*, 172–173; Danforth, "Roxbury Church Records," 88.

6. Hull, "Diary," 211, 215; 220–221; Danforth, "Roxbury Church Records," 163–165; Morton, *New Englands Memorial*, 177, 180; Hubbard, *General History of New England*, 642; Love, *Fast and Thanksgiving Days*, 179.

Thomas Minor of Stonington, Connecticut, counted twenty-nine snowfalls.[7]

The summer of 1670 was "very droughty," but it was followed by a winter which was quite moderate, as was the winter of 1671–1672. The spring of 1671 was rainy, while the summer of 1672 began dry. All the crops, except for the hay, were saved in 1672 by timely rain, and the winter of 1672–1673 was again very mild. The spring of 1673 was very cold, so much so that linen hung out to dry was found frozen stiff on the line on the morning of 15 June. Many cattle died because hay was short on account of the heavy rains and an extremely high tide of the preceding fall. In August there were devastating floods "drowning the meadows," but the ensuing winter was again mild in temperature, though with much snow and wet weather.[8]

The winter of 1674–1675 seemed almost like a return to the harsh winters of the 1640's. It began mild, but February saw the coldest weather for many years; it was "so dry and windy that the dust blew like snow." Increase Mather wrote of such scarcity of grain in New England, Long Island, and Virginia that cattle were dying for lack of food. The spring was also raw and cold until the very end of April. The peach blossoms appeared on 13 May. The summer was hot and dry, "yet pretty fruitful."[9] The winter of 1675–1676 began with a devastating hurricane, which Simon Bradstreet said caused several thousands of pounds damage. The weather was very sharp and stormy in the beginning, creating additional hardships in King Philip's War, but January and February had spring-like warm spells.[1] The circum-

7. Hull, "Diary," 223, 225–226, 228, 230; Minor, *Diary*, 76–78, 88–89, 92–95; Danforth, "Roxbury Church Records," 298–301; Simon Bradstreet, "Memoires," *New England Historical and Genealogical Register*, IX (1855), 44–45; and J. Hammond Trumbull, ed., *The Public Records of the Colony of Connecticut, from 1665 to 1678* (Hartford, 1852), 89–90.

8. Hull, "Diary," 230, 232, 234–235, 237; Danforth, "Roxbury Church Records," 301, 360–363; Hubbard, *General History of New England*, 648; Rev. William Adams of Dedham, Massachusetts, "Diary," Massachusetts Historical Society, *Collections*, 4th Ser., I (1852), 12; Edward Taylor, "Diary," in John H. Lockwood, *Westfield and Its Historic Influences, 1669–1919* (Springfield, Mass., 1922), I, 134–135.

9. Hull, "Diary," 239–241; Increase Mather, "Diaries," Massachusetts Historical Society, *Proceedings*, 2d Ser., XIII (1900), 343, 399.

1. Hull, "Diary," 240–241; Thomas Minor, *Diary*, 131; Bradstreet, "Memoires," 47–48; Increase Mather, "Diaries," 402; and Peter Easton, "Diary," Rhode Island His-

stances of the winter of 1676–1677 are unknown, but the blast on wheat and barley was again a problem in the summer of 1677. The winter of 1677–1678 was mostly moderate, with several snowstorms. Little is known about the winter and spring of 1678–1679 except that there were storms in April and May.[2]

During these three decades, then, English colonists could see a pronounced melioration in their weather. There were many very mild winters, and none of the exceedingly cold winters they had seen in the 1640's. The springs were too often cold, frequently with the addition of too much rain, and this created difficulties in agriculture. The greatest problem was the blast attacking the wheat crop, which colonists saw as weather-related.[3] As a consequence, the Indian corn crop provided a safety-valve of the greatest importance. Several times the harvest was saved by the onset of hot, dry weather in the mid-to-late summer. But with the apparent end of the extreme cold that the earliest settlers had known, it is easy to see how New Englanders such as Edward Johnson could believe that European occupation of the land was changing the climate for the better.

Another way we can gain insight into the colonists' sense of their impact on the land is to see how people from the vantage point of the 1650's and 1660's described the period of the pioneers. These writings repeatedly use rhetorical phrases such as "howling wilderness," "howling desart," "hideous and desolate Wilderness," "desart wildernesse," and "waste and uncouth wildernesse," to describe the land encountered by the original settlers. They had acquired enough distance from this experience to begin romanticizing it. The modifiers distinguish these from other uses of "wilderness"—the religious connotation of a place of refuge or inspiration, or the English sense of a maze in a formal garden, "in which one may become happily and amusingly

---

torical Society, *Collections*, XI (1918), 78–80; Benjamin Church, *Diary of King Philip's War, 1675–76*, ed. Alan and Mary Simpson (Chester, Conn., 1975), 95, 100–102.

2. Hull, "Diary," 243; Thomas Minor, *Diary*, 146, 152, 154; Peter Thatcher, of Milton, Massachusetts, Diary, 1678–99, 10–14, 16–17, (microfilm of typescript), Massachusetts Historical Society, Boston.

3. Josselyn, *Two Voyages to New England*, 336; Robert Hooke, "Method for Making a History of the Weather," 1663, in Thomas Sprat, *History of the Royal Society of London, For the Improving of Natural Knowledge* (London, 1667), 175.

bewildered."[4] The psychological distance from the frontier experience after mid-century was due to broad areas of action, such as clearing the land and building towns, but the climate's apparent melioration must have contributed to a sense of mastery over the environment.[5]

This sense of accomplishment in changing the climate ended in the 1680's and 1690's as New England, along with northern Europe, was plunged into the worst decades of the Little Ice Age. The winter of 1680–1681 was said by Increase Mather to have been the coldest for forty years. Samuel Sewall also said it was the coldest for many years.[6] It signaled the return of very cold weather, in fact apparently much colder than had been known before. Coming as it did in decades of profound upheaval and self-doubt, this climatic shift had a very great impact, both psychologically and physically, on the settlers and their situation. It is necessary to describe the changes in weather and the colonists' understanding of those changes in order properly to understand the socio-economic and psychological realities of the last two decades of the seventeenth century.

4. Peter N. Carroll, *Puritanism and the Wilderness: The Intellectual Significance of the New England Frontier, 1629–1700* (New York, 1969); Ann Leighton, *Early American Gardens: For Meate or Medicine* (Boston, 1970), 180; Heimert, "Puritanism, Wilderness, and Frontier," 370–371.

5. For the howling wilderness image, see Johnson, *Wonder-Working Providence*, sig. A2, 18, 19, 23, 59, 81, 84, 104, 191, 209–210; Morton, *New Englands Memorial*, 13, 14, 83; Hubbard, *General History of New England*, 52; "Early Records of Charlestown," in Young, ed., *Chronicles of Massachusetts Bay Planters*, 375; Michael Wigglesworth, "Autobiography," *New England Historical and Genealogical Register*, XVII (1863), 137; and his "God's Controversy with New England," Massachusetts Historical Society, *Proceedings*, 1st Ser., XII (1871–1873), 83–84; Increase Mather, *A Brief Relation of the State of New England* (London, 1689), 3–4, 12; and his "To the Reader," in Samuel Torrey, *An Exhortation Unto Reformation* (Cambridge, Mass., 1674), sig. A2; Thomas Shepard, *Eye-Salve: Or, A Watchword from our Lord Jesus Christ unto his Church* (Cambridge, Mass., 1673), 11; "Petition from the Town of Northampton to the General Court, April 19, 1665," reprinted in James Russell Trumbull, *History of Northampton, Massachusetts from its Settlement in 1654* (Northampton, Mass., 1898), I, 156–157; John Higginson, *The Cause of God and His People in New England* (Cambridge, Mass., 1663), 10–11.

6. Increase Mather, "Diaries," 409; M. Halsey Thomas, ed., *Diary of Samuel Sewall, 1674–1729*, 2 vols. (New York, 1973), I, 47, 49. Mather stated that 1680 was the worst year ever for the wheat blast in Connecticut, noting that hundreds of acres did not yield enough to feed one family. Mather, "Diaries," 408.

Before we look at the weather experienced in these twenty years, it is important to see how New Englanders thought about weather as opposed to climate. The Royal Society, almost from its beginning, had been calling for a scientific approach to the collection of weather data from all over the world "for the making of comparisons, requisite for the raising Axioms, whereby the Cause of Laws of Weather may be found out." They hoped observers would make daily notes on all kinds of phenomena, using those instruments available in the late seventeenth century.[7] Despite the enthusiasm of early colonial members such as John Winthrop, Jr., and Cotton Mather, and the large number of letters on various subjects which they submitted to the *Philosophical Transactions*, the Royal Society had to wait until the 1720's for systematic meteorological observations from New England.[8] With the exception of John Pike, who noted the date of every snowfall from 1682 through the century, no diarist kept a systematic record of any set of phenomena.[9]

New Englanders lacked instruments to make precise readings until the eighteenth century, but failure to collect the data necessary for investigation of the underlying laws of meteorology had a more fundamental cause. The outlook of the colonists was completely providential. That is, weather phenomena, good or bad, were seen as sent by God and indicative of his will. To understand the weather, they looked at the society and its relationship to God.[1] John Calvin's commentary on Genesis, the English translation of which appeared in 1578, laid down the principle of the providential interpretation of weather: "The intemperature of the aire, yce, thunder, unseasonable raines, drouthe, hailes, and what soever is extraordinarie in the world,

7. Hooke, "Method for a History of the Weather," in Sprat, *History of the Royal Society*, 173–179; Robert Boyle, "General Heads for a Natural History of a Countrey, Great or small," *Philosophical Transactions*, I (London, 1665–1666), 186–189.

8. Raymond P. Stearns, *Science in the British Colonies of America* (Urbana, Ill., 1970), Chaps. 5, 10; John Winthrop to John Winthrop, Jr., Emerson, ed., *Letters from New England*, 135–136.

9. Pike, "Observable Seasons," New Hampshire Historical Society, *Collections*, III (1832), 62–67.

1. See David D. Hall, "Puritanism and Popular Religion in Seventeenth-Century New England," paper delivered to the Organization of American Historians, San Francisco, April 1980.

are the fruites of sinne." The point was emphasized in the marginal note: "Wether untemperate and such like are the fruites of sin."[2] It was a commonplace in seventeenth-century New England that adverse meteorological phenomena were a result of human failings.[3] In fact, much of our information about seventeenth-century weather comes from diarists' notations about days of fasting and humiliation which were called to bring relief from unfavorable conditions, frequently drought. Virtually every journal contains such information, and most saw the rituals as efficacious: that is, the calling of a special day almost always caused improvement in the weather. John Winthrop noted times when the mere setting of the day was enough; the drought broke before the actual rituals.[4] This practice could even elicit divine guidance on specific issues. Samuel Danforth wrote that some people blamed the drought in the summer of 1662 on the calling of the synod, but when the elders met they held a day of prayer and there was then a good rain every week until the harvest, showing that God favored the synod.[5]

Edward Johnson gave a particularly graphic example of the power of these occasions. He wrote of the drought in 1633 in which the crops were being killed by the "extreame parching heate of the Sun." The people, "beholding the Hand of the Lord stretched out against them," held a day of prayer to beg for mercy. The congregation shed many tears and "as they powred out water before the Lord, so at that

2. John Calvin, *A Commentarie of John Calvine, upon the first booke of Moses called Genesis,* trans. Thomas Tymme (London, 1578), 114.

3. Johnson, *Wonder-Working Providence,* 220; John Tulley, *An Almanack* (Cambridge, Mass., 1692).

4. Winthrop, *History of New England,* ed. Hosmer, I, 306–307; II, 81–82, 224; Sewall, *Diary,* ed. Thomas, I, 166–168; John Marshall, "Diary, 1697–1711," Massachusetts Historical Society, *Proceedings,* 2d Ser., I (1884–1885), 150–151, 155; XIV (1900–1901), 32; Cotton Mather, *Diary of Cotton Mather,* ed. Worthington C. Ford, Massachusetts Historical Society, *Collections,* 7th Ser., VII (1911), 165–166; Love, *Fast and Thanksgiving Days.* Hull, "Diary," 185, gives an example in which the ritual was not answered.

5. Danforth, "Roxbury Church Records," *New England Historical and Genealogical Register,* XXXIV (1880), 88. A providential shower of rain helped English soldiers in King Philip's War. Captain Thomas Wheeler, *A True Narrative of the Lord's Providences in Various Dispensations Towards Captain Edward Hutchinson of Boston and my self, And those that went with us into the Nipmuck Country,* 1675 (Boston, n.d.), Old South Leaflets, No. 155.

very instant, the Lord showred down water on their Gardens and Fields." This is a very complicated example, because, in demonstrating both His concern for the colonists and his power, God won the admiration of the Indians who witnessed these events, making the goal of conversion more attainable. William Bradford recorded a similar occurrence in the drought of 1623.

Johnson claimed more than the breaking of one dry spell. He argued that God was changing the fundamental climate of New England in order to make it hospitable to his colonists. In reporting the incident, he began by saying that "the Country is naturally subject to drought." He then went on to say that "the Lord was pleased, during these yeares of scarcity, to blesse that small quantity of Land *they* planted with seasonable showers, and that many times to the great admiration of the Heathen."[6] We have already seen that Johnson believed the climate of New England was changing under the impact of European cultivation. In saying this he combined belief in European technology with his faith in the special destiny of the New England colonists. After he mentioned the theory that cutting down the woods and breaking up the land was changing the climate, Johnson went on, "But Christ have the praise of all his glorious Acts." Later he simply said that Christ had "altered the very course of the Heavens," and that this was done for the comfort of "his poor Churches," "to the wonder of English and Indians, the Winter and Summer proving more moderate, both for heat and cold."[7]

Other phenomena also exhibited the hand of God. When blast or mildew or insect pests attacked the crops, this was widely interpreted as a judgment.[8] Many diarists recorded unusual episodes of lightning, especially when someone was killed or injured. The death of Captain Richard Davenport at Castle Island in 1665 appeared on many lists of

6. Johnson, *Wonder-Working Providence*, 57 (emphasis added); Bradford, *Of Plymouth Plantation*, ed. Morison, 131; *New Englands First Fruits* (London, 1643), 4–5; Hubbard, *General History of New England*, 74, 650.

7. Johnson, *Wonder-Working Providence*, 55, 120, 170–171.

8. Hubbard, *General History of New England*, 662; Morton, *New Englands Memorial*, 172–173, 177, 180; Winthrop, *History of New England*, ed. Hosmer, II, 277; Eliot, "Roxbury Church Records," 65; Danforth, "Roxbury Church Records," 163, 165; Noadiah Russell, *Diary of the Reverend Noadiah Russell of Ipswich, Massachusetts, and Middletown, Connecticut, For the Old Style Year 1687* (Hartford, Conn., 1934), 9.

the most remarkable passages in the history of New England. The Indian who scoffed at Hiacoomes, the Mayhews' first convert, was punished by being struck by lightning, and Simon Bradstreet recorded lightning as evidence of God's power.[9] This being so, one can imagine the consternation of Cotton Mather when he noticed, as he confided to Samuel Sewall, "that more Ministers' " houses "than others proportionably had been smitten with Lightening." He was "enquiring what the meaning of God should be in it."[1]

Phenomena such as earthquakes, comets, and eclipses were seen as portents, even in cases where the mechanisms were known. Samuel Clough's *New-England Almanack* for 1703 had a scientific diagram demonstrating how eclipses occur, and Clough, like most other almanac makers, was able to predict them with great precision. Nonetheless, he went on to describe the awful calamities which would follow the predicted eclipses. Increase Mather doubted that eclipses involved portents because they happen every year, but his writing on comets, as well as those of his son Cotton, shows a mixture of knowledge of the most recent scientific thinking and the strong belief that comets foretell disasters. As Cotton said of thunder: "And indeed, though the natural causes of the thunder are known unto us, yet, there are those notable voices of the almighty God, often sensible in the directing thereof, which it becomes good men to observe with devout resentments."[2]

9. Bradstreet, "Memoires," 43, 44, 46–47, 50; Experience Mayhew, *Indian Converts* (London, 1727), 1–5; Samuel Clough, *The New-England Almanack* (Boston, 1701); Josselyn, *New Englands Rarities*, 113; and his *Two Voyages to New England*, 388–389; Russell, *Diary*, 7–8; Morton, *New Englands Memorial*, 159, 177–179; Hubbard, *General History of New England*, 384, 627–628, 642, 656; Danforth, "Roxbury Church Records," 163, 165–166, 361.

1. Sewall, *Diary*, ed. Thomas, I, 330. See also Cotton Mather, *Magnalia Christi Americana*, ed. Thomas Robbins, 2 vols. (Hartford, Conn., 1853), II, 361–372.

2. Clough, *New-England Almanack* (Boston, 1703); John Tulley, *An Almanac* (Boston, 1693), sig. C; Bradstreet, "Memoires," 43–44, 50; Increase Mather, "Diaries," 408–409; his *Heaven's Alarm to the World* (Boston, 1681); and his *Kometographia. Or A Discourse Concerning Comets* (Boston, 1683), *passim*, especially 20; Cotton Mather, *Magnalia*, ed. Robbins, and his *The Boston Ephemeris: An Almanack* (Boston, 1683); Josselyn, *Two Voyages to New England*, 245, 387; J.F., *Perpetuall and Naturall Prognostications of the Change of Weather* (London, 1591), sig. C3v–C4v; Adams, "Diary," 12; Morton, *New Englands Memorial*, 23, 90–91, 95, 161–163, 170–173, 182, Hubbard, *General History of New England*, 51, 324–325, 339, 420–425, 427, 516–517,

By 1680, New Englanders had experienced three decades of much milder weather than that of the founding decades. Since they believed that all such phenomena were directly controlled by God, they were able to interpret this melioration as evidence of divine favor for the work they were engaged in. It is the argument of this paper that in the final two decades of the century a drastic deterioration in the weather combined with other events to create the profound disillusionment and self-doubt among the colonists which many other historians have described. To discuss this period without understanding the weather conditions faced by the colonists is to omit a crucial part of the picture.

We have already seen that the winter of 1680–1681 was very cold, the coldest winter for forty years. It was followed by a summer drought in which much corn and grass was lost in Connecticut, though John Hull said there was a "competent harvest." The next summer's harvest was plentiful. There were damaging floods in the spring of 1683, and storms with higher tides than anyone could remember in the spring of 1684.[3] The winter of 1684–1685 was very cold, with Boston harbor frozen so hard that 900 people went to Castle Island and back on the ice. The winter of 1685–1686 proved even colder. Samuel Sewall said the frozen sacramental bread rattled on the plate as it was being passed. Coaches went to Charlestown and Noddles Island on the ice "for a considerable time together." The hard winter was followed by a great drought, during which fires in the swamps burned underground to a depth of six feet.[4] We know little of the rest of the decade, except that the spring and early sum-

642–648. See Perry Miller, *The New England Mind: From Colony to Province* (Boston, 1961), 142–146, 180, 438; and Keith Thomas, *Religion and the Decline of Magic: Studies in Popular Beliefs in Sixteenth- and Seventeenth-Century England* (Harmondsworth, England, 1973), especially Chapter 4.

3. Increase Mather, "Diaries," 409; Bradstreet, "Memoires," 50; Hull, "Diary," 249; Sewall, *Diary*, ed. Thomas, I, 55; Thomas Minor, *Diary*, 17, 183; John Pike, "Journal, 1682–1709," Massachusetts Historical Society, *Proceedings*, 1st Ser., XIV (1875–1876), 122–123; William Vaughan, "A Letter from William V., Esq., containing a Journal of Transactions during his Imprisonment, etc., to Nathaniel Weare, Agent in London," in George E. Hodgdon, *Reminiscences and Genealogical Record of the Vaughan Family of New Hampshire* (Rochester, N.Y., 1918), Appendix I, 88.

4. Sewall, *Diary*, ed. Thomas, I, 90–95; Increase Mather, "Diaries," 410; Clough, *New-England Almanack*, 1701.

mer of 1687 were rainy with flooding, the winter of 1687–1688 was warm and rainy with a dry spring, and December of 1690 was extremely cold. The winter of 1691–1692 was cold in December and January and then warm. The summer of 1692 was visited by drought. The winter of 1692–1693 was mixed, and the summer was again dry and hot. Weather was mixed in the winter of 1693–1694 and in the following summer. The winter of 1694–1695 was marked by repeated great snowstorms and cold weather.[5]

The worst years of the century were 1696, 1697, and 1698. The winter of 1695–1696 was very cold and windy with great snowstorms continuing until late April when the snow from a storm on 22 April remained on the ground for three days.[6] The winter of 1696–1697 was again cold. Thomas Hutchinson in his *History* said it was the coldest winter since the first arrival, with sleighs able to go on the ice as far as Nantasket. Cotton Mather tried to perform a secret fast on 2 February, "But so extremely cold was the weather, that in a warm Room, on a great Fire, the Juices forced out at the End of short Billets of Wood, by the Heat of the Flame, on which they were laid, yett froze into Ice, at their coming out." He was forced to give up his exercise.[7] The spring was very cold, with a killing frost in late June, and was "a time of scarcity," with high prices for grain. The summer of 1697 saw a "sore" drought, and in October there were forest fires that burned for more than a week, filling the air with smoke. By the time there were heavy rains in November, water was badly needed for the mills, cattle, and wells.[8]

5. Sewall, *Diary*, ed. Thomas, I, 155, 166, 266, 272, 285–286, 293, 297, 304–306, 311–312, 316–317, 326–330; Pike, "Observable Seasons," 63–64; Cotton Mather, *Diary*, ed. Ford, 166; Russell, *Diary*, 6–8.

6. Cotton Mather, *Diary*, ed. Ford, 191–193; Samuel Clough, *New-England Almanack*, 1701, and his *Kalendarium Nov-Anglicanum, or an Almanack of the Coelestial Motions* (Boston, 1705); Sewall, *Diary*, ed. Thomas, I, 348; Pike, "Observable Seasons," 64.

7. Hutchinson, *History of Massachusetts-Bay*, ed. Mayo, II, 76n.; Mather, *Diary*, ed. Ford, 216.

8. Hutchinson, *History of Massachusetts-Bay*, ed. Mayo, II, 76n.; Sewall, *Diary*, ed. Thomas, I, 369–382; Manasseh Minor, *The Diary of Manasseh Minor, Stonington, Conn., 1696–1720* (n.p., 1915), 21–23; Clough, *New-England Almanack*, 1701; Daniel Travis, *An Almanack* (Boston, 1721); Marshall, "Diary," Massachusetts Historical Society, *Proceedings*, 2d Ser., I (1884–1885), 150–152 and XIV (1900–1901), 32.

Many would have nominated the winter of 1697–1698 as the coldest of the century. The bay was frozen from late January to mid-March, and Samuel Sewall many times crossed on the frozen river to Charlestown in January and February. It was also very snowy, with between twenty and thirty snowfalls. The snow cover lasted from mid-December to late March; in February snow was three and one-half feet deep on the level. On 2 February, Sewall noted that Michael Wigglesworth chose for his text: "Who can stand before his Cold? Then by reason of his own and peoples sickness, Three Sabbaths pass'd without publick worship." Samuel Sewall began his entries for many days with "very cold" or "extream cold," and he visited friends in early March whose sheep, "having been so long kept from the ground, are sick, some dye. Others will not own their Lambs." Sheep continued to die in the wet spring and on 21 May Sewall composed a verse while he was lying in bed:

> To Horses, Swine, Net-Cattell, Sheep and Deer
> Ninety and Seven prov'd a Mortal yeer.

The winter of 1697–1698 became famous for its severity. The Earl of Bellomont wrote from New York to the Lords of Trade that only the severe weather had prevented the French from taking Albany and Schenectady. The snow at Montreal was said to be higher than a man. In 1750, Peter Kalm found general agreement in America that the winter of 1697–1698 "was the coldest and the severest which they had ever felt."[9] There was great scarcity in the spring, and the summer was hot and wet. Some found this good for husbandry; others not. Sewall remarked that the rivers were very high in August, and in October there were violent storms and the worst floods in memory, according to John Pike.[1]

9. Earl of Bellomont in E. B. O'Callaghan, ed., *Documents Relative to the Colonial History of the State of New York* (Albany, 1854), IV, 409; Peter Kalm, *Peter Kalm's Travels in North America*, ed. Adolph B. Benson, 2 vols. (New York, 1937 [orig. publ. 1750, trans. 1770]), I, 277; Manasseh Minor, *Diary*, 26–28.

1. For descriptions of this year's weather, see Sewall, *Diary*, ed. Thomas, I, 384–390, 393–394, 396–397; Marshall, "Diary," Massachusetts Historical Society, *Proceedings*, I, 152; Clough, *New-England Almanack*, 1701; Pike, "Observable Seasons," and "Journal," 132–133; Cotton Mather, *Diary*, ed. Ford, 247; William Brattle, "Records of the First Church, Cambridge," *The Genealogical Magazine*, I (1906), 359; Manasseh Minor, *Diary*, 26–28.

The mild winter of 1698–1699 offered some relief from the battering, but the final winter of the century was again very cold. It began with a storm of freezing rain in early December, which caused many thousands of pounds damage. In mid-February the colonists had the coldest three days for many years. "Some say Brooks were frozen for carts to pass over them, so as has not been seen these Ten years. Ground very dry and dusty by the high wind." March was also cold and dry.[2]

This reconstituted weather pattern shows very high correlation with the mean temperatures for central England worked out by Gordon Manley. The mid-1680's and the middle and late 1690's were among the coldest years of the century, as were the 1640's. We have already seen that the winter of 1607–1608 was very cold on both continents. The evidence so far seems to indicate that Little Ice Age conditions were being felt in eastern North America as well as in Europe.[3]

King Philip's War of 1675–1676, with its devastating toll in casualties and the subsequent shrinking of the frontier, marks the beginning of the Puritans' loss of the sense that they were on a special mission for God. It coincided with the first of the bad winters of the end of the century. That the Indians attacked the settlements was seen as a judgment of God against them, a rebuke.[4] Tensions were continued and heightened by the outbreak of King William's War in 1689, in which the combined French and Indian enemy kept outlying settlements in constant fear. Cotton Mather attributed that war also to bad

2. Sewall, *Diary*, ed. Thomas, I, 417–418, 419, 421–425, 427–428; Brattle, "Cambridge Church Records," 360; Cotton Mather, *Diary*, ed. Ford, 334; Richard Brown, "Diary," in Joshua Coffin, *A Sketch of the History of Newbury, Newburyport, and West Newbury, from 1635 to 1845* (Boston, 1845), 167.

3. Gorden Manley, "Central England Temperatures: Monthly Means, 1659–1973," *Quarterly Journal of the Royal Meteorological Society*, C (1974), 389–405. See also Thompson Webb, III, "The Reconstruction of Climatic Sequences from Botanical Data," *Journal of Interdisciplinary History*, X (1979–1980), 749–772. Susan Swan has found some evidence of Little Ice Age patterns in colonial Mexico. "Mexico in the Little Ice Age," ibid., XI (1980–1981), 633–648.

4. William Hubbard, *The History of the Indian Wars in New England*, 1677, 1685, ed. Samuel G. Drake, 2 vols. (New York, 1971 [orig. publ. 1865]), II, 256–257; Increase Mather, *The History of King Philip's War*, ed. Samuel G. Drake, (Boston, 1862), 47; Carroll, *Puritanism and the Wilderness*, Chapter 10.

living and neglect of New England's special relationship to God, as did the General Court.[5] That war with the Indians created anxiety about fulfilling the founders' purpose can be seen in the many covenant-renewal ceremonies of March 1676.[6] The end of King Philip's War left the settlers with a truncated mission. It signalled too clearly for any mistake that the Indians had not and would not abandon their own culture and religion wholesale and accept Christianity. The founders' belief that they were God's agents carrying Christianity to the heathen and thereby fulfilling a requirement for the consummation of history no longer held. That mission was at best postponed indefinitely.[7]

Following King Philip's War, there was increasing talk of the colonists' being tested or punished to recall them to the path of righteousness set out in the early years.[8] The revocation of the Massachusetts Bay Charter was the greatest calamity of the seventeenth century. Not only did it threaten the special relationship of New England to God, but it also called all social, political, and economic relationships into question. The anxiety generated by this blow sent people back into the churches in large numbers.[9] There was a feeling of being beset on all sides by uncertainty and misfortune. T. H. Breen sees continuing upheaval even after the new charter of 1692 because of the heavy and novel burden of taxation to pay for King Philip's War and subsequent continuing warfare. The taxation caused people to question the old leadership and to enter the public arena in unprecedented numbers. There was no turning back to the old ways.[1] By

5. Cotton Mather, *The Present state of New-England* (Boston, 1690), 28–29. Mather reprinted the proclamation of the General Court. Ibid., 47–49.

6. Sacvan Bercovitch, *American Jeremiad*, 81.

7. Edmund S. Morgan, "The American Indian: Incorrigible Individualist," in his *The Mirror of the Indian* (Providence, 1958); Richard R. Johnson, "The Search for a Usable Indian: An Aspect of the Defense of Colonial New England," *Journal of American History*, LXIV (1977), 623–651, especially 643.

8. Increase Mather, *Heaven's Alarm*, 13; Cotton Mather, *Magnalia*, ed. Robbins, II, 336; Bercovitch, *American Jeremiad*, 76–77, 84–85.

9. Robert G. Pope, "New England vs. the New England Mind: The Myth of Declension," in Alden T. Vaughan and Francis J. Bremer, eds., *Puritan New England: Essays on Religion, Society, and Culture* (New York, 1977), 318, 321; David Thomas Konig, *Law and Society in Puritan Massachusetts: Essex County, 1629–1692* (Chapel Hill, N.C., 1979), 158, 168.

1. T. H. Breen, "War, Taxes, and Political Brokers: The Ordeal of Massachusetts

the end of the 1690's, Cotton Mather felt the colonists had strayed too far from the true path ever to return of their own volition.[2]

It is against this background that we should look at the harsh weather experienced during the 1680's and 1690's in New England. The taxation was not just unprecedented in the amounts demanded, but it also came at a time when the colonists were least able to bear it. The agricultural base on which the colonists depended was declining "precipitously," while they were being asked to provide more in public monies. From 1680 on, the towns studied by David Grayson Allen ceased to produce an agricultural surplus, and the nature of farming changed from mixed agriculture to reliance upon pastures and orchards. New England generally was an importer of corn, wheat, rye, barley, oats, and peas by the 1690's.[3] Moreover, the population had increased dramatically, probably quadrupling from the end of the Great Migration to the end of the century, so the numbers reliant on that food supply were swollen.[4] When the end of the century brought several consecutive years of bad harvest, as happened in the mid-1690's, the spectre of famine was very real indeed. In 1696, 1697, and 1698, there were food shortages which were the result of several years of short harvest even before 1696. The *New-England Almanack* of 1701 recorded that in the summer of 1696 the price of wheat went up to eight or nine shillings per bushel, and maize was at five to six shillings, prices as much as one and one-half

Bay, 1675–1692," in his *Puritans and Adventurers: Change and Persistence in Early America* (New York, 1980); Richard L. Bowen, "The 1690 Tax Revolt of Plymouth County Towns," *New England Historical and Genealogical Register*, CXII (1958), 4–14; Johnson, "Usable Indian," 625–626; James Axtell, *The European and the Indian: Essays in the Ethnohistory of Colonial North America* (New York, 1981), 314–315.

2. Bercovitch, *American Jeremiad*, 88–89.

3. David Grayson Allen, *In English Ways: The Movement of Societies and the Transferal of English Local Law and Custom to Massachusetts Bay in the Seventeenth Century* (Chapel Hill, N.C., 1981), 228–229; Carroll, *Timber Economy*, 93.

4. Kenneth L. Lockridge, "The Population of Dedham, Massachusetts, 1636–1736," *Economic History Review*, 2d Ser., XIX, (1966), 327–328; Susan L. Norton, "Population Growth in Colonial America: A Study of Ipswich, Massachusetts," *Population Studies*, XXV, (1971), 435; Terry L. Anderson and Robert Paul Thomas, "White Population, Labor Force and Extensive Growth of the New England Economy in the Seventeenth Century," *Journal of Economic History*, XXXIII (1973), 634–667; and Gary M. Walton and James H. Shepherd, *The Economic Rise of Early America* (Cambridge, 1979), 51–52.

to two times normal. The *Almanack* further noted that grain was scarce even at those prices and many were reduced to "very great straights." Some people had no bread for weeks in Boston.[5] The food shortage also tested the communal spirit of the New Englanders. During this "terrible Famine" Cotton Mather wrote to the ministers in Connecticut asking them to use their influence to "remitt the Embargo which they have laid upon their Corn unto our exceeding Detriment."[6] The winter of 1696–1697 saw the highest prices for grain and great scarcity of food, according to Hutchinson's *History*, along with great losses in trade. Samuel Sewall recorded the summer of 1697 as a time of scarcity.[7] The winter and spring of 1697–1698 saw the deaths of many animals, particularly sheep, and there was a great shortage of hay. In 1698 people were forced to give their corn to the cattle despite its scarcity, though it was down in price to four shillings a bushel.[8]

So the bad weather of the 1690's and, to some extent, of the 1680's caused more than just discomfort. It certainly compounded the distress which colonists felt from other causes and increased their sense of being out of control of events. Given the fact that New Englanders

5. Clough, *New-England Almanack*, 1701. For comparative prices, see Pike, "Journal," 117–118; *Records of the Towne Meetings of Lyn, 1691–1701/2* (Lynn, Mass., 1949), 29, 39, 44, 52, 73–74; *Records of Massachusetts Bay*, II, 12, 27, 181, 254, 286; Nathaniel B. Shurtleff, ed., *Records of the Colony of New Plymouth in New England, Miscellaneous Records, 1633–1689* (Boston, 1857), 123, 125, 131, 134, 138, 142, 144, 146, 153, 156–157; John Graves, "Diary," ed. Annie Kelsey Maher, *The Connecticut Magazine*, X (1906), 18–22; Hubbard, *General History of New England*, 246; Darrett B. Rutman, "Governor Winthrop's Garden Crop: The Significance of Agriculture in the Early Commerce of Massachusetts Bay," in Vaughan and Bremer, eds., *Puritan New England*, 160, 162; William B. Weeden, *Economic and Social History of New England, 1620–1789* (New York, 1963 [orig. publ. 1890]), II, Appendix A. Dearth conditions may have partly motivated the attempt on the part of the Boston selectmen and the legislature to erect a controlled public market in 1696. See Gary B. Nash, *The Urban Crucible: Social Change, Political Consciousness, and the Origins of the American Revolution* (Cambridge, Mass., 1979), 130–131; G. B. Warden, *Boston, 1689–1776* (Boston, 1970), 53–54; Karen J. Friedmann, "Victualling Colonial Boston," *Agricultural History*, XLVII (1973), 189–205.

6. Cotton Mather, *Diary*, ed. Ford, 191–193.

7. Hutchinson, *History of Massachusetts-Bay*, ed. Mayo, II, 76n.; Sewall, *Diary*, ed. Thomas, I, 374–375.

8. Sewall, *Diary*, ed. Thomas, I, 358–359, 389–390, 393–394; Clough, *New-England Almanack*, 1701; Brattle, "Records of First Church, Cambridge," 359.

interpreted weather phenomena as indicators of God's favor or dis-
favor, their experience of this harsh weather, following as it did on
the optimistic self-assured middle decades, must have seemed powerful evidence of God's adverse judgement on them. When combined
with their other misfortunes, the message must have been unmistakable. In the natural world, as in the political and social, the evidence
that New England had strayed from its special role was clear; the
colonists had not fulfilled their mission and even nature had turned
against them.

Samuel Sewall's *Verses upon New Century* opened with this plea:

> Once more! Our God, vouchsafe to Shine:
> Tame Thou the Rigour of our Clime.
> Make haste with thy Impartial Light,
> And terminate this long dark Night.
>
> Let the transplanted English Vine
> Spread further still: still Call it Thine.
> Prune it with Skill: for yield it can
> More Fruit to Thee the Husbandman.[9]

9. Sewall, *Diary*, ed. Thomas, I, 440–441.

◆◦ JOAN THIRSK ◦◆

# Patterns of Agriculture
# in Seventeenth–Century England

ALTHOUGH they could not see so far into the future, American colonists leaving England in the seventeenth century departed in the course of a long, hundred years of economic difficulty and prolonged agricultural depression. In such times, alternative ways of making a living are urgently needed; people must use their ingenuity in order to survive. These circumstances slowly but steadily brought variety of a new kind to the agricultural economies of seventeenth-century England. The opening up of the New World, at the same time, served to broaden opportunities farther, for not only did America offer new plants for cultivation in England, but it also provided another place where innovative ideas, simmering in England, could be tried out. Englishmen, thus, had an agricultural reason, as well as many others, to look with zest at the prospect of life across the Atlantic. They had the chance to experiment with another mix of farming activities, one which they thought to be feasible because it was being tried successfully in England and perhaps might be still more productive in America because of the different climatic environment.

The agricultural depression in seventeenth-century England was brought about by the falling prices of two staple products, grain and wool, which continued to decline throughout the first half of the eighteenth century. Prices of livestock and livestock products were disturbed—but were not generally as discouraging—and some, indeed, were remarkably stimulated. The fall in the general level of

Joan Thirsk is Reader in Economic History Emerita, Oxford University.

agricultural prices is clearest from 1640 onwards. Whereas the general level rose 600 percent between 1500 and 1640, it rose by only two percent between 1640 and 1750. Grain fell by twelve percent, and wool by thirty-three percent. On the other hand, pig prices rose by seventy-one percent and cattle prices by thirteen percent, although the rise in cattle prices was not evenly distributed as a benefit among all livestock producers. In the second half of the seventeenth century, the effects of the Irish Cattle Act of 1667 undoubtedly assisted breeders in the north and west of England at the expense of the fatteners in south and east.[1]

Certain classes of farmers in sensitive regions perceived, and took early action to protect themselves from, the full depression of grain and wool prices, just as a later generation anticipated before 1750 the recovery of grain prices, a fact not obvious to all until after that date. So the year 1640, which is used in these price indices to divide two periods of rising and then stable (or falling) food prices, serves as a rough signpost only to a watershed between two very different agricultural experiences. Generally, conventional agriculture had been profitable in the sixteenth century, when the demand from a rapidly rising population for basic foodstuffs could hardly be satisfied. Then, from about 1600, or perhaps somewhat before, new agricultural opportunities were being seized for a number of different reasons; not all were prompted by premonitions of a depression ahead. Some pioneers of new crops were driven on by a gambling spirit and a sense of adventure, awakened by an acquaintance with foreign novelties. Some already had firm experience of the current commercial value of new plants on the Continent. But all bold ventures shared (or might share) the same attractions in the new conditions that prevailed more generally after 1640, when traditional foodstuffs were in surplus and prices were sagging. Alternatives could save the situation.

The problem of food surpluses may seem surprising, coming as it did at the end of a long period of continual anxiety about the adequacy of food supplies. Yet, production had been greatly stimulated

1. For the detailed evidence, see Joan Thirsk, ed., *The Agrarian History of England and Wales*, V, *1640–1750* (Cambridge, 1984), chapters 13 and 16.

in the sixteenth century, and farmers did not relax their efforts in the seventeenth, when natural population growth slackened. Contemporaries thought that losses in the civil war and migrations to plantations overseas aggravated the fall of prices by reducing demand. Evidently, they were not totally misled in making these complaints. E. A. Wrigley and R. S. Schofield, in their recent book on English population history, suggest that sixty-nine percent of the natural population increase occurring in the period 1640–1699 was lost to England by emigration to North America.[2]

In the course of the seventeenth century, an increasing number of farmers, who lived by producing conventional agricultural products, had to cast around for ways of overcoming the discouragement of low prices. Some, in order to feed more animals, secure more and better manure as a result, and so improve the fertility of their cornfields, followed much the same routine as before but achieved higher production by growing the artificial grasses—clover, rye grass, lucerne, and sainfoin—in their arable rotations. The general effect of these improvements was to increase grain yields and so offset the fall in unit price. For the most part, however, this solution was only suitable for large farmers cultivating good soils. For the rest, a remarkable growth occurred of alternative or supplementary pursuits. These represented a partial diversion from the mainstream development of corn-livestock farming.

The ideas for such alternatives came from the earlier period—the sixteenth century—when the standard of living of the well-to-do was rising very considerably, and, among other things, the upper classes became interested in diversifying their diet. Two of the new foodstuffs were fruit and vegetables, which came into fashion as food for the rich, when before they had been only the fare of the poor. These things won favor among the rich as a result of lively contacts, newly established by English gentlemen and scholars with the Continent. It all started as a fashion and then became an intellectual interest, finally being transformed into a commercial opportunity.

The intellectual interest rested upon the argument that vegetables

2. E. A. Wrigley and R. S. Schofield, *The Population History of England, 1541–1871: A Reconstruction* (London, 1981), 175.

and fruits provided a healthier diet than the fancy foods previously eaten by the rich; they were easily digested and did not drive men "to seek pepper as far as India." Herbs and other plants, like licorice and rhubarb, were recommended as medicines since they did not have to be brought all the way from Jerusalem and Turkey. "Every poor man had the right remedies growing in his [own] garden."[3] Other rewarding new crops served industrial uses: coleseed for oil; hops for beer; dye plants like woad, weld, saffron, and madder for textiles; teasels for finishing cloth; and hemp and flax for the making of rope, canvas, and linen. Nor should nut trees be overlooked: they provided food *and* timber (walnut trees being especially valued for fine furniture). Woodland trees, too, received more serious attention after 1660 as an increasingly profitable way of using certain kinds of land.[4]

All these plants made their own special demands on labor, land, and equipment, and so could not be grown by everyone everywhere. Thus, the experiments to find the right niche for each were prolonged. In cases where we can follow the early trials with new plants, we soon learn to understand why they made slow progress. One of the reasons for welcoming new plants was the notion that they would be a miraculous panacea for turning derelict or barren land to good account. It was not an auspicious beginning for plants with cultivation needs not yet properly understood.

Optimism shown towards the transformation of neglected land was fostered first of all by the known successes in improving marshes and fens in various parts of Europe, especially in Italy and Holland. Drainage enterprises could be observed nearer to home when work began in 1563 to drain Erith and Plumstead marshes in Kent and, still more, when ambitious drainage plans for the fens around the Wash were laid from the 1580's onward.[5]

Confidence was firmly expressed by John Norden in *The Surveyor's Dialogue* of 1607, in which he proclaimed his "opinion that there is

3. Barnaby Googe, *Foure Bookes of Husbandry* (London, 1577), 67.

4. Thirsk, ed., *Agrarian History of England and Wales*, V, chapter 19.

5. C. W. Chalklin, *Seventeenth-Century Kent* (London, 1965), 13–14; H. C. Darby, *The Draining of the Fens*, 2d ed. (Cambridge, 1968), 13ff.

no kind of soil, be it never so wild, boggy, clay or sandy, but will yield one kind of beneficial fruit or other."[6] Norden's book was written as a dialogue between a surveyor (the author himself) and a bailiff in charge of a gentleman's estate. Both, together, walked over the fields, the surveyor constantly rebuking the bailiff for his negligence whenever they came upon land lying idle and waste. Moorish, boggy land full of weeds needed draining with new trenches. In another place congested with alders, the bailiff was eager to show how quickly he was learning lessons from his companion and suggested rooting them out. But no. The surveyor urged caution here, because alders were useful for hop poles, ladders, and rails. In other odd corners, he urged the growing of willows. Low and spongy ground, when trenched, was recommended for hops; the possibilities could already be seen in Suffolk, Essex, and Surrey. Hot and sandy land was recommended for carrots, already growing around Ipswich and along the Suffolk coast. Little crofts overgrown with nettles, mallow, and thistles could be used for hemp and mustard. Hedges should grow fruit trees as in Kent, Worcestershire, Shropshire, Gloucestershire, Somerset, and Devon. "There is not a place so rude and unlikely," concluded Norden, "but diligence and discretion may convert it to some profitable end."[7]

Whenever a new crop was taken up as an experiment, adventurers (who were usually youngish gentlemen or merchant sons of gentlemen) started the search for derelict land on which trials might be made. Hopes were high of miracles being wrought on barren land. But, in addition to this, it was plainly difficult to find well-cultivated land available for such risky ventures. Farmers, who knew what it was to suffer food shortages in bad years, could not be expected to gamble lightly. Nor did landowners look with favor upon new-fangled crops that were suspected of impoverishing soils. Novelties, in consequence, could be tested only on neglected pieces of ground, which others did not value highly enough to want to keep for more conventional, but more certain, crops. A good deal of persuasion was needed before people were prevailed upon to lease land for new

6. (London, 1607), 205.
7. Ibid., 185, 204, 207–209.

crops. When, for example, the tobacco experiments were started around Winchcombe, Gloucestershire, in 1619, a lot of talking and coaxing by the young son of a local gentleman became necessary before he found sufficient parcels of land. One owner, whom he finally cajoled, with the help of a friendly intermediary, agreed to lease a piece of land he happened to own in Worcestershire; thus, tobacco moved from Gloucestershire into a new district.[8]

For two different reasons, therefore, new crops were usually tried on poor land. When woad-growing commended itself because of the high prices prevailing in the markets of the 1580's and 1590's, two hundred acres of land, formerly a rabbit warren in Berwick St. John, Wiltshire, was used for woad. Another site used for the same crop at the same period was Blagdon Park in Cranborne Chase, Dorset, partly in pasture, partly in rabbit warren. In this case, Robert Cecil was the owner of the land—by 1605, if not earlier. It is tempting in an example like this to suspect that a conjuncture of several circumstances accounts for the experiment. Blagdon Park was "disparked" in 1570. Cecil had an estate in Cranborne. Land in the area was found to grow this novel crop at a time when it was known to be profitable and when it was also deemed in the national interest, in order to reduce imports, to encourage it for industrial purposes. Robert Cecil's father had earlier been much concerned with policy-making in connection with woad and may have financed a venture of his own.[9] In other words, it is not impossible that courtiers who laid their hands on crown estates often found themselves with land that was not very profitably cultivated and was ideally suited for a gamble of this kind. In court circles, financial speculations were continually under discussion. Adventurers looking for run-down land to rent, for their part, shrewdly turned their attention first to the estates of

8. Public Record Office, London, C24/498/22. For a general account of the tobacco-growing venture, see Joan Thirsk, "New Crops and their Diffusion: Tobacco-Growing in Seventeenth-Century England," in C.W. Chalklin and M.A. Havinden, eds., *Rural Change and Urban Growth, 1500–1800* (London, 1974), 76–103.

9. J. H. Bettey, "The Cultivation of Woad in the Salisbury Area during the Late Sixteenth and Seventeenth Centuries," *Textile History,* IX (1978), 113–115; Joan Thirsk, *Economic Policy and Projects: The Development of a Consumer Society in Early Modern England* (Oxford, 1978), 86–87; *Calendar of State Papers, Domestic, 1581-1590* (London, 1865), 532.

absentee owners, of which the first to spring to mind would be crown estates or ex-crown estates. Thus did new agricultural ventures, in their pioneering phase, become associated with the great landowning courtiers.

Run-down land also features in experiments with the growing of madder, starting in the 1620's. The site first chosen was Appledore, Kent, on the edge of the Rother levels alongside Romney Marsh. Another madder plantation was sited at the same period at Barn Elms along the Thames, still another wet, riverside area. A madder experiment of the early 1650's was progressing in a similar riverine position at Deptford beside the Thames, farther east. In the end, madder found a satisfactory niche on the Isle of Ely in newly-drained fens near Wisbech. There, it flourished for a brief period between 1663 and 1678, when the harvest of Dutch madder was dramatically reduced and prices became prohibitively high.[1]

When Robert Reyce described the craze for growing hops in Suffolk in 1618, he conceded that some people were planting hops "in the best meadow ground," but he also described other men who were "draining unprofitable marshes and moors . . . to plant there." Others "planted not in good ground but in the best they had or could spare which was somewhat dry or hard." When the weather ruined the harvest of hops for several years, people quickly put their best land back to other uses and grew hops "upon waste ground otherwise not to be better employed."[2]

When Benedict Webb experimented in the years between 1610 and 1625 with coleseed oil for cloth making, he grew the plant in Kingswood Forest and the Forest of Dean. In a plea of 1624 for more planters of coleseed, he urged its value for enriching barren land, for it "best prospers upon dry sandy ground which affordeth small comfort to the husbandman."[3]

---

1. Thirsk, ed., *Agrarian History of England and Wales*, V, chapters 16 and 19.

2. Robert Reyce, *Suffolk in the XVIIth Century: The Breviary of Suffolk by Robert Reyce, 1618; Now Published for the First Time from the MS. in the British Museum, with Notes by Lord Francis Hervey* (London, 1902), 31–33, as cited in Joan Thirsk and J. P. Cooper, eds., *Seventeenth-Century Economic Documents* (Oxford, 1972), 335–336.

3. Esther Moir, "Benedict Webb, Clothier," *Economic History Review*, 2d Ser., X (1957), 262–263; Thirsk and Cooper, eds., *Seventeenth-Century Economic Documents*, 220–221.

It is not surprising, then, that trials with new plants encountered many setbacks. Only after many decades of experience did writers in the later seventeenth century, like John Worlidge, give wiser advice, stressing that new crops, such as clover, needed the best start on well-prepared, well-manured land.[4] Yet however ill-founded they were, the expectations and assumptions lying behind the experiments in the early seventeenth century form the background not only for English agricultural development but also for the agricultural schemes which emigrants carried to America. They shared the same underlying optimism when contemplating putting virgin land to agricultural uses. A lot of new plants were becoming commercially profitable in England. At the same time, the difficulties of finding land, on any considerable scale for growing new crops, were irksome. The pioneers in England had to collect small bits and pieces of ill-favored land here and there. The census of woad growers in 1585–1586 showed very clearly that the land most readily forthcoming for this plant consisted of small scattered fragments, often of only an acre or two; the example of Robert Cecil's two hundred acres was exceptional.[5] Although many crops benefitted from being grown in small parcels—for this meant that they were more carefully tended—the possibility of larger plantations that could be set up across the Atlantic was contemplated with relish.

The new crops attracting notice at this time were numerous but may be classified readily according to the differing purposes they served. Some were providing food for the discriminating palate and were diversifying diet more generally. Some were valued for medicinal purposes. Some were providing vital raw materials, hitherto imported, for the use of old established industries. Coleseed was among these, being offered as a substitute for imported olive oil, which was becoming too expensive. At first it was used in cloth finishing, but it ended up as an invaluable oil for lighting purposes.[6] Mulberry trees were being tried in the hope of setting up a new

4. John Worlidge, *Systema Agriculturæ; The Mystery of Husbandry Discovered* (London, 1675), 26.

5. See, for example, the Wiltshire return in Public Record Office, London, E163/15/1.

6. Thirsk, *Economic Policy and Projects*, 71–72.

industry, silk manufacture. All held out enticing hopes of a fortune to be made in contrast with the poor returns from grain. But these novelties can also be classified according to the classes of farmers who favored them, for, in the end, when their needs in terms of land, labor, and capital were fully assessed, they tended to be taken up by distinct social groups. The gentry played a leading part in first raising the standard of cultivation of fruit and vegetables. When these foods became a fashionable interest during the course of the sixteenth century, orchards and vegetable gardens attached to gentlemen's houses were objects of expensive attention, and gardeners were often brought from abroad to maintain them. These vegetable gardens and orchards then had considerable influence locally because their gardeners were allowed to sell produce, plants, and seeds to others. In this way, new and better varieties were spread around the district. More small-holders then became market gardeners, since the requirements in land exactly suited their circumstances. Vines were also a serious interest with which gentlemen and parsons long persisted—certainly into the 1650's. Mulberry trees were tried by some gentry, out of loyalty to the crown, when James I went to great lengths to foster them. James had sent a Frenchman, Monsieur Verdon, around the country talking to Lords Lieutenant and J.P.'s, and taking orders for trees he imported from Languedoc. The Frenchman wrote a careful and candid report of his reception in the various countries from Hertfordshire to Cheshire and Lancashire. Historians treat the scheme as a joke, but the experiment did not fail for want of careful planning. People persisted for a long time with mulberry trees and silk worms, and they had some carefully written pamphlet literature to guide them. Fresh hopes were raised whenever another variety of mulberry tree was discovered. At one stage, it was a new American variety from Virginia. Then came news of someone successfully feeding silk worms on lettuce. Yet, at last, mulberry trees could not compete with other fruit trees for the same ground, and they faded out. Nevertheless, in the 1650's, gentlemen here and there proudly sported waistcoats made from their home-produced silk.[7]

7. Thirsk, ed., *Agrarian History of England and Wales*, V, chapter 19.

The meticulous cultivation needed in horticulture called for intensive labor, which the gentry found too expensive to contemplate beyond the gardens and orchards required for feeding their domestic households. In general, their favored activities were those that called for extensive land but little labor. Thus, they took a revived interest during the seventeenth century in maintaining fishponds, either refurbishing old neglected ponds or making new ones. (Roger North, for instance, writing in 1713, expected a return of £6.5s. an acre from a fishpond, compared with £2. from meadows.) They also favored wildfowl decoys, especially in eastern England. Daniel Defoe, however, in the 1720's described two ponds newly laid out at great expense in the West Country, in Dorset, yielding "an infinite number of wild fowl such as duck and mallard, teal and widgeon, brand geese, wild geese etc." which "are sent up to London: the quantity indeed is incredible." Deer parks were refurbished, especially after 1660, and seem to have had a somewhat more commercial purpose by the end of the seventeenth century. They not only supplied venison for the house and made gifts for friends, but also furnished a surplus for sale as well. Rabbit warrens, too, were carefully maintained, and the income from them was calculated down to the last penny. Woodlands were more professionally managed for profit after 1660.[8]

Yeomen preferred enterprises that required medium quantities of capital, modest amounts of land, and moderate labor. A decisive factor in the selection of some of these was the way their labor requirements fitted into slack periods in the farming year. Dye crops, coleseed, and hops were eminently satisfactory in this respect. In northeast Kent, for example, where madder flourished for some years in the early eighteenth century, this was not only because the price was right but because madder was harvested after hop picking had come to an end. Canary grass, much in demand for canary seed to feed to caged birds—a fashion that was brought in by the Dutch in the late sixteenth century—dovetailed well on farms where bread grains were a major crop, for it was harvested after cereals. Fruit orchards, too, were much favored by yeomen as a sideline and spread

8. Ibid.

noticeably in the West Midland counties of Gloucestershire, Worcestershire, and Herefordshire, as well as in Somerset and Devon. Cider fruit was grown to satisfy an increasing number of cider drinkers, when cider became a fashionable drink (as opposed to a common peasant drink) after the Royalist soldiery, including its officers, acquired a taste for it in the course of their West Midland campaigns during the 1640's. In the later seventeenth century, it was a recognized article of commerce. Hops, which had first found a home in Kent and East Anglia, settled also in the West Midlands in the course of the seventeenth century; Worcester became a major hop market, competing seriously with markets in Kent. Some trials were even made in Shropshire. To take but one example, the vicar of Cleobury Mortimer first grew hops in 1658; by 1662 he had received tithe hops from others in the parish. In this area, however, the crop did not prove to be as successful as fruit.[9]

Yeomen also developed a greater interest in keeping dovecotes in the later seventeenth century, at a time when manorial lords seem to have failed to preserve their monopoly. A number of surviving dovecotes are of later seventeenth-century date and reflect both the high value set on pigeon dung and the energetic search for alternative agricultural pursuits sought by all classes in the seventeenth century. A tithe dispute in 1682 not only gives a precise figure for the number of pigeons one owner disposed of each year but also summarizes the same farmer's diverse sources of income, reflecting a resourceful exploitation of varied enterprises. George Clements of Weston-sub-Edge in Gloucestershire held very strong Parliamentarian sympathies in the Interregnum, which he maintained after the Restoration. He avoided tithe payments for thirty years until he was finally presented in the Court of Exchequer. His annual produce from two-and-a-half yardlands was then carefully calculated. He harvested wheat, barley, and pulses, had a dairy herd of eight cows and two yearlings (reckoning to get between four and seven calves a year), kept a flock of

9. Ibid.; Thirsk and Cooper, eds., *Seventeenth-Century Economic Documents*, 86; K. W. G. Goodman, "Hammerman's Hill: The Land, People, and Industry of the Titterstone Clee Hill Area of Shropshire from the Sixteenth to the Eighteenth Centuries" (D.Phil. thesis, University of Keele, 1978), 175.

one hundred sheep, and owned between one and three mares (which gave him at least one colt a year). In other words, he had an ordinary mixed farm of a size appropriate to a man of yeoman standing. But, he had many useful extras: his dovecote, from which he drew eight dozen pigeons in a flight and four flights in a year (384 birds altogether); and between five and eight stocks of bees, which, when sold, yielded five to six shillings apiece. Furthermore, he kept cocks, hens, ducks, and turkeys; had reserves of wood; and expected to gather about eight bushels of apples each year, which were sold for eight shillings.[1] Tithe disputes are full of such brief glimpses of very varied sources of farm income: conventional produce stood at the center of the enterprise, with a number of valuable sidelines on the fringe.

Finally, among small and very small landholders, vegetables, herbs, and tobacco were the favorites, for these required next to no capital and small amounts of land but employed much labor, which such people could usually find within the family. A town market was needed near at hand for the sale of vegetables, but demand built up steadily. Carrots and cabbages were even growing as field crops in the period 1670–1690 in parts of Somerset, probably destined for Bristol.[2]

An eloquent collection of letters from a somewhat later date shows a Scottish gentleman, living in London, writing to his gardener at Ormistoun near Edinburgh in 1735, urging him to cultivate a more discriminating taste for vegetables and soft fruits among his customers in Scotland. John Cockburn was urging his gardener to teach them to be more finicky and appreciative in their purchases. By offering them vegetables out of season and fruits of a new kind, they gradually could be coaxed into coming back for more. It all involved "drawing in the people to a better taste for particular varieties, thus putting an end to the dull conviction that an apple is only an apple and people don't distinguish." Cockburn had learned these lessons by watching the London market gardeners, who took infinite pains in growing and marketing their crops, even, he said, softening their

1. See Public Record Office, London, E134, 34 Charles II, Easter 9.
2. Thirsk and Cooper, eds., *Seventeenth-Century Economic Documents*, 179.

water because they thought it improved the crop. Moreover, they ensured that their vegetables were not "wet, bruised, or broiled in the sun" in the course of transport. Mulberries were recommended as fruit for the table, quinces were said to be more profitable than apples, better kinds of pears and apples were favored because they yielded more than the common kinds, peas and beans that could be got ready in July and August rather than later fetched higher prices, and raspberries were in demand for raspberry brandy. In these lessons offered in Scotland in the early eighteenth century, we see the process by which vegetable growing in southern England became a more commercial enterprise in the seventeenth.[3]

Finally, hemp and flax were industrial crops that suited smallholders admirably and undoubtedly were favored in a number of different areas where expanding local industries provided a strong demand for ropes and canvas wrappings of all kinds. In Devon and Cornwall, hemp growing was linked with fishing and in Staffordshire with a varied selection of metal, clay- and coal-using industries.

Not all the hopes pinned on these many new crops in the seventeenth century were fulfilled. The mulberries did not establish a silk industry; vineyards were gradually abandoned. Safflower, for use as a pink dye for silk, did not establish itself against German safflower, which was cheaper because the labor cost less. Madder only succeeded when Dutch prices were abnormally high. But throughout the seventeenth-century depression, indeed, until about 1750, when rapid population growth started again and the demand for conventional grain and livestock revived, all these alternative crops were valued supplements to farm incomes, and all the counties as far north as Yorkshire and Lancashire showed an interest in some of them.

Thus, the agricultural regions of England in the period 1640–1750 present a much more varied mix of enterprises than in the years 1500–1640. Southern and eastern England boasted the greatest variety, because these counties had been the first to experiment in the sixteenth century. Foreign influences had been earliest and strongest there; thus, the regions of Kent and Sussex were numerous and

3. James Colville, ed., *Letters of John Cockburn of Ormistoun to his Gardener, 1727–1744,* Scottish History Society, *Publications,* XLV (Edinburgh, 1904), *passim.*

diverse, growing hops, cider fruit, cherries, hemp and flax, providing asses' milk for tender stomachs in Canterbury and wheat ears for fancy tastes in Tunbridge Wells. Nearer to London, especially in Middlesex, more diverse regions still were concentrated in yet smaller areas. Here the vegetable gardens and plant nurseries proliferated.

By the end of the seventeenth century, the West Midland and the southwestern counties were also finding a place for many of these alternative enterprises. Teasels occupied 155 acres of Winscombe parish in Somerset in 1700. Potatoes settled firmly in Somerset at the same time, having been brought there from Lancashire. They first appeared in some quantity in the 1660's, and by 1712 it was said that one acre of potatoes that "hit right" could be worth as much as three acres of wheat. The production of all vegetables was urged on for the same sound economic reasons, and the market paid for quality. Sometimes, vegetables showed an eighteen-fold difference between the highest and the lowest prices early and late in the season.[4]

Impressive agricultural improvements in the sixteenth to eighteenth centuries were matched by horticultural innovations that were just as significant in the long term. The two together represented ingenious responses to the mass demand for conventional foodstuffs in the sixteenth century and, then, in the seventeenth century, to the more discriminating demand of a less rapidly growing population. The innovations all had great potential for the future. Some gave much new work to women and children, thereby introducing more than one wage earner into the family. And the high standards of cultivation set in gardening offered many lessons to farmers who later copied them in the fields. The new enterprises spread steadily, but not swiftly, for they were scrutinized and slowed down at every turn by shrewd farmers asking themselves what this or that innovation offered them in particular. In consequence, cautious yeomen and more husbandmen decided that the risks were greater than the benefits.

Many of the alternative enterprises receded into the background after 1750, when mainstream agriculture returned to prosperity. This

4. Thirsk, ed., *Agrarian History of England and Wales*, V, chapters 11 and 18.

fact at once reveals the importance of the particular conjuncture of economic and social circumstances that had favored their development in the seventeenth century. When once conventional farming recovered its impetus, fruit, vegetables, wildfowl, game, rabbits, and the like did not receive the same attention as before; gentry ploughed up the rabbit warrens they had laid out on some of their better land and did not again view them with the same favor until the later nineteenth century, when another depression loomed.[5]

Some historians are inclined to dismiss the alternative activities in seventeenth-century agriculture because they did not continue to expand at the same rate after 1750. But three generations of farmers found in these things veritable lifesavers. The financial rewards are well illustrated in the early eighteenth century by the return from hops compared with grains. On one mixed farm in Kent, at Milstead, profits per acre for hops between the 1720's and early 1740's amounted to £6.10s and in the later 1740's to £7.12s. per acre. This can be compared with a profit of £6 for wheat per acre (but wheat cannot be grown every year on the same land) and somewhere between £2 and £4 per acre for oats, barley, beans, and peas.[6]

Interest in, and fresh attitudes towards, new crops colored the thinking of all classes in rural society in the seventeenth century; consequently, they influenced the thinking of the emigrants to America. Items like mulberries, vines, woad, hemp, flax, orchards, and walnut trees all featured in the earliest correspondence of settlers in the New World. As early as January 1620, the Virginia colonists were reported to be busy clearing ground not only for grain but also for tobacco, vines, and mulberry trees. When a Gloucestershire gardener from England contracted to settle in Virginia the same year, he was promised land that was sufficient for setting up orchards, gardens, and vineyards for growing woad, flax and hemp, olives, and cotton, as well as grain, and for the keeping of silkworms. When, in the 1650's, Samuel Hartlib advertised agricultural experiments and advo-

5. John Sheail, "Rabbits and Agriculture in Post-Medieval England," *Journal of Historical Geography*, IV (1978), 351–354.

6. D. A. Baker, "Agricultural Prices, Production, and Marketing with Special Reference to the Hop Industry: North-East Kent, 1680–1760" (Ph.D. thesis, University of Kent, 1976), Part II, 536 ff., but especially 567–570.

cated fresh plant varieties, the plants so named belonged in this same group of new enterprises that were the subject of common talk and many experiments in England.[7]

In the event, the immigrants were disappointed in their hopes of establishing great commercial enterprises with the new plants and produce now in demand in England. Still, when William Penn's Quakers arrived in the late seventeenth century, the fruits and vegetables were already a sufficiently well-established element in English diets at home to ensure that care was promptly given to providing the same foodstuffs for domestic households in the new environment. In West New Jersey, farms newly created between 1675 and 1682 possessed "unsurpassed orchards of apples, peaches, and cherries, . . . and already Jerseymen were known for their excellent cider."[8] Emigrants took across the Atlantic a whole bundle of innovative agricultural and horticultural ideas that were born and nurtured in the depressed conditions of agriculture at home in the seventeenth century.

7. Susan M. Kingsbury, ed., *Records of the Virginia Company of London*, 4 vols. (Washington, D.C., 1906–1935), III, *1607–1622* (1933), 109, 394, and also I, *1619–1622* (1906), 258; Samuel Hartlib, *Samuel Hartlib his Legacie: Or An Enlargement of the Discourse of Husbandry Used in Brabant & Flaunders*, 2d ed. (London, 1652), 17 ff. and Appendix.

8. Carl Bridenbaugh, "The Old and New Societies of the Delaware Valley in the Seventeenth Century," *Pennsylvania Magazine of History and Biography*, C (1976), 162.

◄§ DAVID GRAYSON ALLEN §►

# "Both Englands"

THROUGHOUT the seventeenth century some of New England's best known observers described the region as a "second England," one of the "two Englands," or linked this New World region as one with the mother country—"Both Englands."[1] While these remarks were clearly not promotional, the Winthrops, Johnsons, and Hubbards who made them never went on to describe the parallels or close relationships they saw between the two. The countless subtleties that made up a common "English" experience on both sides of the Atlantic may have been too obvious or seemed too time-consuming to comment upon. Conversely, since these observers were not historians, comparative geographers, sociologists, anthropologists, or men who had necessarily travelled widely throughout the kingdom, such distinctions as did exist may not have been readily apparent. For the most part, then, the story of "both Englands" must come from other, less literary sources such as local records, legal material, and contemporary maps, and similar forms of documentary evidence.

1. For examples of this language, see John Winthrop, *The History of New England from 1630 to 1649* . . . , ed. James Savage, 2d ed., 2 vols. (Boston, 1853), II, 91, 378; J. Franklin Jameson, ed., [Edward] *Johnson's Wonder-Working Providence, 1628–1651*, Original Narratives of Early American History (New York, 1910), 210, which is echoed later in the century by William Hubbard in *A General History of New England from the Discovery to MDCLXXX*, Massachusetts Historical Society, *Collections*, 2d Ser., V–VI (Boston, 1848 [orig. publ. Boston, 1815]), 541. Other commentators, such as Samuel Maverick, were equally guilty in failing to discuss perceptively New England in light of old England even though he and other writers wrote detailed descriptions of New England localities ("A Briefe Diescription of New England and the Severall Townes Therein, Together with the Present Government Thereof," Massachusetts Historical Society, *Proceedings*, 2d Ser., I [1884–1885], 231–249).

David Grayson Allen is Executive Vice President of The Winthrop Group, Inc., Cambridge, Massachusetts.

At first glance, of course, the differences between seventeenth-century England and New England seem to overwhelm any similarities. Was not England overcrowded and land hungry, susceptible to a high rate of mortality, characterized by an all-embracing state church, and run at the local level by resident gentry: ingredients that were absent in New England? While overcrowding and land hunger were not universal in England, they were likely to exist in woodland-pasture areas and generally on the lands in the south and east, respectively. Yet land scarcity in seventeenth-century New England was not uncommon. Land certainly was available, but often not enough of the *right kind* existed, which meant, as we shall presently see, that town settlers were sometimes faced with one of two choices: either to migrate or to change their agrarian way of life. As for mortality, despite occasional and devastating harvest cycles and periodic outbreaks of epidemic disease, England's population rose from approximately two and one-quarter million in the early 1520's to three and one-half million by 1603 and to five and one-half million by 1688. While the rate of growth slowed down after 1640, high mortality almost ceased to exist in England at the same time. By contrast, the English population in New England did not increase during the earliest decades after settlement. Then it would quadruple during the final decades of the century. In both areas, population underwent upward growth throughout the century, a circumstance which produced comparable implications for agriculture and land use. In matters of religion, no monolithic Puritanism existed in New England, while, in England, Puritan parishes from Yorkshire and East Anglia to the West Country appear to have operated in a localistic manner—in some cases for generations—without regard to an all-embracing Anglican church. Lastly, on the importance of local, resident gentry in England (and their absence in New England), much evidence has been uncovered to suggest that few local gentry resided in many parts of the realm, particularly in areas from which the greatest numbers of Puritans emigrated. If the demographic and social fabric of old and New England was not identical, it was in many ways quite similar.[2]

2. For population estimates, see Joan Thirsk, *Economic Policy and Projects: The De-*

Late sixteenth- and early seventeenth-century England was, in addition, a highly localized society. New industries, new crops, new occupations, and improved technical advances in agriculture brought growth in specialized agriculture and renewal to localities. This growth in specialization was triggered by falling or fluctuating prices for traditional farm products, livestock and grain. In turn, it helped to reestablish regional and subregional market towns as centers for many new products of English agriculture.[3] At the same time that Englishmen became deeply involved in the burgeoning market agriculture, "a new complexity emerged in the social differentiation of rural communities." As distinctions of education, religion, attitudes, and manners developed among the wealthier members of local communities, a polarization of village society took place. Higher wealth and status in communities enabled some to participate increasingly in the political and cultural life of the county and nation, while those at the middle or lower end of the social spectrum remained bound to their geography, becoming "culturally different" from their social superiors.[4] For the great lot of lesser folk who, by and large, made up the Great Migration to New England in the 1620's and 1630's, the transatlantic move did not heighten their social and economic horizons, for they continued in New England to employ their time and energies in traditional, localized ways. National issues and wider influences may have been important to a limited extent, such as when

---

*velopment of a Consumer Society in Early Modern England* (Oxford, 1978), 159 and sources cited; and Terry L. Anderson and Robert Paul Thomas, "White Population, Labor Force and Extensive Growth of the New England Economy in the Seventeenth Century," *Journal of Economic History*, XXXIII (1973), 655–657. Many of the points in this paragraph are discussed in other connections by David Grayson Allen, *In English Ways: The Movement of Societies and the Transferal of English Local Law and Custom to Massachusetts Bay in the Seventeenth Century* (Chapel Hill, N.C., 1981), *passim.*

3. Thirsk, *Economic Policy and Projects*; Alan Everitt, "The Marketing of Agricultural Produce," in *The Agrarian History of England and Wales*, IV, *1500–1640*, ed. Joan Thirsk (Cambridge, 1967), 466–592. While English villagers operated upon localistic premises, such as what to grow for the nearby agricultural market, it is not clear whether they were consciously aware of similarities in nearby communities or of regional or subregional economies. Thus, what may have been localism to them might be more aptly described as having a wider geographic basis than the single locality.

4. Keith Wrightson and David Levine, *Poverty and Piety in an English Village: Terling, 1525–1700* (New York, 1979), especially Chapter 1, "The National Context," 2, and 1–18 *passim.*

Laudian interference intruded upon their distinctive local Puritan practices, but, for the most part, these humbler men, women, and children were caught up in the day-to-day particularities of life which marked their region or subregion and continued to do so, to a greater or lesser extent, once they came to America.[5]

5. This world of 17th-century England and New England, expressed in similar language in my *In English Ways*, has been vigorously criticized by David Thomas Konig (review, *American Journal of Legal History*, XXVI [1982], 264–268) who argues that my interpretation of English local life is based upon "questionable (or outdated) assumptions," is filled with "statistics of dubious use" regarding wealth and wealth distribution in old and New England, misguidedly discusses local "traits," and "grossly" misuses a quotation about the judicial prerogatives that some New England selectmen took upon themselves.

Konig's first argument should be placed in light of the preceeding textual discussion as well as many parts of *In English Ways* that he ignores, such as what I have to say about county-local conditions in Norfolk (pp. 70–71). He criticizes me in that instance for not using A. Hassel Smith's book-length study of Norfolk, which in fact I had read though only citing in my text his more pertinent article on Norfolk J.P.'s. Smith's book adds very little about conditions in pre-migration Hingham to the many other local sources that I used.

Concerning my dubious statistics, Konig insists that I used glebe terriers to make comparisons of wealth distributions. Such a feat would be impossible. As the book repeatedly makes clear, the terriers provided a representative view of *landholdings* in different parts of England. The comparative wealth figures were based on extensive inventory evidence on both sides of the Atlantic and, in one instance, on a tax rate list. Regarding my Massachusetts probate data, he claims that my "sample" was too small and that my characterizations of wealth distributions were too arbitrary. My tables and text are *clearly* limited to the first generation and say so. The extant (not "sample") inventories that I used have been tested at several points for their representativeness (pp. 23n.-24n., 135n.), a point Konig wholly ignores. The fact that the top 10% of first-generation inhabitants with inventories controlled between 27 and 49% of all inventoried wealth, *depending upon the town*, enables me to state that inhabitants from a town like Rowley retained a North Country "consciousness of social place," particularly when such evidence is linked with other, corroborative circumstances like the social placement of houselots, the geometrically-proportioned size of landholdings, and the unusual ratios of moveable to real property found in inventories. Konig has tried to discredit my claims by broadening them beyond recognition without carefully understanding the impact of accumulated details that underscore my interpretation. He further distorts my story in arguing that many local "traits" (his word), like attitudes about timber conservation, should be seen as essentially English, and not as regional characteristics. Yet he fails to note the different reasons for establishing such regulations in three of my towns—Rowley (a tradition of wood scarcity in Yorkshire); Hingham (the presence of a woodcrafting industry in old and new Hingham); and Newbury (the fear of squatters taking over more common land).

Another example of "dubious statistics" concerns my view of a weak county and colony government during the early years after settlement, although, as I state, this

New England settlers were also able to carry on many English local traditions because of a variety of reasons attributed to their method of migration and the conditions they found in New England. Explanations range from a conservative family organization and the lack of outside threats to their stability to the absence of such entice-

---

situation was increasingly modified as the century progressed. Instead of taking on the whole argument, Konig questions a relatively minor point raised in a single sentence concerning the low rate of probate filings in the decades after the establishment of the county courts, a statistic that, in passing, I suggested as indicative of the initial weakness of the institution. After two paragraphs of discussion on this single point, Konig has not supplied us with a useful alternative interpretation because he has not taken into account two obvious factors, the relatively high death rate experienced in the colony during the first two decades after settlement and the age distribution of the settlers, many of whom were middleaged or older. Had he tested my viewpoint against my list of 1636 multi-aged Watertown land grantees, for instance, rather than the 1642 list of *young* (p. 182) Newbury proprietors, his results would have been different. Oddly, Konig also thinks that I ought to compare patterns of testacy in Massachusetts and in English localities, a task that would require laborious population reconstructions and complicated English probate research (see p. 79n. for details) for reasons of doubtful importance and probably unsatisfactory results.

Finally, Konig claims that I argue that my Massachusetts towns were "fully able to order [their] own affairs" by exercising powers "previously attributed only to higher levels of authority." But I quite explicitly point out the latitude that colony law and *earlier* town practices gave to townsmen in governing themselves. That each of my five towns showed so many striking differences in local administration and governance should be adequate proof that local government was practiced with a wide degree of discretion. Whether, as in the instance he cites, the Watertown selectmen ever called themselves a "court" is quite irrelevant if *in fact* they took upon themselves, as I say, a "most conspicuous judicial role in dealing with" a variety of matters, as their records abundantly show. Konig seems to think that these selectmen were mere agents of the county court when, in *a few* instances, they enforced county orders. Yet since other selectmen's records do not show such actions, I am more inclined to think that these particular town leaders, who ran their community like the select vestries in East Anglia, regarded illegal actions of their inhabitants as, in effect, a part of their responsibility, too.

By attacking *In English Ways* on minor, often irrelevant, misleading, or tactless points, Konig fails to perceive the broader themes and implications of the book. Convinced that Anglo-American history of the period must be viewed through county (or higher) institutions and through the socially and economically more powerful men who ran them, Konig construes the seventeenth century as virtually devoid of the yeomen, husbandmen, small tradesmen, and other humbler folk whose daily activities centered around their agricultural pursuits and local personal and institutional relationships—not trips to courts, shire towns, or provincial capitals. Whether *these* Englishmen, some of whom later settled in New England, were concerned with the wider issues and world that Konig refers to remains for him to prove.

ments as staple crop farming and mining, to name but a few.[6] But of singular importance was their method of settlement. Towns in New England were often founded by a Puritan minister, his English followers, and others from neighboring parishes or regions. Of course, not all New England towns were established in this manner. Some large communities like Boston, Charlestown, and Salem were clearly heterogeneous societies filled with highly transient populations. Others were "quasi"-heterogeneous communities like Dorchester and Cambridge, peopled by homogeneous groups that settled sequentially in these towns. For example, a wave of West Country immigrants first settled Dorchester, but upon their removal to Connecticut several years later, another group, this time from Lancaster, came to inhabit the town. The transition from one group to another was evidenced in bylaws that indicated an abrupt change in certain field regulations. In 1633, the dairy farming West Countrymen had established a fencing regulation that required cattle owners to build fences around marsh land in proportion to the number of animals they owned. By 1637, after nearly all of these men had left, the few remaining cattle owners were required to fence against "the Major" part of the town, now corn or grain growers, "at [their] own perill."[7] In addition, some smaller towns, away from the main disembarkation points, such as Reading and Sudbury, appear to have had mixed or heterogeneous populations from the beginning, representing various English regions and institutional experiences.

By far the greater number of communities founded in the Bay Colony before 1650, as judged from surviving manuscript records, local histories, and genealogies, seem to have been highly homogeneous towns. To cite several examples: Wenham, Roxbury, Chelmsford, Springfield, and probably Dedham appear to have been settled

6. T. H. Breen, "Transfer of Culture: Change and Design in Shaping Massachusetts Bay, 1630–1660," *New England Historical and Genealogical Register*, CXXXII (1978), 3–17; Allen, *In English Ways*; David Grayson Allen, "*Vacuum Domicilium*: The Social and Cultural Landscape of Seventeenth-Century New England," in Jonathan L. Fairbanks and Robert F. Trent, eds., *New England Begins: The Seventeenth Century*, 3 vols. (Boston, 1982), I, 1–10, and catalog entry, 49.

7. For the Dorchester bylaws, see *Dorchester Town Records 1632–1687*, Boston Record Commissioners, *Report*, IV, 2d ed. (Boston, 1883), 1-2 (3 April 1633), 23 (2 May 1637).

and governed by men from particular areas in East Anglia; Andover by men from Wiltshire, Hampshire, and Berkshire; Haverhill by settlers from Devon, Dorset, and Wiltshire; Marblehead by townsmen from Devon, Dorset, and Somerset; and Woburn by individuals from East Anglia and counties near London. No doubt this list would include most early Massachusetts communities if others, like Medford, Lynn, Malden, and Manchester, had records that survived from the earliest years, or if our genealogical information about the English origins of settlers was more complete than the roughly ten to twenty per cent of all emigrants for which such evidence has been found.[8]

Eastern Massachusetts was not, of course, the whole of seventeenth-century New England. But this rich mosaic of English regional and subregional variations of population extended to other New England colonies. While these patterns perhaps were not duplicated throughout the region, particularly in places not settled by main line Puritan groups, the distinctive characteristics noted in Massachusetts were also present in Connecticut towns—and to a *more* varied degree, in many respects, than has been noted previously in the Bay Colony. Although local-colony relations differed somewhat from those in Massachusetts, notwithstanding the fact that its founders were "twice purged from the complications of government in England" (to use Charles McLean Andrews's phrase), and despite a "second sifting" (again Andrews's words) of many who had already remigrated several times before, Connecticut settlers continued to carry on local traditions in agriculture, landholding, local government, and lawmaking with which they had long been familiar in England.[9] Much of the remainder of this essay will focus upon a detailed look at

8. For documentation on all 29 towns founded in the Bay Colony before 1650, see David Grayson Allen, "In English Ways: The Movement of Societies and the Transferal of English Local Law and Custom to Massachusetts Bay in the Seventeenth Century" (Ph.D. diss., University of Wisconsin, 1974), 415–426.

9. For the most current reappraisal of local-colony relations in Connecticut, see Thomas Jodziewicz, "Dual Localism in Seventeenth-Century Connecticut: Relations between the General Court and the Towns, 1636–1691" (Ph.D. diss., William and Mary College, 1974); Charles McLean Andrews, *The River Towns of Connecticut: A Study of Wethersfield, Hartford, and Windsor, Johns Hopkins University Studies in Historical and Political Science*, ed. Herbert B. Adams, 7th Ser., VII–IX (Baltimore, 1889), 27.

Connecticut to expand some ideas about the Englishness of early New England life. A final section will explore some additional, general factors that contributed to the continuity of seventeenth-century local life in the region as a whole.

As in Massachusetts, many Connecticut communities were established during the first two decades of settlement. Here, too, they were clustered along the river valleys and coastline. A substantial number of early local records exist for communities like the two river towns of Windsor and Hartford, and two societies founded along the Sound, Guilford and Milford. Each of these communities was settled in the 1630's by an English minister and his local followers. By the spring of 1636 Windsor had been established permanently by the Reverend John Warham; shortly thereafter, Thomas Hooker and his adherents settled in adjoining Hartford, a community begun the previous year by an advance party of East Anglians with ties to Cambridge, Massachusetts. In 1638, the Reverend Peter Prudden and his church congregation left the so-called "Hertfordshire Quarter" in New Haven to settle Milford, and, in the following year, the Reverend Henry Whitfield and his ministerial flock formed the township of Guilford.

Of course, not all of the settlers who came to live in these towns left from the same English region or subregion, but, for the most part, the ministers, substantial men, and those who would later govern the town, make land divisions, survey the lots, and participate in other major town decisions did. Wareham's group, which settled originally in Dorchester, had come from a three-county area in the West Country including western Dorset, south-central and western Somerset, and a few communities in eastern Devon. Although Windsor had originally been settled by a small party from Plymouth Colony in 1634, the Dorchester men quickly assumed control and made the town operate along traditions and practices with which they had been accustomed. By contrast, in the adjoining town of Hartford, Hooker's followers were primarily from mid-Essex. Prudden's group had come from another three-county area in the east Midlands—northern Hertford, southern Bedford, and eastern Buckinghamshire. Lastly, Whitfield's congregation hailed from yet another distinct English region, the Wealden country of Surrey, Sussex, and especially Kent.[1] What marked all of these new societies as they matured throughout the seventeenth century was not their adaptation to the New World environment—that was an eighteenth-century development—but, rather, how each continued patterns of life established elsewhere in their corners of English experience (See Figure 1).

The men, women, and children who came to Windsor in late 1635 and early 1636 had already lived in New England for over half a decade at Dorchester, a community established even prior to Winthrop's initial settlement at Charlestown. By 1635, if not earlier, there were indications that the agricultural economy these West Countrymen had created in Dorchester could not survive: the pasturage was severely limited and substantial pressure existed on what was available. Dorchester's problems with land scarcity were offset by attractions that migration to Connecticut offered: not only was the amount of pasturage much larger, but settlers might even have been drawn there by reports about the red sandstone-based soils of the Connecticut River valley, not duplicated elsewhere in New England, which closely resembled in appearance, though not in chemical composition, the red clay soils of their native English vales.[2]

1. On the geographic origins of the earliest settlers of the four Connecticut towns under discussion, see, among other sources, Charles Edward Banks, *The Planters of the Commonwealth: A Study of the Emigrants and Emigration in Colonial Times* . . . (Boston, 1930) and his *Topographical Dictionary of 2885 English Emigrants to New England, 1620–1650*, ed. Elijah Ellsworth Brownell (Philadelphia, 1937); and the *New England Historical and Genealogical Register*, I to date (1847–      ). Lists of early settlers and information on their English origins come also from several town histories and genealogies, including: Henry R. Stiles, *The History of Ancient Windsor, Connecticut*, . . . (New York, 1859), 122–140 and *passim*, and his *A Supplement to the History and Genealogies of Ancient Windsor, Conn.*, . . . (Albany, N.Y., 1863); Maude Pinney Kuhns, *The 'Mary and John': A Story of the Founding of Dorchester, Massachusetts, 1630* (Rutland, Vermont, 1943); William DeLoss Love, *The Colonial History of Hartford Gathered from the Original Records* (Hartford, Conn., 1914); J. Gardner Bartlett, "The English Ancestral Homes of the Founders of Cambridge," Cambridge [Massachusetts] Historical Society, *Publications*, XIV (1919), 79–103; Lucius Barnes Barbour, *Families of Early Hartford, Connecticut* (Baltimore, 1977); *Families of Early Milford, Connecticut*, compiled by Susan Woodruff Abbott, edited and prepared for publication by Jacquelyn L. Ricker (Baltimore, 1979); and Bernard Christian Steiner, *A History of the Plantation of Menunkatuck and of the Original Town of Guilford, Connecticut, Comprising the Present Towns of Guilford and Madison*, . . . (Baltimore, 1897), especially 12–13, 17, 41–48, 124–131.

2. Barbara Kerr, *Bound to the Soil: A Social History of Dorset, 1750–1918* (London,

Fig. 1. The English Origins of Immigrants to Windsor, Hartford, Guilford, and Milford, Connecti

Once the new town had been established, these West Countrymen continued to operate a town government very much like that which they had set up in Dorchester. Selectmen or "townsmen" (as they were called in Connecticut throughout most of the century) were, as judged from surviving lists of those elected, a small, close-knit group, exempted from the usual duties expected of other inhabitants. In addition, they usually promulgated local bylaws which were later confirmed (and on rare occasions, voted down) by the town in meeting. Long terms in office for these town officials was not uncommon; another officer, the Windsor town clerk, held his position for at least a quarter of a century.[3] Most inhabitants received good-sized parcels of land, measured in acres and rods, during their lifetimes; nearly all of it is noted as pasture or meadowland, and much of it was subdivided from "fields" in the township, though these were not fields in the Midlands or "common field" sense of the word.[4]

Although the Windsor settlers came originally from a three-county area, most were clustered in western Dorset and south-central Somerset, both of which formed a single agricultural region which spread as far east as Wiltshire. This was dairying country, producing large quantities of butter and cheese on land devoted largely to pasturage and only secondarily to arable endeavors, especially the growing of fodder crops. Common fields were absent, and land was enclosed for grazing and cropping. Orchards and their produce as well as pig-

1968), 50–67, especially 53–55; A. J. Buckle, "Agriculture," in *The Victoria History of the Counties of England, Dorset*, ed. William Page (London, 1908), II, 275; Eric Kerridge, *The Agricultural Revolution* (London, 1967), 117–118; Edward Hitchcock, *Final Report on the Geology of Massachusetts* (Amherst and Northampton, Mass., 1841), 17, 434.

3. On similarities in governmental practices with Dorchester, see *Dorchester Town Records*, 3 (8 October 1633), and "Annals of the Town of Dorchester by James Blake, 1750," Dorchester Antiquarian and Historical Society, *Collections*, No. 2 (Boston, 1846), 12, for examples. On early town government, see Windsor Town Acts, 1650–1714, Connecticut State Library, Hartford, Conn., *passim*, and extracts from those records in Stiles, *History of Ancient Windsor*, 141–162. For the role of townsmen in early Windsor, see Andrews, *River Towns of Connecticut*, 88n, 97–98, and on their continuity in office, Linda Auwers Bissell, "Family, Friends, and Neighbors: Social Interaction in Seventeenth-Century Windsor, Connecticut" (Ph.D. diss., Brandeis University, 1973), 168–169, 172–173, 176.

4. On Windsor's land divisions and the landholdings of individuals, see Windsor Register of Deeds, Vol. 1, 1640–1682 (microfilm), Connecticut State Library.

fattening formed minor but important activities for farmers in this region.[5]

Seventeenth-century inventories of Windsor's inhabitants clearly show the continuity of this West Country agricultural economy in the New World, and as the evidence from other communities will later indicate, also the distinctiveness of Windsor's agrarian life in seventeenth-century Connecticut. Dairy cattle were the most prominent and valuable single type of livestock. Meadowland was highly valued: eight acres in Plymouth Meadow was worth £32; seventeen acres in the Great Meadow was listed at £85; and in another section of the same meadow a sixteen and one-half acre parcel was valued at £130! Grains and crops such as corn, wheat, and peas are listed in inventories but not in great quantities, suggesting that what was produced was for home consumption, for both man and beast. Important secondary pursuits included pig raising and the cultivation of orchards. Apples, cider and cider presses, and vinegar are noted in the inventories. Butter- and especially cheese-making are also much in evidence: utensils, cheese presses, tubs, vats, and the cheeses themselves, sometimes numbering as many as twenty-three, indicate how important this activity was in seventeenth-century Windsor. Large quantities of hay, most likely produced from the more nutritious English grasses, filled Windsor barns for the winter months. Dairy cattle and swine predominated among Windsor livestock, with sheep a distant third. Horses played a minor role in the town's agricultural economy.[6]

The inventory evidence of Windsor's agricultural economy is corroborated to a great extent by extant tax rates, which reflect valuations of agricultural products made in the final decades of the cen-

5. Joan Thirsk, "The Farming Regions of England," in *Agrarian History of England and Wales*, IV, 65, 68, 71, 73–75; Kerridge, *Agricultural Revolution*, 115–121, 149–150. For an account of other New England settlers from the same general area but with very different occupational interests, see R. D. Brown, "Devonians and New England Settlement before 1650," Devonshire Association for the Advancement of Science, Literature and Art, *Report and Transactions*, XCV (1963), 219–243.

6. Stiles, *History of Ancient Windsor*, 147. For some inventories illustrating the dimensions of Windsor's early economy, see Connecticut Probate Records, Nos. 1640 (1667), 2139 (1656), 2140 (1673), 2198 (1683), 3896 (1688), 4268 (1683), 4419 (1662), 4610 (1662), 4611 (1673), and 6179 (1655), Connecticut State Library.

tury. Windsor's 1686 list, for example, shows the persistence of the dairying economy throughout the century as presumably other lists, had they survived, would have shown the continuity of different agricultural patterns in other towns. Cows, as distinct from other types of cattle, were clearly the most numerous and valuable form of livestock in the town. Horses were conspicuous, but, except for a few cases, they appear merely to have supplied the needs of personal use. On the average, each household possessed less than one ox, which suggests that many were borrowed for plowing purposes and that Windsor men devoted less attention to farming the arable than did settlers in other towns. Lastly, pigs nearly equalled the number of cows, indicating that this activity formed an important secondary interest of Windsor farmers. These farming patterns were evident in the way in which land in the town was used. Of the acreage that was rated (and therefore in some productive use by Windsor farmers), eighteen percent consisted of home lots, in some cases extensively enlarged and enclosed from the original house lot division. Arable or "upland" contributed only twenty percent of the total rateable land, while all of the meadow divisions—land valued often in excess of twice the price of arable—comprised sixty percent of the productively used land in the town.[7] As this list suggests, continuity of English agriculture persisted in Windsor throughout the seventeenth and perhaps into the eighteenth centuries. Of the four towns studied here, however, only Windsor's lists seem to have survived; unfortunately, no lists of colony valuations of all four towns are available from the first half of the eighteenth century so that we might be able to discern the continuities or discontinuities of seventeenth-century patterns in the later colonial period.

In general, noticeable differences existed in adjoining Hartford. Here, as in the pastoral town of Windsor, a small group of townsmen dominated local government and quickly assumed control of decision-making in the community.[8] Landholding practices, however, varied

7. Compiled from the 1686 tax list, printed in *Documents of and Relating to the Town of Windsor Connecticut, 1639–1703* (Hartford, Conn., 1930), 143–192.

8. *Hartford Town Votes, Volume I, 1635–1716,* Connecticut Historical Society, *Collections,* VI (Hartford, Conn., 1897), 3, 8–9, 12, 28, 46, 69–70, 80–81, 121; cf. Wrightson and Levin, *Poverty and Piety,* 104–110.

somewhat. "Messuages" and other divisions of land, measured out in acres, roods, and perches, were modestly parcelled out of small enclosed fields, though none of these fields were apportioned among the proprietors equally, as was usual in classic common fields. Despite the fact that many of the colony's wealthy and influential leaders lived in Hartford, land distribution was not highly stratified, but moderate, like such East Anglian communities as Watertown in Massachusetts. And like East Anglian towns, sales in lands and indications of consolidation and further enclosure became numerous after the first few years of settlement.[9]

The agricultural economy of Hartford reflected the woodland-pasture pursuits of mid-Essex, from where most of the town's inhabitants originated.[1] For whatever religious and political reasons Hooker and his followers left Massachusetts, Hartford families, like their neighbors in Windsor, seem to have come to Connecticut less for tillable land and more for its rich meadows. Inventories reveal much activity in stock breeding and raising, primarily of cattle, but also of hogs, some horses, and some sheep. Hartford farmers did devote more attention than did Windsor men to the raising of grains, especially wheat, some barley, and oats and malt, but the significance of this activity was only slightly greater than that shown by the West Country men. Clothmaking, however, was an important byemployment—more so than in Windsor but much like that demonstrated in Guilford inventories. For instance, Richard Butler's estate contained quantities of "cloath & serge not made up," while John White's indicated yards of "hoom mead cooten cloth." William Wadsworth's

9. Land distribution practices are based on a compilation of grants from the early divisions, *Hartford Town Votes*, especially 22–24, 49–53; and Love, *Colonial History of Hartford*, 131–150. For small group enclosure in Hartford, see *Hartford Town Votes*, 44, 60–61 for examples; and on practices in Watertown, Allen, *In English Ways*, 128–129. For land sales and exchanges in early Hartford, see *Original Distribution of the Lands in Hartford among the Settlers, 1639*, Connecticut Historical Society, *Collections*, XIV (1912), *passim*, especially in the index, 633–716, where such activities are arranged under individual landholders. For some specific but random examples of individuals and their sales and exchanging pursuits, see Richard Lord, ibid., 65–66, John Talcott, 76–82, and Richard Goodman, 82–89.

1. Thirsk, "Farming Regions of England," 54–55; Kerridge, *Agricultural Revolution*, 89–91.

inventory listed 117 pounds of cotton wool. Numerous others contained spinning wheels, cards, and flax and hemp in sizeable quantities.[2]

By way of contrast, Milford created and developed a society at the mouth of the Hoosatonic River which was very different from the predominantly pastoral towns of Windsor and Hartford. Settled by Englishmen from the east Midlands, Milford exhibited many of the classic characteristics of Midland common-field mixed agriculture.[3] Here the town meeting, or "General Court," as it was called, seems to have decided all important questions. Apparently no independent powers were given to the townsmen. The primary concern was over the ordering of the fields, a process accomplished by the same constellation of actions, procedures, and people seen in other common-field towns like Rowley, Massachusetts.[4]

The fields in Milford were, however, much larger than those in Rowley. East and West fields, for instance, were divided up into numerous "shots" or furlongs, then subdivided into smaller parcels, measured in acres, roods, and poles, for inhabitants. The "Creek Shott" of West Field, for instance, measured forty-two and one-half acres and was divided up into sixteen parcels with an average size of less than three acres. The "Cove Shott" of the same field contained thirty and one-half acres and was divided into seven parcels averaging about four acres in size (See Figure 2). Lot layers were obliged by the town to place at least half of an individual's arable land in the field nearest his house. The town also required that land could not be sold unless it had first been entered into the town book. Noncompliance brought a fine equal to twice the price of the land. If the sale was not

2. Connecticut Probate Records, Nos. 1036 (1684), 5928 (1684), and 5605 (1675). For some other representative inventories, see ibid., Nos. 1025 (1648), 2320 (1689), 2725 (1693), and 5371 (1660); and J. Hammond Trumbull, ed., *Public Records of the Colony of Connecticut*, I (Hartford, Conn., 1850), 448–449, 455–456, 488–489.

3. Leonard W. Labaree, *Milford, Connecticut: The Early Development of a Town as Shown in its Land Records* (New Haven, Conn., 1933); Thirsk, "Farming Regions of England," 50–52; Kerridge, *Agricultural Revolution*, 91–113.

4. Labaree, *Milford, Connecticut*, 8; and for examples of town meeting actions, see Milford Register of Deeds, Vols. 1–2, 1639–1707, 19 Jan. 1645[6], 19 June 1646, 24 October 1651, and 7 October 1653 (microfilm), Connecticut State Library; Allen, *In English Ways*, 38–54.

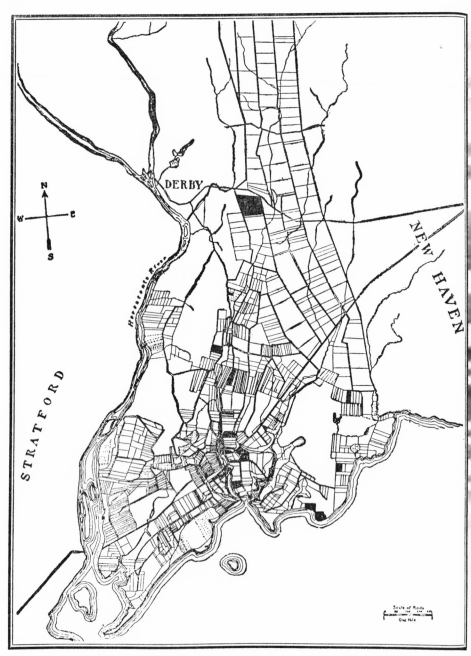

Fig. 2. Land Divisions in Early Milford, Connecticut. (From Leonard W. Labaree, *Milford, Connecticut: The Early Development of the Town as Shown in its Land Records* [New Haven, Conn., 1933], p. 12.)

approved within twenty days, the town was required to buy the property.[5]

Milford inventories indicate what can only be described as a community teeming with many different agricultural activities, a situation which also characterized the mixed-farming practices of the English Midlands. Like its east Midland counterpart, Milford was committed to livestock raising, including horse raising, but also was equally devoted to the products of tillage. Inhabitants produced larger quantities and a wider assortment of crops than in other Connecticut towns, though sizeable amounts were grown for fodder, such as oats and peas. For instance, before his death, George Clark had planted five acres of Indian corn, seven of winter wheat, four of peas; three and one-half acres of peas, oats, and flax were growing in the "new field," and six acres of wheat and three acres of oats had been sown in another location. Milford livestock was both diverse and plentiful. John Baldwin's typically average but highly detailed estate contained white-faced, red-faced, black, and brown cattle; heifers, yearlings, calves, and steers; and "horseflesh" in both barn and the woods. There were also large numbers of sheep and lambs. Horses were noted in almost every estate and many, apparently, were raised for export. The town was widely known for its exporting activities. Inventory takers for Richard Baldwin, for example, listed a horse, valued at £14/15/09, sent to the Barbadoes. There is evidence of clothmaking activity as well as an occasional churn or other dairy implement, but neither was a substantial pursuit and at best satisfied little more than home consumption. As in other common-field towns, the products of the land—the corn and cattle—figured more significantly in the inventories than did the land itself. In Milford, the value of land amounted to approximately one-third of the estate in comparison to one-half to two-thirds in many pastoral town inventories.[6]

5. Milford Register of Deeds, Vols. 1–2, 77–99, especially 82–84; *History of Milford Connecticut 1639–1939*, compiled and written by the Federal Writers' Project of the Works Progress Administration for the State of Connecticut (n.p., 1939), 23–24.

6. Connecticut Probate Records, New Haven District, No. 269 (1665), 15114 (1690); New Haven Probate Records, in 12 vols., 1647–1781, vol. 1, part 2, 83–84 (1681) (microfilm), Connecticut State Library; Maverick, "A Briefe Diescription of New England," 245. For some other examples, see New Haven Probate Records,

Few other Connecticut towns so literally were founded on such a rocky foundation as was Guilford. Of all early Connecticut towns only a few can be said to have been established on such poor soil. But even in these few cases—the towns of Saybrook, New London, and Stonington—the rationale for settlement was largely military or political. About three-quarters of Guilford's territory was either very stony or mountainous land or stony, hilly terrain of light-textured glacial till soils. About half of it was unsuitable even for pastureland and another twenty percent was only marginally productive. While most New England settlers might shun this kind of land, at least during the early years of colonization, Guilford's inhabitants, derived largely from the densely wooded and populous Wealden country of Surrey, Sussex, and especially Kent, were used to the conditions of poor soils and operated an agricultural society largely based on byemployment.[7]

While Milford's agricultural economy fostered an array of activities, Guilford's economic life, as suggested in inhabitants' inventories, appears to be almost lacking in diversity. According to the town's "book of the Terryers," settlers received small- to medium-sized parcels of upland and meadow which were often enclosed by a cooperative group effort of several farmers, as in such similar eastern English regions as Kent and East Anglia. Upon their land they raised some grain, engaged more extensively in stockraising (cattle and sheep) and dairying, and grew some vegetables, hops, apples, and

vol. 1, pt. 2, 3–4 (1666), 29–30 (1672), 73–75 (1679), 101–102 (1683), 138 (1684), 147–148 (1686); vol. 2, pt. 1, 74 (1690), 83 [1683].

7. Bruce C. Daniels, *The Connecticut Town: Growth and Development, 1635–1790* (Middletown, Conn., 1979), 186–190; Allen, "*Vacuum Domicilium*," catalog entry, 41–42. On characteristics of Wealden agriculture and society, see Thirsk, "Farming Regions of England," 57–59; Kerridge, *Agricultural Revolution*, 132–133; Alan Everitt, "Farm Labourers," in *Agrarian History of England and Wales*, IV, 410–411; Alan R. H. Baker, "Field Systems of Southeast England," in Alan R. H. Baker and Robin A. Butlin, eds., *Studies of Field Systems in the British Isles* (Cambridge, 1973), 384–393; and especially C. W. Chalklin, "The Rural Economy of a Kentish Wealden Parish 1650–1750," *Agricultural History Review*, X (1962), 29–45. Like East Anglia and because of the same open manor environment, strong local leadership at the parish or town level developed in the Weald. For the corresponding occurrence in Guilford, see Guilford Town Records, Vol. A, 1645–1664, pt. 2, 9 (microfilm), Connecticut State Library; and Steiner, *History of Guilford*, 78–79.

tobacco. As in Kent, crop farming was not a primary focus of Guilford men; indeed, the town finally required that each owner of upland lots had to "subdue" a half acre of land per year or else forfeit ten shillings. This appears to have followed the practice in Wealden Kent, where tenants were usually required by covenant in their leases to improve the land by rotting down the remains of the grain harvest and to manure the land.[8]

By and large, however, clothmaking and its products and equipment were featured prominently in Guilford estates. John Scranton's inventory lists eleven and one-half pounds of wool yarn, twenty-one of linen, twenty-five of "toe" yarn, and eight pounds of cotton "yearn," as well as some other scattered quantities of material found in different places in his house—linen yarn, eight more pounds of cotton wool, and three and one-half pounds of flax, as well as the clothmaking equipment. Still other inventories list as much as thirty-two pounds of flax and varieties of cloth, including kerseys, serges, and "home made cloaths." Yet perhaps the most unusual features of these inventories are the frequent references to woodworking tools and, especially, to iron and ironmaking: pairs of bellows, large supplies of "old iron" or scrap, and a surplus of iron tools—handsaws, broad and narrow axes, scythes, pitchforks, hoes, spades, and hoops, as well as substantial numbers of nails. The Guilford economy, which relied heavily upon byemployment, seems to have carried on intact ironmaking activities which had been a part of the Wealden society for over one hundred years.[9]

The overall impression left by such details of individual lives and the activities of like-minded men in the same community is one of a more varied local life than we have previously assumed. For instance, settlers seem to have come to the Connecticut River valley not for tillable lands, as some contemporaries and nearly all historians have

8. Register of Terriers, Vol. 1, 1648–1684 (microfilm), Connecticut State Library; Guilford Town Records, Vol. A, pt. 2, 9, 12–14 (n.d.); Steiner, *History of Guilford*, 88, 90, 167, 247; Allen, *In English Ways*, 63–64; Guilford Town Records, Vol. A, 132, Vol. B, 13; Chalklin, "Rural Economy of a Kentish Wealden Parish," 36.

9. New Haven Probate Records, Vol. 1, pt. 2, 41–43 (1671); Thirsk, *Economic Policy and Projects*, 24–25. For some other examples, see New Haven Probate Records, Vol. 1, pt. 2, 13–14 (1668), 37 (1670), and 124–125 (1684).

long contended, but rather to create several pastoral economies on adjoining, if not almost identical land. Our insensitivity to the workaday world of seventeenth-century New England farmers is largely attributable to our misuse or nonuse of data from ordinary and relatively accessible data, such as inventories. Earlier attempts to use such information were hasty and inaccurate: less than a dozen and a half have been studied to determine the agricultural character of the whole Connecticut colony! It is not surprising, therefore, that one recent writer concluded that throughout the seventeenth century, Connecticut agriculture "remained unspecialized by region or town," that "cultivation was the mode of production," and that "little profit was seen in horsebreeding."[1] These generalizations simply ignore this earlier specialization based on English regional and subregional backgrounds of the settlers that only gradually changed to other forms of local specialization in the following century as certain types of land became scarce and as new agricultural demands and markets were created.

What we really need to know, therefore, is how could all of this diversity in agriculture be supported in seventeenth-century New England? The general inertia of settlers to change will not sufficiently explain why such specialties survived and apparently thrived in New England during the first century after settlement. Somehow, this varied pattern of specialization continued to work for generations. But how were surpluses exchanged for other agricultural products and imported goods? Perhaps the only way that we might know how this system worked is to understand how agricultural products were marketed. At this stage the answers still remain elusive.[2]

1. Percy Wells Bidwell and John I. Falconer, *History of Agriculture in the Northern United States, 1620–1860* (Washington, D.C., 1925), 32–37; Bruce C. Daniels, "Economic Development in Colonial and Revolutionary Connecticut: An Overview," *William and Mary Quarterly*, 3d Ser., XXXVII (1980), 429–434, especially 431–432.

2. One of the few historians who has given the patterns of internal and external trade of agricultural produce some attention has been Darrett Rutman, "Governor Winthrop's Garden Crop: The Significance of Agriculture in the Early Commerce of Massachusetts Bay," *William and Mary Quarterly*, 3d Ser., XX (1963), 396–415. For some related issues in the different agricultural economy of eighteenth-century Massachusetts, see Bettye Hobbs Pruitt, "Agriculture and Society in the Towns of Massachusetts, 1771: A Statistical Analysis" (Ph.D. diss., Boston University, 1981), especially Chapter 1, "Farmers and the Farm Community," 6–40.

Our knowledge about the marketing of seventeenth-century agricultural produce in New England can be summarized as follows: Within the first two decades after settlement, New England was producing an exportable surplus and had established several markets for domestic and foreign trade. A weekly market was held at Hartford starting in 1643, annual fairs were established at Hartford, New Haven, and Providence, and Thursday was appointed the weekly market day in Boston in 1633, to which two other days were added in 1696. Furthermore, we know that much agricultural produce, including that grown throughout the Connecticut River valley, was often funnelled through Boston, and that Edward Johnson often described Massachusetts communities in terms of their distance from (and hence, their difficulty in reaching) the "Towns of trade" or "Mart Towns." Certain towns, ill-defined by contemporaries, apparently served as trading centers, while others simply may have collected produce for shipment elsewhere. But in what ways did these towns facilitate farmers? Were they like English market towns or something quite different? As a 1709 visitor to Boston observed, the "Country People" were opposed to setting up market days because of the possible glut and cheap prices that their produce might bring. They preferred, instead, to come in to town "as they think fit."[3]

Still other approaches must be employed to help understand the non-agricultural dimensions of localism and continuity in the seventeenth-century New England experience. The impact of the migration upon occupational structure is one example. For some time historians have argued that the disruptive pattern of migration and resettlement created a displacement of occupations and statuses in the New World. While some shifting occurred, this was primarily a society of rural English in a rural New England setting. Continuity prevailed.[4] Edward Johnson, for instance, mentions that Hingham

3. Howard S. Russell, *A Long, Deep Furrow: Three Centuries of Farming in New England* (Hanover, N.H., 1976), 80, 120–121; *Johnson's Wonder-Working Providence*, 179, 196, 249; Nathaniel Uring, *History of the Voyages and Travels of Captain Nathaniel Uring* . . . (London, 1745), 111.

4. T. H. Breen and Stephen Foster, "Moving to the New World: The Character of Early Massachusetts Immigration," *William and Mary Quarterly*, 3d Ser., XXX (1973), 189–222. Something like this occurred at New Haven, where London mer-

supplied Boston with timber, a pursuit that appears little different from what inhabitants in Hingham, Norfolk, were doing when they sold wood for pipestaves to fishing interests on the Norfolk coast. Johnson also noted that Hinghamites "want not for Fish for themselves and others also," but inventory and other evidence makes clear that this presumably "new occupation," based on a new coastal (rather than inland) environmental setting, was all but nonexistent. Coastal towns could still (and did) maintain the inland pursuits with which they were familiar.[5]

Self-imposed limitations, perhaps unconscious, on extracommunal contacts also helped to insure continuity and localism throughout the seventeenth century. There were well-known exceptions, of course, as both John Hull's and Samuel Sewall's diaries make clear, but for the great majority of seventeenth-century New Englanders, their social worlds or perceptions of the larger New England landscape were exceedingly confined and appear to be related to their occupation and position in society. For instance, after finally settling in Stonington, Connecticut, farmer Thomas Minor rarely set foot outside his community except for occasional trips to neighboring towns like New London. While Milton minister Peter Thacher's world was somewhat larger—he had been raised on Boston's North Shore, served as minister on Cape Cod, and took a short trip to England—his day-to-day life was largely confined to his parish and occasional visits to colleagues in Dorchester, Weymouth, Boston, and Cambridge. Charlestown merchant Lawrence Hammond recorded an occasional trip to Cape Cod to visit his parents-in-law,

---

chant interests tried to establish a commercial center to rival Boston. The attempt failed and settlers there were obliged either to leave or turn to husbandry (Hubbard, *General History of New England*, 317–327, 527). Conversely, some settlers found new opportunities available in the New World and turned to new occupations on at least a part-time basis (Allen, *In English Ways*, 102–103). By and large, however, New England settlers came from rural backgrounds, and those from boroughs were often refugees from the countryside. In a world in which occupational distinctions were still fluid, borough men were never far away from agriculture, and tradesmen carried on part-time activity in livestock and grain growing (ibid., xv–xvi).

5. *Johnson's Wonder-Working Providences*, 116; Allen, *In English Ways*, 79 (sources cited).

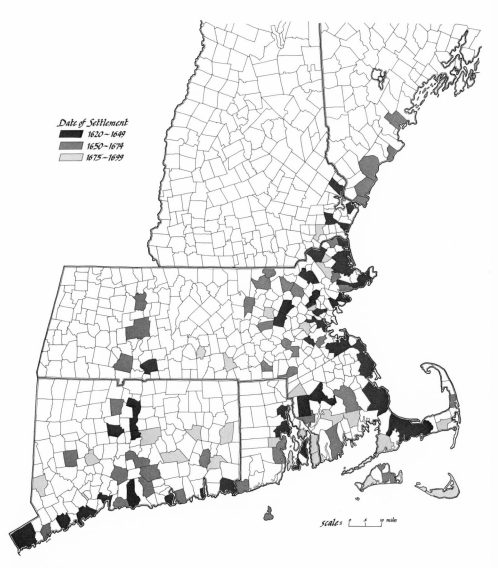

Fig. 3. The Establishment of Towns in Seventeenth-Century New England, Based on Present-day Town Boundaries.

but remarkably little else.[6] Even a century later, John Quincy Adams commented on the rootedness of New Englanders as he travelled from Haverhill to Cambridge via Lincoln. As he turned on to the Lincoln road, he was

very much surprised, to see that very few persons knew, any thing about Lincoln, although it is not more than 22 miles distant from Andover: I met a man whom I judg'd by his appearance to be turn'd of sixty: when I enquired of him the road to Lincoln; his answer was, that he knew of no such place: how many mortals [Adams went on, reciting from Pope's "Essay on Man"],

> On the self same spot,
> Are born, take nurture, propagate, and rot,

entirely ignorant of every thing that lies ten miles beyond it?[7]

Another contributing factor to seventeenth-century localism and continuity was the size and character of New England communities. By English standards, New England towns were huge and isolated communities, and few in number. Once families resettled in towns after leaving disembarkation points in coastal Massachusetts or the river towns of Connecticut, the vast majority of them tended to remain in their new community for several generations. Towns founded throughout the century remained clustered along the coast and inland along rivers where meadow was plentiful. Occasionally, a dozen or so families might move outward to such places as Groton, Deerfield, or Dover, but, as Indian warfare intensified in the 1670's, these settlements were burned or abandoned, and were rebuilt and resettled only in the final decades of the century. Of the 133 communities incorporated in New England colonies throughout the seventeenth century, nearly half of them were founded during the

6. *The Diary of Thomas Minor, Stonington, Connecticut. 1653 to 1684.*, Sidney H. Miner and George D. Stanton, Jr., eds. (New London, Conn., 1899); [Peter] Thacher's Journal," in A. K. Teele, ed., *The History of Milton, Mass. 1640 to 1887* (Boston, 1923), 641–657; "Diary of Lawrence Hammond," Massachusetts Historical Society, *Proceedings*, 2d Ser., VII (1891–1892), 144–172. For examples of men with wider or more limited social worlds, see carpenter John Marshall's diary, ibid., 2d Ser., I (1884), 149–165; Peter Easton's journal, Rhode Island Historical Society, *Collections*, XI (1918), 78–80; and that of John Paine, *Mayflower Descendent*, VIII (1906), 180–184.

7. David Grayson Allen *et al.*, eds., *The Diary of John Quincy Adams* (Cambridge, Mass., 1981), I, 323.

first two decades of Puritan settlement and only about a fifth of them were established during the last quarter century (see the accompanying table and Figure 3). In contrast to the decline in the number of settlements was the rapid increase in New England's population during the second half century: it rose four-fold in five decades.[8]

To some extent, this lack of geographic or spatial mobility was caused by poor roads and channels of transportation, as Madam Knight's journey from Boston to New York so graphically illustrates. Town records amply testify to the fact that connecting roads between towns started to concern many communities only in the final years of the century. Even relatively short distances seemed insurmountable to some. As late as 1716, Hartford officials expressed concern about the town's distance from Yale College, "being So Very remote and the Transporting anything by Water thither being so Uncertain there being but Litle Communications between these Countys and New Haven." Even so, travel by water seemed to some preferable to taking a land route, even through the latter went through a relatively populous countryside. For more than five decades, people seemed to prefer going from Boston to North Shore towns by boat rather than overland.[9]

But poor or under-utilized channels of transportation do not readily explain why extra-town social relationships were severely limited in the seventeenth century. In Rowley, for instance, except for a few wealthy members of the community who had social connections on the outside, it was not until the decades of the 1720's and 1730's that half of the marriages of community members involved a partner from another community. During the seventeenth century, only one couple

8. Anderson and Thomas, "White Population," 655–657. As the number of new towns created dropped precipitously during the last quarter of the century, second- and third-generation New Englanders continued to live in the towns of their fathers and grandfathers. Only with the rise of the fourth generation and the temporary hiatus in inter-colonial rivalries and Indian threats were a substantial number of new towns founded. This occurred for the most part after 1713. See *In English Ways*, 232–235.

9. Sarah Kemble Knight, *The Journal of Madam Knight* (Boston, 1972); Isabel S. Mitchell, *Roads and Road-Making in Colonial Connecticut* (New Haven, Conn., 1933), especially 19, 29–30; *Hartford Town Votes*, 235, 240, 322, *passim*; Winthrop, *History of New England*, ed. Savage, I, 181–182, 333; M. Halsey Thomas, ed., *Diary of Samuel Sewall, 1674–1729* (New York, 1973), I, 16, 161, 174, 175.

**TABLE 1**

## Decline in the Formation of New England Towns During the Seventeenth Century

| Period | Massa-chusetts | Plymouth Colony | New Hampshire | Rhode Island | Maine | Connect-icut | Totals | % of all 17th-century New England Towns |
|---|---|---|---|---|---|---|---|---|
| 1620–1649 | 30 | 9 | 4 | 4 | — | 14 | 61 | 46% |
| 1650–1674 | 20 | 5 | — | 3 | 5 | 10 | 43 | 32% |
| 1675–1699 | 9 | 8 | 2 | 2 | — | 8 | 29 | 22% |
| | 59 | 22 | 6 | 9 | 5 | 32 | 133 | |
| % of all towns created in 17th-century New England | 44% | 17% | 4% | 7% | 4% | 24% | | |

SOURCES: *Historical Data Relating to Counties, Cities and Towns in Massachusetts* ([Boston], 1966); Elmer Munson Hunt, *New Hampshire Town Names and Whence They Came* (Peterborough, N.H., 1970); *Rhode Island Manual* (Providence, R.I. 1981); Maine State Archives, *Public Record Repositories in Maine* (Augusta, [1976]); Bruce C. Daniels, *The Connecticut Town: Growth and Development, 1635–1790* (Middletown, Conn., 1979).

in forty-two married between 1639 and 1659, six couples in sixty-nine between 1660 and 1679, and twenty-one of 116 between 1680 and 1699 involved a partner from outside the community. Nearly all of these extra-communal marriages involved Rowley inhabitants of exceptional wealth and standing, or, as in a few instances, of partners from an adjoining community. Susan Norton has shown that a similar pattern of endogamous marriage continued in many other communities throughout the greater part of the colonial period, and comparable statistics have been compiled for Windsor, Connecticut.[1]

At least one other question remains about New England's localism and continuity: to what degree did English ways of doing things persist? Perhaps the best way to understand this question is to look at it from at least three different levels of persistence. The kinds of customary relationships that have been discussed here are primarily formal and legal. By and large, these depended upon certain social and economic conditions for their perpetuation and persistence. As soon as these conditions changed in the decades between 1680 and 1750, customs and institutions were altered. This is not to say that the customs that Englishmen brought with them were ephemeral, because custom has always been flexible. We have for all too long unquestionably assumed that custom is "immemorial." Yet as historians of continental and English inheritance law have shown us, village people often stretched or changed custom to fit their changing short-term social or economic necessities, and practices died out when conditions inalterably changed. Should New England have been any less immune to a similar fate?[2]

1. Compiled from *Vital Records of Rowley Massachusetts to the End of the Year 1849* (Salem, Mass., 1928), 239–433. See also Susan L. Norton, "Marital Migration in Essex County, Massachusetts, in the Colonial and Early Federal Periods," *Journal of Marriage and the Family*, XXXV (1973), 406–418, especially 410; and Bissell, "Family, Friends, and Neighbors," 140, 142.

2. For examples of social and economic circumstances reshaping inheritance customs, see Susan Amussen, "Governors and Governed: Class and Gender Relations in English Villages, 1590–1725" (Ph.D. diss., Brown University, 1982), Chapter V. Stating the general proposition in another way, would an early 17th-century Yorkshireman have recognized and understood the mid-18th-century Yorkshire landscape any more (or less) than the transplanted 17th-century Yorkshireman might have recognized and understood the society in the Rowley, Massachusetts, of 1750? Both places had changed considerably during the previous century and a quarter, and such developments could, and did, modify preexisting customs.

Another level of persistence of English practices was generational memory and family tradition. Few examples seem to have come to light, but perhaps it is because we have not started looking more closely for them. In his autobiography, Daniel Denison recounted his own migration and settlement in New England, and the life histories and activities of his relatives and ancestors during the previous century—some serving in European wars and the Civil War, others living in Ireland, still others residing in other parts of New England. All of this was retold for his fatherless grandchildren so that, as Denison stated, "you may perceive you need not be ashamed of your progenitors, who have in many respects been eminent in their times." Young Samuel Sewall always singled out "Hampshire" men from the other Englishmen he met, no doubt because such men came from his mother's native county. Later, when he visited England, he travelled to the county shortly after his arrival and saw the local sites and homes of his ancestors. Finally, in one other example of English memory in the seventeenth-century New England mind, when James Kingsnorth came over from Staplehurst in Kent to Guilford at mid-century as his uncle's heir, he was, according to local records, "examined by the [town] Court here as to his knowledge of places and things there [i.e., Kent], of which he gave a satisfactory account to the Court, plainly implying a mutual familiarity with that vicinity."[3]

At still a different and final level of persistence, there are the day-to-day cultural forms which were transmitted from one generation to another but which were so deceptively simple, yet abiding, that historians have hardly discovered (let alone written about) them. We see these English borrowings particularly in material culture,[4] but also in such common and unexplored characteristics as older language forms and the spellings of words, so evident in wills, inventories, and court records. Two centuries after New Englanders had settled on Long Island, "an Easthampton man might be known from

3. Daniel Denison Slade, communicator, "Autobiography of Major-General Daniel Denison," *New England Historical and Genealogical Register*, XLIX (1892), 127–133; Sewall, *Diary*, ed. Thomas, I, 1, 10, 17, 61, 201–203; Steiner, *History of Guilford*, 59.

4. See generally Fairbanks and Trent, eds., *New England Begins: The Seventeenth Century*, 3 vols. (Boston, 1982).

a Southampton man as well as a native of Kent may be distinguished from a Yorkshire man," despite the fact that the two communities shared a common border.[5] Social customs, folk literature, and oral traditions, also long ignored, must be explored more fully, because for many reasons their endurance on New England soil for centuries may yet be the strongest case for "English Ways."

5. E. B. O'Callaghan, ed., *Documentary History of the State of New York* (Albany, N.Y., 1849) I, 678.

◆ DANIEL VICKERS ◆

# Work and Life on the Fishing Periphery
# of Essex County, Massachusetts, 1630–1675

ONE spring day in the year 1666 found two fishermen, Samuel Dutch and John Meager, conversing at Meager's lodgings in Gloucester on Cape Ann about the prospects for the coming season. Both men were single, in their early twenties, and accustomed to the rough ambience of the waterfront. Dutch began by proposing that Meager join him and his brother, Hezekiah, in a mackerel voyage off Cape Cod. Meager, a testy individual with a quick temper, refused at first, claiming that he could find steadier work, "both winter and summer," down the coast at Salem. Dutch then grabbed him by the hand and pleaded the advantages of the unfettered fishing life at Cape Ann—in his own words: "we are all three young men and Can goe when we will and Com when we will."[1]

"When we will." This snippet, recorded by the clerk of the Essex County court, reflected more than mere youthful enthusiasm. In most of Puritan New England, young, unmarried men were not free to come and go as they pleased, let alone to declare that freedom was an ordering principle in their lives. Those who did, wrote Thomas Shepard, "while they live loosely, and are guided by their own wis-

---

1. George Francis Dow and Mary G. Thresher, eds., *Records and Files of the Quarterly Courts of Essex County*, 9 vols. (Salem and Worcester, Mass., 1911–1975), III, 328.

Daniel Vickers is Assistant Professor of History at Memorial University of Newfoundland.

An earlier version of this paper was read at the colloquium of the Institute of Early American History and Culture in October 1981. This version benefited by suggestions from David Hall, John Murrin, Philip Morgan, and Thomas Doerflinger, and from an extended critique by Edward Ayres.

dom for their own ends, according to their own will," may have found this liberty very sweet, but they were hardly fit citizens in a commonwealth which was to serve as an example to the world.[2] What Samuel Dutch was heard to utter ran clearly against the spirit of the New England way.

In holding to such views, Dutch was not alone. Indeed, a spirit of license and undisguised self-interest that truly disturbed the Puritan leadership seemed to spring up in every village that the fishery touched. A particular minister, in a story told by Cotton Mather, once berated the congregation of a coastal settlement northeast of Boston: "Approve yourselves a religious people," he told them, "otherwise you will contradict the main end of planting this wilderness!" Thereupon, a local resident cried out: "Sir you think you are preaching to the people at the Bay; our *main end* was to *catch fish*."[3] The tale may be apocryphal, but, in Mather's mind at least, it captured the cultural gap which split the tough and worldly fishing periphery of New England from its settled Puritan core.

The distinction between core and periphery was something that Englishmen of the seventeenth century felt in their bones. In a less mobile age than our own, people who moved out to earn their livings on the geographical fringes of society were thought to bear a wholly different character from those who remained. The more settled portions of society—the independent husbandmen and craftsmen who worked together with their families on the property they owned, most often within a few miles of where they themselves had grown up—were usually judged the cornerstones of social order. Bound to the region in which they lived by the possession of land, these households were the community's chief agencies for the transmission of culture, leadership, skills, and property from one generation to the next. Around the periphery of this established world, however, there circulated another and more transient crowd of men and women with a rather less savory reputation. Forced off their small holdings in

2. John A. Albro, ed., *The Works of Thomas Shepard . . .* , 3 vols. (Boston, 1853), III, 293–294.

3. Cotton Mather, *Magnalia Christi Americana; or, The Ecclesiastical History of New England*, 2 vols. (Hartford, Conn., 1853), I, 65–66.

the difficult times of the late sixteenth and early seventeenth centuries, these dislocated individuals wandered up and down the countryside in a continuous search for work and subsistence. In the towns and seaports, the forests and colliery districts, or even out on the heath they gathered—anywhere, in short, where they could live unmolested by the parish machinery and where their inexpensive labor was in demand. Persons of casual habits, often without families, brushing shoulders daily with others they scarcely knew, they flouted the accepted traditions of the settled community. Lead miners in the Mendip Hills of Somerset, for example, struck the local justices of the peace as "lewd, vagrent and wandering persons," bent on idling their time away at the ale house, not only upon the Sabbath, but on "other days and times when they should be at their work."[4] Forest-dwellers, who divided their year between weaving and woodcutting, were thought to be a stubborn and uncivil crowd: "mean people [who] live lawless, nobody to govern them, they care for nobody, having no dependence on anybody."[5] Respectable opinion was irked both by the unfamiliarity of this peripheral world and by its apparent lack of restraint. That people of uncertain character with little material stake in the communities through which they passed should have been free to do as they pleased seemed an invitation to disorder.

As vocal as any Englishmen in this chorus of complaint were the Puritans. Reborn ministers and their lay brethren, who found in work "the primary and elemental form of social discipline, the key to order, and the foundation of all further morality," condemned the world of migrant labor at every turn.[6] Men with irregular work habits they termed idlers. Drifters with no settled occupation offended their sense of the calling. Squatters, who chose to live distant from any church, and sailors, who spent long periods at sea, seemed to deny religion altogether. Single men and women, preferring a life of casual labor to the service of others, were, in the judgment of

4. Quoted in J. W. Gough, *The Mines of Mendip* (Newton Abbott, England, 1967), 122–123.

5. Quoted in Joan Thirsk, "The Farming Regions of England," in *The Agrarian History of England and Wales*, IV, *1500–1640*, ed. Joan Thirsk (Cambridge, 1967), 111.

6. Michael Walzer, *The Revolution of the Saints: A Study in the Origins of Radical Politics* (Cambridge, Mass., 1965), 211.

Richard Sibbes, no more than "wild creatures, ruffians, Cains and the like."[7] The wandering life epitomized for men like Sibbes the failings of a wicked and degenerate England.

Regeneration was possible only with the subjection of every man and woman to a godly discipline. For the Puritan individual, this meant the subordination of self to the interests of one's household and community, and, in one's working life, the glorification of God through continuous labor in a fixed calling. These obligations, however, were more than principles of mere personal conduct. Since the Lord rewarded nations only as they cleaved to His Word, the rest of society had to be bent to the same rule. Preachers therefore exhorted magistrates to discipline their disorderly countrymen; as Richard Eaton of Cheshire argued, "the execution of justice upon riotous and inordinate livers is for the present a sweet-smelling sacrifice unto God."[8]

Punishment at the parish level was, nevertheless, an imperfect solution. Only when vagrants and idle laborers were brought under the control of upright men could their sinfulness finally be curbed. The master's firm hand would ensure faithful attendance at public worship upon the Sabbath, regular employment the rest of the week, and orderly behavior throughout. The Lord had ordained that men should live in families. No community which permitted laborers to live unattached to any household, free from the obligations of regular work and prayer, would meet with Puritan approval.

Most propertied Englishmen, of course, would have shared in these sentiments. What set these radical Protestants apart was their willingness to act. In the old country they had proved unusually quick to exercise coercion not only on their families and churches, but through the courts and even in politics in order to fit society to the proper mold. And in the 1630's, when the prospects for reform at home began to dim, thousands of them decided to move to the New

7. Christopher Hill, *Society and Puritanism in Pre-Revolutionary England* (New York, 1964), 457.

8. Quoted in R. C. Richardson, *Puritanism in North-West England: A Regional Study of the Diocese of Chester to 1642* (Manchester, England, 1972), 144.

World, where, free from interference, they might at last order their lives in accordance with God's Word.

On the far side of the Atlantic the Puritan colonists meant to establish a *new* England—a society like that which they had left behind but purged of its vicious elements and composed of none but freeholding producers. Public policy was geared to this end. The founders distributed sufficient land to individuals deemed appropriate but reserved the right of denying it to others who were not. They required all single persons to dwell as servants in established households or face banishment from the colony. And they attempted to outlaw idleness, sexual dalliance, and drunkenness—indeed all the classic trademarks of loose living.[9] In brief, they sought to discourage the obviously unacceptable from entering the Bay Colony at all. Earlier plantations, wrote John Winthrop, with Virginia and Newfoundland in mind, had failed because "they used unfitt instruments . . . a multitude of rude and misgoverned persons, the very scumme of the land."[1] If he and his followers were successfully to transplant the best elements of England's agricultural core onto Massachusetts soil, they could not afford to make the same mistake.

The founding fathers would have preferred the colony to be self-sufficient and insulated as far as possible from the evils of the world outside. But as civilized Englishmen, these early emigrants had standards of well-being that demanded certain goods—fancy textiles, ironware, paper, gunpowder, and so on—which had to come from abroad. To pay for these, as it turned out, the surpluses generated by independent producers in New England's rocky soil were obviously inadequate. If in its material dimension the new Zion was to resemble old England, then the colonists would have to organize an export economy and recruit the necessary workmen to operate it.

9. Nathaniel B. Shurtleff, ed., *Records of the Governor and Company of the Massachusetts Bay in New England*, 6 vols. in 5 (Boston, 1853–1854), I, 88, 109, 186; II, 100–101, 211–212; John Winthrop, *Winthrop's Journal: "History of New England," 1634–1649*, ed. James K. Hosmer, 2 vols. (N.Y., 1908), I, 54; Massachusetts Historical Society, *Winthrop Papers*, 5 vols. (Boston, 1929–1947), III, 216; Percy W. Bidwell and John I. Falconer, *History of Agriculture in the Northern United States, 1620–1860* (Washington, D.C., 1925), 55; Darrett B. Rutman, *Winthrop's Boston: Portrait of a Puritan Town, 1630–1649* (Chapel Hill, N.C., 1965), 78, 157.

1. *Winthrop Papers*, II, 114.

Of all the commodities which the Bay colonists might conceivably have sent abroad, none commanded greater interest than dried codfish. The founders had recognized the market for that "knowen and staple Commoditie" before any of their number set sail for America; and they also understood the coastal waters of New England to be prime fishing grounds.[2] The Puritans, however, were landsmen—mostly farmers and artisans—with little inclination for the sea. How, then, did they propose that the fishery be organized?

During the first decade of settlement, these New England immigrants experimented in several directions. The earliest initiatives, characterizing the years 1629 to 1635, relied, as had the Newfoundland fishery, upon bound servants. Recruited in the fishing ports of the old country, these men were engaged and outfitted by the Massachusetts Bay Company or by such private individuals as Matthew Craddock and Isaac Allerton to serve on yearly contracts under the supervision of the colonists. Through the length of the fishing season they operated out of the harbors on Massachusetts' North Shore. With the approach of autumn they returned with their catch to England.[3]

In its infancy the Bay Colony could never have maintained a fishery without imported help. Free Puritan emigrants willing to labor in subordinate roles were a scarce commodity, and those who knew how to handle a hook and line were rarer still. As late as 1636, John White of Dorchester learned from his New England correspondents, there was hardly a fisherman, master, or servant resident anywhere in the plantation.[4] The few men available for hire, moreover, commanded wages too high for local employers to meet. John Winter, the manager of a fishing plantation in the Gulf of Maine, wrote to his employer in England: "If you do resolve to keep forth fishinge heare, you may please to agree with men at home, for I thinke they are to be hired better Cheepe at home then the[y] will be heare." Fishermen contracted in the old country, whose terms had run out,

2. Ibid., II, 146.

3. *Records of Massachusetts Bay*, I, 395, 402, 403, 404, 406; Winthrop, *History of New England*, ed. Hosmer, I, 119; Sidney Perley, *The History of Salem, Massachusetts*, 3 vols. (Salem, Mass., 1924–1928), I, 232–234.

4. *Winthrop Papers*, III, 322.

never consented to resume work without a raise in pay, Winter complained, for "they give men great wages heare in this country."[5] Only through access to imported servant labor would the New England fisheries ever prosper.

That the capital and labor needed to carry on the business profitably should have originated in London and the West Country was inevitable in a new plantation. But if the servant fishery made money for its English organizers, it did not by that token impress the Puritan fathers. The men it attracted, for one thing, rarely met the standards of probity which the Bay colonists were trying to maintain. The merchants and agents in control of the industry, such as Isaac Allerton, whose "covetousness" so appalled William Bradford of Plymouth, seemed invariably to favor private ends over public interest. Fishermen, like Allerton's "wicked and drunken crue" of 1631 or John Winter's hard-bargaining hands at Richmond Island, never seemed to treat the servant's trinity of obligations—obedience, reverence, and fidelity—with sufficient respect.[6] In matters of religion, moreover, the itinerant fishermen at several plantations proved distressingly attached to the ceremonies of the High Church. Richard Gibson, a cleric, in Winthrop's words, "wholly addicted to the hierarchy and discipline of England," who by his sermons "did scandalize our government," ministered to receptive audiences on the fishing grounds from 1636 to 1642 and found servants at several places willing to pay his salary.[7] Many of these abuses, it is true, occurred outside the bounds of the Bay Colony and beyond the reach of the Puritan authorities, but to men in Massachusetts they intimated visibly the dangers of allowing profits to determine the direction of settlement. All this might have been borne easily enough had Governor Winthrop and his colleagues seen in the nascent fishery much of economic benefit for the colony. Towards local development, however, it contributed almost nothing. Owned, financed, and operated

5. James Phinney Baxter, ed., *The Trelawney Papers*, in *Documentary History of the State of Maine* (Portland, Maine, 1884), III, 33.

6. William Bradford, *Bradford's History of Plymouth Plantation*, ed. William T. Davis (New York, 1908), 277–278, 283–284.

7. Winthrop, *History of New England*, ed. Hosmer, II, 61; Baxter, ed., *Trelawney Papers*, 86, 86n.

by Englishmen, it channeled both the capital and the skills accumulated in New England waters back to the mother country. All the factors of production were imported, and all returned in one form or another to Europe.

Accordingly, about 1635, the colonists began to consider the establishment of a resident fishery. Hugh Peter and a number of civic-minded friends set about to organize a "magazine" that would furnish local seamen with inexpensive supplies and purchase their fish as it arrived on the wharf.[8] Later, the General Court decided to exempt from taxation all colonial vessels engaged in the taking and transporting of fish—not, as Winthrop explained, "to encourage foreigners to set up fishing among us, (for all the gains would return to the place where they dwelt) but to encourage our own people to set upon it."[9]

The key aspect of the new program, however, was the careful management of land grants. In 1635, the General Court decided to permit fishermen who would settle in Marblehead "to plant and improve such grounde as they stand in neede of," an offer of considerable appeal—too much, as it turned out, for the land-hungry mariners began at once to enclose all the land they could; and as the established colonists soon discovered, fishermen who acquired the means to economic independence on shore rapidly lost their taste for the sea. In 1637, therefore, the town of Salem (which had jurisdiction over Marblehead until 1648) declared that "the better furthering of the fishery" could not be reconciled with "the inconvenience . . . found by granting of land for fishermen to plant." Henceforth, a house lot and two acres of planting land were the most a prospective fisherman might expect. Similar provisions soon applied to Ipswich and Nantasket: such carefully measured parsimony, it was hoped, could induce fishing families to settle without causing them to stray from their calling. Married men were bound to raise the moral tone of the fishery, and their earnings would flow back directly into the colonial economy.[1]

8. Winthrop, *History of New England*, ed. Hosmer, I, 165, 169; *Records of Massachusetts Bay*, I, 158, 230.

9. Winthrop, *History of New England*, ed. Hosmer, I, 310; *Records of Massachusetts Bay*, I, 257–258.

1. *Records of Massachusetts Bay*, I, 147, 326–327; William P. Upham, ed., "Town

In practice, however, the attempt to set up a respectable house-holding fishery failed. Colonists of good character and orthodox religious beliefs, even when granted fishing lots, rarely followed the sea for very long. Land was too easy for such men to acquire, and the order and security of life on shore too difficult to resist. Between 1636 and 1639, Salem attempted to draw into the fishery a number of local residents—mostly householding church-goers with property else-where in town—by offering them half-acre lots at Winter Harbor for the drying of their hauls. It was hoped that these solid citizens would either organize the labor of their children and servants or prosecute the fishery themselves. The town fathers miscalculated, for only a minority of the grantees, as far as we can tell, ever involved themselves in the fishery in any way. Some died; others moved away; still others pursued careers on merchant vessels (usually in positions of command); but most simply returned to their old land-based trades, if, indeed, they had ever worked at sea in the first place.[2]

Those immigrant fishermen who did take up the colonists' offer usually tended to be little different from the itinerant servants of earlier years and seemed equally wedded to those classic maritime diversions—drinking, smoking, carousing, and profaning the Lord—which the Puritans so despised. These were foreigners in spirit, if not in nationality—hardly, as Winthrop put it, "our own people."[3] What made fishermen different from their landed counterparts? The answer to this problem lies primarily in the organization of their working lives.

Like all industries on the periphery of the European world in the seventeenth century, the cod fishery could be rationally organized only with the aid of merchant capital. The trading community alone possessed the knowledge of business techniques, the personal connec-

Records of Salem, 1634–1659," Essex Institute, *Historical Collections*, IX (1869), 15, 27, 28, hereafter cited as "Salem Town Records"; Thomas F. Waters, *Ipswich in the Massachusetts Colony*, 2 vols. (Ipswich, Mass., 1905–1917), I, 80.

2. "Salem Town Records," 16, 33, 36, 62, 78, 80, 83, 84, 88, 92. The biographical data on these men were drawn from ibid.; *Essex County Court Records*, vol. I; and Perley, *History of Salem*, vols. I, II.

3. Winthrop, *History of New England*, ed. Hosmer, I, 310.

tions, and the financial power to unite the sources of dried cod on the North American coast with markets in the West Indies and Europe. From its founding, therefore, the New England fishery operated on lines of credit extending from London across the Atlantic to Massachusetts and on the reciprocal obligations that flowed back in return. For their part, the English normally agreed to furnish in advance the salt and productive equipment that the fisheries required and to provide the necessary shipping. In turn, the merchants in the Bay Colony contracted to prepare and deliver cargoes of dried cod to the London-owned vessels when they arrived on the coast. Were the transports to arrive before the shipment had been assembled, the New Englanders would be liable for the damages in dead freight and wasted time which the vessel-owners had sustained. And if the ships in their rush to reach the market departed half-empty, then the Massachusetts exporters would be stuck with an inventory of depreciating produce until they could negotiate the freighting with another carrier. The shipments, therefore, had to be ready on time.[4]

The obligations assumed in New England, however, could be fulfilled only if they were passed on to the men who actually gathered in the catch. Direct supervision along several hundred miles of shoreline was obviously impossible. Nor could merchants be certain, where land was abundant, that hired fishermen would feel the economic pinch sufficient to drive them in a regular and punctual fashion to their work. Most of these entrepreneurs, therefore, chose not to employ their men on wages, but to engage them as formally independent companies and to shift the risk (as well as the opportunity) onto their shoulders. To each company of fishermen, the individual outfitter advanced the necessary provisions and equipment in return for the promise to sell him at current prices the entire catch for the voyage. From the revenue derived, he then deducted the expenses, divided the net profit or loss into equal shares among the crew, posted these sums to their individual accounts, and claimed the fish to

---

4. *A Volume Relating to the Early History of Boston Containing the Aspinwall Notarial Records from 1644 to 1651*, Boston Record Commissioners, *Reports*, XXXII (Boston, 1903), 24, 79, 217–218, 222–223, 279–280, 361, 390; Bernard Bailyn, *The New England Merchants in the Seventeenth Century* (Cambridge, Mass., 1955), 79–81.

meet his export obligations. Some, such as George Corwin and William Browne of Salem, knew the fishermen by face and dealt with them directly; others, especially those in Boston and Charlestown, preferred to deal through paid agents or independent middlemen in the outports. In either case, the aim of the outfitting merchant was to secure a claim on the fruits of his customers' toil.[5]

Fishermen were happy enough with the offers of financial aid and the opportunity to participate in the generally healthy markets of the mid-seventeenth century;[6] but the requirement that companies sell their produce to their creditors and to no one else met with resentment. In 1662, a pair of fishermen from Cape Ann, John Jackson and John Bryers, provisioned themselves on credit from two different merchants, Jacob Greene of Charlestown and Peter Duncan of Gloucester. With Greene, the two mariners had signed a written bond specifying repayment in fish, but to Duncan the only evidence of their obligation was a debit balance in his books. As soon as the season was over and the fish had been cured, Greene and Duncan both demanded that the entire haul be delivered to their respective warehouses. Instantly, they discovered the nature of their conflicting claims. Each then brought a separate suit of debt against the two fishermen in order to establish his own prior right. Eventually, the courts decided that, bond or no bond, both merchants had equally valid claims and left the two of them to work out their differences in private. The law assumed, therefore, that any individual who financed a voyage, by that very act, established a clear lien on a sufficient quantity of fish to cover the credit he had advanced.[7] This assumption reflected actual practice, as the account books of the period demonstrate, for the produce of every voyage invariably passed into the hands of the out-

5. George Corwin Account Books, 1658–1664, 1663–1672, Essex Institute, Salem, Mass.; *Essex County Court Records*, I, 214–217; III, 330–333; V, 8–11, 246.

6. Daniel F. Vickers, "Maritime Labor in Colonial Massachusetts: A Case Study of the Essex County Cod Fishery and the Whaling Industry of Nantucket, 1630–1775" (Ph.D. dissertation, Princeton University, 1981), Appendix: Cod Prices in Massachusetts, 1634–1775, 326–329.

7. *Essex County Court Records*, II, 386–387, 401–402; Archie N. Frost, ed., *Verbatim Transcripts of the Records of the Quarterly Courts of Essex County, Massachusetts*, 57 vols. (Salem, Mass., 1936–1939), VII, 103, 104, 106, 141.

fitting merchant.[8] Had fishermen in an economy that was labor-poor been at liberty to deal with whomever they chose, they could always have found a host of dealers willing to bid for their produce. By restricting this freedom, the individual merchant could assure himself that the credit he had extended at the season's beginning would be transformed at the lowest possible cost into the fish he needed to meet his commercial obligations.

Merchants could not arbitrarily name their prices or they would shortly run out of customers, but with most of the season's catch committed to them in advance, the upper hand in these negotiations was normally theirs. In the summer of 1666 a disagreement broke out at the Isle of Shoals between the local fishermen and a group of traders from the mainland when the latter, owing to the slowness of international markets, decided to lower their offer for merchantable cod from thirty-two to twenty-six rials (sixteen to thirteen shillings) per quintal. The fishermen were outraged and refused to hand over their hauls except "on ye termes they had payd it to one another"— that is, the old price. A series of public meetings were held at which the leaders of the local companies "proffered some small abatemt," but the merchants, who deemed the fishermen's position "verry unreasonable," refused to compromise. The fishermen finally capitulated, and indeed, no merchantable cod changed hands that season at any other price. The merchants had them cornered; prevented from searching about for other buyers, they had no room to bargain.[9]

The fishery differed, therefore, from the agricultural sector of the economy in that it involved most of its labor force in relations of clientage. While it is true that on many Essex County farms most of the physical work was performed by the maturing generation of dependent children, it is also true that the majority of these offspring could look forward as a matter of course to becoming householders in their own right and beholden for most of life's necessities to no one. In the fishery, by contrast, success derived less from the property

---

8. Corwin Account Books, 1658–1664, 1663–1672; *Essex County Court Records*, V, 11, 372, 419–420; VI, 67; Frost, ed., *Verbatim Transcripts of Essex Court Records*, XL, 138.

9. Corwin Account Book, 1663–1672; *Essex County Court Records*, V, 6–12.

and skill which one might inherit and more from the access to markets and capital that lay in the control of another class into which few seafarers ever climbed. No fisherman at any stage in his career, even if he was in the fortunate minority that owned boats, could have financed, without credit, the purchase of the necessary salt, timber, food, liquor, cordage, and canvas for as much as a single season's operations.[1] Nor could he, without merchant connections, have disposed of his produce overseas. Farm boys depended on their fathers for access to the means of production, but not through the entirety of their working lives. The power that a given merchant could exercise over a landless client fisherman was considerably more permanent.

The fishing industry, therefore, took on a flavor that was quite foreign to the experience of landed New Englanders. Labor at sea under any circumstances would have involved a level of danger, tension, and deprivation to which most settled householders were unaccustomed. The peculiarly erratic structure of work in the Essex County fishery, however, tied as totally as it was to the ebb and flow of prices and credit, demanded of its men a degree of flexibility which the Puritan colonists simply could not have mustered. That we may better understand this point, let us pause to examine the course of the fisherman's year.

The companies sailing out of Essex County ports knew at the beginning of each season that the prices of dried codfish tended to move in a cyclical pattern. They peaked twice in the year, normally at the end of the spring and in late autumn, just before the principal voyages of the year returned, and fell to their lowest point soon after, when the arriving boatloads glutted the market.[2] The sooner that one's catch was delivered into the merchants' hands, therefore, the greater its value would be, while the proceeds from a late haul might not

1. The cost of outfitting a four-man company (three fishermen and one shoreman) usually ran between £100–£150 sterling per year. See Corwin Account Books, 1658–1664, 1663–1672.

2. Seventeenth-century price data are not specific enough by month in order to measure this phenomenon accurately, but see the figures for the eighteenth century amassed in Ruth Crandall, "Wholesale Commodity Prices in Boston During the Eighteenth Century," *Review of Economic Statistics*, XVI (1934), 182, and reworked in Vickers, "Maritime Labor," 84. For an example of seasonal fluctuations in prices during the seventeenth century, see *Essex County Court Records*, V, 9–10.

even cover costs. Under these circumstances, fishermen could not simply gear their work in a casual manner to the natural seasons of the cod. Rather, they had to strive at all times to be first—first out of port, first on the grounds, first to complete their cargo, and first to be home. The pressure of time bore constantly on their efforts.

Accordingly, as early in the year as they could manage, most fishermen attempted to secure themselves a position and begin the job of outfitting. The minority—roughly forty percent—who were lucky enough to own all or part of the vessels they operated found their berths ready-made. The remainder had either to ship themselves with a company that was short a man or team up with others in the same predicament and rent a boat in a partnership of their own. Composed sometimes of kin, more frequently of friends, and often of near-total strangers, these groupings all had to ready themselves for several months of intense cooperative work at extraordinarily close quarters if the season was to be brought to any success.[3] At once, therefore, they plunged into feverish preparations for the voyage to come. The fishing shallops from which they worked had to be repaired and their equipment purchased, assembled, and carted down to the shoreline. Each crew loaded its vessel with lumber, salt, and empty barrels; hooks, lines, leads, and bait; casks of bread and salted meat, bushels of peas and flour, hogsheads of brandy, beer, and rum; and usually a few live hogs. On their own accounts, the men purchased sea-boots, blankets, heavy waterproof clothing, perhaps some tobacco or chocolate, and any other items they thought necessary.[4]

If all proceeded smoothly, the vessel could be ready for the first voyage of the year by the end of December. Some companies liked

3. Corwin Account Books, 1658–1664, 1663–1672. In a sample of 29 voyages outfitted by Corwin between 1660 and 1664, 34 of 87 fishermen (39%) owned shares in the boats they operated. Of 11 fishermen who died at sea between 1645 and 1675 and whose inventories survive, 5 (or 45%) were boatowners. See *Essex County Court Records*, I–VI. For specific examples of partnerships, see ibid., II, 320–387; III, 40–41, 156–157, 209; V, 372–373; VI, 67; Thomas Lechford, "Notebook Kept by Thomas Lechford, Esq., Lawyer in Boston, Massachusetts from June 27, 1638 to July 29, 1641," American Antiquarian Society, *Transactions and Collections*, VII (Worcester, Mass., 1885), 406–407.

4. Corwin Account Books, 1658–1664, 1663–1672.

to work the familiar if somewhat indifferent waters off the Massachusetts coast, but the big money was to be made on the more distant
grounds in the Gulf of Maine; so most fishermen pushed off to the
eastward as early in the season as they could. Winter travel along the
New England coast, however, could be dangerous. Storms blew up
more frequently than at any other season, ice formed easily on the
rigging, driving snow could cut visibility to near-zero, and death
from exposure was a constant possibility. But delaying the start of
one's voyage until March, when the weather improved, meant to
risk a soft market upon one's return. So, fishermen measured off the
relative dangers of shipwreck and financial disaster, and, if the high
incidence of late winter fatalities is any indication, continued to
chance themselves in these early departures.[5]

When fair weather did prevail, companies could reach Monhegan,
Damariscove, Matinicus, and the other important fishing sites in a
few days. There, they built cabins to sleep in; erected stages and
flakes where the fish might be split, salted, and cured; and passed
their time catching bait while they waited for the cod to come in. On
the day when the fish finally arrived on the grounds, there began for
all of them a string of long, difficult days working with hook and line
in an effort to complete their loads in advance of the competition.
Hand over hand, sometimes eighteen or twenty hours a day, the
crew members drew up the codfish on lead-weighted lines from the
ocean floor, as much as thirty fathoms below. When the fish were
plenty, the labor could be almost continuous, and in cold weather,
totally exhausting. Just as taxing on the nerves, if not the body, were
the times when the fish were not biting at all. Every day lost brought
each fisherman closer to the end of the season, when the cod would
depart and his earnings would cease. Through the bitter winds of
February or under the hot July sun, as the men sat idly at anchor and
waited, they must have yearned for the pace of busier times. In a
normal season, the work routine swung back and forth between these

5. William Hubbard, *A General History of New England from the Discovery to
MDCLXXX*, Massachusetts Historical Society, *Collections*, 2d Ser., VI (Boston, 1815),
421; *Essex County Court Records*, II, 368; VII, 78.

two extremes; accommodating oneself to a pace of life this erratic was no easy task.[6]

Serviced by coasting vessels from Boston and Salem, the companies spent up to half a year at a time, working out of temporary stations in the Gulf of Maine, before returning westward to reorganize. A typical venture was that of John Roads and Peter Greenfield. Both men had emigrated from England in the 1650's, married locally, and settled in Marblehead. Together, they purchased in 1659 for £100 an open-decked shallop which they employed on extended voyages to the eastward. In the late fall of 1661 they were outfitted by George Corwin of Salem, and shortly after Christmas, along with a hired man named William Ford, they weighed anchor for Monhegan. There, they set up camp, employed a shoreman to dry the fish, and worked through to April, when they returned to Salem to deliver their catch and purchase more provisions. After completing their business, they hurried back down the coast again to take advantage of the remainder of the spring season. In June the three of them returned for good, conducted their final reckoning with Corwin, and parted company. Any man who signed on for a voyage to the eastward could expect some of the same: months of labor on an isolated stretch of shoreline in exclusively male company, punctuated only by visits from other fishermen or the "walking tavern" and occasional trips home on business.[7]

All three may have shipped out again immediately, but most fishermen chose to spend a week or two at home recuperating. Indeed, in mid-season when the fleet was out, even an ambitious mariner might have to spend time looking about for a position. And when the fall season had finished, almost the entire fishery ground to a halt

6. "Downing's Account of Fish, 1676," *Documentary History of the State of Maine*, Maine Historical Society, *Collections*, 2d Ser., IV (Portland, Maine, 1889), 372–376; G. Browne Goode, ed., *The Fisheries and Fishery Industries of the United States*, Section V: *History and Methods of the Fishery*, 2 vols. (Washington, D.C., 1887), I, 191–194. For daily totals of fish caught per man, see *Essex County Court Records*, III, 103; Baxter, ed., *Trelawney Papers*, 57; Box 1, Folder 1, 1758–1769, Joshua Burnham Papers, Essex Institute, Salem, Mass.

7. Corwin Account Book, 1658–1664. On "walking taverns," see John Josselyn, "An Account of Two Voyages to New England (1638, 1663)," Massachusetts Historical Society, *Collections*, 3d Ser., III (Boston, 1833), 351.

for a month or so before the next year began. The erratic alternation between work and inactivity characterized not simply the daily operations out on the grounds but the entire course of the fisherman's year. Many of these men, declared the General Court in 1674, "when they are at home & not imployed in their callings . . . tended to be spectators, or otherwise idleing, gameing, or spending their time unprofitably whereby such persons as attend their duty, & spend time in that service, are discouraged."[8] Puritan colonists who believed that work was pleasing to God only when performed in a regular and disciplined manner obviously thought this alternation of frantic activity and idleness to be rooted in moral failing. In fact, the irregularity of work patterns was a necessary feature of this seasonal and market-oriented calling.

Such attention to prices and credit not only set fishermen against the clock; it also set them against one another. During the course of a busy season, disagreements between companies broke out continually. In a choice harbor to the eastward, for example, the competition over land and timber could be fierce, and, with no magistrates or constables at hand, petty squabbles and incidents of trespass could flare up into major disputes at any time. Reports of "diverse fishermen . . . pulling downe, ruinatinge and brakeing up of Stages, Flakes and other edifices" filtered into the Maine courts throughout the period.[9] Even in Marblehead, where property rights were more clearly spelled out and justice was relatively close at hand, misunderstandings about moorings and rights around the stages led repeatedly to fisticuffs and legal suits.[1]

Even more disruptive to the life of a fishing company were the tensions which brewed within. A trade that demanded such strict cooperation in a hostile environment, as did working in small boats at sea, was certain to generate levels of interpersonal friction that on extended voyages proved difficult to defuse. There is only one recorded murder in the annals of the early fishery—when Gregory

8. *Records of Massachusetts Bay*, IV, ii, 552.

9. Charles T. Libby *et al.*, eds., *Province and Court Records of Maine*, 6 vols. (Portland, Maine, 1928–1974), I, 52; II, 88, 98–99, 115, 132, 209.

1. *Essex County Court Records*, III, 107–108; V, 109–110.

Caswell felled his employer "with the broad end of an Hamer" at Monhegan Island in 1654—but the escalation in strain to the point of violent conflict, especially when inhibitions had been lowered by drink, was a common pattern.[2] Fully one-quarter of all the violent crimes reported to the quarterly courts of Essex County in the seventeenth century were committed by residents of Marblehead—four times the rate which its population would lead one to expect.[3] John Josselyn, who spent several years on the coast of Maine, advised men of "quality" to steer clear of fishermen under the influence, "for when *wine* in their guts is at full tide, they quarrel, fight and do one another mischief."[4]

Nothing testifies to the power of these internal strains as does the instability of partnerships. Three years seems to have been the maximum lifetime for any company, and many, especially among those who did not own the vessels they operated, broke up after one or two voyages. John Roads of Marblehead, one fisherman whose career can be followed over a number of years, worked in at least seven different companies between 1655 and 1670; William Woods of the same town belonged to a minimum of four, between 1659 and 1668.[5] So constant was this shuffling of personnel, even in mid-season, that in 1679 the General Court had to order "that all fishermen that are shipt upon a winter & spring voyage shall duely attend the same," and those who had signed on for the summer "shall not presume to breake off the said voyage before the last of October."[6] Nevertheless, while the court forbade desertion, it recognized that partnerships might legitimately be reorganized at least twice a year. Such latitude,

2. John Noble and John F. Cronin, eds., *Records of the Court of Assistants of the Colony of the Massachusetts Bay, 1630–1692* (Boston, 1928), III, 61.

3. *Essex County Court Records*, I–VIII. Of 42 cases of "assault," "battery," and "striking," recorded in the years 1640–1642, 1650–1652, 1660–1662, 1670–1672, 1680–1682, 11 (or 26%) involved residents of Marblehead, a town which accounted for no more than 8% of Essex County's population. See Evarts B. Greene and Virginia D. Harrington, eds., *American Population before the Federal Census of 1790* (New York, 1932), 19–21.

4. Josselyn, "Account of Two Voyages," 352.

5. Corwin Account Books, 1658–1664, 1663–1672; *Essex County Court Records*, II, 26.

6. *Records of Massachusetts Bay*, V, 212.

unnecessary in a stable farming community, was essential to the highly competitive fishery.

Needless to say, the overwhelming majority of villagers in the Bay Colony would have found life in the cod fishery intolerable. The erratic pace of work, the flux in personnel, the peculiarly maritime hardships, the occasional necessity of toiling on the Sabbath, the enforced absence from home and church, and the ethic of competition fostered by the industry would clearly have grated on men who placed such value on religion, discipline, and the maintenance of social order. Most important of all, householders who took pride in economic self-sufficiency could never have accommodated themselves to the patterns of employment and obligation which the fishery imposed upon its work force. Given the availability of free land in Massachusetts, few of them had to. The scarcities and inequalities of property ownership, which in old England had served to determine who worked for whom, had far less force in the New World. Where free men found it a relatively simple matter to acquire the land they needed, the supply of laborers willing to toil under the hands of other men tended naturally to diminish. Emmanuel Downing pointed out in 1645 that "our children's children will hardly see this great Continent filled with people, soe that our servants will still desire freedome to plant for themselves and not staye but for verie great wages."[7] This was a problem. In a country where every man seemed bent on individual independence, how could an ample supply of reliable and inexpensive fishing hands be recruited?

The social origins of fishermen are not easy to trace. Their names surface without warning in merchants' accounts and frequently disappear just as quickly. The best way to tackle the problem is to establish, first, who they were not. Hardly any—roughly eleven percent of those who can be identified—were part of the Great Migration of the 1630's, nor did the group contain any blacks or Indian servants or more than a handful of indentured Englishmen. Judging from surnames and the observations of contemporaries, it appears, rather, that

7. *Winthrop Papers*, V, 38.

the great majority of fishermen were drawn from a pool of British maritime laborers who made their living on the North Atlantic and stopped in at the ports of Essex County, not for reasons of political or religious persecution, but to fish.[8] "Marblehead," noted its inhabitants in a petition of 1667, "hath been a place of fishing for many yeares past, on which Acco$^t$ divers persons from England, Newfound Land, and other places have [reso]rted thither, many of them persons undesirable and of noe estates, butt rather indebted."[9] Some chose to stay on and settle; others left at the end of the season; but almost all were, by Puritan standards, outsiders.

The Newfoundland fishery in particular seemed to channel a large number of mariners southward to Massachusetts. West Countrymen who had signed on for a summer voyage to the Grand Banks often discovered at the end of the season that their employers, in order to save on provisions and cargo space, would rather "pack them away to New England" than carry them home. Shipmasters from Boston and Salem, provisioning the Newfoundland fishery and anxious for return freight, were only too happy to offer them passage back to the Bay Colony. A great many of these penniless immigrants stayed for no more than a season or two, but, when markets were healthy, as they normally were in this period, their labor was vital to the fishing economy.[1]

8. The names of 205 fishermen were drawn from the Corwin Account Books, 1658–1664, 1663–1672; *Essex County Court Records*, I–VI; William B. Trask *et al.*, *Suffolk Deeds*, 14 vols. (Boston, 1880–1906); and Lechford, "Notebook." Only fishermen for whom actual voyages could be identified were included. Their origins and careers were traced in Perley, *History of Salem*, I–III; John J. Babson, *History of the Town of Gloucester, Cape Ann, including the Town of Rockport* (Gloucester, Mass., 1860); *Essex County Court Records*, I–IX; *Vital Records of Salem, Massachusetts, to the End of the Year, 1849*, 6 vols. (Salem, Mass., 1916–1925); *Vital Records of Gloucester, Massachusetts, to the End of the Year 1849*, 3 vols. (Topsfield, Mass., 1911–1924); *Vital Records of Marblehead, Massachusetts to the End of the Year 1849*, 3 vols. (Salem, Mass., 1903–1908); Essex County Probate Files, Registry of Probate, Essex County Courthouse, Salem, Massachusetts; "Salem Town Records"; William H. Bowden, ed., "Marblehead Town Records, 1648–1683," Essex Institute, *Historical Collections*, LXIX (1933), 207–329.

9. *Essex County Court Records*, V, 373.

1. W. Noel Sainsbury *et al.*, *Calendar of State Papers, Colonial Series* (London, 1860), *American and West Indies*, V, *1661–1668*, 559, 560; VII, *1669–1674*, 257; IX, *1675–1676*, 600; XI, *1681–1685*, 294; XIX, *1701*, 529–530; XXX, *1717–1718*, 318; XXXIX, *1732*, 225.

Two considerations drew these men to New England's shores: the high rate of earnings and the ease of obtaining credit. Essex County fishermen in the mid-seventeenth century earned on average about £20 sterling (room and board, such as it was, included) for no more than ten months' work in the year.[2] Compared to the incomes of freeholding landsmen, this was hardly an enormous sum, but nowhere in the North Atlantic—on merchant vessels, in the servant fishery at Newfoundland, or on the London docks—could a common mariner do as well.[3] "There being great wages given to men in New England," wrote one Newfoundlander in 1700, "makes men desirous to go there, and frequently attempt it."[4] The same could have been said for the entire period after 1645.

Fishing merchants did not offer such terms out of generosity but because the scarcity of mariners had forced them to enter the Atlantic labor market and to bid high. The colonists were competing for hands, not only with their counterparts across the ocean, but with one another as well. Every outfitter of ambition had to devote much of his energies towards drawing fishermen away from the patronage of others and into his own fold. He could have accomplished this easily enough by reducing the prices he charged on supplies or paying higher sums for fish. This would have been expensive, however, and most merchants preferred another tack. We have already noted the way in which credit was bestowed on companies to regulate the delivery of their produce; it was also used in individual accounts as an agent in the recruiting of men.

Fishermen who appeared to be good risks could normally obtain supplies from a given creditor for their personal use, often in sums exceeding several years' earnings, interest-free, on practically no col-

2. This average was calculated from a sample of 51 annual incomes drawn from the years 1666–1671 in Corwin Account Book, 1663–1672. Here as elsewhere in this paper, Massachusetts currency values were converted into British sterling using John J. McCusker, *Money and Exchange in Europe and America, 1600–1775: A Handbook* (Chapel Hill, N.C., 1978).

3. Ralph Davis, *The Rise of the English Shipping Industry in the Seventeenth and Eighteenth Centuries* (London, 1962), 135, 151–152; Harold Innis, *The Cod Fisheries: The History of an International Economy* (Toronto, 1929), 70n–71n, 101; Gillian T. Cell, *English Enterprise in Newfoundland, 1577–1660* (Toronto, 1969), 16.

4. *Calendar of State Papers, Colonial, 1700*, XVIII, 522.

lateral, if they would agree to deal with him alone. These merchants were generally prepared to let these obligations stand for years on end; indeed, for as long as the mariners who held them continued to deliver the fish. Farmers and artisans, too, were frequently debtors but generally for much smaller sums. As the table below demonstrates, fishermen, both active and retired, were much more likely to possess book debts when they died than were their neighbors on the mainland.[5] The account books of George Corwin, one of Salem's wealthiest merchant outfitters, point in the same direction: sampling

### Credit Position of Inventoried
### Essex County Decedents, 1645–1775

| | Percentage by Credit or Debit Balance | | | | |
| | Credit | | | Debit | |
| | £20+ | £5–£20 | £5–(£5) | (£5)–(£20) | (£20)+ |
| --- | --- | --- | --- | --- | --- |
| Non-Maritime Sample | | | | | |
| 1645–1675 (n=45) | 15 | 6 | 43 | 13 | 23 |
| Active Fishermen | | | | | |
| 1645–1675 (n=20) | 5 | 10 | 15 | 30 | 40 |
| 1676–1725 (n=22) | 5 | 14 | 46 | 32 | 9 |
| 1726–1775 (n=14) | 7 | 7 | 78 | 7 | 0 |
| Total Fishermen | | | | | |
| 1645–1675 (n=24) | 4 | 8 | 25 | 30 | 33 |
| 1676–1725 (n=48) | 6 | 2 | 50 | 21 | 21 |
| 1726–1775 (n=32) | 9 | 6 | 56 | 16 | 13 |

SOURCES: The inventories in the non-maritime sample were drawn at random from *Essex County Court Records*, I–VI; those of fishermen were taken from ibid., I–IX, and the Essex County Probate Files. Only fishermen for whom actual voyages could be identified from the sources in footnote 8, p. 102, and from other account books in different Essex County repositories (see Vickers, "Maritime Labor," 353–355, for a complete listing) were included. Fishermen were deemed "active" if their death occurred in the same quarter century (e.g., 1676–1700, 1751–1775) as their last recorded voyage.

5. *Essex County Court Records*, I–IX; Essex County Probate Files. Fishermen in "mid-career" were defined as those whose estates were probated within ten years of their last recorded voyage. For the techniques of sampling used, see Vickers, "Maritime Labor," 140, n. 102.

the ledger balances of those who brought in fish and farm produce in the years 1658 and 1661 shows that fishermen had accumulated an average of £35 sterling in debts, while the comparative figure for farmers was only £14.[6] In some cases the amounts that Corwin and his competition were willing to advance individual fishermen could be staggering. John Slater, a young man of twenty-nine who lived with his new wife in a sparsely furnished house at Marblehead, died in 1665 owing Corwin almost £90 sterling, the equivalent of more than four years' wages. John Roads and Henry Trevett, both of whom worked for the same merchant between 1660 and 1675, were almost invariably between £75 and £200 in debt.[7] Granted, sums this high were unusual, but fishermen/creditors were rarer still.

Was this indebtedness rooted in poverty alone? Although fisher-

6. Corwin Account Book, 1658–1664. For sampling techniques, see Vickers, "Maritime Labor," 140, n. 104. By the second quarter of the eighteenth century, as the Table makes clear, the indebtedness recorded in the probated estates of fishermen had greatly diminished. The account books of merchants tell a similar story: the phenomenon of chronic indebtedness, so characteristic of Corwin's era, had almost disappeared by the middle of the following century.

| | Persistent Debtors | Mixed | Persistent Creditors |
|---|---|---|---|
| George Corwin (Salem) 1659–1660 | 18 | 10 | 2 |
| Miles Ward (Salem) 1745–1760 | 0 | 10 | 0 |
| William Stevens (Gloucester) 1769–1775 | 2 | 8 | 6 |
| William Knight (Marblehead) 1767–1775 | 0 | 5 | 3 |

Obviously, credit was no longer essential to the manning of the fishery. As more and more mariners decided to settle in the outports, marry, and raise up their sons in the trade, the scarcity of labor began to ebb. Merchants no longer had to compete with one another over the fishing hands they needed, and their generosity in advancing goods evaporated. The precise timing of this transition is hard to pinpoint, but the plethora of debt cases involving fishermen heard before the Essex County Inferior Court of Common Pleas in the 1720's and 1730's suggests that it was in the course of these two decades that the purse strings were drawn. See the George Corwin Account Book, 1658–1664; Miles Ward Account Books, 1736–1745, 1745–1753, 1753–1764; William Stevens Account Book, 1769–1775; and William Knight Account Book, 1769–1775, all in the Essex Institute, Salem, Mass.; Files of the Inferior Court of Common Pleas for Essex County, Essex Institute, Salem, Mass.; and Vickers, "Maritime Labor," 211–215.

7. Corwin Account Books, 1658–1664, 1663–1672; *Essex County Court Records*, III, 102, 103, 267–268.

men were certainly among the poorest inhabitants of Essex County, the facts indicate a more complicated explanation. For one thing, relatively flourishing mariners were no more likely to be free of debt, judging from inventories, than their less prosperous neighbors. In fact, three of the five wealthiest fishermen in the probate records— William Charles, Job Hilliard, and Edmund Nicholson—were also among the five most indebted.[8] William Nick, a shoreman and client of Corwin, who died in 1683 owning a well-appointed house, an orchard and field, two stages, two boats, a fishyard, and a warehouse, worth £545 sterling together, counted the most liabilities, £204, of any man involved in the fishery during the period.[9]

The true function of debt and credit in the industry was stated in its plainest fashion by John Josselyn:

if fishermen save a Kental or two to buy shooes and stockins, shirts and waistcoats with, 'tis well, otherwayes they must enter into the Merchants books for such things as they stand in need of, becoming thereby the merchants' slaves.[1]

Josselyn spoke in exaggerated terms, but the system worked much as he described: each merchant advanced cloth, food, liquor, and other supplies to his fishermen in excess of their income so that he might establish his claim over the produce of their labor in the season to come. To the entrepreneur, advances of this nature did constitute a cost, but they also served an important purpose: in an economy that was chronically short of men, they created a structure of long-term indebtedness and a resultant series of labor obligations that provided him with much of the help he needed. For years on end, men like John Slater, Henry Trevett, and Peter Greenfield returned to their patron's warehouse to purchase supplies and hand over their fish;

8. *Essex County Court Records*, I–VI. Mean wealth and indebtedness were calculated for the 24 fishermen whose estates were inventoried between 1645 and 1675.

|  | Physical Estate | |
| --- | --- | --- |
|  | Above Average | Below Average |
| Indebtedness: Above Average | 5 | 4 |
| Below Average | 4 | 11 |

This shows no positive (and possibly a weak negative) correlation between debt and poverty.

9. Essex County Probate Files, No. 19,545.

1. Josselyn, "Account of Two Voyages," 352.

when they died, their liabilities were almost always concentrated in his hands.[2] The credit connections which individual fishermen held with their outfitters could be lifetime affairs, far more stable, in fact, than the partnerships they formed with one another.

Fishing merchants were not naturally open-handed. They were simply drumming up business and dispensing credit in measured amounts towards that end. Some mariners capitalized on the opportunity this afforded and built moderately prosperous careers for themselves within the fishing community that would have been unthinkable without financial assistance. Had George Corwin refused him credit, William Woods could never have acquired a shallop worth £33 in 1670, nor could John Roads have purchased the bricks, boards, hinges, and shingles with which in 1662 he built himself a house.[3] Similarly, Andrew Tucker needed advances from William Browne, Sr., of Salem to buy his house and fishyard on Marblehead Neck, erect a stage and warehouse, and purchase vessels of his own. Eventually, he was able to retire from the sea, earn his living purely as a shoreman, and leave his descendants enough property to ensure their security through the following century.[4]

For projects that might reduce the clients' dependence on maritime work—especially agricultural ones—the enthusiasm of these merchant creditors tailed off swiftly. Most Essex County fishermen managed to acquire during their active careers neither fields nor farm animals. Even those who had retired from the sea and were casting about for other means of maintenance rarely accumulated more than a garden or an orchard with perhaps a cow or a few pigs.[5] Further-

2. Corwin Account Books, 1658–1664, 1663–1672; *Essex County Court Records*, I–VI. Of 14 fishermen for whom probate records survive and who were indebted to identifiable individuals at the time of their deaths, 9 owed more than 50% of their debts to one creditor.

3. Corwin Account Books, 1658–1664, 1663–1672.

4. Essex County Probate Files, No. 28,248; *Essex County Court Records*, VII, 411; VIII, 194–195; IX, 199–200. See also the references to Tucker's descendants in the valuation lists of 1735 and 1749 contained in "Tax and Valuation Lists for Massachusetts Towns Before 1776," Harvard University Microfilm Edition, Reel no. 12.

5. *Essex County Court Records*, I–IX; Essex County Probate Files. Of 13 inventories of fishermen who died at sea, only 4 contained land or animals. Of 20 fishermen who worked at sea before 1675 and lived to age 50 or older (meaning those who had retired), 14 possessed animals, but on average worth only £4.9 sterling; and though all 20 had some real estate, few owned more than an acre or two.

more, after 1645 hardly any immigrant fishermen managed to penetrate the agricultural interior. To the end of the colonial period such
family names as Bartoll, Brimblecombe, Pedrick, Trevett, Cally,
LeGros, Dolliver, and Meek, descended from these early seamen,
were unknown in New England outside its coastal villages.[6] Although
these mariners could move about at liberty from one port to the
next, their freedom to leave the sea and establish themselves outside
the Massachusetts fishing periphery was severely circumscribed.

There is little evidence that this denial of landed independence
entailed much formal coercion. Yet, it is easy to imagine the chilly
welcome that communities such as Dedham or Salem Village would
have accorded to fishermen whose ways and habits so thoroughly
violated their standards of proper conduct. Informal exclusiveness
could be every bit as effective in keeping the unwanted out of a given
community as any formal legislation. Mariners did aspire to the security that land could offer. In Maine, where the force of the Puritan
social ethic was considerably muted, a recent study has demonstrated
that fishermen were able to move rather easily into farming, of an
admittedly hardscrabble nature, if they so wished.[7] Many of their
counterparts in Essex County would have chosen the same opportunity—had it existed.

Thus, although fishermen in Salem, Marblehead, and Gloucester
enjoyed a level of comfort and prosperity unusual within the Atlantic
maritime community, they found the broader promise of economic
independence largely beyond reach. The Puritan colonists were interested in them only for their ability to produce an exportable surplus; otherwise, they would rather that this disorderly crowd had
stayed away. It was hunger for English goods which forced the
founders to compromise. Fishermen would be allowed and even encouraged to stay in Massachusetts but only as long as they kept to

6. Movement of these families out of Marblehead, Gloucester, and Salem was measured, using Bettye Hobbs Pruitt, ed., *The Massachusetts Tax Valuation List of 1771*
(Boston, 1978). See Vickers, "Maritime Labor," 142, n. 120.

7. Edwin A. Churchill, "Too Great the Challenge: The Birth and Death of Fal-
mouth, Maine, 1624–1676" (Ph.D. dissertation, University of Maine at Orono,
1979), 289–290.

themselves out on the colony's periphery. The sanctity of the Puritan experiment in the core would not be disturbed.

On the ocean fringes of Essex County fishermen formed communities of their own. There, the principles which directed society in the villages of the interior—the enforced homogeneity of religion, the stress upon regular work habits, the strengthening of the household, the stern standards of public authority, and the provision of economic independence for each family—were wholly inappropriate. The social virtues, which a capitalist fishery encouraged and which Puritan exclusiveness reinforced, bred in the town of Marblehead and in the maritime quarters of Salem and Gloucester a radically different way of life.

Perhaps the most striking feature of fishing society in this early period was its instability. Two-thirds of those who arrived before 1675 were under the age of thirty when they first came; three-fifths left no trace of a family in the region; and almost four-fifths had disappeared from Essex County, either by death or departure, within ten years of their arrival.[8] "The concourse of many strangers especially in the summer season," as the Marblehead selectmen put it, must have reminded contemporaries more of other seaports around the North Atlantic than of the agricultural communities across the harbor.[9]

Of the hundreds of mariners who spent time in the Essex County fishery, a small portion chose to stay on permanently and settle. Robert Bray of Ipswich in England, for example, was working for George Corwin during the late 1660's when he decided to send for his wife "Thomazin" and their two children. In the spring of 1670

8. Corwin Account Books, 1658–1664, 1663–1672; *Essex County Court Records*, I–VI; Perley, *History of Salem*, I–III; Babson, *History of Gloucester*; *Vital Records of Salem*; *Vital Records of Marblehead*; *Vital Records of Gloucester*; "Salem Town Records"; "Marblehead Town Records." Fishermen were identified and their presence in Essex County traced through all of these sources. Ages at emigration were calculated for those 42 fishermen whose ages were noted in the court records. For example, "Edward Woolen, aged thirty-four years" in 1659 (*Essex County Court Records*, II, 186) who fished for Corwin between 1668 and 1670, first appeared in Essex County in 1651 (Perley, *History of Salem*, I, 211). His age at emigration was, therefore, 26.

9. *Essex County Court Records*, VIII, 318.

she sailed from Plymouth to rejoin her husband in the New World. Together they made their home near Winter Harbor and founded a family of mariners who skippered vessels out of Salem well into the nineteenth century.[1] Another fisherman named Elias Fortune, though single when in 1660 he first appeared in Marblehead, managed to marry locally before the end of the decade. In an eighteen-foot-square cottage which he and his wife erected on town land, the two set up housekeeping and were able somehow in these cramped quarters to raise a family of eight children.[2] Similarly, Paul Mansfield came to Salem as a bachelor about 1650, married Damaris, the widow of Timothy Laskin, built himself a house on the South River, and maintained a household there in fairly comfortable fashion by working the fishery off Misery Island in Salem Sound.[3] Although prospective householders like Mansfield, Fortune, and Bray accounted for only thirty-nine percent of immigrant fishermen between 1645 and 1675, their longer residency in the colony meant that they played a relatively greater role in the fleet. In this period, married men, returning to the sea year after year, filled roughly half of the berths available, a proportion that seems gradually to have increased as more and more mariners decided to cease their wanderings and settle down.[4]

These, however, were not households of the same variety as existed elsewhere in Essex County. For one thing, they were much poorer. The estates of married fishermen probated between 1661 and 1681 reached a median average of only £66 sterling, considerably less than the comparable figure of £113 recorded in the same period for estates throughout the county as a whole.[5] Furthermore, the households in

1. Ibid., VII, 30; IX, 145, 349; Perley, *History of Salem*, III, 48–49; Corwin Account Book, 1663–1672.

2. Essex County Probate Files, No. 9780; *Essex County Court Records*, II, 390; Sidney Perley, "Marblehead in the Year 1700, No. 6," Essex Institute *Historical Collections*, LXXII (1911), 165.

3. *Essex County Court Records*, I, 256; III, 14; Perley, *History of Salem*, I, 314; II, 13; III, 240; Essex County Probate Files, No. 17,639.

4. Vickers, "Maritime Labor," 119, 143n–144n.

5. *Essex County Court Records*, I–VIII; the Essex County figure was calculated from David Warner Koch, "Income Distribution and Political Structure in Seventeenth-Century Salem, Massachusetts," Essex Institute, *Historical Collections*, CV (1969), 53–56.

fishing villages were generally not working units. A few sons joined
with their fathers in voyages to the banks, and in-laws could occasionally share in the rental or purchase of a boat, but far more frequently the membership in a given company was governed by other
considerations—availability, convenience, friendship, mutual appreciation of talent, and so on—that had very little to do with family
structure. Farm boys worked within the household in which they
had been raised until they were ready to start a family of their own.
Any young fisherman, by comparison, could secure a berth simply
by purchasing an outfit on credit and signing on with a vessel short
of hands. Once he had come of age, he did not have to work in his
father's boat (if, indeed, his father owned one or was even living in
New England); he did not have to obtain his father's consent to work
for somebody else; and he could keep his earnings for himself. This is
not to say that fishermen were totally free. As was argued earlier,
they depended heavily on others for access to productive equipment,
but these "others" were merchant creditors, not their fathers. This
fact above all—that the basic unit of production consisted not of the
conjugal household, but of a partnership between the members of a
company and their outfitter—underlay the institutional weakness of
the family within the fishing community. And this constituted the
chief social distinction between the agricultural core of Essex County
and its ocean periphery.

When two sectors of society were related to the process of production in such different ways it was probably inevitable that their
cultural horizons would have differed too. Fishermen stood almost
entirely outside the established church. In the seventeenth century the
numbers of converted, even among Essex County's permanent fishing population, reached no more than one in fifteen.[6] So few were
the freemen of Marblehead that on two occasions the General Court
had to pass special exemptions enabling that town to recruit its office-
holders from the populace at large.[7] Cotton Mather saw no mystery

6. Fishermen identified in the sources mentioned in n.8, p. 102, were traced in
Richard Pierce, ed., *Records of the First Church in Salem, 1629–1730* (Salem, Mass.,
1974).
7. *Records of Massachusetts Bay*, II, 57; V, 8.

in the fact that the premier fishing town in New England should have possessed no organized church before 1684: The inhabitants, he declared, were "generally too remiss to form one."[8]

Fishermen were not necessarily irreligious, but, for the strictly reformed temper of the New England Way, they had little patience. Although they usually attended church when at home and sometimes even owned Bibles, they often found the opportunity to snub Puritan tradition difficult to resist. George Harding of Marblehead, for example, was obviously spoiling for a fight when he declared in 1649 that he intended to apply for the christening of his dog. Similarly, one wonders about the religious sensibilities of a fisherman like John Bennett, who was fined in 1653 for lighting up his pipe during Sunday meeting, or Matthew Coe, whom the magistrates prosecuted for "hunting and killing a raccoon in the time of the public exercise."[9] Marblehead in particular accounted for a number of religious offenses —mostly blasphemy and Sabbath-breaking—that was vastly disproportionate to its size.[1] Cotton Mather, at the beginning of the following century, granting that the local fishermen might be better-mannered than their counterparts in other colonies, insisted nonetheless that they spoke far too "Filthily" and "Profanely," and that their "Clipt Oaths" ought to be curbed.[2]

What really bothered the established colonists, however, was not that fishermen stood outside their church—so did most of the world —but that they replaced Puritan orthodoxy in part with suspect cultural forms of their own. Men who earned their living on the sea, engaged as they were in one long battle with fate, found the Puritan trust in God's arbitrary pleasure insupportable. Forms of spirituality —the invocation of Saints' names, for example, or the use of certain lucky charms and ceremonies—which involved the individual's own supplications, spoke far more directly to those for whom economic uncertainty and physical danger were continual threats.[3] In the face

8. Cotton Mather, *Magnalia Christi Americana*, quoted in Samuel Roads, Jr., *The History and Traditions of Marblehead* (Boston, 1880), 9.

9. *Essex County Court Records*, I, 134, 170, 320.

1. Ibid., I, II.

2. Cotton Mather, *The Fisherman's Calling* (Boston, 1712), 44.

3. Ibid., 42–43; Cotton Mather, *Sailour's Companion and Counsellour* (Boston, 1709), vi.

of such superstition, serious Puritans were horrified. Not only did it deny the sufficiency of Scripture, but it also seemed to imply the existence of spiritual powers beyond those which the reformed tradition attributed to God alone. Cotton Mather knew exactly what these customs meant: "Rites of Sorcery" and "Black Defiances of Heaven" he termed them—the work of the devil.[4] Fishermen could truthfully disclaim worshipping the devil, but there was no denying the spiritual gulf which separated their world from that of their Puritan neighbors.

Maritime culture further distinguished itself by the importance it placed upon organized social drinking. Both at home and on voyages large quantities of alcohol consumed in the company of one's friends provided fishermen with their single greatest source of formal relaxation. While off on the deep, the typical boat's crew furnished itself with enough beer, cider, and brandy to provide each member with at least a quart of beverage every day.[5] The demand for drink in the port towns, moreover, supported enough tavern-keepers—fourteen in Salem and eight more in Marblehead during the 1670's—to inspire a whole series of complaining petitions and periodic regulation by the authorities.[6] Marblehead generated close to three times the number of liquor-related offenses that one would have expected from a town of its size.[7]

Why did fishermen drink? Probably the degree of anxiety in their lives and the level of physical stress inherent in seafaring each played a certain role. It is interesting, however, to note that drunkenness was a problem not just in the cod fishery but in all the export industries of New England's peripheral zone. The timber industry in New Hampshire, the merchant marine of harborfront Boston and Salem, the fur trade in the interior, and the whale fishery of Nantucket all consumed quantities of alcohol that frightened the colonial establish-

---

4. Mather, *Sailour's Companion and Counsellour*, vi; Mather, *Fisherman's Calling*, 43.

5. Corwin Account Books, 1658–1664, 1663–1672.

6. *Essex County Court Records*, V, 223; VII, 70–72.

7. Ibid., I–V. Liquor-related offenses were counted for sample periods, 1650–1652, 1660–1662, 1670–1672. Of 63 offenses, 17 (27%) were committed by inhabitants of Marblehead.

ment.[8] Each of these export economies relied not on the original settlers and their descendants but on Indians and imported Englishmen to perform most of the work; the drinking habits, therefore, of laborers in these peripheral communities derived in all likelihood from their position as outsiders. For men reminded daily of their subordinate status, the heavy consumption of cider and flip, and the tavern life which accompanied it, provided a realm of sociability in which *they* might set the rules.

Insofar as drunken and rowdy behavior intimidated the establishment enough to keep it at a distance, it did serve a purpose—but only at considerable social cost. After all, drink in quantity was not cheap, nor did it lead to higher productivity; and it certainly did not raise one's credit-worthiness in the eyes of the merchant class. For the effectively powerless fishing community, it provided a peculiar brand of independence. Like a wild, roundhouse punch, it gained them little in the long fight but may temporarily have cleared a bit of room.

The spirit of exclusiveness cut both ways. The more firmly the magistracy tried to impose standards of good Puritan order upon the colony, the more doggedly fishermen refused to conform. Such was the degree of mutual suspicion in this period that almost no movement of men between the two communities ever took place. At no time in the seventeenth century did more than the lightest scattering of these immigrant mariners or their descendants penetrate the agricultural heart of Essex County, nor did farmers ever make a practice of sending their sons out to work on the banks. This was not, it must be stressed, a relation of mutual advantage. The husbandmen of New England rejected the fishery by choice, for they disliked both the work and the relations of clientage it engendered. Fishermen, by contrast, stayed out of agriculture because, in the world which the Puritans had ordered, they found substantial freeholds nearly impossible to acquire. Their frequently single status, hard-drinking habits, customary improvidence, and lack of spiritual orthodoxy combined

8. Charles E. Clark, *The Eastern Frontier: The Settlement of Northern New England, 1670–1763* (New York, 1970), 114; *Records of Massachusetts Bay*, II, 172; III, 184; Francis Jennings, *The Invasion of America: Indians, Colonialism and the Cant of Conquest* (New York, 1975), 40, 40n; Vickers, "Maritime Labor," 168–169.

to disqualify them as neighbors, land recipients, or even as legal residents in every village of the Bay Colony's agricultural core.

As the colonial period wore on, the sharp distinctions between the agricultural core of Essex County and its maritime periphery gradually softened. In the farming villages of the interior there surfaced in spite of all orders to the contrary many of the social problems that the founders had once hoped to confine to the colony's ocean fringe. Rates of mortality rose; lack of property increased; and young men departed for new lands to the west and north—all of which testified to the difficulties which eighteenth-century colonists encountered in attempting to maintain their families in comfortable independence. After 1700 a growing number of farmers' and artisans' sons, for lack of opportunity at home, were even prepared to invest a part of their youth in the fishery—something that their fathers and grandfathers would never have contemplated. Under the pressure of need the old exclusive impulse was breaking down.[9]

The maritime community, oddly enough, was moving at the same time in the direction of greater stability. As more and more fishermen took up permanent residence in the county and began to raise their sons in the same trade, the industry ceased to rely on imported help, and the coastal villages lost their air of transiency. Churches were founded, schools established, and a wide variety of tradesmen drawn to set up shop in every fishing settlement on Massachusetts' North Shore. By 1766 John Barnard, the pastor of the First Church in Marblehead, could observe that his lifetime had seen the character of that community greatly altered. At the beginning of the century, he recalled:

the town was always in dismally poor circumstances, involved in debt to the merchants more than they were worth; nor could I find twenty fam-

9. This description of eastern Massachusetts in the eighteenth century draws especially on Kenneth A. Lockridge, "Land, Population, and the Evolution of New England Society, 1630–1790," *Past and Present*, XXXIX (1968), 62–80; Robert A. Gross, *The Minutemen and Their World* (New York, 1976), 68–108; Douglas Lamar Jones, "The Strolling Poor: Transiency in Eighteenth-Century Massachusetts," *Journal of Social History*, VIII (1974–1975), 28–54; Philip J. Greven, Jr., *Four Generations: Population, Land, and Family in Colonial Andover, Massachusetts* (Ithaca, 1970), 175–258; Maris A. Vinovskis, "Mortality Rates and Trends in Massachusetts before 1850," *Journal of Economic History*, XXXII (1972), 195–202.

ilies in it that, upon the best examination could stand upon their own legs; and they were generally as rude, swearing, drunken, and fighting a crew, as they were poor.

In the subsequent decades, however, all of this had changed; the ways and manners of the inhabitants in his estimation were now "vastly mended." Not only had "many gentlemanlike and polite families" moved into town, but even the fishermen by this time scorned "the rudeness of the former generation."[1] Barnard may have been playing the local booster and, perhaps, romanticizing his own pastorate, but there was truth in his words. Marblehead and the other fishing communities of Essex County were still troubled by poverty and related social problems, but they now resembled the other towns in the colony far more than they had a century before. Demographic maturation and the waning of Puritan exclusiveness were beginning to lessen the gap between core and periphery.

In this perspective, the origin of the earlier tension between the two sectors stands fully revealed. The founders of Massachusetts wanted to enjoy the benefits of a capitalist fishery without incorporating it physically into their community. Given the freedom to leave their callings and move into the heart of the Bay Colony, not only would these mariners have sullied the purity of the "City upon a Hill," but they would also have left the fishery as labor-poor as before they arrived.[2] The limits of opportunity, as much within this corner of the New World as within others, had to be strictly set. Fishermen were free to move about from port to port and to build their futures around the colonial rim, but not to move beyond. The peculiar manner in which the exclusionary impulse interacted with the problem of labor scarcity produced in seventeenth-century Essex County two distinct social systems—a dominant core and a subordinate periphery

1. John Barnard, "Autobiography of the Reverend John Barnard," *Massachusetts Historical Society, Collections*, 3d Ser., V (1836), 240. Barnard's picture is confirmed in his obituary in the *Essex Gazette*, 30 January–6 February 1770. The most complete portrayal of this process of stabilization can be found in Christine Heyrman's forthcoming study, *Commerce and Culture: The Maritime Communities of Colonial Massachusetts, 1690–1750*.

2. John Winthrop, "A Modell of Christian Charity," in Perry Miller and Thomas H. Johnson, eds., *The Puritans: A Sourcebook of Their Writings* (New York, 1963), I, 199.

—that were interdependent economically but distinct in personnel. The difficulty which the Puritan colonists experienced in combining aspirations for independence with a level of material civilization that only capitalism and its subservient labor force could generate would in one form or another trouble Americans into the present century. The various balances that were struck at different times and in different places would determine as much as anything what it meant to be a laborer in the New World.

•◦ COLE HARRIS ◦•

# European Beginnings in the Northwest Atlantic:
# A Comparative View

IGRATION is a spatial means of changing the relations of people and property that *in situ* change more or less rapidly with the passage of time.[1] In medieval and early modern Europe, when changes in property relations were rapid, they were likely to have been unpremeditated and uncontrollable, as after war, plague, or accident; when they were slow, they were usually bound by rules of inheritance or by long-term adjustments in the relative costs of factors of production. Migration, on the other hand, could substitute new land—new property—for both chance and time, as it did, in a limited way, when people moved from the open field lowlands of southeastern England to the more forested western uplands, or as it would do, more decisively, when they moved overseas. Transatlantic migration changed the relationship between people and property more drastically than the Black Death and more rapidly than any system of inheritance.[2] For many, this was North America's

1. Growing out of musings and readings scattered over a number of years and of recent editorial involvement with volume one of the *Historical Atlas of Canada*, this paper is not easily footnoted. Largely for reasons of expediency, I finally have decided to footnote it minimally. Direct quotations and references are noted, some wider literatures are introduced by a few key references, and here and there mention is made of specialized studies. Where the most accessible reference on a particular topic will be a plate in the *Historical Atlas of Canada* (forthcoming, 1986), it is so footnoted. I have been particularly sparing of references to early New England, as most readers of this paper will know the literature on that area better than I do.

2. E. P. Thompson, "The Grid of Inheritance," in Jack Goody, Joan Thirsk, and E. P. Thompson, *Family and Inheritance: Rural Society in Western Europe, 1200–1800* (Cambridge, 1976).

Cole Harris is Professor of Geography at the University of British Columbia.

attraction: the opportunity to bypass both the confining grid of custom and power that dominated European property and the vagaries
of chance that, at the personal level, usually turned on relatives' life
spans. The opportunity could be seized individually—to improve
one's lot in the world—or collectively—to impose, untrammelled, a
European social vision on a new setting. Perceptions of opportunity
were rooted in European custom and thought, but emigrants found
themselves in new settings where people and property could not be
recombined as in Europe. The change was quick and pervasive.
Those of European descent in North America at the end of the seventeenth century spoke European languages and practiced countless
European ways while living in societies without precise European
equivalents.

It was not only, or even primarily, that they had moved back into
the forest, although of course they had. There is something of northwestern France before the eleventh- and twelfth-century clearances
or of Anglo-Saxon England when beaver, bears, boars, and wolves
were still in English forests and commoners hunted freely there, in
the experience of seventeenth-century Europeans in North American
middle latitudes. When William the Conqueror established royal
forests and forbade hunting in them, "the rich," reported the Anglo-
Saxon Chronicle, "complained and the poor lamented."[3] They also
became poachers and over the centuries reached into dwindling forests for turf, wood, lops, faggots, berries, fish, and game and practiced
their innumerable evasions against the constables, rangers, foresters,
woodwards, verderers, regarders, and game keepers—to use English
names for offices that were European—who were there to protect
trees and game: another's property.[4] In seventeenth century North
America, forests again were relatively open for gathering, chopping,
and hunting but, of course, early modern rather than medieval
Europe participated in this transatlantic reencounter. Commercial
capital vigorously crossed the Atlantic, and with it came the tech-

3. Cited by Juliet Clutton-Brock, "The Animal Resources," in David M. Wilson,
ed., *The Archaeology of Anglo-Saxon England* (London, 1976; pbk ed., Cambridge,
1981), 391.

4. For an example of the pressure on the forest and of the steps taken to protect it,
see E. P. Thompson, *Whigs and Hunters: The Origin of the Black Act* (London, 1975).

nologies of resource exploitation, the laborers and settlers, and the trade that placed the early European settlements on the edge of North America within a seventeenth-century transatlantic web of prices, laws, institutions, and values.

Yet when seventeenth-century Europeans settled in eastern North America, their context was drastically altered. There was forest where there had been cleared land; sparse, isolated populations where there had been dense, continuous settlement; and beginnings in strange places where there had been continuity in familiar ones. There were unknown, neolithic people, missing European ways, and new relationships among the factors of production and with markets. Europeans were no longer in Europe. If European elements could be reestablished overseas, Europe could not—not even the fullness of any of its local regions. The context of life was different, and perhaps the most basic assertions that can be made about this pervasive change are that the relationships between people and property had changed and, following therefrom, the relationships between people as well.

The question then is raised of whether there was pattern in these changes and, if so, in what elements of European life overseas and at what scale? While the literature on European settlement in seventeenth-century North America frequently toys with the possibility of pattern,[5] it trusts local or regional studies that emphasize the variety of European experiences overseas. There is wisdom in such caution. Yet were a more vigorous comparative and interdisciplinary literature to develop, it would have to rest on the assumption that individual settlements were not entirely unique, and also on some tentative assessment of the nature of their common patterns and of the processes that created them. This is a daunting order, but I think my own field, historical geography, has been young and brazen enough to take a few steps in this direction.[6] If they are combined

5. The recent literature on early New England emphasizes local variety and the transatlantic persistence of local English ways, yet embodies a certain ambivalence. To take one example, in T. H. Breen, *Puritans and Adventurers: Change and Persistence in Early America* (New York, 1980), both the persistent localism of early New England and the influence of "the American environment" are stressed.

6. For a review of the main recent literature in North American historical geography, see Cole Harris, "The Historical Geography of North American Regions," *American Behavioral Scientist*, XXII (1978), 115–130.

with the historians' far larger and, overall, more mature literature on early North America perhaps an analytical framework for comparative study can be discerned. In any event, such presumption forms the basis of this paper.

Its essential premise is that the ideas implicit in European cultures were mobile, and that emigrants carried them far and wide to new settings that then exerted selective pressures. By "new settings" is meant the new relations among land, labor, and capital in which immigrants found themselves or, succinctly, their new relations with property. It is assumed to be in response to this nexus of New World relationships, rather than in response to the influence of the physical environment itself, that new settlements and societies emerged in the northwestern Atlantic area in the seventeenth century. Certainly, in the view presented here, the nature of New World societies cannot be deduced from an understanding of Old World ideas. If most of the details of seventeenth-century European settlements in northeastern North America were European, their compositions were not, and new compositions reflected selective pressures imposed in new settings.

The first part of this paper considers three characteristic settings within which the seventeenth-century European immigrants and their descendants worked out their New World lives. It outlines what might be expected to happen to Old World ways when seventeenth-century French and English people moved overseas to (1) work in staple trades, (2) live in towns, or (3) develop mixed family farms where there was little commercial opportunity. The second part of the paper briefly explores the relevance of these sketches to particular New World societies. Were I more familiar with early New England, these explorations would be located there. As it is, I must enlarge the scale to include territory I know better and touch on the whole theater of European settlement in seventeenth-century North America from New England north. The resulting paper is far too crowded but, in the circumstances, inevitably so.

Seventeenth-century European capital sought resources in the lands bordering the Northwestern Atlantic and, where it found them, developed societies that reflected specialized strategies of resource exploitation. While these strategies were as diverse as the staple trades involved, all were labor intensive and, as in England or France at the same time, this labor was a high percentage of product cost.[7] Some of the demand for labor might be satisfied by natives, although this strategy was less successful in the Northeast than it had been in the Caribbean and in Central America. Invariably, European labor was needed, and the fulfillment of this demand generated European settlements that were dominated by specialized modes of production. In such settlements the staple trade was the focus of work. Its rhythms divided time; its organization divided people. These cells of specialized work were not bounded, as they would have been in Europe, by other European people about other pursuits, but by wilderness, ocean, and native North Americans. Nor were they constrained by tradition. They were units of seventeenth-century European production abstracted from Europe. As such they acquired their own momentum, shaping new societies around their own productive relations.

In settings where there were neither constraints of custom nor alternative employments, capital acquired a particular leeway. There was no recourse to village custom; in particularly remote, ephemeral settlements, people lived beyond the reach of law. Distance from markets and, in some cases, the forbidding environments into which the staple trades had penetrated eliminated most alternative economic opportunities. A few people fled to live with the Indians; more slipped away to practice largely subsistent farming or to return to Europe. Because land available for family farms invariably bid up the price and increased the independence of labor, capital restricted this opportunity as much as possible—by the employment of Indian labor; by the seasonal transportation of white labor, hired at European rates, to the New World; by the use of long-term labor contracts, signed in Europe at European rates, coupled with severe punishments for desertion; and even by recourse to slavery. If laborers could be insulated from land, the societies associated with staple trades would

7. A helpful introduction (with an ample bibliography) to the English economic background of seventeenth-century North America is in D. C. Coleman, *The Economy of England, 1450–1750* (Oxford, 1977).

be sharply stratified by position in the productive system. They would come closer than other European settlements in the seventeenth century to creating a proletariat and, on both sides of the Atlantic, they would make some men wealthy. Social stratification would lose most of the European nuances—family name, the myriad subtleties of education, honorifics, etiquette, and vocation—and would be tied instead to wealth and position in a single system of production.

Because most of the settlements associated with staple trades required seasonal male labor, their demographic profiles were severely imbalanced. White women and children—white nuclear families—were rare at first; then slowly more common. Where opportunity presented itself, there was white-Indian miscegenation, the children almost always remaining with their Indian mothers; then less miscegenation as the white demographic profile became more balanced. Initially, labor was geographically mobile. Single men worked out contracts and returned to Europe or contracted with a new employer in a different location; only as white women became more available would populations become more rooted. Occupational specialization eliminated most European trades. The nature of migration—characteristically young, single men hired in the dockyards and hinterlands of European ports—and the initial weakness of the nuclear family further reduced the possibility of local cultural transfers. These people were known more for what they did than for where they came from; their workplaces dominated and largely obliterated their regional backgrounds. In particular circumstances, there were partial exceptions. Where labor came from the same source region and had few New World contacts with other people, isolation protected some elements of local European tradition—accent, for example—that were independent of the staple trade itself. In this way, parts of local European cultures could long survive within settlements dominated by the technique and routine of specialized work. In general, tradition was weak in these settlements; individuals were exposed and easily exploited.

Such settlements depended on urban connections but not necessarily with towns on the western side of the Atlantic. Management could long remain in Europe, and European ports could remain the urban outlets of New World settlements. The mercantile town planted on the edge of the forest was not an inevitable hinge of New World development,[8] and the level of urbanization in the European settlements in northeastern North America in 1700 was low: well under ten percent, less than half the English level of urbanization at the same time. Retarded urbanization reflected in some areas the continuing delegation of urban functions to towns across the Atlantic, and in others the emergence of substantially subsistent agricultural economies with weak urban requirements. Yet, New World towns had developed as foci of commercial and administrative attachment to Europe, as entrées to resource hinterlands or as regional centers of administration and trade. Contemporaries likened them to provincial towns in France or England, and they were, undoubtedly, the most comprehensive European transplantations to northeastern North America in the seventeenth century.

Compared to the workplaces of the staple trades, these towns were heterogeneous settings of Europeans overseas. Docks and warehouses lined their waterfronts, and successful merchants, together with their families and servants, lived in substantial houses. The civil and military paraphernalia of colonial government were usually in evidence, as were churches and associated hospitals, orphanages, and schools. Such places supported many employments: laborers, tradesmen, and artisans connected with the port, with construction, and with the provision of those consumer goods and services that could not easily be transported across the Atlantic; wholesale and retail merchants; professionals and clerics; and, in a few crown appointments to senior colonial office, members of the European nobility. Amid this occupational and economic range, European assumptions of status, honor, and deference found relatively congenial settings. An edge of European polish reemerged in these towns, to be reflected in street plans, architecture, and the domestic accoutrements of the well-to-do.

Occupationally diverse and socially highly stratified, these towns admitted more European details than elsewhere in seventeenth-cen-

8. James E. Vance, *The Merchant's World: The Geography of Wholesaling* (Englewood Cliffs, N.J., 1970). See also Carville V. Earle, "The First English Towns of North America," *Geographical Review*, LXIX (1977), 34–50.

tury North America—and quickly began to recompose them. They were new, barely three generations old in 1700, and small, only Boston then having more than ten thousand people. Age and scale were shaping factors as, compared to European towns, were the high cost of labor, the related weakness of gentility and nobility, and the distinctive migrations that peopled these new towns.

As long as labor was relatively expensive, as it was whenever employers had to counteract the attraction of available agricultural land, there would tend to be less poverty and fewer servants per capita in these New World towns than in equivalent French or English ports. There would be fewer occupations, imports replacing some local manufactures because of the high cost of local labor, the smallness of the local market, and the absence of really wealthy patrons. There would be less elegance, in some cases because profits were still returning to Europe, in others because New World entrepreneurship was still building from modest beginnings and, in the background, because the refinements of European gentility and nobility were so largely irrelevant to the practical challenge of building in new places and so largely unsupported by the drastic New World change in the relative cost of land and labor. Hence the social range compacted a little, losing the glitter at the top and the worst wretchedness at the bottom, and the occupational structure thinned. The institutional accretions of centuries that gave some European towns a good deal of administrative autonomy and regulated much of their commercial and social life were more drastically reduced, if only because immigrants had come from such different institutional backgrounds. The collective memory of established custom was broken, and, institutionally, this meant an increased reliance on a smaller number of institutions—some, such as the nuclear family, that were widely accepted and easily transported, and others, such as courts, that were convenient vehicles for public order—and a tendency to support this contracted institutional legacy by legal definition rather than by custom. Seventeenth-century migration to most French or English towns was largely local; therefore such towns considerably reflected the regional cultures in which they were set, and only the largest metropoli departed from this pattern. In this respect the small seventeenth-century towns in northeastern North America resembled London or Paris much more than European towns their size: they, too, drew people from varied, distant sources and mixed, regional cultures. At the level of the vernacular regional traditions of France or England, the New World town was a locus of cultural assimilation where particular regional accents, superstitions, vocabularies, dietary preferences, and the like either would disappear or would be recombined in distinctive blends.

The third principal setting of European life in northeastern North America in the seventeenth century emerged more inadvertently than the other two but eventually involved more people. It was the mixed farm worked, essentially, by nuclear families who brought agricultural techniques, crops, and stock from northwestern Europe to settings where the relationships among land, labor, and markets were suddenly changed. Land was far cheaper, a reflection of lower population densities. If natives, an enormous forest, and an intimidating fauna often stood in the way, these unwelcome ingredients of new land could be pushed back and farms established with small capital outlay, simple tools, and relentless family labor. On the other hand, hired labor was expensive, partly because population was low but, principally, because relatively cheap land attracted labor and raised its price. Finally, European markets for European foodstuffs raised overseas were shielded by transfer costs and, after the third decade of the seventeenth century, by generally falling prices. Local New World markets were usually small and easily satisfied. In short, against landed opportunities were set high labor costs and weak or inaccessible markets.[9]

In such circumstances, settlements of mixed family farms were relatively detached, in comparison with those in Europe, from commercial or landed power. They participated, weakly, in North Atlantic trade; whereas the staple trades built lines of direct transatlantic dependence, these relatively subsistent societies weakened them

9. I have previously argued parts of the case presented in this section. See R. Cole Harris, "The Simplification of Europe Overseas," *Annals, Association of American Geographers,* LXVII (1977), 469–483; and also R. Cole Harris and Leonard Guelke, "Land and Society in Early Canada and South Africa," *Journal of Historical Geography,* III (1977), 135–153.

because they attracted little external commercial capital. Nor was older, landed wealth drawn to settings where labor was expensive and land cheap; European nobles found that tracts of New World wilderness with Old World titles did not soon translate into estates and privilege. The officials representing French and English crowns, disinclined to bear the cost of governing distant colonies that contributed little to the wealth of the mother country, might legislate vigorously but enforce weakly and erratically. Consequently, local rural society found itself freed from many of the external fiscal and legal demands that capital and nobility placed on its European counterpart. The centralizing tendencies of a Stuart court suddenly would be remote, the royal charges (the *taille*) that took a third of the French peasant's income would not be levied. Manorial and seigneurial institutions would be weak or absent. The bourgeoisie would own far less of the countryside. Youths would be less likely to be pressed into service; the forest would no longer have a watchful game keeper. Poor people would still live closely bounded lives but, in comparison with Europe, boundaries would have relatively more to do with local circumstances and relatively less to do with the power of crown, manor, or merchant.

There was opportunity, therefore, towards the middle and lower ends of the French or English social hierarchies, and toward the more vernacular side of rural life.[1] However intimidating the initial encounter with the forest, the prospect of land was at hand. Labor that in France or England earned the annual rent for a hectare or two had come to settings where, after a few years, it was often possible to acquire title to a considerable tract of land and provisions to tide over a small family until there were crops in first clearings. Perhaps at the end of a lifetime there would be ten or fifteen cultivated hectares—a farm. Life was rude where a frail technology opened niches of settlement along a wilderness edge and Indian raids were sometimes calamitous, but after a generation or two most people ate better, lived

1. For an admirable summary of the recent English literature, see Keith Wrightson, *English Society, 1580–1680* (London, 1982). For an erudite introduction to the French countryside in the late seventeenth century, see Pierre Goubert, "Les cadres de la vie rurale," in Fernand Braudel *et al.*, *Histoire économique et sociale de la France, 1660–1789* (Paris, 1970).

longer, married younger, owned more livestock, and worked more of their own arable than most European peasants. Anchored now by land, the wandering, begging poor virtually disappeared. If hardly anyone attained the income of the prosperous yeoman or *laboureur* in England or France, the circumstances of the husbandman or, perhaps, after two or three generations, of the poorer yeoman, were relatively available to those and their descendents who brought labor and sought land. As long as land was available and commercial opportunities were weak, these societies would have little socio-economic range. Time diminished such differences if they had accompanied immigrants or delayed their emergence if they had not. Family after family would have a small farm, none would rise very far above the common level, and the complex socio-economic gradient of the European countryside would be confined to a narrow stratum. The rural landscape would lose much of its European complexity.

There was nothing mysterious about this process; new men were not being created. Land had been relatively cheap in relation to labor at various times and in various places in Europe, with approximately similar results. The closest temporal comparison may be with the century after the Black Death when depopulation raised the price of labor and reduced that of land, thereby creating relatively favorable conditions for ordinary people.[2] The closest spatial comparison was with those areas where population pressed less heavily on land, where a good deal of forest or waste remained, and where clearing was still going on, as in the western, more pastoral lands of seventeenth-century England. Rural society there was more egalitarian than that

2. If there is little doubt that the century after the Black Death was a time of relative opportunity for the poor of northwestern Europe because the pressure on land had relaxed and the value of labor had risen, the extent of this opportunity, at least in relation to later North American experience, easily can be exaggerated. Control of land remained elusive for many people, as numerous peasant revolts testify. Only thirty years after the Black Death in Hertfordshire, peasants revolted against their landlord, the abbot of St. Albans, to obtain more common pasture, bridle paths, and hunting and fishing privileges, demands that were granted under the pressure of a mob then quickly withdrawn. *The Peasant Revolt in Hertfordshire: A Symposium*, Hertfordshire Local History Council, *Occasional Paper*, No. 51 (Stevenage Old Town, Herts, 1981).

in the densely populated champion lands of the southeast.[3] Of course, on both sides of the Atlantic, such conditions were temporary. The demographic clock was ticking, and as population pressure increased land values, improved local markets, and enhanced commercial opportunity, socio-economic differentiation increased in proportion. But transatlantic migration had effected a particularly sudden and particularly extreme transformation of the relationship between land and labor with the result that throughout the seventeenth century, and well beyond, the man-land equations on the two sides of the Atlantic were out of phase. As French and English populations rose rapidly in the sixteenth and early seventeenth centuries, land increased in value and real wages fell. The number of rural landless grew, and rural society became increasingly polarized between a prosperous or wealthy few and far more who struggled at the edge of destitution.[4] For some, emigration broke this pattern by placing them and their descendents in settings where the relationship of land to labor was very nearly opposite. Where markets were also weak, the result was not social polarization but rather convergence around a minimal, family-centered sufficiency. Eventually, land values would rise—sooner near the towns than farther away, sooner where immigration was considerable than where it was not, sooner where a coasting trade could develop than farther inland—but nowhere in northeastern North America at the end of the seventeenth century had the relative cost of land for mixed farming and of labor to work it reverted to their characteristic European relationship.

The still vigorous regional cultures of seventeenth-century France and England also would be difficult to transplant overseas. In the staple trades they had suddenly encountered an overriding technology and economy; in the New World settlements dependent on

3. Joan Thirsk, "The Farming Regions of England," in *The Agrarian History of England and Wales*, IV, *1500–1640*, ed. Joan Thirsk (Cambridge, 1967), 1–112. For an example of life in a pastoral village during this period, see D. G. Hey, *An English Rural Community: Myddle under the Tudors and Stuarts* (Leicester, 1974).

4. The rate of population growth declined abruptly after about 1640 and, overall, conditions for the poor probably improved slightly before the end of the century. The labored but essential study of the demographic vital statistics for this period in England is in E. A. Wrigley and R. S. Schofield, *The Population History of England, 1541–1871* (London, 1981).

peasant farming, the economic environment exerted less dramatic pressures on transplanted memories of local ways. Because wood was at hand, construction emphasized this material and in so doing perpetuated some elements of European technique at the expense of others. Where it was no longer so essential to extract the last gleaning from fields, the agricultural emphasis shifted. Stock browsed and grazed untended in the forest and their genetic quality declined. Rotations tended to simplify, and labor-intensive crops made belated appearances. Agricultural land looked rougher and less cared for, a quality that long occupied the commentaries of visiting European agronomists. Indeed, it was, in part because the recent battle with the forest was not entirely over, but also because, within the limits of a stable agricultural technology and the cost of clearing, land was being substituted for labor. And the relative availability of land meant that those collective elements of European agricultural practice—common lands and open fields with stubble grazing rights—that protected the poor's access to land were suddenly unnecessary. Just as European farmers tended to move away from these constraints on individual decision-making when they felt economically secure enough to do so and when they could consolidate scattered holdings, so their North American counterparts exercised the same option in settings that provided unusual opportunity for poor people to acquire enough contiguous land to support their families. At most, open fields would survive for a generation or two. The tendency, therefore, was toward individual rather than collective farming, toward dispersed rather than agglomerated settlement, and toward an increasing social emphasis on the family. All such structural adjustments to new economic environments cut across the grain of Old World regional cultures.

Moreover, regional Old World cultures depended on common memories that were difficult to reassemble in new places. Sometimes the majority of immigrants to a particular settlement shared a local, Old World background, but, more often, they did not. Where immigrants' local regional backgrounds were diverse, many memories quickly slipped away, the collective European heritage thinned, and vernacular cultures combined elements from different source regions supplemented by a few borrowings from the Indians. In these circumstances, European ideas that were not regionally specific tended to receive New World emphasis. The sentiment of the family—nuclear with modest extensions—the craving for land—a means to family-centered security in pre-industrial society—and a sense of private property—these were fairly ubiquitous assumptions that became more salient when people of different local backgrounds converged in New World settings that could not nourish uncommon memories but that did provide unusual, if limited, economic opportunity for ordinary people.

As long as land was available locally, there would be little economic incentive for the young to move far from the parental farm. The extreme displacement of transatlantic migration could be succeeded by a period, the length of which would depend on the rate of population growth in relation to the amount of locally available land, in which most movements would be very short: young people would move to adjacent land. This local infilling would increase consanguinity and, whatever the mix of European elements, would tend to create pockets of very local, homogeneous, New World cultures. In the longer run, adjacent land would not be available. Then many of the young would depart, usually going to new land farther west. These longer moves and the settlements that resulted from them again mixed people of different backgrounds and, as the pace of westward migration accelerated, tended to blend them into an increasingly common culture while spreading it over a considerable territory. The general pattern, therefore, was one of very local cultural pockets around first settlements coupled, as time went on, with increasingly blended regional extensions.[5]

The eighteenth century would accentuate these dichotomies, but even in the seventeenth century the tendency to reshape the spatial pattern, as well as the content, of French and English regional cultures can be discerned. In rural France or England in the seventeenth century young people commonly moved away from their place of birth.

5. On the importance of stability as well as mobility, see Philip J. Greven Jr., *Four Generations: Population, Land, and Family in Colonial Andover, Massachusetts* (Ithaca, N.Y., 1970).

Most of these moves were short, characteristically within nearby parishes and infrequently, unless the destination were a town, more than fifteen or twenty kilometers.[6] At this scale, most migration was inserted within regional cultures. Those who moved farther were usually few enough, relative to the receiving population, to be culturally absorbed. High rates of geographical mobility in rural societies did not entail, therefore, the rapid convergence of established regional cultures. But in the northwestern Atlantic, white settlement was superimposed on wilderness—the Indians being displaced—and initial settlements were detached from regional contexts. In these circumstances, internal migration was culturally expansionistic. Because there were no established regional cultures, but at first only settlements, those who left such settlements moved away from their cultural support. If they encountered only wilderness, they would tend to reproduce what they had known, but if, as was much more common, they also encountered other people with other backgrounds, different memories would mix, and an increasingly blended culture would expand inland. The result, sooner or later, would be a convergence of different people, a mixing of ways and, overall, a simplification of cultural memories as some persisted and many others disappeared. Without cultural resistance and with new land drawing settlers, new blends would spread over far larger territories than was characteristic of regional cultures in Europe. At the other extreme, as long as individual settlements exported but did not import people, distinctive ways could survive there for generations, in some cases perhaps in more cultural isolation than anywhere in England or France.

In sum, however diverse the experiences of individual Europeans in northeastern North America in the seventeenth century, most lives were worked out in settings approximately like one of those just described. It is useful to consider that there was neither one nor an endless variety of North American settings, but rather a few common types within which most people lived their lives. These different

6. R. H. Smith, "Population and its Geography in England, 1500–1730," in R. A. Dodgshon and R. A. Butlin, eds., *An Historical Geography of England and Wales* (London, 1978), 221–224. Also R. W. Malcolmson, *Life and Labour in England, 1700–1780* (London, 1981), 71–74 and 93–96.

settings shaped different societies, and people in each of them experienced North America differently. But all of these settings, even the
towns, were severe abstractions from Europe. As I have tried to show
in these sketches, the complex texture of Europe was gone, though
European elements were established wherever Europeans settled. In a
sense, North America disaggregated Europe, relocating parts here
and there, detaching them from former social, economic, cultural,
and regional contexts. The people who lived within these lean, re-
emphasized selections of Europe would begin to experience and to
measure the world as Europeans did not.

If there is something in Louis Hartz's conception of the fragmentation of European culture overseas,[7] as I am sure there is, the case
should not be argued as Hartz tried to argue it. He is probably wrong
about the process of fragmentation, which would seem to have little
to do with the hiving off of ideas in Europe that then were transplanted overseas, and far more to do with selective pressures in New
World settings. And the scale of Hartzian pronouncement is far too
grandiose. Given his assumptions about the process of fragmentation,
he is forced to define his fragments in broad European social and
intellectual categories: New France was "feudal," New England was
"liberal-bourgeois." Such labels are metaphors that point back to
Europe, emphasize elusive European categories and deflect attention from what really was going on in the New World. The pockets
of European settlement in seventeenth-century North America, like
others later, are better taken on their own terms. Their economic,
social, and demographic details are to be worked out; their folklores,
material cultures, settlements, landscapes, and regional patterns are to
be appreciated. As such understanding grows, it does become apparent that the complex texture of European life had not been reestablished overseas, but rather elements of it—fragments, if you will—
that in new settings were being composed in new ways. This pervasive
reorganization permeated the detail of European lives overseas. But,
if the myriad details are seen primarily as responses to selective pressures in new settings, if the essential characteristics of new settings are

7. Louis Hartz, *The Founding of New Societies: Studies in the History of the United
States, Latin America, South Africa, Canada, and Australia* (New York, 1964).

seen to be changed relations among the factors of production, and if the factors of production in the early enclaves of European settlement overseas fell into a small number of characteristic patterns, then an analytical framework emerges that may have some comparative potential.

At the beginning of the seventeenth century, a seasonal European fishery had operated in the northwestern Atlantic for about a hundred years. As early as the 1530's, Basque fishermen and whalers established seasonal stations along the north shore of the St. Lawrence, and long before the end of the sixteenth century thousands of fishermen from ports from Bristol to Lisbon crossed the North Atlantic each year to fish for cod.[8] Out of the fishery developed an intermittent, then increasingly pursued, fur trade. By 1530, Iroquoians from the St. Lawrence Valley were trading with Breton, Basque, and Norman fishermen at the Strait of Belle Isle; by 1550, trade had shifted west to the mouth of the Saguenay, where, by 1580, French merchants came expressly to trade for furs. In 1600, they built a trading post at Tadoussac and, in 1608, another at Quebec.[9] The Great Lakes Basin began to receive French goods via the St. Lawrence and Dutch goods via the Hudson. Indian groups that controlled this inland flow reaped deadly bonanzas. The Iroquoians at Stadacona (Quebec) and Hochelaga (Montreal), the earliest middlemen of the St. Lawrence fur trade, were wiped out by more westerly Indians sometime about 1580. By 1615, along parts of the Atlantic coast, and, by the 1630's in the Great Lakes Basin, European diseases were running through native popu-

8. The outstanding general description of this fishery is Henri Louis Duhamel du Monceau, *Traité générale des pêches et histoire des poissions qu'elles fournissent, tant pour la subsistance des hommes; . . .* (Paris, 1772). The most comprehensive modern treatment, though far from the easiest to read and increasingly dated, is Harold A. Innis, *The Cod Fisheries: The History of an International Economy*, rev. ed. (Toronto, 1954). On the French fishery, see Charles de La Morandière, *Histoire de la pêche française de la morue dans l'Amérique septentrionale*, 3 vols. (Paris, 1962–1966); and on the early English fishery, Gillian T. Cell, *English Enterprise in Newfoundland, 1577–1660* (Toronto, 1969) and C. Grant Head, *Eighteenth Century Newfoundland: A Geographer's Perspective* (Ottawa, 1976).

9. Henry Percival Biggar, *The Early Trading Companies of New France: A Contribution to the History of Commerce and Discovery in North America* (New York, 1965 [orig. publ. Toronto, 1901]).

lations, leaving remnants in their wake.[1] In New England, Puritan divines, observing the epidemics' deadly course, attributed them to a kindly Providence opening the wilderness to the Puritan's special errand. The Huron, sole middlemen of the French fur trade by the early 1640's, were destroyed by the Iroquois League in 1649, and other Iroquoian speakers in the Ontario peninsula were dispersed soon after. Before 1660, diseases and warfare had depopulated much of northeastern North America as far west as the Michigan peninsula and the Ohio Valley.[2] European settlement expanded into this relative vacuum. In Newfoundland, the fishery now left behind a resident population. Around the Bay of Fundy a handful of French immigrants dyked and farmed the marshlands. Along the lower St. Lawrence, the continuing artery of the fur trade, farms spread out along the river from Quebec to Montreal. And in New England, focus of far more immigration than the other settlements combined,

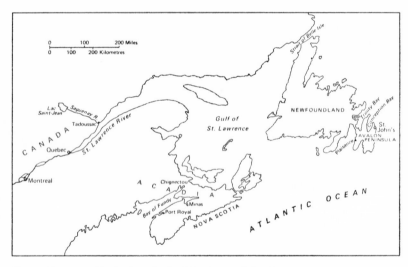

Fig. 4. European Beginnings in the Northwest Atlantic.

1. See articles on particular groups in Bruce G. Trigger, ed., *The Handbook of North American Indians, Northeast* (Washington, D.C., 1978), XV.

2. For a cartographic indication of the extent of depopulation, see Conrad Heidenreich, "Trade, Warfare, and Epidemics, 1600–1653," *Historical Atlas of Canada* (Toronto, forthcoming), I, plate 35.

agriculture expanded slowly inland, while a carrying trade spread through much of the North Atlantic.

By the seventeenth century, the inshore Newfoundland fishery was operated by French and English fishermen, most of whom sailed from French ports in the Gulf of St. Malo or from the southern English ports of Poole and Dartmouth. This fishery recruited labor from as far as forty or fifty miles inland—orphans or boys whose families could not provide better for them were often placed in the fishery in their early teens—and sent fishermen across the Atlantic on seasonal contracts.[3] A few of them were left behind to tend shore properties while wintering in Newfoundland. Gradually a resident population developed: a few French settlements, the largest at Plaisance, along the south shore; and more English settlements, the largest at St. John's, along the east shore of the Avalon and in Conception and Trinity Bays. There were not many residents involved—at the end of the seventeenth century perhaps a thousand wintered over in the French settlements and four to five thousand in the English—and all of them were dependent on the ships that came each year from Europe and on wages earned from catching and processing cod. Apart from gardens there was no agricultural opportunity in Newfoundland. At first, other New World settlements were inaccessible and external connections were entirely transatlantic. By about 1650, the growing connection with New England began to trouble employers,[4] for it opened an otherwise closed system and bid up the price of labor. Even so, no European settlements in seventeenth-century North America were more completely dominated by a European staple trade. Essentially, European capital had brought labor and technologies worked out in the northeastern Atlantic to resources and workplaces in Newfoundland.

These populations were strikingly mobile. A cove that was continuously settled was not necessarily populated by the same people over many consecutive years. Men would stay for a few years and

3. W. Gordon Handcock, "An Historical Geography of the Origins of English Settlement in Newfoundland: A Study of the Migration Process" (Ph.D. thesis, Birmingham, 1979).

4. Innis, *The Cod Fisheries*, 95–138.

then return to Europe; others would take their place. Every summer the population would be multiplied by seasonal fishermen from Europe. Some men had wives in France or England, but even when wives came out and children were born in these settlements, there was still a great deal of transatlantic mobility, if not quite as much as before. In most settlements at the end of the seventeenth century, women and children accounted for less than ten percent of the population. Of the some six hundred people who wintered over in St. John's in 1675, three-quarters were migratory fishermen there for the winter. Most of the rest were male servants and laborers who were somewhat less mobile. Only about ten percent of the winter population was made up of planters and their families, most of whom were also part of the transatlantic ebb and flow.[5] Resident fishermen obtained supplies on credit and lived with annual, often accumulating, debts to creditors on both sides of the Atlantic. By the end of the seventeenth century, there were some local merchants, *habitants-pêcheurs*, the French called them, who owned shallops and hired men. The larger merchants lived in comfortable homes in Granville or Poole, while some of their agents and most of their labor force worked on this side of the Atlantic.

These settlements were unembellished workplaces. The shore drying of cod was particularly labor-intensive, and the larger centers of this activity in the migratory fishery may be thought of as seasonal, man-powered factories to which, in the permanent settlements, houses and gardens were added. At the end of the seventeenth century, Plaisance had a tiny church and a pallisaded fortification containing the governor's residence, a chapel, and a garrison, but it was essentially a settlement of *habitants-pêcheurs*, most of whom owned three or four shallops and hired a few fishermen. Wharves and sheds lined the inner harbor with simple wooden houses and kitchen gardens behind. There were twenty women and seventy children in Plaisance in 1698. A few of these women had been born there; others came from various parts of northwestern or interior France, the Basque

5. John Mannion, "St. John's," *Historical Atlas of Canada* (Toronto, forthcoming), I, plate 28.

coast, Canada (the St. Lawrence colony) or England.[6] Presumably little of their cultural backgrounds survived in this sparse fishing settlement of some three hundred winter residents, most of whom were migratory laborers. Every summer, Basque fishermen dried cod on the Plaisance beaches. At other sites of the migratory fishery, wharves, sheds, and drying platforms were sites of labor-intensive summer activity, and then were left to a few retainers until the next fishing season. There was not much ornament or much of European regional culture where the trappings of a European fishery perched on the edge of a severe New World land.

Whereas the seventeenth-century fishing stations along the Atlantic coast of Nova Scotia were much like those in Newfoundland, the settlements on the marshlands around the Bay of Fundy were extreme examples of another characteristic type of European settlement overseas.[7] Out of range of the commercial fishery and, after the consolidation of the St. Lawrence route to the interior, marginally located for the fur trade, they depended on agricultural land obtained by dyking or clearing. Freshened marshland soils were fertile, and occasional inundations maintained yields. The climate was well suited to pasture and to the hardy European grains, vegetables, and fruits. A few immigrants seized this limited opportunity and established mixed farms on the marshland. There were not many people involved: some three hundred at Port Royal in the early 1650's and perhaps twelve hundred in all the Fundy settlements by 1700. Almost all of these settlers were descended from a few dozen families. Tucked away in a corner of the northwestern Atlantic, the Acadians' only regular trade was with New England. They built shallops and sailed them illegally to Boston, while Boston merchants operated unhindered in the Bay of Fundy. By means of their New England commercial connection, Acadian cattle, wheat, wood, furs, feathers, and fish reached outside markets, but the volume of this trade must have been small. Even in the eighteenth century, when the French fortress

---

6. La Morandière, *Histoire de la pêche française*, I, 481–484.
7. The basic accounts in English are: Andrew H. Clark, *Acadia: The Geography of Early Nova Scotia to 1760* (Madison, Wisc., 1968); and Naomi Griffiths, *The Acadians: Creation of a People* (Toronto, 1973).

at Louisbourg created a large, relatively accessible market for food-stuffs, the Acadian settlements in the Bay of Fundy were minor suppliers. The Acadians were not self-sufficient, but their local economy probably was as nearly subsistent as that of any European settlement in seventeenth-century North America. Agriculture provided for families and produced small surpluses that, now and then, some Acadians were able to market.[8]

This meager economy would not attract European capital or interest European governments. A buffer between New France and New England, Acadia had some geopolitical significance and changed hands frequently in the seventeenth century. No matter which flag flew at Port Royal, where there was usually a governor and a few soldiers, the Acadians were left alone. Occasionally, some of them may have billeted soldiers, but there is no evidence of this or any other royal exaction, although men at Port Royal did serve irregularly in the militia. Much of Acadia was conceded *en seigneurie*, and some seigneurs probably sub-granted land. Now and then, seigneurial rents may have been paid, but there is no evidence that they were, that a seigneurial court was ever held, or a banal right exercised. As settlement spread up the Bay after 1670, any vestige of French seigneurialism must have been left behind and, without bailiffs or notaries, an illiterate people could have retained only drastically simplified elements of the *coutume de Normandie* or any other body of French customary law. Priests collected tithes, kept minimal parish records, at least at Port Royal, and must have arbitrated many civil disputes. Often these poor priests were all that survived of the bourgeois, seigneurial, ecclesiastical, and royal power that weighed on the French peasantry.

What was left was a peasant society drawn from here and there in

8. In detail the volume of Acadian trade will never be known. A. H. Clark, reacting to a view of the Acadians as simple, subsistent farmers, emphasized their commercial connections, but we do know that in the eighteenth century the Acadians supplied less than 10% of the foodstuffs for Louisbourg, a considerable potential market close at hand. As none of those who left accounts of the Acadian settlements make any mention of the prosperity that, for some at least, would have been the likely corollary of a considerable trade, it is still the most plausible inference that Acadian agriculture was primarily subsistent.

northwestern France, and maintained on the Fundy marshes. In the early years, some settlers took Micmac wives, but the demographic profile soon balanced in this society of farm families, and most of the Acadians' material culture came from France. Dykes and sluice gates were similar to those in the marshy *landes* of coastal western France; the techniques of squared log, timber frame, or wattle and daub construction employed to build the Acadians' tiny houses were well-known in northwestern Europe; and Acadian food, more varied and abundant than the diets of the poorer French peasantry, presumably was prepared and served in French peasant ways. Items of French rural culture relevant to the lives of poor farm families on the Fundy marshlands had been retained, whereas French privilege had faded. Apart from the fort at Port Royal, which was always of contemporary military design, there was hardly a suggestion of French architecture. Visitors mistook the church at Port Royal for a barn. Acadian buildings, like most of the rest of Acadian material culture, were products of local materials, French peasant techniques, and the failure of a substantially subsistent economy to generate wealth.

Unlike the fishermen, these people were soon detached from a transatlantic migration field. Their sons and daughters stayed in Acadia, intermarried, and farmed the marshland. Clusters of consanguineous settlement emerged around parental farms, and when some progeny moved to new marshes they took an increasingly common Acadian culture with them. If some of the settlers at Port Royal in 1650 retained accents of Aunis or Poitou, at the end of the century their descendents at Minas or Chignectou, the Acadian settlements near the head of the Bay of Fundy, shared a vernacular culture in an inbred society. Years later, when some of the deported Acadians were resettled on the Ile de Ré near La Rochelle, neither the local peasant culture nor the differentiated and deferential society in which they found themselves were part of their experience, and most soon left for Louisiana.

In Canada, the French colony centered on the St. Lawrence River, furs and hides were the only seventeenth-century exports, and still made up eighty-five percent of the value of exports at the end of the

French regime.[9] Until the destruction of Huronia in 1649, this trade depended on Indian middlemen. Thereafter, it was carried on by French traders who, well before 1700, were familiar with the Ohio Valley, the Mississippi, and some waterways beyond Lake Superior. After 1670, they had faced English competition from Hudson Bay, as well as the Hudson River, and responded by pushing inland. The fur trade depended on Indian hunters; the French were middlemen, and they required white inland labor to transport trade goods, man posts, and procure furs. The size of this labor force is debated but probably consisted of about three hundred men a year at the end of the seventeenth century. These men operated westward out of Montreal, part of a transatlantic trading system based in La Rochelle and passing through the St. Lawrence towns to interior trading posts and, finally, to Indian bands.[1] Both Montreal and Quebec depended on this trade as well as on the Crown's civil and military expenditures. At the end of the seventeenth century, perhaps a fifth of a Canadian population of about seventeen thousand lived in these towns. Of the thirteen to fourteen thousand in the countryside, a few, near Montreal, were siphoned off each year by the fur trade and, well down-river from Quebec, a few others participated in the Gulf fishery. The great majority farmed—as had their parents and would their children—in this colony created by a staple trade that, long before 1700, could employ only a tiny fraction of its growing population. Canadian farms raised much the same crops and livestock as the Acadians but in a more ample territory where, in this most interior of seventeenth-century European colonies in the northwestern Atlantic area, external markets were out of reach, and local ones were soon satisfied.

In many ways, the fur trade and cod fishery were diametric opposites: the one maritime and stationary in the territory it exploited;

9. James Pritchard and Thomas Wien, "North Atlantic Trade," *Historical Atlas of Canada* (Toronto, forthcoming), I, plate 48.

1. General accounts are William J. Eccles, *The Canadian Frontier, 1534–1760* (New York, 1969); and Edwin E. Rich, *The Fur Trade and the Northwest to 1857* (Toronto, 1968). The organization of the fur trade in Montreal is best described by Louise Dechêne in *Habitants et marchands de Montréal au XVIIe siècle* (Paris, 1974). Estimates of the trade's white manpower are disputed; data are fragmentary and where quantitative records exist it is not clear what fraction of the trade they represent.

the other continental and expansionistic; the one indifferent or hostile to the Indians; the other dependent on them and on their technology; the one competitive; the other inclined toward monopoly. Yet both were staple trades that drew men to remote resources. As in the fishery, most fur trade labor was seasonal; men returned to the lower St. Lawrence, just as fishermen returned to Europe. The seventeenth-century fur trade left behind children of mixed blood but not yet a permanent white population in the interior, although some of the Orkney Islanders in posts on Hudson Bay would stay for several years. Wages in the St. Lawrence fur trade were higher than those in the fishery, a reflection less of the arduous, dangerous nature of the work—for these qualities also characterized the fishery —than of the availability of land and, hence, of alternative employment, along the lower St. Lawrence. Most *engagés* made their first trip west in their early twenties, and most made only one trip; the 170 or so livres they earned for four months of paddling were perhaps enough for some of them to buy the few stock, the seed, and the tools with which to begin a farm.[2]

At the end of the seventeenth century, there were approximately two thousand people in Quebec and just over one thousand in Montreal. In Quebec, commercial and administrative functions were separated by a cliff at the base of which were warehouses and docks, and the laborers, artisans, shop and innkeepers, and merchants associated with the port. Above them were the fort, hospital, governor's residence, seminary, and a remarkable array, for so small a New World place, of the baroque architecture and geometric gardens of seventeenth-century France. Newer, smaller, and closer to the fur trade, Montreal was rougher, but both these towns, through which passed a trade that in good years sent furs to the value of well over a million livres to La Rochelle and that together reproduced most of the governmental apparatus of a French provincial town, housed defined, stratified societies.[3] The colonial governor, the intendant, and their retinues lived in Quebec. There were troops

2. Gratien Allaire, "Les engagés de la fourrure, 1701–1745: une étude de leur motivation" (Ph.D. thesis, Concordia University, Montreal, 1981).
3. Dechêne, *Habitants et marchands*, 353–413.

and officers. In both towns there were a few nobles, some of them created in Canada and almost all of them living well beyond their means in a colony where land could not support ease, or engaging in activities that in France would have been unacceptable for people of their rank. Some nobles were indigent wards of the crown, and only a few left estates as large as those of the more prosperous artisans. There were priests and sisters of several orders and some fairly well-educated laymen: notaries, doctors, bailiffs. There were merchants, men of frugal, unostentatious habits, who commonly left fifteen to thirty thousand livres and sometimes more than one hundred thousand livres and were the wealthiest people in the colony. There were tradesmen and artisans, shopkeepers and, at the bottom of the social hierarchy, laborers, domestic servants, *engagés* recently arrived from France and working out their contracts, and sailors. Probably the occupational mix was leaner and certainly it was somewhat different, but there is no doubt that Montreal and Quebec reproduced much of the social fabric of a French provincial town during the *ancien regime*.

Rural society was far less occupationally diverse and stratified. With weak markets and a growing number of subsistent farmers, only crop failures consistently relieved the slide in agricultural prices.[4] Land was available almost everywhere. Even at the end of the century, uncleared land was worthless except within a radius of the urban demand for firewood. The price of cleared land reflected the labor cost of clearing it but had no speculative value. After the heavy immigration of the 1660's and early 1670's the pace of land sales slowed: the Canadian countryside expanded in direct proportion to the population and in almost as much commercial isolation as the marshland farms around the Bay of Fundy. Such a countryside attracted neither capital nor privilege, both of which remained urban. The massive bourgeois penetration of rural France had a meager Canadian counterpart: about twenty percent of the farmland within a few kilometers of Quebec and Montreal and some neglected seigneuries. Nor was nobility drawn to seigneuries that, in themselves,

---

4. Dechêne, *Habitants et marchands*, 521; Jean Hamelin, *Économie et société en Nouvelle-France* (Quebec, 1960), 61.

did not impart status, and that could not support its social pretensions. Ecclesiastical seigneurs were more patient, knowing that unpaid rents or land would be retrieved sooner or later and having an institutional base for long-term management. At the end of the century, Montreal Island, with forty-five hundred people—by far the most populous Canadian seigneurie—was beginning to turn an annual profit of ten to fifteen thousand livres. As its Sulpician seigneurs pressed their rights a little harder and *censitaires* procrastinated as they could, population growth created conditions a little more like those in France.[5] In the Gulf of St. Lawrence some seigneuries were developed as fishing stations. Overall, the seigneurial system, which even in relatively small French seigneuries required a manager, an attorney, an assistant attorney, a clerk, a sergeant, lieutenants, and perhaps a gaoler, hung over seventeenth-century Canada in a state of suspended animation, its legal structure intact, unlike Acadia, but the conditions that would give it life not yet in place.[6] There were no royal taxes, although families near the towns billeted soldiers and most men served intermittently in the militia. The bishop saw to the erection of parishes and the establishment of resident priests, who would be supported by tithes of one twenty-sixth of the grain harvest, where numbers warranted. Canada was not Acadia; far more French institutional apparatus was in the Canadian countryside, where it would remain a somewhat ghostly presence as long as an essentially subsistent economy was unable to create wealth and land was available for ordinary people.

After the early 1670's, the Canadian population grew largely from natural increase at an average annual rate of two and a half percent, doubling in just under thirty years. Most of this increase was absorbed by the countryside where young people could expect their own labor to reproduce the family farm of their upbringing. Farm lots were available in most seigneuries for the asking, and the low seigneurial

5. Dechêne, *Habitants et marchands*, 241–258.

6. R. C. Harris, *The Seigneurial System in Early Canada: A Geographical Study* (Madison, Wisc., 1966). For a different view see, Fernand Ouellet, "Seigneurial Property and Social Groups in the St. Lawrence Valley, 1663–1760," in Michael S. Cross and Gregory S. Kealey, eds., *Economy and Society during the French Regime to 1759: Readings in Canadian Social History* (Toronto, 1983), I.

rents charged for them often went uncollected for years. Provisions, stock, and tools might be obtained by wage labor or, more usually in a system of partible inheritance, from a share, or an advance on a share, of the value of the parental property. The considerable variation in the size of cleared landholdings along the lower St. Lawrence in the seventeenth century depended, for the most part, on the stage of farm development. Small farms were being cleared; larger farms bore a generation or more of work. Where farms were the same age, there was a remarkable sameness: similar houses were at the fronts of similar lots amid similar fields growing similar crops. There were no really large *habitant* farms, nothing comparable to the holdings of the *coq du village* in France: but in established areas there were many farm families with fifteen or twenty cleared hectares, most of them planted in a two-course rotation of wheat or peas and fallow. These farms also contained considerable kitchen gardens, each of which included a few fruit trees, and there would be a few chickens, sheep, swine, a cow or two, a pair of oxen, and, perhaps, a horse. In most years, such a farm produced a small surplus for sale while providing for most of the subsistent needs of the family. There was no luxury or ease anywhere, but the marriage age, the infant and adult mortality rates, and the comments of visitors all suggest a standard of living above that of most French peasants.[7]

From the beginning, agriculture was individual rather than collective, a sharp accentuation in a setting where ordinary people could obtain land, of the tendency toward individual farming in northwestern France. There were no open fields with strip allotments, and commons, locally important where there was good but limited riparian pasture, were a small part of the whole agricultural economy. The *assemblée des habitants*, whose principal function in France was to apportion the burden of externally imposed charges, became in Canada no more than the *fabrique* (church vestry) that attended to parish affairs. In time, informal communities of close kin would develop in the lines of settlement along the river; more essentially, the nuclear

7. Hubert Charbonneau, *Vie et mort de nos ancêtres: étude démographique* (Montreal, 1975).

family and its local extensions found breathing space in the agricultural land along the lower St. Lawrence.

Almost half the people who lived in Quebec, Montreal, or the surrounding countryside came from Normandy or the Ile de France in the north, or from Aunis or Poitou in the west; and almost all the rest came from other parts of northern or western France. The great majority of these immigrants were young, single men who crossed the Atlantic as soldiers or as *engagés* and came from poor but not quite destitute backgrounds. Only one man in twenty and one woman in five was or had been married when they embarked for Canada; after 1673, female migration virtually ceased, averaging, thereafter, three women per annum to the end of the French regime.[8] Therefore, when nuclear families reformed in Canada, characteristically husband and wife came from different French regions or a French man married a Canadian girl. Such families lived among others of equally diverse background, and in the second generation their offspring intermarried, further mixing the brew. In this way, the local cast of particular French backgrounds was soon lost; like their Acadian counterparts, the second- and third-generation Canadians who moved from older parishes near Quebec to land on the South Shore, or lads near Montreal who signed on for a season in the fur trade were culturally far more homogeneous than their recent emigrant ancestors. Here, broadly, were two migration fields—one around the Bay of Fundy, the other along the lower St. Lawrence—distributing North American cultures fashioned in somewhat different settings out of immigrant French people from, as far as we know, much the same backgrounds. Whether in Quebec or Montreal there were enough people of common regional stock to delay this process for a generation or two is unknown but improbable.

At first glance, there seems to be little relationship between early New England and the small, scattered, rather adventitious settlements that developed out of the cod fishery or the fur trade in Newfoundland, Acadia, and Canada. New England received a far larger, far

8. Hubert Charbonneau, "French Origins of the Canadian Population," *Historical Atlas of Canada* (Toronto, forthcoming), I, plate 45.

more family-dominated migration, and many of these people travelled from a common source region to a common local destination.
Many of them brought some means and education. They came relatively early in the seventeenth century, leaving time for several seventeenth-century generations, and for a good deal of New World
population growth. Many of them were Puritans who had been
drawn across the Atlantic by a vision of social and religious regeneration. Such motivation gave early New England a deductive overtone
that was completely absent farther north. And, while some New
Englanders depended on the cod fishery, many more on essentially
subsistent family farms, and a few on the fur trade, the most vigorous
motor of the New England economy was probably the coastal carrying trade. Certainly, New Englanders and Canadians had no use for
each other. They fought, considered each other the devil's agents,
and would have resolved the French- or English-speaking destiny of
northeastern North America much sooner had they been able to get
at each other's throats more easily.

And yet, English immigrants to New England found themselves in
settings that corresponded approximately to one or the other of the
three types discussed in the first part of this paper. If that description
of the selective pressures exerted by these settings has some general
value, then early New England should reveal some of their characteristic effects. Apparently it does, and what follows is a short, unembellished list. Of course, my analysis does not include Puritanism, and
while this is inexcusable, I know—rather like writing on Winnie the
Pooh without mentioning honey—the omission does at least permit
the inference that where my remarks and the reality of early New
England diverge, Puritanism was perhaps the cause.

The absence of a sizeable staple trade and the weakness of the rural
economy encouraged autonomy at two scales: of colonies from England and of local countrysides from royal officials, landed gentry and
nobility, and commercial capital. The New England fishery was not
large enough, and the New England coasting trade was not manage-
able enough to encourage close, English control of these transatlantic
colonies, with the result that there were long periods of virtual autonomy followed by those resented bursts of attempted control that

culminated in the War of Independence. The matter of local autonomy seems less clear. From Sumner Chilton Powell to the present,
some authors emphasize the relative independence of local communities from the common sources of power in the English town and
countryside,[9] whereas others stress the complexity and power of centralized control.[1] Perhaps both are correct. It would follow from the
arguments presented in this paper that the principal source of the
centralized control of local life in the agricultural settlements of rural
New England, to the extent that such control existed, must have
been Puritanism. Puritan control would diminish as settlement spread
and opportunities for individuals unfolded.

The cheapness of land, the cost of labor, and limited occupational
options created countrysides in which the socio-economic range was
much less than in England. Puritanism would not affect this change
except to bring across the Atlantic some prosperous yeomen and artisans who would receive larger shares of new town lands than most of
their fellows. Such migration could establish a considerable socio-
economic range in the developing countryside, but the difference between one man who received two hundred hectares and another who
received twenty was not nearly as substantial as it would be a few
generations later when the land was cleared and far more valuable. In
many townships, no one would be very rich, few would be desper-
ately poor, and the prevailing middle would not vary far from a
common, marginal sufficiency. Near the towns, and with time, differentiation would increase. The fishing settlements would be sharply
stratified by occupation in the fishery but, because there was some
agricultural alternative to fishing, fishermen's wages would be higher
than in Newfoundland or England. Social differentiation, increasingly
based on wealth, would be most pronounced in the port towns.
Everywhere the relative availability of agricultural land would tend
to improve the standard of living of the poorer peasantry, a change

9. Sumner Chilton Powell, *Puritan Village: the Formation of a New England Town*
(Middletown, Conn., 1963).
1. For example, David T. Konig, "English Legal Change and the Origins of Local
Government in Northern Massachusetts," in Bruce C. Daniels, ed., *Town and Coun-
try: Essays on the Structure of Local Governments in the American Colonies* (Middletown,
Conn., 1978), 12–43.

that, as in Canada, would be measured by the basic demographic statistics.

Collective rural traditions would weaken in New England, where poor farmers held more land than their English counterparts. In such circumstances commons or stubble grazing after harvests on open fields would suddenly be less important, the pressure on land would relax, and rights defended clamorously on the other side of the Atlantic would slip away. In those townships where most settlers came from open field backgrounds, collective traditions would be reestablished, and then would be replaced, often within a generation, by more individualistic agriculture as the reality of different circumstances sank in. Even the nucleated village, long taken to be the tangible geographical expression of the New England rural community, would be rare in New England before the late eighteenth century.[2] In New England and Canada the basic pattern of rural settlement appears to have been the same: nuclear families lived on their own farms and services were dispersed among them.

The cultural traditions of English regional custom would blend in New England as people mixed, intermarried, and moved through migration fields that distributed the new vernacular culture. This process would be delayed where people of similar English background settled together, and might be delayed further if subsequent movement generated local migration fields within townships. Sooner or later, different backgrounds would tend to merge; in city and countryside local cultural convergence would be the rule, local cultural isolation the exception. Presumably, long before the van of settlement reached the western Connecticut of Charles Grant's study,[3] East Anglians, Yorkshiremen, and Hampshiremen would have disappeared. Long before the end of the eighteenth century a relatively common New England vernacular culture would be poised to spill out of New England.

In rural areas, the smaller occupational and economic range, the

2. Joseph S. Wood, "Village and Community in Early Colonial New England," *Journal of Historical Geography*, VIII (1982), 333–346.

3. Charles S. Grant, *Democracy in the Connecticut Frontier Town of Kent* (New York, 1961).

weakening of traditional local cultures, and the common, generational movement of new families to new land would change English patterns of deference. First, they would reduce their range and fine tuning simply because the range between rich and poor had diminished and because there was far less occupational variation. Second, deference would have less to do with tradition—family name, vocational status, and the like—and more to do with personal traits and with income. In new settings it would be far easier to know whom one liked or who was rich than to classify people in terms of their social pedigrees. Third, deference would become more symbolic, being associated less with an ongoing, organic society in which people had familiar places than with the idealization of such a society. Is this an interpretation of the meeting house with its innumerable sermons about Christian community set amid a society of dispersed farming families who made their own agricultural and market decisions, tended their own property, and provided as they could for their own children? At the other end of the scale of deference, could the crown have become, in time, simply an irrelevant symbol rather than the culmination of an organic society that no longer existed?

Finally, by abstracting Puritanism from its English social context, New England would change the Puritan meaning of community: the English social order (within which a Winthrop assumed the City of God) would not be in the minds of Puritan divines who preached community in late seventeenth-century New England. Their community, I should think, would have become either more visionary or more local and personal. If anything, the work of pioneering and the practical achievements it demanded would reinforce the ascetic materialism of the Puritan tradition, while the growing salience of the nuclear family and proportional decline of the organic community would emphasize the privatism in the Puritan encounter with God. Sooner or later, such religion would become emotional and evangelical.

Here, then, are some steps toward a simple and fairly comprehensive analytical framework that may have some value for the comparative study of early modern European settlements in northeastern North

America. The framework can be much elaborated, of course, particularly regarding the towns. Some of its present inferences may prove to be wrong; at most, they should be used suggestively rather than deductively. But perhaps it is clear that the seventeenth-century European colonies north of New Spain, including those south of New England, present a singular opportunity for comparative study. Data are abundant, new settlements were isolated from each other, and new societies reflected fairly clear responses to the selective pressures of different settings. Perhaps, too, such studies may shed some light on a subsequent North America, partly because they deal with the roots of later experience; partly because seventeenth-century settings had later equivalents that exerted similar pressures and had similar effects. The seventeenth-century settlements bordering the northwestern Atlantic introduce modern North America chronologically and geographically, and, conceivably, the study of them may also introduce North America analytically.

◄◦ LILLIAN B. MILLER ◦►

# The Puritan Portrait:
# Its Function in Old and New England

IN St. Andrews and Blackfriars Hall in Norwich, England, hangs an array of portraits on four long walls, all similar in costume, pose, and accessories, but dating, as they tell us, over a hundred-year span from the early sixteenth to the seventeenth century. Here they stand or sit, mayors of Norwich or benefactors, priests, bishops, merchants, sheriffs, or magistrates, Norwich's pride painted at municipal expense as examples of virtue and honor for future generations to emulate. With their hands resting on a skull (Figure 5), they speak to human vanity and testify to the human condition; they hold the gloves of the gentleman, the book of the scholar, the bell, book and candle of the man of the church (Figure 6), the staff of the magistrate. Here in the center of the Puritan rebellion, the heart of East Anglia, we find splendid examples of English provincial art, which in pose, style, and accessories remind us of portraits hanging in Boston today.

In the Ashmolean Museum at Oxford, we find a portrait of an unknown woman (Figure 7), a member of the Trandescant Family,

Lillian B. Miller is Editor of the Charles Willson Peale Papers, National Portrait Gallery, Smithsonian Institution.

Research in England for this paper was supported by a grant from the Smithsonian Institution's Fluid Research Fund. I am grateful to Dr. S. Dillon Ripley, Secretary of the Smithsonian, for making this research possible. Most of the New England portraits mentioned in this paper are illustrated in the Museum of Fine Arts, Boston, exhibit catalog, edited by Jonathan L. Fairbanks and Robert F. Trent, and entitled *New England Begins: The Seventeenth Century*, 3 vols. (Boston, 1982).

whose portraits by De Crivitz were collected early in the seventeenth century by Elias Ashmole to become the basis of Oxford's first museum. She reminds us of Boston's *Mrs. Freake and Baby Mary* (Figure 8), although Boston's lady is more finely wrought, more delicately conceived and chiseled.

At the National Portrait Gallery in London may be found Robert Walker's portrait of Oliver Cromwell, the Puritan leader and Parliamentary Protector of the British Empire (Figure 9). At the Museum of Fine Arts, Boston, is the portrait by an unknown limner (probably Thomas Smith) of Major Thomas Savage (Figure 10), which in pose and manner is reminiscent of the Walker. The American portrait lacks the assurance of the English one, but the relationship between the two is clear: perhaps they both were modelled after a portrait of Thomas Wentworth, First Earl of Strafford by Van Dyck (Figure 11); or perhaps the prototype for the American painting was the portrait of John Leverett (Figure 12), painted while he was agent at the English court between 1655–1662 by a follower of Lely.[1]

We may continue to match American portraits against English prototypes. The emphasis on detail in costume in, for instance, *Mrs. Freake and Baby Mary*, we see in many Elizabethan paintings such as those by George Gower or Marcus Gheeraerts the Younger. Elizabeth Paddy Wensley (Figure 13) is presented in the full frontal pose in bright light that Queen Elizabeth insisted upon out of superstitious dislike of shadows.[2] The reliance of Tudor and Jacobean artists on pattern and line may be seen in the checkerboard floor tiles, the narrow bands of lace, the balanced sleeve shapes and inserts—even the symmetry of the neatly-tied hoods—that provide a rhythmic design in the portraits of the Gibbs children and the group portrait of the Mason children (Figure 14); and the English artists' interest in color applied strongly and directly to outline shapes and fill in pat-

1. *Catalogue of Portraits in the Essex Institute, Salem, Massachusetts, Covering Three Centuries*, introd. by Henry Wilder Foote (Salem, Mass., 1936), 117.

2. Nicholas Hilliard, *A Treatise Concerning the Arte of Limning*, Walpole Society, *Publications*, I (1912), 29; quoted in Roy Strong, *The English Icon: Elizabethan and Jacobean Portraiture* (London, 1969), 13. Hilliard describes how Elizabeth chose to sit for her portrait in "the open alley of a goodly garden where no tree was near, nor any shadow at all."

terns is expressed clearly in Mrs. Freake's portrait with its bright
yellows, reds, and greens.

Symbols in American pictures remind us of symbols in sixteenth
and seventeenth century English portraits: the flowers on the table in
Mrs. Wensley's portrait may be compared to those in the portrait
of Mrs. Baker (1675: Massachusetts Historical Society), painted in
London and sent to her grandaughter Mrs. Shrimpton in New England. The two roses that have fallen out of the vase in Mrs. Wensley's picture may indicate two dead children, roses denoting either
the transient values of the flesh, or "the word Divine made incar-
nate." The two tulips remaining in the vase probably refer to the
future resurrection of the children while the other flowers testify to
the fact that Mrs. Wensley has given birth to five children in all—
which, indeed, she did between 1664 and 1675.[3]

The flower held by little Abigail Mason in *The Mason Children*
appears in many English portraits of women and children from the
Tudor and Jacobean periods, such as *Edward VI* from the studio of
William Scots (circa 1546: National Portrait Gallery, London) or
*Elizabeth of York* (Figure 15). The gloves and cane of David Mason
are accessories associated with the gentleman in England, and may be
found in portraits of cavaliers dating from Elizabeth's time or earlier,
as in the portrait of Sir Walter Raleigh and Son (1602: National
Portrait Gallery, London). Joanna Mason's fan, which traditionally
denoted a highborn lady, is held by Queen Elizabeth in the famous
"Ditchley" portrait by Marcus Gheeraerts the Younger (Figure 13).
Henry Gibbs's bird (Figure 14) frequently was painted into portraits of young children, the bird being a soul symbol that occasionally accompanied other natural symbols, such as the finch with
the eglantine in the sixteenth-century English portrait of *Elizabeth
Brydges* by Hieronymus Custodis, painted when she was about six-

3. James Savage, *A Genealogical Dictionary of the First Settlers of New England Showing Three Generations of Those who Came Before May, 1692*, 4 vols. (Boston, Mass.,
1860–1862), IV, 483; Inventory of John Wensley's estate, 24 May 1686; Administration of John Wensley's estate, 27 April 1711, executrix Mercy Bridgham, widow
[Wensley's daughter], Suffolk County Probate Office, Boston; Fairbanks and Trent,
eds., *New England Begins*, III, 466.

teen years old (1589: Duke of Bedford Collection; illus., Strong, *Icon*, p. 197). The eglantine symbolizes chastity; together with the bird, it probably relates to the purity of her soul.[4]

The equating of the soul with the image of the bird was a common seventeenth-century metaphor that had its origin in biblical psalms, as in Psalm 142:7, where an angel released a soul from a wicker cage. In medieval English church wall paintings, the dove represented the Holy Ghost, and even though iconoclasts destroyed these images, the metaphor remained.[5] Cotton Mather, when writing about death, compared the soul to a bird "which has been habiting its full time, When *Time* for it [death] arrives, the *Shell breaks* and the *Bird* then does *Fly Away*."[6] Carvings of wings on New England gravestones depict Mather's metaphor, which with slight variation appeared frequently in sermons delivered on both sides of the Atlantic: ministers pictured the soul nesting in the tree of life, just as medieval artists pictured the Holy Ghost as a dove nestling in God's lap.[7]

Other accessories in New England portraits appear in their English prototypes. The open book with thumb inserted as if to suggest a pause in a continuous activity was a common way for English portraitists to signal that their sitters were "ladies" or "gentlemen," as well as to indicate the occupations of clergyman, writer, or magistrate. Swords and canes symbolized power and status as well as occupation, while rings, shields, and other heraldic devices established family and class positions.

The stylistic relationship between English sixteenth- and early seventeenth-century portraits and those painted in New England in the

4. In the portrait of Elizabeth of York, the white rose represents the house of York; her husband, Henry VII, holds the red rose of Lancaster in his portrait at the National Portrait Gallery, London. Portraits of Queen Elizabeth I contain many of the symbols that appear in later English portraits: the eglantine (a single white rose), emblematic of chastity; a pillar, symbolizing constancy and fortitude; the sword of justice; the olive of peace; and spring flowers, emblematic of youth, the Golden Age, everlasting calm. See Roy Strong, *The Elizabethan Image: Painting in England 1540–1620* (London, 1969), 46; Mary Ann Dwight, *Introduction to the Study of Art* (New York, 1856), 199–233.

5. John Phillips, *The Reformation of Images: Destruction of Art in England, 1535–1660* (Berkeley, Calif. 1973), 27, 152, 186, 190.

6. Cotton Mather, *The Soul Upon the Wing* (Boston, 1733), 10.

7. Allan I. Ludwig, *Graven Images: New England Stonecarving and its Symbols, 1650–1815* (Middletown, Conn., 1966), 202–216.

Fig. 5. *Thomas Anguish, Mayor of Norwich.* Unknown artist, 17th century English School, 1612. Oil on panel, 36¾×26 ins. Norfolk Museums Service (Norwich Castle Museum).

Fig. 6. *Archbishop Matthew Parker.* Unknown artist, 16th century English School, 1573. Oil on panel, 24×19½ ins. Norfolk Museums Service (Norwich Castle Museum).

Fig. 7. *Jane, first wife of John Tradescant the Younger.* Unknown artist, 17th century English School, ca. 1640. Oil on canvas, 24×28 ins. Ashmolean Museum, Oxford.

Fig. 8. *Mrs. Freake and Baby Mary.* Unknown artist, Boston, ca. 1671–1674. Oil on canvas, 42½ × 36¾ ins. Worcester Art Museum, Worcester, Massachusetts. Gift of Mr. and Mrs. Albert W. Rice.

Fig. 9. *Oliver Cromwell*. Robert Walker, c. 1659. Oil on canvas, 49½×40 ins. National Portrait Gallery, London.

Fig. 11. *Thomas Wentworth, 1st Earl of Strafford.* Unknown artist; after Sir Anthony van Dyck, 1636. Oil on canvas, 50 1/2 × 40 ins. National Portrait Gallery, London.

Fig. 10. *Major Thomas Savage.* Attributed to Thomas Smith, 1679. Oil on canvas, 42 × 37 1/8 ins. Museum of Fine Arts, Boston. Bequest of Henry Lee Shattuck in memory of the late M. Gray.

Fig. 12. *John Leverett*. Unknown artist (possibly Peter Lely), c. 1655. Oil on canvas, 43½×35 ins. Essex Institute, Salem, Massachusetts.

Fig. 13. *Elizabeth Paddy Wensley*. Unknown artist, Boston, 1670–1680. Oil on canvas, 41⅝ × 33⅛ ins. The Pilgrim Society, Plymouth, Massachusetts.

Fig. 14. *The Mason Children, David, Joanna and Abigail*. Unknown artist, Boston, 1670. Oil on canvas, 39½ × 42¼ ins. The Fine Arts Museums of San Francisco. Gift of Mr. and Mrs. John D. Rockefeller 3rd.

seventeenth century seems very clear, and it has been noted by such scholars as Louisa Dresser and Samuel Green.[8] Similarities in style and symbolism underscore the English origins of American culture, and remind us that whatever religious disagreements existed between the Puritans and the English church, American Puritans remained transplanted Englishmen in their tastes and cultural interests.[9] In coming to America, they did not erase from their memories things seen and experienced at home—the visual environment that had entered into their consciousness as they went about their daily routines of work and worship. In small churches and large cathedrals, in manor houses, town halls, guildhalls, universities, and professional institutions, they had observed and visually absorbed the art of sixteenth- and seventeenth-century England. Public celebrations, pageants, and parades had impressed on their memories colors and images that further contributed to their awareness and understanding of the meaning and function of the visual arts. When they came to America, the settlers brought with them this awareness, and, when circumstances permitted, they attempted to duplicate their earlier experiences with the arts in their new homes. And because this art reflected the values and purposes of their new community as well as those of their former society, the colonists encountered no prohibitions or restrictions in its patronage.

The art that the Puritans knew in England and patronized in New England was the art of portraiture. Frowning upon luxurious indulgences that diverted men from the spiritual purposes and goals of life, American Puritans, like their English counterparts, were gen-

8. Louisa Dresser, *XVIIth Century Painting in New England: A Catalogue of an Exhibition Held at the Worcester Art Museum . . . July and August, 1934* (Worcester, Mass., 1935); Louisa Dresser, "Portraits in Boston, 1630–1720," in *Journal of the Archives of American Art*, VI (1966), 1–34; Louisa Dresser, "The Background of Colonial American Portraiture: Some Pages from a European Notebook," American Antiquarian Society, *Proceedings*, LXXVI (1966); Samuel M. Green, "English Origins of Seventeenth Century New England," in Ian M. G. Quimby, ed., *American Painting to 1776: A Reappraisal* (Charlottesville, Va., 1971), 15–69.

9. See Perry Miller and Thomas H. Johnson, eds., *The Puritans*, 2 vols. (New York, 1963), I, 7, 10; Louis B. Wright, *Middle-Class Culture in Elizabethan England* (Ithaca, N.Y., 1958), 14–15.

erally not receptive to the fine arts of painting and sculpture. They opposed religious art—particularly attempts to give divinity (God, Christ, or angels) a corporeal representation—considering such art as idolatrous and a transgression of the second commandment. As heirs to an iconoclastic tradition that stretched back to medieval times, to such reform movements as fourteenth-century Lollardy and fifteenth-century humanism, in their own time—from the mid-sixteenth century to the Civil War—they had been witnesses to and had participated in an iconoclastic campaign that resulted in almost total destruction of all religious images and paintings.[1]

In 1586, for example, the English religious reformer Sir Edward Hoby urged princes (and those who would emulate princes) to avoid "statues, images, and wanton pictures" because they were "the teachers of vanitie, of lyes, deceite, and abominations."[2] A half century later, Dr. William Ames, the Puritan theologian whose textbook, *The Marrow of Theology*, provided Harvard students for many generations with lessons in proper religious behavior, warned that "representative images at or before which God is worshiped" were not to be introduced into Christian service.[3] Thus, when at the end of the seventeenth century, the New England minister Samuel Willard rhetorically questioned: "How is it possible to rightly shadow a Spirit? who ever was able rightly to decypher the form or shape of a being which is invisible!" and reminded his congregation that it was "mad-

1. The mid-sixteenth century suppression of images may be said to have begun in 1538 when pilgrims' shrines were destroyed, but the formal iconoclastic campaign got underway on 21 February 1548 with the order of the Privy Council for the removal of images, sent to Archbishop Cranmer. See Strong, *The Elizabethan Image*, 14. Even when the reformists were no longer in control, however, the official Anglican position in relation to images reflected the iconoclastic enthusiasm unleashed by the Reformation. In Jewel's *Apology* of 1562, for instance, the value of images in teaching the illiterate is pointed out, but it is also argued that it is better to remove images since they lead to idolatry. Wright has suggested that when "Fanatical asceticism swept England in the 1640's . . . Cavaliers and Roundheads alike were guilty of vandalism." Wright, *Middle-Class Culture*, 14. See also Phillips, *Reformation of Images*, 1, 9, and *passim*; Strong, *English Icon*, 2–3.
2. Matthieu Coignet, *Instruction aux Princes*, transl. Edward Hoby, in G. Smith, *Elizabethan Critical Essays* (Oxford, 1904), I, 342–344.
3. William Ames, *The Marrow of Theology*, transl. John D. Eusden from the 1629 Latin edition (Boston, 1968), Book II, Chapters 38–44, 282–83. For Ames's portrait, see Fairbanks and Trent, eds., *New England Begins*, II, 157–158; illus., 114.

ness and wickedness to offer any image or Representation of God,"
he was speaking within a long and well-defined tradition.[4]

None of these men was averse to having his portrait painted.
Hoby had his portrait painted twice; one of these was transformed
into a morality lesson with the inclusion of an allegory of peace in
the cutout (Figure 18). Dr. Ames's likeness appeared as the frontispiece to most of the early seventeenth-century editions of his book.
In 1633, he sat to the Dutch artist Willem van der Vliet for a portrait
that eventually was presented to Harvard College (Figure 19); and
a half century later, Harvard commissioned Thomas Smith to make
a copy of Ames's "effigies."[5] And however "lofty" the Reverend
Willard could become in his tirade against images, he obviously did
not resist having his portrait taken (Harvard University Portrait
Collection), from which an engraving was made for the frontispiece
to his *Compleat Body of Divinity* (1726), "the first folio volume of
theology published in this country."[6] Perhaps even more striking in
this regard are the many portraits existing of Oliver Cromwell, the
instigator of the most destructive iconoclasm ever practiced in England
and spokesman for English Puritanism (Figure 9).[7]

4. Samuel Willard, *A Compleat Body of Divinity* (Boston, 1726), 54.

5. Dresser, *XVIIth Century Painting*, 135. The curators at the Museum of Fine Arts,
Boston, believe that the 1680 copy is not the same image as the van der Vliet, Fairbanks and Trent, eds. *New England Begins*, II, 157.

6. Justin Winsor, ed., *The Memorial History of Boston*, 4 vols. (Boston, 1881), I, 208
and illustrations.

7. Oliver Cromwell was painted by Sir Peter Lely on commission from James
Waynwright soon after his installation as Protector on 16 December 1653. Lely's
image became to a limited extent the official one from which many copies were taken
(illus., Oliver Millar, *Sir Peter Lely, 1618–80* [London, 1978], 47). Lely's portrait was
probably copied from Samuel Cooper's miniature taken from life. Cromwell is supposed to have said to Cooper, "Paint my picture truly like me. & not Flatter me at all,
but . . . remark all these ruffness pimples warts & every thing as you see me." (ibid.)

It is interesting to note that Lely was not inhibited by a sense of Puritan disapproval
of portraiture; with two other artists he is supposed to have proposed to the Long
Parliament before its dissolution in April 1653 that he paint a series of pictures to be
placed in the palace of Whitehall representing all the memorable achievements since
the Parliament's first sitting, including pictures of principal battles and sieges of the
Civil War— "beset" with portraits of appropriate generals and commanders. The artists also suggested two large group-portraits for the Banqueting House, one of the
"whole Assemblie of Parliament" and another of the "Council of State." This offer
was not accepted. Millar, *Lely*, 14.

The portrait survived the anti-art fever in England for various reasons. One of these was certainly its relative cheapness and small scale. Even while he was spending money lavishly on all kinds of artistic projects, Henry VIII had found it necessary to encourage the pillaging of monasteries and church property for economic reasons: the court was near bankruptcy and the church's wealth was essential for its maintenance. The economic chaos of the country that followed his death continued to limit the funds available for artistic commissions on a large scale. Any aesthetic interest that may have existed in landscape, history, or allegory had, of necessity, to be funneled into the crafts, which continued to be practiced because they required less expenditure and could be justified as being useful.[8]

The portrait also escaped prohibition because it was regarded as a craft. Up to the eighteenth century in England, portraitists were perceived as craftsmen. Called variously painter, painter-drawer, painter-stainer, limner, or scrivener (who was more frequently a clerk), such artists enjoyed the same privileges as other craftsmen in the towns in which they resided. They were not highly paid workers, but neither were they the lowest paid. Rather, they occupied a status somewhere in the middle of the economic and social scale of their towns. Ancient Salisbury in Wiltshire, for example, had been home to a craft guild of "Lymbners" since 1440; when Henry VI found it necessary to call on all the twenty-three guilds in town for money to "complete the great ditch" for the defense of the city, the "Lymbners" contributed a sum below that given by the highest ranking group and the most prosperous, the merchants and the brewers, and below, as well, the goldsmiths and the embroiderers, but above what

8. Strong, *English Icon*, 1; F. C. Dietz, *English Government Finance, 1455–1558* (Bloomington, Ill., 1920); and his *English Public Finance* (New York, 1932). Portraiture dominated English art up to the eighteenth century and even later. When Lely arrived in England from the Netherlands in the mid-seventeenth century and tried to pursue "the natural bent of his *Genius* in *Landtschapes* with *small Figures*, and Historical *Compositions*," he found "the practice of *Painting after the Life* generally more encourag'd" and so "apply'd himself to *Portraits . . . ,*" according to the seventeenth-century observer Richard Graham. Quoted by Millar, *Lely*, 9. The cavalier poet Richard Lovelace commiserated with Lely on the necessity to paint portraits instead of other kinds of pictures in "an 'un-understanding land', where only portraits were in demand." *A Panegyrick to the best Picture of Friendship Mr. Pet. Lilly* (London, circa 1647–1660).

was contributed by the saddlers, carpenters, masons, and others employed in the building trades. Prices paid for portraits also suggest that they were valued as a good, but not exceptional, commodity: the highest price seems to have reached £10; the average was £5; and occasionally a bust portrait went for less than a pound.[9]

The situation seems to have been the same elsewhere. In Reading, Berkshire, where a guild of painters-stainers existed in the early seventeenth century, and in Norwich, Norfolk, one of the more important artistic centers outside of London (and the heart of the Puritan rebellion), the painter-stainers and limners enjoyed a middling prosperity, not much different from that experienced by similar craftsmen. They were frequently called upon to paint church pews and do decorative work on public buildings. When they did take portraits, they did not sign their paintings, nor were their names associated with specific pictures. But in the small towns in which they lived and carried on their craft, they were surely known and their work understood.[1]

9. From about 1250 on in England, when painters began to leave the monasteries where they were employed by monks and became itinerant workers, they took on both the social status and condition of other craftsmen—scribes, servers, goldsmiths, glaziers, etc. According to Ernest William Tristram, the wages of all craftsmen in the thirteenth century were "practically on the same scale, the average earnings of skilled workers being from four pence to seven pence. A scribe working on inscriptions in a painted chamber at Westminster received five pence a day." (*English Medieval Wall Painting*, 3 vols. [London, 1950], I, 419ff).Tristram's conclusions are born out by a study of the account books at Canterbury Cathedral of fees paid to workers, including "paynters-stainers," as late as the sixteenth century. Also see Charles Haskins, *The Ancient Trade Guilds and Companies of Salisbury* (Salisbury, 1912), 59–61 for entry relating to raising money for the great ditch; for subscriptions taken in 1607 to send deputations to London, which lists donations of guilds and craftsmen, see N. J. Williams, ed., *Tradesmen in Early Stuart Wiltshire: A Miscellany* (Trowbridge, 1960), 76–77. For status and incomes of London painters, see Mary Edmond, *Limners and Picture-makers*, Walpole Society, XLVII, *Annual Volume* (London, 1980), 60–242. Also see Strong, *English Icon*, 24–25, 49–50.

1. Wills, inventories, parish records, and cathedral account books were studied in the records offices at Kent, Trowbridge, Reading, Norwich, and Cambridge; at Oxford University Library, Cambridge University Library, Canterbury Cathedral, the Council House, Salisbury, and Salisbury Cathedral. Estates of the few painters, stainers, and limners listed were generally quite modest. See "Wills, Administrations, Bonds and Inventories in the Archdeaconry of Wiltshire, 1557 to 1779," Typed. ms., London, 1961; "Index to Wills etc. from the Salisbury Diocesan Registrar," Typed ms., 1971; Index to Bishop's Register for Diocese of Salisbury, including Parishes in

The limner's trade was a familiar one, then, to Englishmen coming to the New World; as New Englanders, they continued to treat the limners as craftsmen, seldom referring to individual artists by name (except for that one time when Harvard College commissioned Thomas Smith), and, although there were no guilds in America, they probably did not pay the limner more for his work than they had in England.[2] The craft nature of the portrait—the sense that it was an article of use—removed from it the onus of extravagance or ornamentation associated with historical or religious painting, and made it more acceptable as an art form to a middle-class community eager to assert its prosperity but limited by religious scruples.

That the usefulness of the portrait was what made it most acceptable to both English and American Puritans seems clear when we realize that an important corollary of Puritan belief was the necessity to find purpose in their pastimes. Nothing was good for its own sake; all experience, as Perry Miller has pointed out, "was given of God" and therefore had "some reason behind it," some use it served.[3] In sixteenth- and seventeenth-century England, the portrait was use-

---

Berks and Wilts Counties''; Sub Dean of Sarum, "Index to Wills,"—all in Wiltshire County Record Office; Miss M. A. Farrow, comp., *Index of Wills Proved in the Consistory Court of Norwich . . . 1604–1686* ([Norwich], 1950); "Norwich Diocesan Archives, Probate Inventories, 1688–1849," listed by Thomas F. Barton for Norwich Consistory Court.

2. The little we know about the role of the painter in seventeenth-century New England corroborates the craft status we find he held in England. The "painter-stainer" Thomas Child of Boston, for instance, was responsible for the establishment of a house painting business that trained apprentices in decorative painting; Joseph Allen was described by Nathaniel Mather to his brother Increase as a craftsman with "a good skill in watchmaking, clockmaking, graving, limning, & that by his owne ingenuity & industry chiefly. . . ." (Massachusetts Historical Society, *Collections*, 4th Ser., VIII [Boston, 1868], 52). In the accounts of Simeon Stoddard Account Book, Stoddard Papers, Massachusetts Historical Society, Boston, we find the notation "paid the limner," but Stoddard did not bother to note the name. Harvard College paid Smith £4.4 for his copy of Dr. Ames's portrait (Harvard College Accounts, in Massachusetts Historical Society, *Proceedings*, 1st Ser., VI [1862–1863], 340). Also see Abbott Lowell Cummings, "Decorative Painters and House Painting at Massachusetts Bay, 1630–1725," in Ian M. G. Quimby, ed., *American Painting to 1776: A Reappraisal* (Charlottesville, Va., 1971), 71–117.

3. Perry Miller, *The New England Mind: The Seventeenth Century* (Cambridge, Mass., 1954), 90, 173; Michael Zuckerman, "Pilgrims in the Wildnerness. Community, Modernity, and the Maypole at Merry Mount," *New England Quarterly*, L (1977), 265.

ful because it met political, familial, and social needs. It served similar purposes in seventeenth-century New England.

During the reign of Queen Elizabeth, English nationalism encouraged the portrait, for it became the vehicle through which the crown and nation could be glorified. The court required art to impress visiting emissaries and establish its national prestige, and portraiture, which did not require such large expenditures as tapestries or mural works, answered this purpose. Presented visually as the "most Royal queene or empresse," through the portrait Elizabeth was transformed into an icon, symbol of the splendor and strength of the British nation. Portraits of the country's eminent citizens also enhanced British nationalism; dressed in rich materials, shining armor, and elaborate robes of office, and identified by the heraldic device designed to establish status and family position, they appeared as superior beings, the pride of a bold and prosperous nation.[4]

The Elizabethan portrait also expressed the Englishman's concern with history, and the prevailing assumption that a knowledge of history and heroic feats contributed to public morality. "Portraitures, Pictures, and other Monuments were devised to ornifie Temples, Cities, and Princes pallaces," wrote the portraitist William Segar; "they were made to retaine in memory, the excellent Actions of such men, as had lived honourably, and died vertuously."[5] In 1595, Sir Philip Sidney, whose *Defense of Poesie* expressed authoritatively "the literary commonplaces" of sixteenth-century humanist thought, defined a similar function for the portrait: "For as the Image of each Action stirreth and instructeth the minde, so the loftie image of such woorthies must enflameth the minde with desire to bee worthie." Portraits, in Sidney's view, were capable of moving "man toward virtue" and, like "the heroical best poetry," taught "what is good and true and which most induces man to act accordingly."[6] "The

4. Strong, *English Icon*, 37.

5. William Segar, *Honor Military and Civill* (London, 1602), 254–255. Segar was quoting Scipio. See also Wright, *Middle-Class Culture*, 297–334.

6. Sir Philip Sidney, *A Defence of Poetry*, ed. J. A. Van Dorsten (London, 1966), 11, 25, 47; Andrew D. Weiner, *Sir Philip Sidney and the Poetics of Protestantism* (Minneapolis, Minn., 1978), 37–39.

beautiful Sidney," as the New England poetess Ann Bradstreet characterized him, had many admirers in the New World, and his defense of art and poetry as serving didactic purposes by reminding people of great historical deeds must have fallen on receptive ears.[7]

From the beginning, history and biography had been important intellectual concerns for the Englishmen who settled Massachusetts Bay. Almost immediately upon landing in America, Governors Bradford and Winthrop had begun to chronicle the history of their respective colonies, so that future generations would be aware of the reasons behind the migrations and the hardships that the first migrants had suffered in order to establish these new commonwealths. After 1660, the desire to record the past and the achievements of the founders seems to have increased in intensity. Ministers began to urge their congregations to give attention to the study of New England's history, so that, as Urian Oakes preached in 1673, the memory of God's "almost unexampled and unparall[el]ed mercy" would be transmitted to Posterity "that the memory of them may not dy and be extinct with the present Generation."[8] Cotton Mather justified his biographies of New England saints by explaining that his *Magnalia Christi Americana* (1702) would portray "the exemplary LIVES of many Magistrates, and of more *Ministers* who so Lived, as to leave unto Posterity *Examples* of everlasting *Remembrance*." Their biographies would provide *"the whole World,"* he believed, "with vertuous Objects of Emulation." Mather specifically associated Governor John Winthrop's portrait that was hanging, as he said, "with honour in the State-House of his country," with the late governor's "wisdom, courage, and holy Zeal," which rendered him a worthy example for his successors.[9]

7. (1638). Joseph R. McElrath, Jr., and Allan P. Robb, eds., *The Complete Works of Anne Bradstreet* (Boston, 1981), 149–152. The idea that the arts should be used to inspire men to what Dr. Ames called "good action" was contained in the doctrine of "technologia," which, according to Perry Miller, "carried the emanations of divine energy into things, from things to the mind of men in the form of the arts, where it galvanized them into right conduct. . . ." *The New England Mind*, 173–174.

8. Urian Oakes, *New-England Pleaded With* (Cambridge, Mass., 1673), 23.

9. Cotton Mather, *Magnalia Christi Americana, or, the Ecclesiastical History of New England* (London, 1702), Bk. I, 163; Bk. IV, 9. See also Sacvan Bercovitch, *The Puritan Origins of the American Self* (New Haven, Conn., 1975), 8–14. The Winthrop portrait

Fig. 15. *Elizabeth of York.* Unknown artist, late 16th century English School. Oil on panel, 22¼ × 16⅜ ins. National Portrait Gallery, London.

Fig. 16. *Elizabeth I.* Marcus Gheeraerts the Younger, c. 1592. Oil on canvas, 95 × 60 ins. National Portrait Gallery, London.

Fig. 17. *Henry Gibbs*. Unknown artist, Boston, 1670. Oil on canvas, 40¼ × 32¾ ins. Private Collection. Photograph courtesy, Museum of Fine Arts, Boston.

Fig. 18. *Sir Edward Hoby*. Unknown artist, 1583. Oil on panel, 37½×29¾ ins. National Portrait Gallery, London.

Fig. 19. *William Ames, 1576–1633*. Attributed to Willem van der Vliet, 1633. Oil on white oak panel, 33¾×25¾ ins. Harvard University Portrait Collection. Gift of Ephraim Hyde.

Fig. 20. *Captain George Corwin*. Attributed to Thomas Smith, Boston, 1675. All but head repainted by Hannah Crownshield about 1819; retouched by Howarth, Boston, 1864. Oil on canvas, 49×39 ins. Essex Institute, Salem, Massachusetts.

Fig. 21. *Unknown Gentleman. Thought to be Sir George Downing.* (Also called *Elisha Hutchinson*). Attributed to Thomas Smith, 1675–1690. Oil on canvas, 43½×35⅞ ins. Harvard University Portrait Collection. Gift of Robert Winthrop.

Fig. 22. *Self-Portrait*. Captain Thomas Smith, 1670–1691. Oil on canvas, $24\frac{1}{2} \times 23\frac{3}{4}$ ins. Worcester Art Museum, Worcester, Massachusetts.

It is interesting that just about this time—after 1660—three portraits were commissioned in Boston and Dorchester as memorials of great Puritans and their achievements. All three are associated with Augustine Clement (circa 1600–1674), a painter from Reading, England, who came to Boston in June 1635 and lived in Dorchester and Boston for the remainder of his life. Clement had served as an apprentice painter in Reading and Eton, where he would have had the opportunity to observe some fine portraiture, since both towns were important artistic centers outside of London. We do not know what Clement did in the New World, except that he kept a shop in Boston around 1665, the year traditionally assigned to the portrait of John Endicott (State House, Boston; copy at the American Antiquarian Society).[1]

Called by the nineteenth-century historian Edwin L. Bynner "the most stern and uncompromising Puritan of them all," John Endicott had arrived in Salem from Dorchester, England, in 1628, as leader of the first emigrants to the colony of Massachusetts Bay. Almost immediately, he visited disorderly Mount Wollaston, renamed Merry Mount by its leader, Thomas Morton, and cut down its offensive maypole. Named governor of the colony in 1629, he maintained control over the little settlement at Salem until Governor Winthrop's arrival in 1630 and never actually relinquished his vigorous leadership until his death in 1665. It was Endicott who "packed all the Episcopalians home to England; who cut the cross out of the

---

which Mather discussed was later destroyed by fire. A portrait of Winthrop, presumably taken from life in England, circa 1629, is at the American Antiquarian Society.

Mather's historical goals were pursued through the eighteenth century. When Thomas Prince began his *Annals* of New England in the 1730's, he dedicated the first volume to the ruling heads of Massachusetts Bay's government—Governor Jonathan Belcher, Lieutenant-Governor Spencer Phipps, and members of the Council and House of Representatives of the colony—in the hopes that these officials would continue "the same vital and pure Christianity and liberty both civil and ecclesiastical" followed by their predecessors, and imitate "their virtues." (*A Chronological History of New-England in the Form of Annals . . . from the Discovery of Captain Gosnold, in 1602, to the Arrival of Governor Belcher in 1730 . . .* 3d ed. (Boston, 1852), v–vi.

1. Sidney M. Gold, "A Study in Early Boston Portrait Attributions: Augustine Clement, Painter-Stainer of Reading, Berkshire, and Massachusetts Bay," *Old-Time New England*, LVIII (1968), 61–78; Edith Gaines, ed., "Collector's Notes," *Antiques* (November, 1968), 662, 666, 668.

flag in his insensate rage against the old faith . . . who knew no fear of prince or potentate . . . and who was deservedly one of [the colony's] most esteemed and respected leaders." In his portrait, the "uncompromising Puritan" looks sternly frontward, holding prominently the glove of the gentleman, its ornate cuff and the ring on his little finger the only ornaments in an otherwise severe scholarly portrait.[2]

The second portrait attributed to Clement of an important public figure of Massachusetts Bay is that of Dr. John Clark (Boston Medical Library in the Francis A. Countway Library of Medicine), which, according to tradition, was painted in Boston just before Clark's death in 1664 and in his sixty-sixth year. Dr. Clark came to New England in 1637 and served as an eminent surgeon and magistrate in Ipswich and Newbury before coming to Boston around 1650. The first physician in America to perform the operation of trepanning the skull, he holds in his hand the surgical implement for cutting round pieces out of broken skulls in order to recover the fragments which have been driven in. On the table is a bone saw, another instrument denoting his profession. Like the Endicott portrait, this likeness is associated with Clement because the artist owned a lot adjacent to Clark's house in Boston—circumstantial evidence to be sure, but suggestive, especially since both the Endicott and the Clark portraits are obviously the work of a professionally-trained artist. Despite the ravaged condition of both portraits, and especially that of Endicott, there is little doubt that these works demonstrate the fine artistry of a trained studio-painter capable, as Jonathan Fairbanks has pointed out, "of rendering complex visual illusions."[3]

The third portrait, which has been assigned by tradition to the years 1660–1669, is that of Richard Mather (American Antiquarian

2. Winsor, ed., *Memorial History of Boston*, I, 541, 82, 94; portrait illus., 308. A copy of Endicott's portrait by Smibert (1737) is at the Massachusetts Historical Society; in 1873, the original was in the possession of a descendant, William P. Endicott of Salem. Copies are also in Essex Institute and Senate Chamber of Massachusetts. See William C. Endicott, American Antiquarian Society, *Proceedings* (1873), 113.

3. Fairbanks and Trent, eds., *New England Begins: The Seventeenth Century*, III, 416.

Society), pastor of Dorchester Church, one of the most beloved ministers in Massachusetts, and progenitor of New England's most famous ministerial family. Clement had signed the Dorchester Church covenant soon after his removal to Dorchester, which must have taken place by 7 October 1668, when he was elected to town office. When Mather died in 1669, Clement and one John Smith were asked by the church to erect a memorial gravestone to their revered leader. The familiar woodcut print of Mather made by John Foster may have been taken at the same time from an earlier Clement portrait as a way of distributing the minister's image to his parishioners.[4]

The Endicott, Clark, and Mather portraits were painted just before the death of the sitters. Coming toward the end of their careers, the portraits seem designed to remind the community of the contributions these men had made to New England's history. In style as well as purpose, the portraits remind us of the pictures hanging in Norwich, or of Robert Peake the Elder's portrait of *Sir Edward Grimston* (1590: The Earl of Verulam Collection; illus., Strong, *Icon*, 232), or of Tudor portraits of clergymen and savants by Holbein and his followers. In their stark black and white quality, they also suggest to us engravings which served as frontispieces to books, such as those of Francis Quarles or Robert Vaughan, or of the Puritan martyr Hugh Peter, a copy of whose image by James Franklin in relief cut was circulated broadly throughout New England in the early eighteenth century. They follow a convention established for portraits of civilian heroes—sober bust or half-length canvasses of a size appropriate for book publication; they are not designed as ornament but rather limned to recall the mind, character, occupation, and achievement of public men. Emphasis is placed, therefore, on the heads which dominate the canvas, and on iconographical elements— an open book, skull, surgical instruments, glove—which are not separate decorative items but are so integrated into the entire design that they become part of a unified conception.

4. According to David Hall, Increase was playing "political games" in publishing this biography of his father; but even if he were, he must have conceived that such a biography would be effective. (Letter to the author.) The Foster woodcut of Mather is illustrated in Wendy J. Shadwell, *American Printmaking: The First 150 Years* (Washington, D.C., 1969), Plate 1.

A second group of paintings illustrating another important function of the portrait in both old and New England consists of portraits of children and their parents, painted between 1670 and 1674, perhaps by the same hand. Roy Strong has pointed out how for the Elizabethans "the portrait cult [was] another aspect of the genealogical mania which beset them. . . . Pride of family with an eye to posterity inspired the commissioning of portraits."[5] Family was also important for the Puritans, as we know from studies made of Puritan society, theology, and church structure. Believing that the family was the first social organization created for mankind by God after the Fall, the Puritans made the family the foundation of both church and state. To ensure the continuity of families in church governance, the Half-Way Covenant of 1662 made the family rather than the individual the basis of church membership. Although the church was the place for public worship, the family in its home, as Samuel Sewall's diary so graphically reveals, was the place for private devotions and religious education. Studies of English Puritanism have demonstrated how household religion culminated, actually, in Independency: "family prayers and catechising," according to Christopher Hill, "offered an alternative to public worship, especially when the worship itself left so much to be desired as that of the Laudian Church."[6] In New England, as Edmund S. Morgan has demonstrated, the stress on family religion resulted in such a complete retreat to the household that the original missionary purpose of the group suffered. Such phrases as "a Church in his house" or "Ministers in their families," indicate the extent to which the emphasis on family-based religion could be carried.[7]

Students of the Puritan family in England have concluded that the concern for family characterized especially the middle and upper classes: "the poor could not hold a conception of a unified family because of the great social and economic disabilities to which they

5. Strong, *English Icon*, 29.

6. Christopher Hill, *Society and Puritanism in Pre-Revolutionary England* (New York, 1964), 454. See also R. C. Richardson, *Puritanism in North-West England* (Manchester, England, 1972), 90–91.

7. Edmund S. Morgan, *The Puritan Family* (Boston, 1944), 134–136, 173–174; Richardson, *Puritanism in North-West England*, 92–93.

were subject," nor could they afford the luxury of indulging their children as was the practice in middle class families. Puritanism found favor, therefore, as Joan Thirsk has argued, in middle class families located in urban areas or in those parts of the English countryside where "the typical economic unit was the farmhouse rather than the village." It was from such urban and "weakly manoralised" areas that New England Puritans—essentially a middle class group —emigrated.[8]

Puritans not only observed as a religious duty the biblical injunction to honor one's parents, but extended it to include affection towards all family members. The desire for family portraits emanated from this sentiment.[9] When, for instance, Elizabeth Roberts of London married Colonel Samuel Shrimpton of Boston and left home to come to live in the New England town, her father, the London merchant Nicholas Roberts, was urgent in his efforts to arrange an exchange of portraits.[1] The Reverend Nathaniel Mather of Dublin and London (1630–1697) had difficulty finding a limner in Dublin to satisfy his American relatives' desire for his likeness. He finally located one and, in 1683, two years after receiving a portrait from Increase Mather in Boston (perhaps one similar to the line engraving of Increase by Thomas Emmes done in 1702), he was able to fulfill his promise.[2]

The imminence of death made family portraits all the more desirable, especially portraits of women and children. Among the group of family portraits that Roberts sent to Elizabeth Shrimpton in Boston was one of her dying sister Katherine, who died soon after her portrait was taken. "Wee little thought," he wrote to Elizabeth, "ye curtaine would be so soon drawn over yet being intended for you hath sent it yt you may see by ye shadow what a sweet likely

---

8. Joan Thirsk, "The Family," *Past and Present*, 27 (1964), 118.

9. Morgan, *Puritan Family*, 19–21.

1. Nicholas Roberts to Samuel and Elizabeth Shrimpton, July 1671; 10 October 1674, Shrimpton Papers, Massachusetts Historical Society, Boston.

2. Nathaniel Mather to Increase Mather, 26 March 1684, Massachusetts Historical Society. Morgan has pointed out the importance placed by the Puritans on maintaining kinship relationships, especially when separations occurred. *The Puritan Family*, 150.

babe it to live. . . ."[3] The portrait of *Elizabeth Eggington* (1664: Wadsworth Athenaeum, Hartford, Connecticut), Cotton Mather's niece, was presumably taken after her death to retain her likeness for her absent seafaring father.[4] These, and probably other family portraits, testify to the concern of families to retain likenesses of departed members as well as to the realistic recognition—taught at an early age to New England children in such texts as *The New England Primer* (1727)—that

> Youth forward slips
> Death soonest nips.

Henry, Margaret, and Robert Gibbs were the children of the Boston merchant Robert Gibbs. Henry (1668–1723) (Figure 17) became a minister; Robert (1665–1702) (1670: Museum of Fine Arts, Boston) followed his father's mercantile occupation; and Margaret (1663–?) (1670: Private Collection) died young, perhaps soon after her portrait was taken at age seven.[5] The portrait of the Mason children (Figure 14) was taken in 1670, the same year as the Gibbses'; not more than four years later, two portraits of members of the Freake family (Figure 4) were painted, similar in style to the Gibbs and Mason portraits.[6]

All these canvasses are in the tradition of English sixteenth-century painting, which has been called Tudor-Jacobean, Elizabethan, or

3. 3 May 1675, Shrimpton Papers, Massachusetts Historical Society.

4. Louisa Dresser, "Portrait of Miss Eggington, Granddaughter of John Cotton," Wadsworth Athenaeum, *Bulletin*, 5th Ser., III (1959), 1–9. Also see Dresser, "Boston Portraits," 9. A label on the back of this picture identifies the portrait as John Cotton's granddaughter "taken after death." The curators of the Museum of Fine Arts, Boston, believe that the portrait, or possibly just the head, was taken from life. Given the awkward assembling of the head and the rest of the body, I would agree with the nineteenth-century inscription until further evidence is available. Fairbanks and Trent, eds., *New England Begins*, III, 457. The custom of taking portraits from death beds, particularly of youngsters, continued into the eighteenth century: Charles Willson Peale was occasionally asked to do so, and only reluctantly consented.

5. J. L. Sibley, *Biographical Sketches of Graduates of Harvard University*, 3 vols. (Cambridge, Mass.), III, 327–334, s.v. Henry Gibbs; Walter Kendall Watkins, "The Robert Gibbs House, Boston," *Old-Time New England*, XXII (1932), 193–196; Fairbanks and Trent, eds., *New England Begins*, III, 458–459.

6. Fairbanks and Trent, eds., *New England Begins*, III, 460–462, 462–463. The portrait of John Freake, circa 1674, is at the Worcester Art Museum, Worcester, Mass.

medieval, but which, in any case, is marked by the flat and linear style that characterized English painting up to the 1630's and, as Roy Strong has pointed out, continued to exert "its vitality" in the provinces "down to the outbreak of the Civil War and beyond."[7]

There seems to be no question that the painter of the Gibbses, Mason, and Freake portraits was a studio-trained artist, one who had probably received his education in the English provinces, where the old-fashioned style still prevailed, and not in London, where the new artistic developments brought to England by Van Dyck were encouraged. Or else, having come to New England in the early 1630's, he had remained unaware of the new and fashionable style. As a "neo-medievalist," he gave careful attention to the rendering of materials, especially the design of clothing, perhaps in an effort to indicate the status and position of his sitter; but he was not concerned with three-dimensional reality. His linearly-drawn outline of facial features, however, with just a hint of shading, must have provided sufficient resemblance to satisfy his Puritan patrons.

Given the Puritan's education in neo-Platonic philosophy—a way of seeing and experiencing that consistently linked the idea of something to the thing itself, and that regarded material reality as emblematic or symbolic—an emphasis on the objective facts of three-dimensional reality, on body and flesh, would probably have not been welcome. To the Puritan, knowledge of what existed was innate; all that an individual conditioned to think in Platonic or Ramean terms required was a simplified or diagrammatic representation of appearance. The rest the mind provided. Just as Puritanism internalized the Christian ritual as embodied in the life of Christ rather than externalized it as did Catholicism, so did seventeenth-century Puritan art call upon the individual's innate knowledge of forms, finding no need for objective, or external, reproduction.[8] In the portrait of *John Davenport* (1670: Yale University Art Gallery), for instance, the

7. Roy Strong, *English Icon*, 27.
8. See Miller and Johnson, eds., *The Puritans*, I, 19–41, especially 29–31; Miller, *The New England Mind*, 154–180, especially 165–169; Bercovitch, *Puritan Origins*, 9–10; E. H. Gombrich, "Icones Symbolicae: The Visual Image in Neo-Platonic Thought," *Journal of the Warburg and Courtauld Institutes*, XI (1948), 163–192.

features seem merely sketched; the position of the hand and the costume tell us all we have to know about the Puritan minister.

This kind of art recalls the artistic forms of thirteenth- and fourteenth-century Siena, which tell their story simply, clearly, and as illustration, revealing little concern for what Bernard Berenson has called "tactile values," but showing a remarkable feeling for line and color.[9] The religious imagination of medieval Siena, like the religious imagination of seventeenth-century Puritans, supplied what was visually absent.

English pride in family combined with the English sense of history to produce a third group of portraits in seventeenth-century New England—three-quarter-length standing figures finely dressed as was suitable to their rank and social position and bearing the symbols of their prosperity and virtue. Most of these portraits also carry the family coat of arms, a convention early introduced into the English portrait to underline aristocratic status. The inclusion of such heraldic devices suggests a purpose that the portrait was intended to serve; as one English sixteenth-century gentleman explained, he commissioned his portrait because he wanted his son and his son's descendants to know "the stock he and they are derived from."[1]

Portraits in this group include the painting of Major Thomas Savage (1606–1682), Captain of the Ancient and Honorable Artillery Company, deputy to the General Court, a successful merchant and an early settler, having come to Boston in 1635 (Figure 10); Captain George Corwin (1610–1684), prosperous shipowner, businessman, captain in the militia, and deputy to the General Court (Figure 20); and an unknown gentleman (Figure 21), at one time identified as Sir George Downing but now called by the Boston Museum of Fine Arts "An Unknown Gentleman" (probably Elisha Hutchinson)[2]—all three seemingly by the same hand and attributed to Major Thomas Smith (died circa 1691) who, it is surmised, was painting in the Boston vicinity in the 1670's and 1680's.

9. Bernard Berenson, *Italian Painters of the Renaissance* (Cleveland, Ohio, 1962), 153.
1. Quoted in Strong, *English Icon*, 29.
2. Fairbanks and Trent, eds., *New England Begins*, III, 472.

Art was not Thomas Smith's major activity in the New World; the estate indicated in his inventory[3] was too large to have been amassed simply from portraiture. As ship's captain, he must have learned something about art in either England or Holland, and have practiced it as an avocation, probably using mezzotint engravings to remind him of postures and other formal considerations. Despite his effort to establish his figures within three-dimensional space, his portraits remain essentially two-dimensional; and although he obviously knew something about shadowing to achieve roundness and volume, he was not able to create these convincingly. His portraits are drawn flat against the drapery, as in an engraving, and the folds of the cravats are more decorative than actual, except perhaps in "An Unknown Gentleman," where he was able to create a sense of fullness. The structure of Smith's portraits, his obvious effort to suggest depth and distance through the use of the cutout, and his understanding of chiarascuro indicate knowledge of the change that had taken place in English painting from the older styles characterizing the Freake limner's work to the newer continental or baroque style introduced into England by Anglo-Dutch painters, and particularly by Van Dyck. Smith's capacity to invest head and eyes with a life-like immediacy gives his portraits a physical reality that indicates quite clearly that the artist knew how to use light and shade for special purposes.

Smith's portraits combine the limner concern with decorative design with a baroque interest in modelling and volume. But the three paintings are also interesting in the way they purposely demonstrate the rank of the sitters through ornate uniforms, symbols of power (such as baldrics and swords) and symbols of wealth (such as jewels, ribbons, fringes, and lace). The three-quarter length pose, with the head turned conventionally to the right and the hand resting with assurance on a sword or cane, and the size of the canvas itself, to-

3. Will of Thomas Smith, 20 October 1688; and Inventory of Thomas Smith, 25 April 1691. Suffolk County Probate Court Office, Boston. A mariner's career was the assumption of Dr. F. L. Weis, who found a Thomas Smith, mariner, mentioned in Bermuda manuscripts. See Dresser, *XVIIth Century Painting*, 135. Smith's occupation is corroborated by his will, which calls him mariner, and by the items included in his inventory which suggest a life involved in overseas trade, including trade with Holland.

gether with the actual inclusion of a coat of arms in the Savage painting, clearly underscore the function of the portrait as an expression
of pride in family and social status. It was generally accepted in
England in the sixteenth and seventeenth centuries that the painter
was obligated to portray his subjects in pose, accessories, costume
and manner suitable to their place in society. Even tombs in their
size, design, and material had to be appropriate to "the qualitie and
degree of the person deceased," according to John Weever in 1631.[4]

The prevailing belief that the portrait was reserved for the great is
revealed in the frequently-told story of how the Reverend John Wilson refused to have his portrait painted: "What! Such a Poor, Vile
Creature as I am! Shall my Picture be drawn?" he is reported to
have exclaimed when entreated by his relative Edward Rawson "to
let his *Picture* be drawn." Rawson, who was secretary of the Commonwealth, was himself portrayed by the limner in three-quarters
length holding the glove of the gentleman (1670: New England
Historic Genealogical Society, Boston; illus., Winsor, I:381); and his
daughter Rebecca was also limned, perhaps just before her marriage
and departure for England in 1679 (circa 1670: New England Historic Genealogical Society, Boston; illus., Winsor, I:519). Cotton
Mather, who reported Wilson's refusal to be portrayed, delighted in
the minister's humility;[5] but the conviction that a portrait was reserved for individuals of rank and achievement continued into the
eighteenth century, when Massachusetts Governor Jonathan Belcher
wrote angrily to his son in England reprimanding him for having
his portrait by Phillips engraved and distributed. The elder Belcher
was fearful that such a distribution would be considered by his political opposition an act of overweening vanity.[6]

It may be suggested that such portraits acted as a kind of social
control, not only providing *exempla* of greatness, but also instilling
a sense in their viewers of the sitters' God-given right to command
and prosper. When hung in legislative halls or public buildings, such

4. John Weever, *Ancient Funerall Monuments* (London, 1631), 10.

5. Mather, *Magnalia Christi Americana*, Bk. III, 50.

6. Alexander D. Wainwright, "Jonathan Belcher: Notes on a Recently Acquired
Portrait of an Early Benefactor of the Princeton Library," Princeton University Library, *Chronicle*, XIV (1953), 169–176, especially 172.

portraits surely fulfilled the portrait's purpose of providing examples of virtue to emulate, and of demonstrating the power and authority of leaders. When privately commissioned, however, and hung in the newly-built mansions of their wealthy owners, they seem only to indicate the sense of superiority held by members of the Massachusetts elite, their perception of their own worth. Certainly, neither humility nor fear of criticism seems to have affected Savage, Corwin, or "An Unknown Gentleman." Self-assured and confident of their right to be thus portrayed, they flaunt their prosperity and power with undisguised arrogance.

There seems to be no question that the New Englanders who had their portraits painted in the seventeenth century composed a distinct class group. They were magistrates, merchants, clergymen, militia officers, ships' captains—a ruling elite who came from fairly comfortable English backgrounds, emigrated to this country with servants, intermarried, and continued to maintain leadership in the colony at least through the middle of the next century. As William H. Whitmore wrote in 1881, with genealogical enthusiasm: "It can safely be said that those of our colonists who were of the gentry at home, kept to the traditions of their class here, in a measure. They lived in better style than the others, they held most of the offices, and they intermarried so as to constitute an allied section of the community. The clergy and other graduates of Harvard were generally admitted to the same circle, and naturally the richest part of the merchant class could not be excluded."[7]

That it was primarily the New England elite who had their portraits painted is demonstrated by a study of Charles Knowles Bolton's three-volume catalog of portraits of founders which were either brought over to the colonies or drawn in America before 1701.

7. Frank R. Holmes, comp., *Dictionary of the Ancestral Heads of New England Families, 1620–1700* (Baltimore, 1974); William H. Whitmore, "Boston Families Prior to A.D. 1700," in Winsor, ed., *Memorial History of Boston*, I, 557–588. Many studies have built on Whitmore's lists. See Frederick C. Jaher, *The Urban Establishment: Upper Strata in Boston, New York, Charleston, Chicago, and Los Angeles* (Urbana and Chicago, 1982), 15–20; James Henretta, "Economic Development and Social Structure in Colonial Boston," *William and Mary Quarterly*, 3d Ser., XXII (1965), 574–582; Bernard Bailyn, *The New England Merchants in the Seventeenth Century* (Cambridge, Mass., 1955), 135–139.

His collection reveals that of the New Englanders included among the sitters (and this group constituted the largest percentage of portraits), about one-third had a college education, most were from the upper classes, and all were leaders and achievers: clergymen, merchants, military officers, and government officials. These were the men whose images deserved to be recorded, whose exploits would help guide further generations in righteousness—and who also could justify having theirs or family members' portraits painted because they enjoyed incomes of over £200.[8]

The relationships among the sitters also suggest the way in which the portraitist moved within families. The Winthrops (whose portraits are at the Massachusetts Historical Society), for example, were related to the Downings through Lucy Winthrop Downing, John Winthrop's sister and mother of Sir George Downing ("*An Unknown Gentleman*"). Governor Winthrop's niece Mary Downing, first wife of Anthony Stoddard, recorder of Boston and for nineteen years a representative at the General Court, was the mother of Simeon Stoddard (illus., Winsor, I:583), who married Elizabeth Roberts, widow of Colonel Samuel Shrimpton (Massachusetts Historical Society); Anthony Stoddard's fourth wife was the widow of Captain Thomas Savage, Mary Shrimpton, the Colonel's cousin, married the young Robert Gibbs (Museum of Fine Arts, Boston), who became a merchant like his father. Robert's mother, Elizabeth Sheaffe, daughter of Jacob Sheaffe, "one of the wealthiest settlers," married Jonathan Corwin of Salem, whose father Thomas was portrayed by Thomas Smith. Sarah Shrimpton married the son of Dr. John Clark, who took as his second wife Elizabeth Hutchinson, daughter of Elisha Hutchinson ("*An Unknown Gentleman*"). Hutchinson's second wife was Elizabeth Freake, widow of John Freake and daughter of the wealthy merchant Thomas Clark.

Not only were these families among the forty singled out by Whitmore as "entitled to precedence" in Boston, but they were

8. Charles Knowles Bolton, *The Founders: Portraits of Persons Born Abroad who Came to the Colonies in North America before the Year 1701*, 3 vols. (Boston, 1919, 1926); Rosamond Humm, *Children in America: A Study of Images and Attitudes* (Atlanta, 1978), 12; Fairbanks and Trent, eds., *New England Begins*, III, 458.

among Boston's wealthiest residents, involved in land purchases, trading ventures, mills, forges and the manufacture of rum.[9] Generations built on the success of their predecessors, and in doing so, introduced luxuries into their homes and lives that made possible patronage of art in the form of the portrait. When, for instance, Henry Shrimpton, Samuel's father and one of Massachusetts Bay's first settlers, died in 1666, his estate, which amounted to over £3,313, consisted in part of a warehouse filled with rugs, skins, hats, cloth, curtains, gingham, satin, fustian, leather bags and rum. His personal estate included money, gold and gold rings, a silver box, thirteen pairs of shoes, and books.[1] Thirty years later, when his son Colonel Samuel Shrimpton died, the younger Shrimpton's estate ranged from properties that included Exchange Tavern, Noddle Island, and brick warehouses[2] to eight small pictures and five alabaster images.[3] The inventory of his wife's estate when she died in 1714 consisted of jewelry—three diamond rings, a diamond girdle buckle, a gold locket and watch chain, and a pearl necklace—and twenty-eight pictures. Of the latter, four were the family pictures of the Robertses and Bakers sent from England, one was a portrait of her grandson, Master Yeomans, valued at £28, three were pictures painted on glass, and the others were probably engravings.[4]

The same story is repeated in inventories and wills of other

9. Whitmore, "Boston Families," in Winsor, ed. *Memorial History of Boston*, I, 559–588.

1. Inventory of Estate of Henry Shrimpton, 24 July 1666, Suffolk County Probate Office, Boston.

2. Will of Samuel Shrimpton, 5 June 1697; Inventory of Samuel Shrimpton, 22 January 1704; Executors Accompt., May 1712; Accmpt. Estate Samuel Shrimpton Dec'd, 15 May 1712, Suffolk County Probate Office.

3. From the mid-fourteenth century to the Reformation, alabaster carvings in the form of small panels or figures were produced in various centers in England. Intended as altar pieces, they frequently were made in series narrating incidents in the lives of saints. Norwich churches and the cathedral owned such works. See P. Lasko and N. J. Morgan, eds., *Medieval Art in East Anglia 1300–1520* (Norwich, 1973), 30; illus., 41, 42, 55, 56. The presence of such images in Shrimpton's estate, and in others in the early eighteenth century, suggests the secularization process taking place in former Puritan families: Henry Shrimpton, the family's founder, had been a member of the Boston congregation.

4. Will of Elizabeth Stoddard, 11 April 1713; Inventory of Elizabeth Stoddard, 15 July 1713. Suffolk County Probate Office. Also see Inventory in Stoddard Papers, Massachusetts Historical Society.

wealthy New Englanders. We find a similar succession and enlargement in the ownership of things: elaborate furnishings such as curtains, quilts, bedcovers and linens, books, precious stones and jewels, china, porcelains, silver spoons, pewter, brass and ironware, valuable rugs and cloths, and by the second or third generation, alabaster images and pictures—all of which testify to an expanding comfort and elegance of life for those favored families who had profited most from New England's developing economy.[5]

Bernard Bailyn points out that by the eighth decade of the seventeenth century, Boston's wealthy families, for the most part, had "separated themselves from the Puritan style of life" and "took the pattern for their conduct . . . from their picture of life in Restoration England." If so, the portrait as a statement of social distinction would have become important in such a lifestyle. Whether or not these families remained "Puritan" is, of course, a question. Even if they did, however, given the function of the portrait as providing examples of virtuous achievement, there would have been no religious bar to having their portraits taken.[6]

There is still one further purpose that the portrait served in New England society—as it did in late Elizabethan and Jacobean England: that is, the *memento mori*. Roy Strong believes that the introduction of the *memento mori* theme in English painting of this period enabled sitters and artists to "counter the portrait image with its overtones of human glory with a stern moralistic message," reminding both the sitter and viewer "that all earthly things are transitory." Strong also suggests that the *memento mori* portrait is "midway between the portrait proper and the subject picture"—as in *The Judd Memorial* (Dulwich College Picture Gallery, England; illus., Strong, *Icon*, p. 39), where "the portrait element is made wholly subject to the allegory."[7]

5. *Early Records in Probate*, New Series, I; Abbott Lowell Cummings, ed., *Rural Household Inventories* (Boston, 1964); Abbott Lowell Cummings, *Bed Hangings* (Boston, 1961).

6. Bailyn, *New England Merchants*, 139–140.

7. Strong, *English Icon*, 37–41; also see *ars moriendi* files at Warburg Institute Photographic Library, University of London on the numerous 16th and 17th century Italian, Dutch, and English paintings that include the *memento mori* symbolism.

Death's heads were frequently introduced into Dutch paintings—portraits such as Frans Hals' *Portrait of a Cavalier* (National Gallery, London) or his *Portrait of a Man* (National Gallery, London), or allegories such as Harmen Steenwyck's *Still Life: An Allegory of Human Life* (National Gallery, London). Holbein's great painting *The Ambassadors* (National Gallery, London) spells out explicitly the meaning of the death's head, as do illustrations in such seventeenth-century books printed in England and distributed in Massachusetts as John Payne's title page to *The Mirror which flatters not . . .* by Jean Puget de la Serre (1639), or the frontispiece drawn by Thomas Cecill for John Weever's *Ancient Funeral Monuments* (1632). And in the portraits of Norwich's mayors and magistrates, the death's head is a prominent image, included conventionally to counter the pride in achievement represented by these city leaders with warning of their common mortality (see Figure 5).

Thomas Smith's *Self-Portrait* (Figure 22) falls into this tradition, and, because it contains a verse, his painting also reflects the tradition of the emblem. Created during the Italian Renaissance, the emblem was a pictorial image accompanied by a verbal commentary. The idea expressed by the commentary expands, interprets, and complicates the meaning of the visual image, turning what may at first appear to be a straightforward painting into an allegory, or extended metaphor.[8] In Robert Janny's portrait (Figure 23), which hangs with those of other mayors of Norwich in St. Andrews' Hall, we see the skull, a grinning skeleton, and a verse relating to death relieving the pain of life for all who are worthy. Thomas Smith's poem is more personal:

> Why why should I the world be minding
> therein a World of Evils finding;
> Then farewell World: Farewell thy Jarres
> thy Joies thy Toies [Toiles?] thy Wiles thy Warres.
> Truth sounds Retreat: I am not Sorye.

8. For discussion of the emblem and its tradition, see Mario Praz, *Studies in Seventeenth-Century Imagery* (Rome, 1964); R. Freeman, *English Emblem Books* (London, 1948). For meanings of emblem in the seventeenth century, see Henry Cockburn, *The English Dictionarie of 1623* (New York, 1930), 59; Edward Phillips, comp., *The New World of Words: or, Universal English Dictionary* (London, 1706).

the Eternall Drawes to him my heart
By Faith (which can thy Force subvert)
To crowne me (after Grace) with Glory.

The verse gives the naval battle illustrated in the cutout window another dimension. I have already suggested that the Puritans easily made the transition from the thing itself to its meaning in symbolic or allegorical terms. Although the battle probably marks an episode in Smith's career as a mariner—perhaps he was engaged in the Dutch war as was Savage, if we read the flags correctly—the significance of the embattled fleet would not have been lost on Smith's contemporaries as a symbol of the battleground of the worldly life that he is rejecting in his poem and as an ideogram of the portrait's meaning.[9]

The moral life for the Puritan involved war with the temptations of the world, the flesh, and the devil. Smith's poem reminds us of the literature on the craft of dying so popular in England from the fifteenth century on.[1] In Thomas Becon's *The Sick Mannes Salve* (1561), a Calvinist interpretation of the art of dying theme, the sick man anticipates his conflict with death, for once the battle is fought and victory obtained, he will have exchanged "the vyle pleasures of this world, for the inestimable joys of the glorious kyngdom of God." To aid him in this war, the dying man's friends pray for him, while the angels pitch their tents in his room (similar to the tents or fortresses seen in Smith's painting), to protect him from the "hellish army." Phrases in *The Sick Mannes Salve* implying deathbed struggle, triumph over death, death as departure, life as "knighthede or warfar" fought "valeantly and mightly" by prayer under "our graunde captayn Christ" suggest the imagery generally utilized by Protestant writers and preachers, not only addressed to the dying man but presented as prescriptions for an *ars vivendi*, as principles that should govern the behavior of the godly while living. Thus, the naval battle image might have encompassed for Smith a number of ideas, all related to living and dying well.[2]

9. Fairbanks and Trent, eds., *New England Begins*, III, 469, 474; Dresser, *XVIIth Century Painting in New England*, 135.

1. See Nancy Lee Beatty, *The Craft of Dying: A Study in the Literary Tradition of the Ars Moriendi in England* (New Haven, Conn., 1970).

2. Quoted in Beatty, *The Craft of Dying*, 2–5, 141, 148–149, 197.

The skull which Smith displays to the viewer possesses no element of realism, as does, for instance, the skull in the painting of Dr. John Clark, which is clearly a reference to Dr. Clark's work as a surgeon. Rather, in its modelling and design, Smith's skull resembles what Peter Benes in his study of Plymouth County gravestones has called a "headstone spirit," or an "after-life spirit," such as were carved on gravestones between 1689 and 1805. For all the variations in design that these skull carvings display, Benes is convinced that "the underlying thematic purpose" was the same: that each was "an illustration or symbol of the spirit released from the body by death, and in some manner anticipating the resurrection." The heart shape which forms Smith's skull's nose, according to Benes, was a symbol of "eternal life" and could appear in a variety of ways, as skull shape, mouth, nose, or ornament.[3]

Thomas Smith's verse, like the epitaph of a gravestone, confirms Benes' interpretation of the meaning of the skull and heart symbol and strengthens the impression that Smith's painting was designed to serve the same purpose as the graveyard stone: a personal memorial, a statement of philosophy or religious expectation, an iconographical expression of "the concepts of grace, resurrection, and salvation," which lay at the heart of Puritan expectations, and perhaps the persistence of medieval belief in magic that continued even while Puritan ministers attempted to discourage tombs and these kinds of epitaphs as suggestive of Popery. In his renunciation of the "World of Evils" as symbolized by the naval battle being waged in the cutout window, the man of "Faith" holds fast to the skull—symbol of eternal life. Like the true Christian described in *The Sick Mannes Salve*, he bids farewell to the world, repents his worldliness, and looks forward to death, grace, and redemption or "glory."[4]

Smith's painting also reminds us of the Puritan (and English) emphasis on usefulness or purpose in art and on the close association

3. Peter Benes, *The Masks of Orthodoxy: Folk Gravestone Carvings in Plymouth County, Massachusetts, 1689–1805* (Amherst, Mass., 1977), 43, 47, 56, 91, 93, 103.

4. Benes, *Masks of Orthodoxy*, 2, 45; Joseph Allard has interpreted this painting as representing a Puritan "saint of the same general category as Cotton Mather." "The Painted Sermon: The Self-Portrait of Thomas Smith," *Journal of American Studies* X (1976), 347.

between seventeenth-century art and funeral rituals.[5] What is most interesting about his painted effigy is the way in which the artist was able to draw upon suggestions emanating from traditional English portraiture—the allegorical tradition of Elizabethan art—as well as the most advanced stylistic developments in English portraiture to create in the painting medium a gravestone carving of the kind that Benes has defined as a "folk art." According to Benes, the gravestone carvers rejected "traditional Christian symbols of beatitude and sanctification" in their desire to avoid the taint of Catholicism, and instead "devised folk substitutes which probably expressed some of the same concepts, but which did so outside of the context of conventional Christian or baroque iconography."[6]

Like these carvers, Thomas Smith executed a design that was deliberate and purposeful in its expression of a "religious attitude and expectation." In his attempt to make his portrait a secular expression of a religious conception, Smith adopted formal baroque forms which he had either learned or picked up information about in England or Holland, or from mezzotints, and transformed them into easily understood folk symbols, resulting in an incongruous combination of worldliness and superstition that may very well mark the late seventeenth-century Puritan.

All societies, primitive as well as advanced, have resorted to art to satisfy, in Sir Herbert Read's words, "an internal world of necessity."[7] New England society in the seventeenth century was no exception, and it is a mistake to say, as students of seventeenth-century literature claim, that "fearful of the magnetic attractions of icons for idolatry," the Puritans expressed their "universal craving for well-

---

5. Martha Gandy Fales, "The Early American Way of Death," Essex Institute, *Historical Collections*, C (1964), 75–84; Edwin Dethlefsen and James Deetz, "Death's Heads, Cherubs, and Willow Trees: Experimental Archaeology in Colonial Cemeteries," *American Antiquity*, XXXI (1966), 502–510; David E. Stannard, *The Puritan Way of Death: A Study in Religion, Culture and Social Change* (New York, 1977), 111–112.

6. Benes, *Masks of Orthodoxy*, 56.

7. Quoted in Marian Smith, ed., *The Artist in Tribal Society: Proceedings of a Symposium held at the Royal Anthropological Institute* (New York, 1961), 124.

wrought mimesis" in literature rather than the visual arts.[8] There is no question that it was the word rather than the painted or sculpted image that more frequently was resorted to by the Puritan imagination. For the most part, Puritans agreed with the young Michael Wigglesworth that it was the "Eloquence" of sermons rather than paint, and oratory rather than carvings, that gave "new luster and bewty, new strength, new vigour, new life unto trueth" and inspired the mind "with a kind of rapture" capable of "catching the will and affections."[9] But despite their greater familiarity with language as a vehicle for imaginative expression, New Englanders, like their compatriots who remained at home, were not fearful of and did not completely reject the visual arts.

Historians who have blamed Puritanism for the slow development of artistic interests in the United States have misunderstood the nature of both portraiture and Puritanism. They have dismissed the portrait as a legitimate art form, relegating it, as did the seventeenth-century Englishman and New England Puritan also, to the status of a craft, probably because it seemed to bear a more immediate relation to usefulness than other kinds of painting. However, we now realize that the portrait is more than a historical document: for whatever purpose it was originally created, once completed, it becomes as much of an artistic illusion, as much an interpretation of life as a subject-piece. As practiced by the most renowned names in the history of western art, the art of portraiture, like all art that has survived, speaks to our imagination and fills our minds with wonder. If seventeenth-century New England did not produce a Raphael or a Van Dyck, a Titian or a Rembrandt, that was not the fault of Puritanism, but the logical consequences of an undeveloped economy and society. The fact that such a large number of portraits have survived from seventeenth-century New England, and so many of charm and interest, suggests that Puritan New Englanders took as much—

8. Norman Grabo, "The Veiled Vision: The Role of Aesthetics in Early American Intellectual History," *William and Mary Quarterly*, 3d Ser., XIX (1962), 499.

9. Michael Wigglesworth, "The Prayse of Eloquence," 1650, in Miller and Johnson, eds., *The Puritans*, II, 674–675. Also see Emory Elliott, *Power and the Pulpit in Puritan New England* (Princeton, N.J., 1975), viii.

if not more—delight in color and form as any other group of people in the same situation, facing similar problems of survival. Puritan portraits are testimony to the power of the painted as well as the written word.

◆ STEPHEN FOSTER ◆

# The Godly in Transit:
# English Popular Protestantism and the Creation
# of a Puritan Establishment in America

THE literature dealing with the Puritans has become so extensive and so articulated that new studies generally seem
obliged to open with a formulaic abjuration of all previous
historiography. Those who came before are generally held to have
done what they did very well after their fashion but to have done it
for far longer than it needed doing. The work in hand can then be
justified as at last breaking fresh ground after so much entirely for-
givable but as yet unredressed overemphasis on this or that aspect of
a topic complex by definition. Since in the present essay the subject
is the religion of the more ordinary sort of English laymen who migrated to New England, the appropriate act of renunciation might
appear to be the avoiding of any and all clerical perspectives on the
assumption that these have for too long been taken as the only possible concerns of the whole Puritan movement. And there is much
to be said for such a tack, provided it is not pursued too aggressively:
it is certainly valuable to bear in mind that the fascination that some

Stephen Foster is Professor of History at Northern Illinois University.

The author would like to thank David Grayson Allen, T. H. Breen, and David D. Hall
for their comments on earlier versions of this essay and to acknowledge with gratitude
the generous support of the National Endowment for the Humanities and Northern
Illinois University in providing the academic leave under which much of the research
presented here was undertaken. He would also like to extend his appreciation to the
staff of the Newberry Library for providing him with essential assistance at a time
when that institution was undergoing massive physical alterations and only the readers
found the process painless.

historians find in what one minister said to, or in refutation of, another minister is no evidence in itself that the contemporary laity also found the matter nearly so compelling. Acts of naïve anticlericalism, however, now as then, can be self-defeating. The current debate over the vitality and relevance of Puritanism in America, for example, pays a curious tribute to the continuing clerical hegemony even as it denigrates the influence of the ministry. The method of attack on the problem (what, if anything, did Puritanism mean to to the mass of the New England population) seems to have been to examine the laity primarily with a view to gauging the extent to which they heeded clerical shalt-nots. When one has identified a sufficient incidence of quarrelsomeness, fornication, acquisitiveness, or whatever to be considered a critical mass, modernity is declared to have begun and Puritanism and the study are over. The impulses that made the godly choose godliness, the things *they* hoped to get out of Puritanism, and *their* degree of fulfillment or frustration are not matters much looked into in this discussion precisely because the rather imperial perspective of the pulpit is still the one that has been unhesitatingly assumed in defining Puritanism, if only to locate the precise moment of its demise. In place of that familiar picture, beloved of bookjackets, of the laity as a mass of eagerly upturned heads grouped around a massive pulpit from which the larger head of the preacher peers down, we now have one where at one point or another the little heads are all turned away, not listening. The outsized pulpit remains squarely at the center, and the laity are still not in focus.

If scholarship does need to shed the constraints of Geneva black, it will not accomplish this difficult feat by ignoring the clergy but only by seeing them for what they were, dynamic, interacting components with the laity in a single protean movement. Properly forewarned, there is actually considerable value in beginning our inquiry with what the clergy had in mind for the laity. Popular religion in England and America was not passively dependent on clerical discourse, but neither was it wholly autonomous, and the clerical programs at least have the advantage of specificity when compared with the more diffuse nature of lay initiates. The proverbial vicarage win-

dow is a better place than most to make a start in understanding so
intricate and varied an entity as Puritanism, providing always that
one remembers to look through it from both sides.[1]

The vicarage selected is Dedham, Essex, in the 1580's, a prime center for the classical organization at the height of Elizabethan Presbyterianism. At full cry, unrestrained by temperamental or tactical
moderation, the Elizabethan Puritans eerily anticipate their equally
uncompromising Puritan successors on both sides of the Atlantic in
the next hundred years. In particular, a classic Presbyterian text, the
Dedham "orders" of 1585, sets down in one place a scheme that
might have served as a blueprint for a large fraction of the edifice
gradually erected in New England over the course of the latter part
of the seventeenth century. Drawn up on 9 August 1585 as a proposed agreement between the two ministers of Dedham and the
"Auncients of the congregation," very evidently at the instance of
the former, the orders were accepted on the 20th of October in "a
profession freely made by the voyces and handes" of the town's nine
leading inhabitants. The signatories undertook to "joyne together"
to enforce a comprehensive set of fifteen articles requiring the cooperation of church and town governors at every stage for "the observation and mayntenance of all christian order," and for "the banish-
ing of the contrary disorder." Several of the articles merely make an
attempt—not a very successful one in the end—to bring a semblance
of decorum to the chaos of Elizabethan parochial worship. (One can
gain some slight sense of the problem from the work of a Puritan
minister belonging to the Bury classis, the northern neighbor of the
Dedham meeting, who composed an authoritative treatise on the
sabbath in which he was obliged to devote pages to persuading the
worshippers not to bring their hunting hawks in to the church during

---

1. My view of the relevant perspectives, like my title, is indebted to an unpublished
but seminal essay by Patrick Collinson, "The Godly: Aspects of Popular Protestantism
in Elizabethan England" (paper delivered at the *Past and Present* Conference on Popular Religion, 1966). Some of the paper's argument and evidence is summarized in
*idem, The Elizabethan Puritan Movement* (Berkeley and Los Angeles, 1967), 372–382.
Collinson's *The Religion of Protestants: The Church in English Society, 1559–1625* (Oxford, 1982), which deals with the same themes at greater length, especially in chaps.
5–6, appeared too late to be more than noted at a few points in this essay.

the service.) To give direction to the newly methodized religious life of the community other orders appointed that the sacrament be administered monthly and that this new communion Sunday should become the focus for disciplining the townspeople in systematic Christianity. On the Wednesday, Thursday, and Saturday before communion "maryed persons or householders" would repair to church at six in the morning to be examined in their Christian knowledge, while the Dedham youth came in for the same treatment on Saturday afternoon. (These educational arrangements were fleshed out in further articles dealing with compulsory catechising of the youth and with the householders' obligation to attend the two weekly lecture sermons with as many of their servants as could be spared from their work.) On Sunday, at the communion itself, the churchwardens were to take a collection for the poor, "after the cuppe be delyvered," while making sure that the communicants "sytte orderly and comly in their places," presumably to prevent them from walking out on their charitable duties. And on the Tuesday following the two ministers and the "auncients" would meet "to conferre of matters concerninge the good government of the towne."

No less than seven of the fifteen articles explain the meaning of good government in the Puritan sense. Two dealing exclusively with the poor are as concerned with reformation as with relief. In proportion to their abilities the townspeople were to invite to their houses "such of their poore neighbors as have submitted themselves to the good orders of the Churche, and walke christianly and honestlie in their calling." Additionally, the two ministers and a few of the ancients, "alwaies accompanied with one of the constables," will make quarterly inspections of the poor, "and chiefly the suspected places, that understandinge the miserable estate of those that wante and the haughtie disposition of disordered persons, they may provide for them accordinglie." Another two articles envision a fully literate Dedham: all the young will be taught to read (the poor at public expense), and any new illiterates will be kept from settling in town by an agreement among the ministers and the "governors" of families to employ only apprentices already able to read. Still other forms of disorder were to be remedied by providing a special ceremony of

public humiliation to be added on to the wedding and baptismal services of couples known to have been guilty of prenuptial fornication
and by an agreement to force out of town unattached individuals
who were neither responsible for themselves by virtue of possessing
a household or honest calling nor "retayned of any" who might
undertake their edification and discipline.

The one remaining article, the eighth in order, will look especially
familiar to students of the New England town. On top of knowledge
and virtue, admission to communion was going to require a pledge
of love and harmony:

> 8. Item. that so many as shalbe admitted to the Communion promise
> and professe to live charitablie with all their neighbors, and if any occasion
> of displeasure arise, that they refraiginge from all discord or revenging by
> wordes, actions or suites will firste make the mynister and two other
> godlie and indifferent neighbors acquaynted with the state of their causes
> before they proceed further by lawe or compleint out of the towne.[2]

With only a slight change in wording and none whatever in substance, item eight might be the third term of the town covenant of
Dedham, Massachusetts, in 1639. However, the context reveals the
significance of the item (and of similar proposed arrangements elsewhere in the same period): so far from representing peasant communalism in Protestant guise, compulsory mediation was very much the
opposite. English villagers playing their favorite and time honored
game of deadly malice against their neighbors were not fit members
of the body of Christ by anyone's standards, Puritan or otherwise,
and should be kept from communion until reconciled, though, in
any case, they often refused themselves to share the sacrament with
their enemies while the recurring cycle of feuding was going on.[3]

2. The "Orders" are printed in Roland Greene Usher, ed., *The Presbyterian Move-
ment in the Reign of Queen Elizabeth as Illustrated in the Minute Book of the Dedham
Classis, 1582–1589* (Royal Historical Society, *Publications*, 3d Ser., VIII [London, 1905]),
99–101. (Item 8 is found at 99.) For the context, see Collinson, *The Elizabethan Puritan
Movement*, 222–239, and for the hawks, Nicholas Bownd, *The Doctrine of the Sabbath
. . .* (London, 1595), 131–132.

3. The covenant of the New England Dedham is reprinted and discussed in Kenneth Lockridge, *A New England Town, the First Hundred Years: Dedham, Massachusetts,
1636–1736* (New York, 1970), 6–9. Similar arrangements may be found at Kilsby in
Northamptonshire and in the proposed "Orders and dealings" for the town of North-

Compulsory mediation was only an abortive attempt to short circuit these quarrels at an early stage before they had hardened into a way of life through tedious prosecution in the church and common law courts. Like the other fourteen articles, item eight was a ministerially inspired device to be imposed from above in order to cure old, and by Puritan lights, bad habits.

Far more interesting than any one article is the concept of order affirmed by all of them jointly. For Dedham to achieve godliness by Elizabethan Puritan standards every available form of institution, civil and ecclesiastical, would have to be employed, and in a coordinated manner. At the root of this enduring Puritan obsession was a severely guarded optimism about human nature. "Great and dillegent teaching" would be necessary "because men are made of dull metal and hard to conteine spirituall and heavenly things." Nevertheless, the perverse heart of man could be reached, bringing salvation for the elect and at least a degree of external decency for the rest, but only by a systematic and continuous assault on all fronts. Most of the elements of the projected Puritan machine are already in place in the Dedham orders: literacy, charity, voluntary regimentation, drill and discipline, as well as the exclusion of the uncontrollable and an extra dose of the universal supervision for the suspect class, the poor. Later generations of Puritans would have found that the Dedham orders, and the various schema of the Elizabethan Puritans in general, struck a relatively one-sided balance between order and love and between participation and regimentation. As the size, autonomy, and reputation of the godly grew, a more equal emphasis would fall on these competing motifs. All of the townspeople would sign the Dedham, Massachusetts, covenant and they would do their godly walking in the name of love as well as of obedience. But in broad outline the Dedham Orders do represent the continuing hopes of the Pu-

---

ampton itself. See W. J. Sheils, *The Puritans in the Diocese of Peterborough, 1558–1610* (Northamptonshire Record Society, *Publications*, XXX [Northampton, 1979]), 56, 120–122; W. Ryland, D. Akins and R. M. Sergeantson, eds., *The Victoria History of the County of Northamptonshire*, II (Westminster, 1906), 44–45. For the problems local feuds caused the ministers of the Dedham classis (as well as their willingness to use coercion when mediation failed), see Usher, ed., *The Presbyterian Movement in the Reign of Queen Elizabeth*, 47, 71.

ritan clergy for the complete reformation of England and the cause supported by their patrons and allies among the landed classes and the urban and parish oligarchies.[4]

It is a vision that might aptly be termed (after Harriet Beecher Stowe) a culture trap—a "plenitude of means" so extensive, subtle, and overlapping that its intended quarry could hardly avoid becoming entangled in some of them and probably, sooner or later, in all of them. Admitting, therefore, that this official style of Puritanism envisioned an austere and comprehensive regimen that even its proponents candidly conceded to be opposed to the natural inclinations of the individuals for whom it was designed, we confront at once our major poser: how did the Puritan movement ever obtain any substantial number of adherents? One possible response—and a good one—is that "adherents" is hardly the appropriate term for the victims, of what was, in effect, a simple exercise of power by their betters. Anyone who has ever dealt with the realities of the seventeenth century will be well aware that England was no more a free marketplace for ideas than the New England that whipped Baptists and hanged Quakers. Quite apart from brutal instances of the application of public and private coercion to decide the matter of religious "preference," in England, at least, and perhaps more than we realize in America, a fragile society inevitably depended on a regular basis on

4. The phrases in quotation come from George Gifford, *A Briefe Discourse of Certaine Points of the Religion . . . which may bee termed the Countrie Divinitie . . .* (London, 1583), f. 84 [i.e., 83]r. The authoritarian, coercive aspects of Puritanism seem curiously absent from New England local studies, especially when one considers the importance assigned the point in the recent English historiography. Cf. Paul Slack, "Poverty and Politics in Salisbury, 1597–1666," in Peter Clark and Paul Slack, eds., *Crisis and Order in English Towns, 1500–1700* (London, 1972), 164–203; Peter Clark, *English Provincial Society from the Reformation to the Revolution: Religion, Politics and Society in Kent, 1500–1640* (Hassocks, Sussex), chap. 5, esp. 173–184; *idem*, " 'The Ramoth-Gilead of the Good': Urban Change and Political Radicalism at Gloucester, 1540–1640," in Peter Clark *et al.*, eds., *The English Commonwealth, 1547–1640: Essays in Politics and Society Presented to Joel Hurstfield* (Leicester, 1979), 167–187; Keith Wrightson and David Levine, *Poverty and Piety in an English Village: Terling, 1575–1700* (New York, 1979). For an overview of this approach see Christopher Hill, "Parliament and People in Seventeenth-Century England," *Past & Present*, 92 (1981), 118–122. But cf. the observations of Patrick Collinson, partly confirmatory, partly skeptical: "Magistracy and Ministry, a Suffolk Miniature," in R. Buick Knox, ed., *Reformation, Conformity, and Dissent: Essays in Honour of Geoffrey Nuttall* (London, 1977), 70–91; Collinson, *The Religion of Protestants*, 153–177, 216–230, 239–241.

more insidious and persuasive forms of compulsion in matters of faith. No doubt, for example, the tenants of Groton manor found John Winthrop's profession to suit their constitutions very well while he held possession of the lordship and patronage of the living. Like just about everything else at the time in the English speaking world, grace often flowed along the lines of blood and clientage. But when due allowance is made for the force of convenience, there were still enough individual mavericks in both England and America and enough wholesale disruptions in both places to demonstrate that there was some degree of freedom left when every agent of necessity had done its work. As a matter of fact, any number of first generation New Englanders could testify that it had not been convenient, that it had cost them a little something to be a Puritan. "Hence I came to New England," a Suffolk mason named Nicholas Wyeth recalled, "being persecuted and courted for going from the place where we lived" in order to "hear them that were most suitable to my condition to stir up my heart."[5] Michael Wigglesworth had a nearly identical story to tell of his godly parents in the North Country, reviled by their ignorant neighbors when they attended worship outside their parish and ultimately forced to give up "a new built house" and "a flourishing trade" to undergo the "distressing difficulties of a howling wilderness, that they might enjoy Liberty of Conscience & Christ in his ordinances."[6] Most of what we know of Edward Wigglesworth and his wife (her name is a bit uncertain) comes from Michael, and he probably had a weakness for edification even in recalling his parents. But they seem to have hailed from Batley parish in Yorkshire, which was the location in the 1630's of perhaps the most fully autonomous lay Puritan gatherings in the

5. George Selement and Bruce C. Woolley, eds., *Thomas Shepard's Confessions* (Colonial Society of Massachusetts, *Collections*, LVIII [Boston, 1981]), 193–194, hereafter cited as Selement and Woolley, eds., *Thomas Shepard's Confessions*. See also the fifteenth of the "Common Grevances Groaninge for Reformation" in Wyeth's home county of Suffolk (Allyn B. Forbes *et al.*, eds., *Winthrop Papers, 1498–1649* [Boston, 1929–1947], I, 304), where complaint is made of "many bad minded people" who "doe take occasion by Justices and ecclesiasticall courtes to ponish and often to [force to] doe pennance" those who leave a sermonless parish to hear a neighboring preacher.

6. "Rev. Michael Wigglesworth, His Memoir, Autobiography, Letters, and Library," *New England Historical and Genealogical Register*, XVII (1863), 137.

West Riding, and they migrated as part of the company of Ezekiel Rogers of Rowley, who described the families who had come with him as having withdrawn from communion in the Church of England "of a long time" on account of its corruptions. Their Puritanism does not sound particularly passive under the circumstances.[7]

The godly in England had perfectly good grounds from their own experience for thinking themselves something more than fish caught in the ministry's net. In their own estimation they were at once the saving remnant preserving the spark of the gospel in an unregenerate society and, simultaneously, participants in a gigantic national experiment employing the combined resources of a godly state and a Protestant religious establishment to raise the state of civility and Christianity of the English nation beyond the merely nominal. Such allegiance as the clergy was able to drum up came from their understanding of the ambivalence of lay piety and their ability to use their own uncomfortable vision to mediate between the conflicting imperatives. When the distinctive, Janus-like culture of the Puritan colonies came to take on a recognizable shape towards the end of the seventeenth century, the triumph was in one sense very much the clergy's, their Dedham orders writ large. Yet the matured New England Way was also very much the expression of the forces that originally gave the Puritan movement its popular following: an integral combination of separation from and engagement with the England of their day. For us, looking back from the other side of a great historical divide, the laity's motivations may seem a union of irreconcilables and their partnership with the clergy a misalliance. But if the double thrust of lay piety is examined in a little more detail, its apparent paradoxality resolves itself into a perfectly natural response to a particular set of historical circumstances, and the essential Englishness of the subsequent Puritan establishment in the colonies emerges quite clearly.

7. The Batley connection is established in "Lane Family Papers," *New England Historical and Genealogical Register*, XI (1857), 110n.–111n. For incipient sectarianism at Morley and Woodkirk chapelries in the parish, see Ronald A. Marchant, *The Puritans and the Church Courts in the Diocese of York, 1560–1642* (London, 1960), 108–111, and for the separatist sentiments of Rogers's company, John Winthrop, *The History of New England, from 1630 to 1649* . . . ed. James Savage (Boston, 1853), I, 335.

Part of the popular attraction of Puritanism (the more obvious part) lay in its minority position. The poor and persecuted people of God, as Nicholas Wyeth and Edward Wiggleworth held themselves to be, enjoyed all of the emotional power of a Christianity that harked back to the struggling apostolic church before the conversion of Constantine. Admittedly, for the church under the cross the Puritan movement boasted too many beneficed ministers in its ranks, not to mention MPs, J.P.'s, and armigerous gentlemen generally. But in the age of the Reformation Protestantism carried a price, actual and potential. For the first Puritans especially, the Marian persecutions were a recent experience that some of them had endured personally, while the memory of the exiles and the victims of those five years was kept alive long after in Foxe's *Book of Martyrs*. A return of Catholicism seemed a real enough possibility throughout the reign of Elizabeth, and the menace loomed up once again in the 1630's and early 1640's in the fear of the "moderate popery" of the Laudian bishops and of a Spanish or Irish invasion. Even in more confident times, Puritanism often attracted a following in the areas, particularly in the north of England, where the Catholics continued to hold their own, open recusancy encouraging the most forward form of Protestantism in response. For example, the Lancashire of Richard Mather, founder of the American clerical dynasty, was the Northern Ireland of the early seventeenth century: in sections of the county where both groups were strong they jockeyed for control of the pulpits and the schools, alternating lawsuits with other forms of harassment and occasionally resorting to outright violence. Mather himself recalled that the Protestant schoolmaster of his native Winwick Parish successfully intervened to prevent his parents from apprenticing him to Catholic merchants on the grounds "that he should be undone by Popish Education." After Mather left the parish to minister to "the Holy Land" of Toxteth Park, a Protestant citadel in the recusant haven of west Lancashire, the nomination of a leading Puritan to the Winwick rectory in 1624 set off a riot between the nominee's supporters and partisans of the candidate of the local Catholic gentry. Winwick, however, turns out to have been a prize worth fighting over: the schools of the parish were a center for preparing would-be ministers like Mather for entering the universities and for training teachers for the whole of Lancashire.[8] In neighboring Yorkshire, the educational foundations similarly divided into warring establishments that owed their existence to the Catholic-Puritan rivalry, and the religious schism fit like a glove over longstanding regional animosities.[9] Further south, the domestic "old church" was mostly a paper tiger, at least by the accession of James in 1603, but anywhere in England at any time to wear one's Protestantism on one's sleeve, Puritan fashion, was to run certain risks in the event of a Catholic revival and in the meanwhile to enroll in the same cause as the Lollards and the Smithfield martyrs.

More often, however, the Christian warfare was a diffuse sort of guerrilla skirmishing between the godly and the "vulgar" or the "multitude." These very terms for their non-Puritan neighbors reveal well enough how the chosen few felt themselves alone in a hostile sea of indifferent formalists and practical atheists who lacked the conviction even to be papists but who could "persecute" the godly with enthusiasm all the same. Visible religious differences always provided a marvelous means in England, just as they one day would in America, for organizing and perpetuating local quarrels. The causes of the disputes were as varied as the locales in which they took place, but the forms of conflict were monotonously similar. Puritan preachers routinely encouraged their hearers to turn from the wicked, and the saints, in their turn, were often drawn to one another anyway for mutual comfort and edification. Puritan "singularity," therefore, meaning an affected clubbing together of pious hypocrites too proud to fraternize with any but their own kind, became a favorite theme in

8. Increase Mather, *The Life and Death of Mr. Richard Mather*, Dorchester Antiquarian and Historical Society, *Collections*, III (Boston, 1850 [orig. publ. Cambridge, Mass., 1670]), 45; R. C. Richardson, *Puritanism in North-West England: A Regional Study of the Diocese of Chester to 1642* (Manchester, 1972), 16–17, 153–176; Mark H. Curtis, "The Trials of a Puritan in Jacobean Lancashire," in C. Robert Cole and Michael E. Moody, eds., *The Dissenting Tradition: Essays for Leland H. Carlson* (Athens, Ohio, 1975), 78–99; Richard Parkinson, ed., *The Life of Adam Martindale* (Chetham Society, *Remains*, IV [Manchester, 1845]), 12, 12n.–13n.

9. J. A. Newton, "Puritanism in the Diocese of York (excluding Nottinghamshire), 1603–40" (Ph.D. diss., Univ. of London, 1955), 293–304; John Bossy, *The English Catholic Community, 1560–1850* (New York, 1976), 88–89.

the manifold forms of harassment and defamation by which feuds at close proximity were generally carried on. One Sussex man had to bring suit in the Star Chamber of 1632 because in a rhymed ballad (to the tune of "Tom O'Bedlam") circulating in the Rye alehouses he was described as a member of "the holie Brotherhood" who used the pretext of private religious conferences for sexual affairs, while "soe holie he is, that he will speak to noe bodie he meets." Another of the brethren, a Surrey man this time, who migrated to Massachusetts in 1638, reported that at home in England upon his being "much affected" with a sermon against drunkenness and forsaking his tippling companions for "private societies of saints," he "found communion with God and His people so sweet that I resolved against ill company and hence was hated."[1]

Such bitter relations were only to be expected. Explaining "this great fray in the world betwixt God's children and world[ly] ones," Paul Baynes in his popular commentary on *Ephesians* attributed the root cause to guilty consciences:

they nickname these [saints], persecute them so far as they dare. Why? Because that the lives of the godly do control [reprove] them, this it is that breadeth the hatred, great estrangement.[2]

And providing the conflict stayed at the level of an occasional nuisance, there was comfort to be found in persecution. An ordinary individual was given importance by his neighbors' hostility, and a weak Christian had his faith affirmed by opposition. Edward Shephard, a Yorkshire sailor come to New England, described himself as

1. Samuel Rawson Gardiner, ed., *Reports of Cases in the Courts of Star Chamber and High Commission* (Camden Society, *Publications*, N.S., XXXIX [1886]), 149ff.; John Stedman of Sutton Survey in Selement and Woolley, eds., *Thomas Shepard's Confessions*, 73–74. See also the divisive impact of Arthur Hildersham's long (if frequently fugitive) ministry at Ashby-de-la-Zouch, Leicestershire, n. 3, p. 208 below, and the discussions in Shiels, *The Puritans in the Diocese of Peterborough*, 131–134; Collinson, *The Religion of Protestants*, 230–239, 252–268; *idem*, "Cranbrook and the Fletchers: Popular and Unpopular Religion in the Kentish Weald," in Peter Newman Brooks, ed., *Reformation Principle and Practice: Essays in Honour of Arthur Geoffrey Dickens* (London, 1980), 171–202; William Hunt, *The Puritan Moment: The Coming of Revolution in an English County* (Cambridge, Mass., 1983), 146–155.

2. *An Entire Commentary upon the Whole Epistle of St. Paul to the Ephesians . . .* , Nichol's Series of Commentaries, XI (Edinburgh, 1866 [orig. publ. London, 1618]), 323.

happiest at sea, isolated among his reprobate shipmates, because "the Lord kept me with a heart desiring to follow him in the use of means. But when I came here [to New England] and not seeing the need and necessity of the Lord I thought myself miserable."[3]

Before expending too much sympathy on these suffering brethren, one should always recur to the example of another North Country man, the nonconformist minister Adam Martindale, who took a special pride late in life in recounting his youthful skill with the quarterstaff. As individuals the saints probably gave as good as they got. But they were also in need of powerful official protection to shore up their legal vulnerabilities. In an age when most prosecutions originated with informers the vulgar were perfectly capable of carrying the infighting into the church courts or occasionally before ordinary criminal tribunals. In his best selling allegory *The Isle of Man*, Richard Bernard described this sort of harassment through the character of "Mr. Outside," a formalist who attended sermons without listening:

This fellow cannot abide any after [sermon]-meditation, or Christian conference with others of that which he hath heard; and if he espie any meeting together for this purpose, then he maketh information against them, and is ready to send the Hue and Cry, as against privie Schismatically conventicling, and unlawfully meeting.[4]

A collection of twenty-four "Common Grevances Groaninge for Reformation" that originated in Jacobean Suffolk put the matter more tersely: grievance number four is entitled simply, in block capitals, MANY UNJUSTLY TRADUCED FOR CONVENTICLES. From as early as 1585 onwards, the characteristic Puritan meetings for "repetition" of sermons, scriptural conferences, or fasting and prayer all potentially fell within the definition of a "conventicle." Oliver Heywood's evocation of the "warm spirit of prayer" at conventicles in Lancashire in the 1630's "in the heat and height of the Bishop's tyranny over godly ministers," like the similar recollections of Nehemiah Wallington of the "praying year" (1640) in London, and of

---

3. Selement and Woolley, eds., *Thomas Shepard's Confessions*, 173.

4. Parkinson, ed., *The Life of Adam Martindale*, Chetham Soc., *Remains*, IV, 46–47; Richard Bernard, *The Isle of Man: or, the Legall Proceeding in Man-shire against Sinne*, 11th ed. (London, 1640), 16–17.

Joseph Lister of the harassment of the godly in Bradford, Yorkshire, about the same time, all bear testimony to the pleasures of suffering in moderate amounts, and especially to the thrill that came with being able to identify with the earliest Christians as besieged knots of the faithful scattered across a heathen landscape.[5]

When the Civil War finally took the lid off, longstanding enmities, brought to a head in the decade of the 1630's, could finally be paid off with interest. The bishops took their share of knocks from the London mobs, but elsewhere it was just as likely to be the saints, a self-confessed remnant, who were at the mercy of those of the multitude with old scores to settle.[6] Under other circumstances, the withdrawal of the godly might have become complete long before either the later stages of the Interregnum or the creation of Dissent by act of parliament in 1662. Before the mid-1640's only a few English Puritans, more consistent than most, or just more beaten about, did take the insistence on separation to its logical, sectarian conclusion and repudiated both the Church of England and any hope of a comprehensive godly society. William Bradford of the *Mayflower* and New Plymouth colony attributed his Yorkshire company's initial turn to outright separatism to their having been "both scoffed and scorned by the prophane multitude" and hauled through the church courts.[7] Yet theirs was never the typical nor even a par-

---

5. *Winthrop Papers*, I, 297; J. Horsfall Turner, ed., *The Rev. Oliver Heywood, B.A., 1630–1702 . . .* , I (Brighouse, Eng., 1881), 98, 156; Nehemiah Wallington, *Historical Notices of Events Occurring Chiefly in the Reign of Charles I . . .* , ed. R. Webb, I (London, 1869), 132–133; Thomas Wright, ed., *The Autobiography of Joseph Lister, of Bradford in Yorkshire . . .* (London, 1842), 8–9. For other instances of conventicling and general discussion, see Stephen Foster, "New England and the Challenge of Heresy, 1630–1660: The Puritan Crisis in Transatlantic Perspective," *William and Mary Quarterly*, 3d Ser., XXXVIII (1981), 626–629, as well as the sources cited in ibid., 626n–627n.

6. For cases of anti-Puritan rioting and other abuse, see Brian Manning, "Religion and Politics: The Godly People," in *Politics, Religion and the English Civil War*, ed. Brian Manning (London, 1973), 91–95. Another instance, not noted in Manning, may be found in Roger Hayden, ed., *The Records of a Church of Christ in Bristol, 1640–1687* (Bristol Record Society, *Publications*, XXVII [Gateshead, Eng. 1974]), 84, 86. And for Puritan participation in violence towards "papists" and the "vulgar," see Brian Manning, *The English People and the English Revolution, 1640–1649* (London, 1976), 238–254; Hunt, *The Puritan Moment*, 284–310, *passim*.

7. William Bradford, *History of Plymouth Plantation* (Boston, 1912), I, 17–18.

ticularly common path, except perhaps during seasons of unusual frustration for the Puritan movement as a whole, such as the period of disappointment after the Hampton Court conference or the high tide of the Laudian repression. Most of the time, without ever becoming so alienated from their society as the expatriate Separatists of the Netherlands, the bulk of the godly managed to weave together a coherent sense of membership in a common cause and still fit snugly within the interstices of the official institutions of church and state. Theirs was not the accommodation of a subject people to a dominant culture—forced, pragmatic, superficial. Nor were they, like the occasional conformists at a later date, merely making the bare minimum of concessions necessary to ward off the penalties of repressive legislation. Rather, for most of the godly, their Puritan allegiance was actually the basis for larger kinds of loyalties rarely available to ordinary people in the culture of their day on any other terms. As important as the sense of exaltation of the chosen was to the Puritan movement, the sense of access to a world beyond the narrow confines of the neighborhood was no less central.

Take the case of John Trumbull, a mariner who eventually found his way to Massachusetts. Living originally in some unnamed English place without a preaching minister or a local group of saints, he was, in his own words, a man who regarded "nothing but back and belly and fulfilling my own lusts." His initial breakthrough came only after he put to sea, when having accepted a copy of Arthur Dent's *Plain Man's Pathway to Heaven*, solely to practice his reading upon it, he was accidentally taken with its substance and pressed on with Dent's *A Sermon on Repentance*. Like Adam and Eve, Trumbull all at once understood his own nakedness—"so saw my misery," as he laconically put it. Accordingly, he moved "to a place where the means were twice," that is, where he could hear a Sunday sermon and a weekday lecture, and the usual internal struggle ensued. He was frustrated by his own weaknesses and tempted by former friends and other carnal men who ridiculed the saints, but eventually he did manage to fall into godly company and profit by the experience. It was another voyage, however, that sealed his conversion: putting into London, he was brought over by hearing Obadiah

Sedgwick, the lecturer at St. Mildred's Bread Street, explain the difference between hypocrites and true believers, and while further
doubts and difficulties inevitably ensued, his fate was effectively secured. Welcomed into the ranks of God's people, he travelled with
them to New England to a respectable position in Cambridge and
Charlestown society and a place at the head of an American family
tree.[8]

Trumbull may seem a little unusual in having been saved by going
to sea, but it was seaborne commerce and the contacts it brought
that represented for him a peculiarly literal link with a universe beyond the nameless place without means of his early life. What he
glimpsed in the Puritan message conveyed by tract and preacher was
a vision that made his previous experience seem ignorant and aimless,
a vision that represented his only real contact with any form of high
culture. If he was alienated from old comrades and old haunts, he
was inducted into a brotherhood national in scope and little short of
cosmic in orientation. Less dramatically, perhaps, but for much the
same reasons, thousands of others made the same choice: by so choos-
ing they simultaneously set themselves apart from ordinary Englishmen, still intensely local and bounded in their loyalties, and made
themselves part of the great struggles of the English nation and
Protestant Christianity. Inward looking and self-concerned as they
may have been, the little societies of the godly flourished best in
these locations most closely tied to the national culture.

The perfect Puritan location is easy to envision, and it would be
anything but an isolated Arcadia: the "plenitude of means" by which
men were saved cost money and required extensive outside contacts.
In the utopia of the godly, a painful learned minister on an adequate
stipend would reside on the site, a grammar school would be nearby,

---

8. Selement and Woolley, eds., *Thomas Shepard's Confessions*, 106–109. The editors
unfortunately confuse this John Trumbull with another man of the same name, a
cooper who hailed from Newcastle and settled at Roxbury. The tangle is unraveled in
J. Henry Lea, "Contributions to a Trumbull Genealogy," *New England Historical and
Genealogical Register*, XLIX (1895), 148–152, but Lea's suggestion, 151, that the Cambridge John Trumbull was born in Wapping does not seem to fit either: the locale
was hardly "without means." See Paul Seaver, *The Puritan Lectureships: The Politics of
Religious Dissent, 1560–1662* (Stanford, Calif., 1970), 186–199.

the closest member of the gentry would be a well-affected justice who suppressed enormities and patronized promising young candidates for the ministry. Not far away could be found a flourishing market town, located, preferably, on some major trade route and supplied with an endowed weekly lecture, a stationer, and, in general, some kind of continuous sampling of what was going on out there, however much filtered through Puritan lenses.[9] The real ligaments of the Puritan movement before the Civil War are to be found here, in the half accidental, always loosely connected network by which the godly associated themselves with each other *and* with the great events of their time. By way of his enemies, for example, we learn that Calvin Bruen, the Puritan sheriff of the city of Chester, owned a copy of Alexander Leighton's inflammatory *Sions Plea against the Prelacy* only a short time after it came off the presses at Amsterdam in 1630. The tract was apparently obtained through the city's only stationer, who made sure that "no Puritanical books [appear] but our citizens get them as soon as any." In the case of the radical Canterbury politician, Thomas Scott, his own memoranda indicate how he kept himself informed by a steady diet of newsletters and tracts, distilling the information throughout the 1620's in circular letters to his constituents. For Colchester in Essex we have the word of yet another episcopal informant that Thomas Cotton, who kept a "privat church" in the town, also maintained a "peevish intelligencer" at London, whose dispatches he proceeded to read publicly at the town market, while about him "the zealants thronge as people use where Ballads are sunge."[1] In the course of the Great Migration to America in the

9. For contemporary verdicts on this point, see Richard Baxter, *Reliquiae Baxterianae* . . . (London, 1691), 88, 89, 90; John Corbet, *An Historicall Relation of the Military Government of Gloucester*, in John Washbourn, ed., *Bibliotheca Gloucestrensis* (Gloucester, 1825 [orig. publ. London, 1645]), 10, 14. On the importance of market towns to the Puritan movement, see Richardson, *Puritanism in North-West England*, 11–14; Margaret Spufford, *Contrasting Communities: English Villagers in the Sixteenth and Seventeenth Centuries* (Cambridge, 1974), 232n; Collinson, "Magistracy and Ministry," in Knox, ed., *Reformation, Conformity, and Dissent*, 73–79; Collinson, *The Religion of Protestants*, 247–248. There is a prudent and well-informed discussion of the social and geographic conditions conducive to religious nonconformity in Spufford, *Contrasting Communities*, 298–318.

1. William Prynne, *A New Discovery of the Prelates Tyranny* . . . (London, 1641), 214; Richardson, *Puritanism in North-West England*, 182–183; Peter Clark, "Thomas

1630's, we can very occasionally observe groups of the faithful serving as recruiting agents or just cheering off their New England bound
brethren and publicizing the good news from the Puritan colonies as
it filtered back across the Atlantic.[2]

Some indication of the way these activities fused theological and
political concerns can be gleaned from the instance of the man who
eventually led the migration to Connecticut, Thomas Hooker, while
he served as a lecturer at Chelmsford in Essex in the late 1620's. By
the admission of his admirers, Hooker was "a great inquirer after
News," although not, we are assured, "out of *Athenian* curiousity,
but christian conscientiousness, to sympathise with the church of
God."[3] In 1626, when the Puritans were increasingly concerned
about England's failure to play its part in the international struggle
with the power of Rome, Hooker in two sermons calling for personal
and national moral regeneration could assume that his audience would
catch his allusions to the details of the Gunpowder Plot of 1605 and
also to the latest fighting on the Continent, the two poles of the
current battle with the Romish Antichrist, as well as to the sale in
1621 of one hundred ordinance in the Tower to the Spanish for use
against the Protestants in the war in Germany. On another occasion
at about the same period he improved upon the poor harvests of the
1620's by attributing them to Charles I's marriage to a Catholic
queen.[4] Hooker had ample opportunity to broadcast his opinions be-

---

Scott and the Growth of Urban Opposition to the Early Stuart Regime," *Historical
Journal*, XXI (1978), 1–26; S.P. 16/276, f. 124r., Public Record Office; Stephen Foster,
*Notes from the Caroline Underground: Alexander Leighton, the Puritan Triumvirate, and the
Laudian Reaction to Nonconformity*, Studies in British History and Culture, VI (Ham-
den, Conn., 1978), 47–48.

2. Cf. Hayden, ed., *The Records of a Church of Christ in Bristol*, 85, 88; *Winthrop
Papers*, II, 178; Roger Howell, Jr., *Newcastle-upon-Tyne and the Puritan Revolution* (Oxford, 1967), 89–94, 102–103; T. H. Breen and Stephen Foster, "Moving to the New
World: the Character of Early Massachusetts Immigration," *William and Mary Quarterly*, 3d Ser., XXX (1973), 206–207, 222; Kenneth W. Shipps, "The Puritan Emigration to New England: A New Source on Motivation," *New England Historical and
Genealogical Register*, CXXXV (1981), 83–97.

3. Oliver Heywood, *Oliver Heywood's Life of John Angier of Denton*, ed. Ernest
Axon (Chetham Society, *Remains*, N.S., XCVII [Manchester, Eng., 1937]), 68–69.

4. George H. Williams *et al.*, eds., *Thomas Hooker: Writings in England and Holland,
1626–1633*, Harvard Theological Studies, XXVIII (Cambridge, Mass., 1975), 49, 67–
70; Kenneth W. Shipps, "Lay Patronage of East Anglican Puritan Clerics in Pre-

yond Chelmsford by way of "divers young ministers" who "spent thire time in private meetings and conferences with him or with such as are of his society and returned home in the end of the week and broch on sundaies what he hath brewed, and trade upon his stocke." At least one of those ministers, Thomas Weld of Terling, encouraged private meetings of the godly of his parish, as did Hooker himself at Chelmsford, where he gathered an exclusive, covenanted "company of Christians" to complement his work as a preacher to the multitude.[5]

Outside of such connections, Englishmen too ordinary to possess extensive family ties or university affiliation had no real alternative foci for involvement in the public concerns of their culture. Without the anomalous element of a Puritan commitment one had little choice but to be content to lie down in the old provincial darkness, unaffected by the thirst for "news" that increasingly spurred the educated public to burst the limitations of primitive communications and repressive government policy. The nearest rival to the loose networks of the godly as a source of mutuality and information alike was the ever more ubiquitous alehouse, which, significantly, those in authority regarded as the source of the same kind of rumormongering and unrest as the sedition-spouting preacher and the schismatic conventicle.[6] Effectively, long before the two became temporarily identified

---

Revolutionary England" (Ph.D. diss., Yale University, 1971), 116; Cotton Mather, *Magnalia Christi Americana, or the Ecclesiastical History of New England . . .* , ed. Thomas Robbins (Hartford, Conn., 1853), I, 345.

5. SP16/142/f.239r., Public Record Office; "Letter of the Rev. Thomas Welde, 1633," Colonial Society of Massachusetts, *Transactions*, XIII (1912), 130–131; John Eliot to Richard Baxter, Oct. 7, 1657, in F. J. Powicke, ed., "Some Unpublished Correspondence of the Reverend Richard Baxter and the Reverend John Eliot," *Bulletin of the John Rylands Library*, XV (1931), 159–160; Shipps, "Lay Patronage of East Anglian Clerics in Pre-Revolutionary England," 116–118, 204 (for the indirect impact of Hooker on the laity of Braintree).

6. The insularity of country life in Stuart England is emphasized, perhaps overemphasized, in Alan Everitt, *Change in the Provinces: The Seventeenth Century*, Leicester University Department of English Local History, *Occasional Papers*, 2d Ser., I (Leicester, 1969). The special role as "brokers" of the national culture that was ordinarily reserved to the professional and landed classes is discussed in Clive Holmes, *Seventeenth-Century Lincolnshire*, History of Lincolnshire, VII (Lincoln, 1980), 47–87; F. J. Levy, "How Information Spread among the Gentry, 1550–1640," *Journal of British Studies*, XXI (1982), 11–34. The beginnings of an educated public eager for "News" has been discussed in many places, but perhaps in its broadest cultural context in D. F. McKenzie, *The London Book Trade in the Later Seventeenth Century*, the Sandars Lectures for 1976

by the laws of Massachusetts and New Haven, sainthood had already become citizenship. Indeed, it was the essential combination of the two—the inescapable fusion of the individual psychomachia with public purpose—that moved men and women to take on the formidable burden of being Puritan. For them the whole clerically sponsored rigamarole was a way, a unique one, towards volition, autonomy, engagement.

In the Elizabethan period the intimate link between participation and separation was palpable enough. An Englishman who took up the cause of the international Reformation was by definition a member of a distinct and often testifying minority in his own country. After the collapse of the Presbyterian movement, as overt militancy subsided and a broad Protestant consensus apparently took hold among all parties, the crucial duality is less immediately apparent. Later generations of Puritan ministers seem on the face of it intent mainly on rapproachment with their church and society. Unable to obtain the single Discipline of the Elizabethans, they substituted the multitude of lesser disciplines that came to be known as practical divinity. Through the use of devotional literature, conference, household religion, the neo-Hebraic sabbath, and the private fast they elaborated an interlocking set of routines designed to turn the believer's simple intellectual assent to doctrine into "operative knowledge" (active, self-generating profession).[7] If the clergy, however, seemed to have abandoned their attempt to replace the government of the church wholesale with a mostly respectable campaign to fashion a pervasive

---

(privately printed, 1982), 1–11. For the ordinary man's other source of information, see Peter Clark, "The Alehouse and the Alternative Society," in Donald Pennington and Keith Thomas, eds., *Puritans and Revolutionaries: Essays in Seventeenth-Century History Presented to Christopher Hill* (Oxford, 1978), 47–72.

7. The classic study of this second, "golden age" of English Puritanism is William Haller, *The Rise of Puritanism; Or, The Way to the New Jerusalem as Set Forth in Pulpit and Press from Thomas Cartwright to John Lilburne and John Milton, 1570–1643* (New York, 1938). A number of works deal in whole or in part with Puritan practical divinity, but all are to one extent or another superseded by the recent publication of Charles E. Hambrick-Stowe, *The Practice of Piety: Puritan Devotional Disciplines in Seventeenth-Century New England* (Chapel Hill, N.C., 1982). See also Collinson, *The Religion of Protestants*, 258–273.

Christian society for the many, the results of their efforts in the golden age of Puritanism were, in fact, merely to heighten the tensions that had emerged in the Elizabethan era. Ironically, such successes as were gained among the laity by the more peaceable methods of the Jacobean era were as likely as not to increase the sense of alienation of the godly from their society and to undermine the clerical control over the Puritan movement that the Elizabethans could take for granted.

In the nature of things the spiritual pilgrimages the clergy hoped to guide often ended up as self-directed adventures. In the long maturation period from weak to strong Christian a believer still unable to apply the promises of scripture personally often ended up acting a bit like a classic valetudinarian whose chronic disease has become an absorbing passion quite independent of the physicians consulted. In the conversion narratives this or that wounded soul drags around from sermon to sermon, listing the key texts but generally leaving the various ministers who preached on them anonymous. So, Alice Stedman, from somewhere in the London area, found herself convicted when very young "by a godly minister," subsequently had fears about her estate and "went to London to a minister" who convinced her she rested on mere duties, underwent a further course of sermon hearing "in the country," and on and on . . . hers is one of the more interminable of the relations endured by Thomas Shepard in gathering his Cambridge church.[8] The narratives are, in fact, very like the boring account of some professional invalid visiting "the doctor," then seeing "another doctor," and after that "a specialist," with the physicians identified by name only when a particularly famous or particularly effective practitioner is consulted. In Alice Stedman's case the successful healer was John Cotton and the crucial text was, "For God so loved the world, that he gave his only begotten Son, that whosoever believeth in him should not perish but have everlasting life." One may be forgiven for suspecting some small degree of self-dramatization when so lengthy and incidented an odyssey culminates in the narrator stumbling across the single most ob-

---

8. Selement and Woolley, eds., *Thomas Shepard's Confessions*, 102–105.

vious text in the New Testament. She was perhaps a trifle self-indul-gent, but hardly unique. What Alice Stedman or anyone else who actively pursued the means achieved was a plot, that is, a coherent structure for one's life, complete with tension, struggle and climax, that made one's previous existence seem so much living "at random." Therein lay the lure of Puritanism, but for all the significance of various preachers in the salvation of any given member of the godly, the narrative as a whole belonged to the individual recounting it: he became the hero of an episodic story whose prescribed happy ending was a strong, self-confident Christian but whose unlooked-for consequence was a substantial degree of both autonomy and cohesion among the godly.

For those caught up in its regime, practical divinity, like so many other aspects of Puritanism, had become both an invitation and an estrangement. The prescribed experiences virtually required aban-doning earlier acquaintances for the continued company of saints, with whom significance and meaning had generally first been glimpsed and among whom the precious gift was subsequently nurtured. Just as the preachers liked to say, the fire was warmer than the warmth of all the individual firebrands taken together. Thus, Anne Erring-ton, another one of Thomas Shepard's redeemed Northerners, was conquered (as she was meant to be) by her abrupt injection, as a servant, into the routine of a Puritan household. "She living in ig-norance till she came to New castle to a godly family and it was harsh to her spirit being bound seven years. And I resolved if ever loose I would be vile." But she was never loose again. A godly hus-band ("who thought me so, but I was not") succeeded the godly family, and then, seeking a more enveloping web of godliness, she left Newcastle for New England: "and feeling not the means work hence I desired hither to come thinking one sermon might do me more good than a hundred there."[9] She had learned the first two lessons of practical divinity, that divinity was best "practiced" in a matrix of means and that there was danger in wandering too far from it. The discovery eventually led her, and others like her, to

9. Ibid., 184–186.

New England in search of an environment where the impact of grace was multiplied by the overwhelming preponderance of the gracious in the population. At home in England this same impulse, derived from an attempt to broaden the Puritan mission, went a long way in the opposite direction, towards creating a separated people well before an immigrant ship crossed the Atlantic. For the first quarter of the seventeenth century the dominant movement was merely a growth in the sense of solidarity among the godly and a lengthening of the agenda that they were required to address. The mechanisms for a more complete schism, however, one that would be realized after 1630, were already there in the very techniques that made practical divinity so appealingly practical.

The clergy pioneered the way, as ever with decided ambivalence. The ministers who warned against private men meddling in affairs reserved to the governors of church and state also exhorted the godly to use their conferences to weigh seriously the works of God as manifested in his latest providences—to undertake "the consideration of his creatures" in Nicholas Bownd's phrase. Bownd meant the weather, neither an inconsequential nor an apolitical topic in Elizabethan or Jacobean times. Drought and flood, good and bad harvests, were God's doing, and disasters especially could be understood as judgments for the failings of an unworthy people. Bownd himself attributed the poor harvests of the 1590's to the magistrates' failure to enforce a strict sabbath, just as in the next run of dearth years, the 1620's, it was possible to locate the cause in a vacillating foreign policy, appeasement of papists, and Charles I's marriage to the Catholic Henrietta Maria.[1]

Fasts, above all, invited topical exposition because by definition they were called in response to some public calamity and because they were often held in defiance of authority. If the authorities failed to require a public repentance, then the prayers and tears of the godly in secret were all the more likely to appease an angry god for the

---

1. Bownd, *The Doctrine of the Sabbath*, 223–230 (the quotation occurs at 224 margin). Cf. Richard Greenham, *A Treatise of the Sabbath*, in *The Workes, Collected into One Volume*, ed. Henry Holland (London, 1605), 213; Hunt, *The Puritan Moment*, 196–202, 274–275.

benefit of the whole nation; at the least, such clandestine activities would preserve the participants themselves in the midst of the deserved general punishment.[2] "These tymes," pronounced one of the greatest of the practical divines, Arthur Hildersham, "may also be justly called tymes of persecution" when Christians could lawfully practice their religious duties secretly in defiance of the magistrate, because "this christian duty of public fasting (which god hath also streigthly commanded to be taught and practiced when such occasions is given) is not only not allowed but oppressed and persecuted." (Hildersham and his supporters at Ashby de la Zouch practiced what he preached to the point where they all ended up in front of the High Commission in 1616.)[3]

Private fasts can be found taking on an unashamedly partisan form by the mid-to-late 1620's, but the origins of what was by this late date a visible fissure in the Church of England can be found decades earlier in apparently uncontroversial and wholesome activity. The believer in company with proven saints was to work out the meaning of scripture, and, through the complete sense of the word understood in terms of his own personal experience and his observation of the world around him, his salvation. When that world and the believer's experience of it came to seem peculiarly menacing, the same individuals who attributed bad harvests to bad royal marriages were liable to possess hearts first melted by misgovernment. A good instance is Richard Condor, a Cambridge yeoman of modest acres who founded a nonconformist dynasty and who frequented a conventicle held regularly in the 1630's on market day at Royston. Meeting in a private room, the participants discussed "how they had hard [heard]

2. Nicholas Bownd, *The Holy Exercise of Fasting* . . . (Cambridge, 1604), 227–229. See Foster, *Notes from the Caroline Underground*, 16–18, 50; Horton Davies, *Worship and Theology in England from Andrewes to Baxter and Foxe, 1603–1690* (Princeton, 1975), 245–249; Collinson, *The Religion of Protestants*, 260–264.

3. Hildersham's remarks may be found at Addl. MSS, 4275, f.289, British Library. In the course of his ministry at Ashby from 1543 to 1631 he was suspended on four occasions, spent the years 1613 to 1625 in prison or in hiding (while carrying on clandestine activities), encouraged a bitter factional dispute in the parish, and patronized conventicles of his following. See Stuart Barton Babbage, *Puritanism and Richard Bancroft* (London, 1962), 185–186; Benjamin Brook, *The Lives of the Puritans* (London, 1813), III, 383n–384n.

on the Sabbath-day, and how they had gone in the week past." When the talk turned to "*by what means God first visited their souls and began a work of grace upon them*," Condor's saving instrument turned out to be the reissued Declaration of Sports:

When our minister was reading it, I was seized with a chill and horror not to be described. Now, thought I, iniquity is established by a law, and sinners are hardened in their sinful ways! What sore judgements are to be expected upon so wicked and guilty a nation! . . . And God set in so with it, that I thought it was high time to be earnest about salvation . . . so that I date my conversion from that time; and I adore the grace of God in making that to be an ordinance to my salvation, which the devil and wicked governors laid as a trap for my destruction.[4]

That so many Puritans should find the revised book of sports their breaking point indicates dramatically the way in which the Puritan movement in its later phases had become identified with a distinctive and largely lay form of behavior. Opposition to the ceremonies—an issue that struck the clergy hardest—was always negotiable, but no ground could be given on the sabbath because it had become the great integrating moment in the Puritan calendar, "the market day of the soul," when, for one day in seven, all of the means came together. Sabbatarianism had not even been an original Puritan tenet, but in the 1630's the defense of this central institution finished off otherwise discrete clergymen who would have been willing to do a bit of business on the ceremonies, ranged layman against authority (Condor's "iniquity is established by a law" would find echoes elsewhere), and pointed migrants in the direction of New England. As John Fessington, a Kentish glover who came to Cambridge, Massachusetts, confessed, "when the book of liberty came forth and being afraid I should not stand in trials, hence I looked this way." Fessington's pastor Thomas Shepard, having looked and then come the same way, made a similar point with less economy of style when he asked a Harvard audience, "how hath that little flock of slaughter, which hath wept for it [the sabbath] and preacht and praied, and done and sufferend for it, been hated and persecuted?" A more palpable "document" (to use a contemporary phrase) of the way in which the new

4. Quoted in Spufford, *Contrasting Communities*, 231–232.

Israel stood heir to the old could not have been imagined than to have stood once a week, every week, as one of the band of Hebrews among the scoffing Canaanites of England.[5]

Renewed official attack on Sabbatarianism in the Laudian years made the weekly rupture in parish religious life acute, turning the inadvertent into the self-conscious, but, it is worth emphasizing, here and in general, the Laudian hegemony only worsened a crisis in Puritanism already extant and growing. Some kind of fusion between the world-as-church of *Barchester Towers* and the sectarian exclusiveness of the Jehovah's Witnesses was the defining irony of the Puritan movement at every stage of its existence, and periodic readjustments between these constituent elements made up much of the history of Puritanism in England. Well before Laud, for example, the more dexterous of the Puritan ministry can be found trying to head off full-blown separatism by indulging the godly in one or another form of distinctive fellowship of their own as a supplement to the comprehensive membership of the parish.[6] But these same longstanding tensions, logically anomalous, historically quite natural, were transferred to America at a moment, the 1630's, when they were peculiarly intense because of the manner in which the Laudian ascendancy compromised the establishmentarian commitment of the Puritan movement. For the first time since the Marian persecution the godly seemed far less the vanguard than the remnant, not leaders but survivors charged with preserving the spark of the gospel with uncompromising purity in a world where moderation and compromise had been decisively proven so many shrewd snares of Antichrist. In the decade when New England was founded the tensions that gave the

5. Selement and Woolley, eds., *The Confessions of Thomas Shepard,* 176–177; Thomas Shepard, *Theses Sabbaticae, Or, the Doctrine of the Sabbath* (London, 1649), 48. On the origins of Puritan Sabbatarianism, see Patrick Collinson, "The Beginnings of English Sabbatarianism," *Studies in Church History,* I (1964), 207–221; and for a general study, Winton U. Solberg, *Redeem the Time: the Puritan Sabbath in Early America* (Cambridge, Mass., 1977).

6. See the instances cited in Foster, *Notes from the Caroline Underground,* 7–8; *idem,* "New England and the Challenge of Heresy," *William and Mary Quarterly,* 3d Ser., XXXVIII (1981), 629, 629n. Cf. also the remarks of Richard Baxter and Thomas Hooker on the separation of the godly: *Reliquiae Baxterianae,* 91; Williams *et al.,* eds., *Thomas Hooker,* 117.

Puritan movement its longstanding vitality were coming to seem insoluble contradictions.[7]

As one of the chief executors in America of the tangled English legacy, John Winthrop betrayed the acute stage the Puritan crisis had reached in the early 1630's in his reply to some sort of Separatist manifesto demanding that the new churches of the colonies unqualifiedly repudiate their English mother and, by implication, the longstanding engagement to reform the many as well as to nourish the few. In one and the same document Winthrop, who very evidently knew how to live with contradiction, found himself arguing both sides of the case simultaneously. On the one hand, he defended the Church of England by the extraordinary claim, possible only in the heyday of practical divinity, that *most* of the members were really weak Christians crying out for the succor of the already converted. Winthrop even attributed this sad neglect of the bulk of the English nation, implicitly worth saving, all of them, to "that spiritual pride, that satan rooted into the hearts of their brethren who when they are converted, doe not, nor will not strenthen them, but doe censure them, to be none of Gods people, nor any visible Christians." But, evidently uncomfortable with this argument from generosity, he also fell back on the traditional defense, wholly sectarian in origin, that separation from the churches of England (in the plural) would be schism because at least some parishes down deep had at their core a nucleus of gathered saints, whatever the carnal dross subsequently added by force of law.[8] The argument was a tortured one, but little else could be expected in the 1630's, when the spiritual pride so loathed by Winthrop was in many ways merely the elation of the newly successful masters of an esoteric wisdom paradoxically avail-

7. I have discussed the crisis of the 1630s and its impact on New England elsewhere. See Stephen Foster, "English Puritanism and the Progress of New England Institutions, 1630–1660," in David D. Hall *et al.*, eds., *Saints and Revolutionaries: Essays on Early American History* (New York, 1983), 3–37.

8. *Winthrop Papers*, III (Boston, 1943), 12–13. For the notion that the English alone among Protestant nations understood the "Practicall part" of religion, "*the power of godlinesse and the profession thereof, with difference from carnall and formall chris-tions*," see Thomas Goodwin *et al.*, *An Apologeticall Narration . . .* (London, 1643 [i.e., 1644]), 4, 22–23; Thomas Hooker to John Cotton, *c.* April 1633, Williams *et al.*, eds., *Thomas Hooker*, 297–298; Shepard, *Theses Sabbaticae*, Sig. A4r.

able for just 1s.6d. a copy (the rough cost of two of the most popular awakeners of dead hearts, Dent's *Plain Man's Pathway* and Lewis Bayly's *Practice of Piety*).

Awkward as their situation was, Winthrop and his associates managed to ride their tiger. The solutions adopted turned out to be among the most unstable in the history of the Puritan movement, but at least they provided a kind of ecclesiastical framework, however improvisatory, for the supercharged commitment of the generation of the Migration, who were far more susceptible to the Separatist argument than their forebears. In the 1630's and early 1640's successive adaptations in the initially fluid religious life of the New England colonies satisfied, and by institutionalization stabilized and limited, the lay militance that a little later would wreck any hope of a comprehensive Puritan establishment in England. By 1640 or so a New England saint had become a saint indeed: his grace was certified by a narration of his spiritual life approved for accuracy by fellow saints, he was accorded the unique privileges of the right to form a church and to turn one of its members into a minister, he alone enjoyed the prerogatives of church membership, and especially access to the sacraments, and in New Haven and the Bay Colony he alone had the right to vote.[9] Inevitably, for the first two decades or so after 1630 most of the life of the imagination in New England went into the founding and shaping of the early churches, replacing the plenitude of means with a single all-encompassing drama carried out over and over again in various separate locations by a sophisticated and rather inbred set of actors. The most vivid single ordinance in the worship of the early settlers was probably neither sacraments, sermons, sabbaths, nor fasts, but the conversion narratives. As Oliver Heywood in his memoirs turned first to the fervency and excitement of the conventicles of his youth, so Captain Roger Clap of Dorchester recalled with similar nostalgia the didactic and communal value of the rapid-fire succession of admissions that marked the early years of the New England churches. Weak Christians, new converts, and an-

---

9. See Foster, "English Puritanism and the Progress of New England Institutions," in Hall *et al.*, eds., *Saints and Revolutionaries*, 17–24.

cient professors alike could all center their religious life on version
after version of the shared heroic adventure:

> Many were Converted, and others established in Believing: many joined
> unto the several Churches where they lived, confessing their Faith pub-
> lickly, and shewing before all the Assembly their Experiences of the
> Workings of God's Spirit in their Hearts, to bring them to *christ*: which
> many Hearers found very much Good by, to help them to try their own
> Hearts or no? Oh the many Tears that have been shed in *Dorchester*
> Meeting-House at such times, both by those that have declared God's
> Work on their Souls, and also by those that heard them.[1]

It is not really surprising that the same period also witnessed quite
a number of bitter church schisms. As they suffered through the
problems of working out the meaning of congregationalism in practice, the New Englanders invested their emotional energies heavily
in their new church foundations, and they would hardly have had
much satisfaction without the excitement of conflict and reconciliation. For a few churches the thrill became addictive, but most managed very nicely on just a row or two, and the process was probably
healthy enough in the long run. The English alternative to this petty
squabbling was the Interregnum.

We are used to seeing the early years of the New England Way
in a special and rather misleading light. If the arrangements of the
1630's and 1640's are taken as normal, that is, if we ignore the long
past of the Puritan movement before the settlement of New England, then the history of the godly after 1650 is in one way or another, and for one reason or another, the story of their progressive
worldliness, though the blame for this development is attributed to
everything from human nature to the passing of one or another village convenience. But if we stop taking our cues from the ministry
in the very act of trying to describe the laity, if we recall the Puritan
movement in its entirety, then the developments of the later seventeenth century become no more than another stage in the ongoing
exchange between ministry and laity. The equilibrium point reached
by the end of the century did come down a little closer to the side

---

1. *Memoirs of Roger Clap* (Dorchester Antiquarian and Historical Society, *Collections*, I [Boston, 1844]), 21.

of Anthony Trollope than of the Prophet Jeremiah, but that was as perfectly acceptable a form of reconciliation of the competing elements within Puritanism as any other.

Compelling as they were for the time, and necessary as they had been to the integrity of the Puritan movement in America, the formulations of the first two decades simply could not persist. In the second half of the seventeenth century the congregations of New England did not succumb to a resurgence of the world, the flesh, and the devil (under whatever name we choose to denominate these social forces); they did, however, for more mundane reasons lose their near monopoly position as the fulcrum for their members' imaginative lives. Most obviously, the number of new admissions, and consequently, the frequency with which the ceremony of the spiritual narration was offered, declined sharply. There were not that many adults left to convert after immigration stopped in 1642, and individuals coming to adulthood after migration or born in New England took their time before announcing that they had the requisite conversion experience. In itself there is no necessary Buffonesque New World degeneracy in this spiritual hesitancy—the elder John Winthrop back in England was thirty before he felt confident to lay hold on the promises.[2] When it is remembered that by about 1670 the majority of those over sixteen (roughly the earliest age at which conversion could be expected) were probably under thirty (roughly the median age in many churches of those first entering into full communion), the ministry's alarm over the need to provide for the rising generation becomes comprehensible.[3] A growing portion of their auditory were still weak Christians needing all the various means that had nourished their parents and grandparents before the migration, the means that had originally laid the basis for the self-sustaining chain reaction celebrated by Roger Clap.[4]

2. *Winthrop Papers*, I, 190–215, III, 342–343.

3. For age at conversion, see Robert Pope, *The Half-Way Covenant: Church Membership in Puritan New England* (Princeton, 1969), 280–285, and the discussion (as well as the sources cited) in Gerald F. Moran and Maris A. Vinoskis, "The Puritan Family and Religion: a Critical Reappraisal," *William and Mary Quarterly*, 3d Ser., XXXIX (1982), 45–46.

4. For a rather dramatic instance of the *scarcity* of means in early New England, see Jonathan Mitchell's advice to his brother in 1649. When the latter brought Mitchell

Ecclesiastical responses to the new realities included extension of the limits of church membership, reinterpretation of the sacrament to revive its importance as a "means," and an attendant expansion in the clergy's conception of itself as a distinct and privileged order. All these developments are well known, much written about, and in no great need of another rehearsal. What does need a little emphasis is the way in which changes within the churches were accompanied by their incorporation as a whole into a much larger, if loosely structured edifice. Increases in population size and density, economic development, and a growth in contacts between the towns all provided mechanisms for transmitting the official culture, for thickening it, in effect, until it became the exclusive medium for noetic activity in New England. Individual spiritual pilgrimages continued at a brisk pace, but increasingly under a greater degree of central definition and direction.[5] The reintegration of Puritan religious life in America is tellingly revealed in three deceptively familiar New England institutions: public days, the printed word, and the law courts. Each was put to a new and distinctively American use in the last half of the century, but the guiding genius in the overall arrangement was recognizably English in origin, and this was so for the simple reason that the challenge addressed was no more and no less than the fundamental, animating Puritan goal of orienting the individual believer within a collective mission.

While the New England colonists are best remembered popularly through the annual repetition of one of their thanksgivings, the other form of public day, the fast, probably strikes most people as the

the classic complaint of formal knowledge with weak feeling, his solution was familiar in outline—a better organized, more intensive and more integrated spiritual life in place of one practiced in snatches—yet curious in detail, barely mentioning or omitting entirely the ministry, good books, the sabbath or any kind of collective activity besides conferences with a single close friend. *Mr. Mitchell's letter to his Brother* (Boston, 1732), 3, 4, 11, 13–14. Cf. the stock consolations of Richard Greenham in a similar situation (*Workes*, 40) or the considerably less solitary regimen proposed by Henry Sands to a troubled John Winthrop (*Winthrop Papers*, I, 198).

5. For a different account of the restructuring of the New England imagination after 1660, emphasizing the unique and American aspects of the process, see Hambrick-Stowe, *The Practice of Piety*, 246–277.

more quintessentially Puritan. The stereotype is, for once, not too far off the mark: far more time was spent discussing the necessity and nature of fasting, and fasts substantially outnumbered feasts in frequency. Thanksgivings merely showed gratitude for mercies already vouchsafed; fasting was the way to get things done in the first place, the most supreme, because most solemn and collective, form of wrestling with God on public occasions. The popularity of private, unauthorized fasts among the English godly at the time of the Migration has already been commented upon, but, significantly, in New England, where the saints ruled rather than prayed behind closed doors, the public fasts initially were not especially frequent. Despite plentiful occasions for calling special days on account of the events of the Civil War at home in England and of all the incidents marking the hammering out of polity in church and state in the colonies, Massachusetts enjoined only fourteen public fasts and three thanksgivings in the entire decade of the 1640's, Connecticut four fasts and one thanksgiving. By way of contrast, in the ten years 1665–1674 the rate at which these extraordinary days were called had almost doubled in the Bay and the disproportion was greater still in Connecticut. The difference cannot be attributed to the occasions for fasts and thanksgivings, because a relatively less eventful ten years was chosen for the later period in order to make the point. (The frequency with which public days were set does not rise dramatically for the next ten year period, the terrible years 1675–1684.)[6] The comparatively modest use of public days in the early years of New England settlement suggests the sharply changed situation the

6. For English Puritan admiration for the New England fasts, see the diary of Samuel Rogers for August 1636, quoted in Shipps, "The Puritan Emigration to New England," *New England Historical and Genealogical Register*, CXXXV (1981), 88. The incidence of public days has been calculated from the table in W. DeLoss Love, Jr., *The Fast and Thanksgiving Days of New England* (Boston, 1895), 466–478. See also Richard P. Gildrie, "The Ceremonial Puritan: Days of Humiliation and Thanksgiving," *New England Historical and Genealogical Register*, CXXXVI (1982), 3–16. The count of fasts and thanksgivings given by Gildrie (ibid., 16 [table]) differs significantly from that derived from Love's table because he includes only those public days called on the authority of the General Court. There are, however, a few instances of fasts set exclusively by the colony's churches acting together on their own initiative, and in quite a large number of cases the Council alone, in between sessions of the entire legislature, appointed days of humiliation or thanksgiving. I have consequently followed the Love table here rather than the more recent study.

migrants found themselves in after they left their fasting, praying
brethren. The English godly of the 1630's envied the Americans their
authorized fasts, but this was precisely the circumstance that deprived
the ordinance of the double-edged quality from which Puritanism
derived its strength. The English in their clandestine fasts were both
testifying to their own righteousness and preserving the whole of
the nation, not to mention enjoying a positively apostolic sense of
persecution. They had, as the Americans did not, a continuing context for these Puritan rites that set the worshipers apart but still dealt
directly with the great crisis of their day, and they could see their
own efforts at personal reformation as, à la Richard Condor, a political act. In New England, the fast at first was merely a way of dealing
with a discrete problem, as the thanksgiving was an acknowledg-
ment of its resolution. Unending conflict of a public nature, to which
the struggle within could have been linked, would have required a
far more potent and persevering enemy, far better established within
New England's borders than anyone actually available. (Louis XIV,
who might perhaps have filled the bill to an extent, came on the
scene much too late to be of help.) But if New Englanders could
find no organizing extended metaphor for themselves in the New
Testament, the Old, as it turned out, contained much to help them.

The Jeremiad tradition, celebrated in a revitalized and more frequent round of public days, signaled the recovery in general of the
public dimensions of Puritanism under the very special conditions,
unique in the history of the movement, of the burden of establishment. In the wayward Israel of the prophetic period the New England ministry found a biblical analogy as perfect for their purposes
as the church before Constantine remained for the Dissenters of England. Like Israel, New England was a theocracy—true religion was
established by authority. Like latter-day Israel, with security and
prosperity New Englanders had grown too comfortable with their
special charge, and so the Lord had obligingly reintroduced an element of risk: multiple afflictions for the present, the threat of being
cast off in the future if this chastisement was not taken to heart. And
like Israel chastened, the cure was found in a general and open recognition of sin in a series of public fasts called as occasions warranted,

accompanied by repentance, individual and collective, and concluded with an earnest pledge of reformation. There would be further episodes of laxity, of course, because there had to be if later calamities were to be woven into the same pattern and a new generation of prophet clergy and their American Israelites were to be given ways to locate their individual destinies within it. By joining the ritual of fasting with the pessimistic strain of prophecy that begins with Amos and culminates in Jeremiah the New Englanders found a tradition that could contain Puritanism's central tension under the extraordinary circumstances of a degree of success.[7]

It is worth recalling—the point has been made before—that this marvelously helpful discovery had remained ready to hand for many years before extensive use was made of it. John Cotton for one was already in 1630 expounding on the special relevance of Jeremiah 2:21 for later generations of colonists, even as he launched the founding fathers on their mission. A year later, Thomas Hooker took as his text for *The Danger of Desertion* Jeremiah 14:19, applying it to the England he was leaving, and in 1645 Thomas Shepard once again fell back on the prophet, applying his message to England with a glance at America, on a day of public fasting "in reference to the good estate of the Lords people in England." (Three years later his youngest son would appropriately be christened Jeremiah Shepard.) The elements of the Jeremiad—the ordinance of fasting, the special relationship with the Lord, the Hebraic analogy in general—were all English and were imported to America with the first English settlers. Their subsequent development in the colonies in the next thirty years or so can only be a matter of conjecture (and has been much conjectured about) because so few fast and election days sermons survive for the period prior to 1660. What can be said, nonetheless, is that

7. The classic account of the Jeremiad tradition is that of Perry Miller, "Errand into the Wilderness," in *Errand into the Wilderness* (Cambridge, Mass., 1956), 1–15; the equally classic revisionist argument on the same subject is Sacvan Bercovitch, *The American Jeremiad* (Madison, Wisconsin, 1978), 3–30. There is, however, an unfortunate tendency to let Miller's short article (originally an occasional piece) obscure the complexity of his full dress statements of the same theme, which do take into account the multiple English strands combined into this New England institution. Cf. *The New England Mind: The Seventeenth Century*, 2d ed. (Cambridge, Mass., 1954), 463–491; *The New England Mind: From Colony to Province* (Cambridge, Mass., 1953), 19–52.

however obvious and necessary, the eventual working of these various items of intellectual baggage into a single integrating theme for New England could occur only when a later generation of New Englanders returned to traditional Puritan concerns so cruelly compromised first by the Laudian hegemony and then by the too complete triumph of the refugee saints in America.[8] Through these repeated rites of mass self-denigration the plight of the believer could again be merged with the survival of the polity and the progress of the church, and the energies of the laity could once again be disciplined into a common quest. The hallmark of the age of declension was the boldest sign that in New England the Puritan movement had entered an era of revival.[9]

Public observance provided the foci for the official culture, the high points at which it was most solemnly and explicitly enunciated. Day-to-day repetition was another matter, no less important, and depending as much on the printed as the spoken word. Reading had always had an important place in the Puritan movement as a significant part of the framework of means constructed around scripture and sermon. No soul was ever saved exclusively by a book, except perhaps in very rare instances the Bible unaided, but reading added informed reflection to the lively teaching of the pulpit and the pious life, as they in their turn breathed full meaning into the otherwise lifeless abstractions of print. In England the Puritan clergy had made full and effective use of the press, giving thanks that "God hath given a marveilous blessing of printing to further his Gospelle." Quite apart from the widespread circulation of Bibles, the printing presses after 1590 or so

8. John Cotton, *God's Promise to his Plantations* . . . (London, 1630), 19; Williams et al., eds., *Thomas Hooker*, 228–252; Thomas Shepard, *Wine for Gospel Wantons; Or Cautions against Spiritual Drunkeness* (Cambridge, Mass., 1668). English Puritans, however, never *systematically* identified their nation, even at its most perverse, with Israel of the prophetic period; indeed, on the eve of the great migration an obvious analogy was the day of humiliation in Joshua 7:6, with the subsequent sanctification of Israel by the stoning of Achan. (The contemporary parallels were not hard to find.) Cf. Henry Burton, *Israels Fast, Or a Meditation upon the Seventh Chapter of Joshua, a Faire Precedent for These Times* (London, 1628); Arthur Hildersham, *The Doctrine of Fasting and Praier, and Humiliation for Sinne* (London, 1633). (The later title takes its text from *Ecclesiastes* but makes extensive use of the seventh chapter of Joshua.)

9. See also Hambrick-Stowe, *The Practice of Piety*, 100–103, 247–249.

brought forth a flood of religious material that dwarfed in volume and availability alike every other form of "popular" literature except the ubiquitous almanacs. When they rejoiced that there was "never such a plentie of so good and plaine books printed, never so good cheape," John Dod and Robert Cleaver, themselves much published, knew whereof they spoke.[1]

America was not quite so fortunate. The early date of a printing establishment at Cambridge has always been a source of pride for collectors of American firsts, but the contribution of that press to the vital piety the Puritans assumed ran on printer's ink was initially very small. After eliminating almanacs, material in Latin or the Indian language, statutes lately made, spelling books, and similar items, the output of the New England presses begins to appear very feeble until after about 1665. In any five year period before 1660 the largest number of English language works that could pretend to any imaginative or intellectual content was never more than eight. That number more than doubled for the five year period 1660–1664, doubled again to thirty-six each for 1665–1669 and 1670–1674, then doubled yet again to sixty for 1675–1679, and seventy-one in 1680–1684, remaining in this general range for the rest of the century.[2] Marmaduke Johnson, the first printer with a commercial aptitude, can take some of the credit, and the rest probably belongs to the transfer of the main print-

1. Josias Nicholls, *An Order of Household Instruction . . .* (London, 1596), Sig. G 7r.; Robert Cleaver and John Dod, *A Godly Forme of Houshold Government . . .* (London, 1630), Sigs. [X5r. – X6v.]. For this literature and its uses, see Helen C. White, *English Devotional Literature (Prose) 1600–1640*, University of Wisconsin *Studies in Language and Literature* XXIX (Madison, Wisc., 1931); Hambrick-Stowe, *The Practice of Piety*, 157–161; Margaret Spufford, *Small Books and Pleasant Histories: Popular Fiction and its Readership in Seventeenth-Century England* (Athens, Ga., 1981), 194–218.

2. These totals are compiled from Charles Evans, *American Bibliography*, I (Chicago, 1903); Roger P. Bristol, *Supplement to Charles Evans' American Bibliography* (Charlottesville, Va., 1970). I have dropped all obvious ghosts from the count, but some spurious titles have undoubtedly crept in anyway, without, however, much altering the general drift of the figures presented in the text. The definition of intellectual and imaginative content is necessarily a bit arbitrary, but these figures do include catechisms, law codes (as opposed to individual statutes), and the minority of proclamations with substantial religious commentary. The omission of all three of these categories would do little except to make the contrast between the earlier and later decades of the seventeenth century more marked still.

ing business of New England to Boston after 1675.[3] The true engine of change, however, was the growth of a market for commercially oriented printers and booksellers to exploit by way of Boston's increasing contacts with the coastal towns and the hinterland. (Johnson complained in 1668 that Cambridge was "a town where no trade, or very little is managed," and repeated the observation in his successful petition for removal to Boston in 1674.)[4]

The increase in English language titles with something resembling a mental content has been taken to indicate a secularizing of New England culture, but most of the new material falls into one or another traditional genre. The sharp rise in the absolute numbers of titles (whatever the slight fluctuation in the "secular" proportion of the total output) really means that in the last third or quarter of the seventeenth century the domestic press was finally fulfilling the essential function that the Puritans had routinely assigned it. For the first three or four or even five decades of settlement the New England colonies must have suffered from a most un-Puritan print drought. Books the immigrants brought over with them undoubtedly played a part in their religious life in the very earliest years, but as these copies wore out and the population increased, the significance of reading must have declined until the expansion in the work of the American presses. The only alternative source of books, English imports, simply was never important if extant booksellers' inventories and manifests are any guide: dating mostly from the last twenty years of the seventeenth century, these lists never include much more than

3. For Johnson, see George Parker Winship, *The Cambridge Press, 1638–1692* . . . (Philadelphia, 1945); Benjamin Franklin, V, ed., *Boston Printers, Publishers, and Booksellers: 1640–1680* (Boston, 1980), 303–309. The history of printing in seventeenth-century New England is an often told story, but for a concise and critical account, see Samuel Eliot Morison, *The Puritan Pronaos: Studies in the Intellectual Life of New England in the Seventeenth Century* (New York, 1936), 110–129. In the ten years prior to Johnson's permanent settlement in 1665, the Cambridge press produced 17 titles in English with some sort of intellectual content; for the ten years 1665 to 1674 (the year of Johnson's death) the number is 72. In the next ten years, 1675–1684, the equivalent is 131 titles, with the large majority coming from Boston, not Cambridge.

4. Carl Bridenbaugh, *Cities in the Wilderness: The First Century of Urban Life in America* (New York, 1938), 32–34; Winship, *The Cambridge Press*, 280–281, 328. See also, Bernard Bailyn, *The New England Merchants in the Seventeenth Century* (Cambridge, Mass., 1955), 95–98.

thirty copies of any English book (most came over in much smaller batches), and even when all the multiple orders of a single title are added up, the largest number of copies (excluding school books) is still only eighty-four for a single piece.[5] The domestic press, like its London counterparts, had the capacity for a thousand or fifteen hundred copies of a work in a single edition, and on occasion could turn out more still: one has only to recall the seventeen hundred copies of the Bay Psalm Book that launched religious printing in New England or the nearly insatiable demand for Michael Wigglesworth's *The Day of Doom*.[6]

In importing English titles the Boston booksellers rendered a valu-

5. The figures are derived from Worthington C. Ford, *The Boston Book Market, 1679–1700* (Boston, 1917), 88–182; Roger Thompson, "Worthington Chauncey Ford's *Boston Book Market, 1679–1700*: Some Corrections and Additions," Massachusetts Historical Society, *Proceedings*, LXXXVI (1974), 68–78. (The eighty-four copies—from five separate entries—are of John Fox, *Time and the End of Time*, a tract by a nonconformist English minister first published in 1670 and running to at least an eighth edition by 1700. For the author—not to be confused with the Elizabethan martyrologist —see *Dictionary of National Biography*, s.v. "Fox, John.") After quantity of individual shipments, the next most interesting figure would be overall frequency of importation, and here the lists in Ford, *The Boston Book Market*, 121–150, are particularly revealing. They are invoices between John Ive (the agent for John Usher) and Richard Chiswell and probably represent the entire transactions for a period of just over a year (3 March 1684 to 13 April 1685) between the most important of the Boston booksellers and the major London wholesaler of books to the colonies. Three lists yield 202 separate entries in all, a total of 1,755 volumes, but only two titles, Charles Hoole's *Sententiae Pueriles* and his edition of Cato, accounted for more than a hundred copies each. (For Hoole's Cato, see Thompson, "Worthington Chauncey Ford's *Boston Book Market*," Massachusetts Historical Society, *Proceedings*, LXXXVI, 69,74). Only twenty-one titles were shipped in lots of 20 or more, and eleven of these are schoolbooks (most, like Hoole, in Latin) or works of reference. Of the ten titles remaining, the leader was an English edition of the Bay Psalm book at 70 copies, followed by James Janeway, *A Token for Children* (60 copies), and *Time, and the End of Time* (50 copies). By 1685 there had already been five *American* editions of the psalms, and there would be another two by 1700, while both Janeway and Fox subsequently went through numerous colonial reprintings. The obvious conclusion would be that the import trade served as a supplement to the products of the domestic presses and not, as is generally supposed, the other way around.

6. For the Bay Psalm Book, see Winship, *The Cambridge Press*, 21–34, 143–149; for *The Day of Doom*, see below, n. 60. For an edition of a 1,000 copies in 1705, see Worthington C. Ford, ed., *Diary of Cotton Mather, 1681–1708* (Massachusetts Historical Society, *Collections*, 7th Ser., VII [Boston, 1911]), 520. A similarly large edition in 1717 may be found at ibid., VIII (Boston, 1913), 462. Other press runs from the first half of the 18th century may be found in Rollo G. Silver, "Publishing in Boston, 1726–1757: The Accounts of Daniel Henchman," American Antiquarian Society, *Proceedings*, N.S., LXVI (1956).

able service to New England by enormously increasing the variety of material available to the relatively small group of genuinely intellectual readers, but they could never have reached anything like a large public. It was in the nature of the trade for the bookseller to thrive on offering small samples of a multiplicity of titles, while the printer lived by volume production. If any Boston book merchant had decided for some reason to act in a downright unnatural manner the disabilities of his colonial situation (really just an extreme version of the predicament of his counterpart in the English provinces) would have quickly frustrated the effort.[7] To begin with, payment for the English imports had to be made in hard coin or high quality bills of exchange on leading London merchants. Neither was especially easy for American merchants to acquire, and bad relations between the Boston men and their London suppliers inevitably ensued: John Usher, for example, the leading New England bookseller, complained about the refusal of his stationer, Richard Chiswell, to accept the bills he had purchased for payment, and Chiswell protested in his turn the delay Usher took in making his returns. In the end, simply to have an acceptable and available means of exchange New Englanders found themselves obliged to spend an ever larger portion of their time and capital on other lines of the transatlantic trade in order to build up the English credits needed to pay for their books, so that, in effect, the entire commerce in imported literature was inherently self-limiting.[8]

In addition to this constraint on the overall size of the trade, a New

7. The discussion that follows is heavily indebted to Graham Pollard, "The English Market for Printed Books," *Publishing History*, IV (1978), 7–48; John Feather, "Cross Channel Currents: Historical Bibliography and *l'histoire du livre*," *The Library*, 6th Ser., II (1980), 1–15. An account of the constraints placed on the import trade at a somewhat later date may be found in Stephen Botein, "The Anglo-American Book Trade before 1776: Personnel and Strategies," in William L. Joyce *et al.*, eds., *Printing and Society in Early America* (Worcester, Mass., 1983), 48–82. (Botein characterizes the book trade before about 1750, p. 16, as "sluggish.")

8. Ford, *The Boston Book Market*, 13–14, 83–84. See also W. T. Baxter, *The House of Hancock: Business in Boston, 1724–1775*, *Harvard Studies in Business History*, X (Cambridge, Mass., 1945), Chaps. II–IV, esp. 45–48; and his "Daniel Henchman, A Colonial Bookseller," Essex Institute, *Historical Collections*, LXX (1934), 1–30. Cf., Pollard, "The English Market for Printed Books," *Publishing History*, IV (1978), 29; Feather, "Cross Channel Currents," *Library*, 6th Ser., II (1980), 6–8; Bailyn, *New England Merchants*, 99–101.

England bookseller simply could not choose to import a large quantity of a few titles. The London stationers on whom the New Englanders necessarily depended maintained something very close to an oligopoly in which they adopted business practices that precluded volume supply in the wholesale market. The Londoners functioned at the same time as retailers for the city's trade, distributors to the provinces and colonies, and, as copyright holders, the publishers (in the modern sense) of most of what came from the English presses. Since in this last case they were financially interested in a select portion of the books they sold at wholesale, they were generally in no hurry to supply the retailers outside London with large batches of competing titles in which they did not have a finger.[9] At the same time in order to obtain titles on which they did not hold the copyright for the benefit of their own retail trade, as well as to limit their risk on the copies they did publish, they engaged in a variety of practices that virtually insured that they would never have a large number of any one book on hand for their wholesale business. Of these devices, the newest but increasingly the most important was the "conger" or sharebook system, a syndicate of wholesalers who pooled their money in order to obtain collective control over the copies—later the copyrights—of selected lucrative titles. (Robert Boulter and Richard Chiswell, the main London suppliers to New England were, in fact, by 1670 members of a very early conger, and Chiswell, the son-in-law of the man usually credited with inventing the form, was the prime mover in gaining a commanding position for the system in the organization of the London book trade.)[1] Stationers formed a conger

9. See Pollard, "The English Market for Printed Books," *Publishing History*, IV (1978), 25–34; Terry Belanger, "Bookseller's Sales of Copyright: Aspects of the London Book Trade, 1718–1768" (Ph.D. diss., Columbia University, 1970), 1–6 (summarizing the state of the trade at the end of the 17th century); *idem*, "Publishers and Writers in Eighteenth-Century England," in Isabel Rivers, ed., *Books and Their Readers in Eighteenth-Century England* (New York, 1982), 7–18.

1. The definitive account of the conger by Cyprian Blagden is hidden away beneath an understated title as Norma Hodgson and Cyprian Blagden, eds., *The Notebook of Thomas Bennet and Henry Clements (1686–1719) With Some Aspects of Book Trade Practice* (Oxford Bibliographical Society, *Publications*, N.S., VI [Oxford, 1953]), 67–100, hereinafter cited as Hodgson and Blagden, eds., *Notebook*. Evidence for the early activities of Boulter and Chiswell may be found in ibid., 216–218. See also Pollard, "The English Market for Printed Books," *Publishing History*, IV (1978), 25–34.

to protect their copyrights against piracy and to prevent price cutting in the wholesale trade, but an incidental effect of their operation was to distribute the available copies of a title equally in small lots among all the members, with a substantial segment being "stocked" (left undistributed) in a warehouse to avoid flooding the market. As a result, a New England bookseller could not have ordered a hundred copies of a popular title under conger control (Bayly's *Practice of Piety*, for example) without applying to as many as ten different London stationers at one time or waiting for a very long period as lot after lot was unstocked, ten books or so at a go. What the New Englander could do—and what he did do—was to obtain from his English sources a broad sampling from that wide range of titles (available in small batches) that trade practices, from the oldest, simple barter between stationers, to the newest, the conger, imposed upon the London wholesalers.[2]

In the eighteenth century the contrasting forms of circulation between imported and native imprints probably contributed to a segmentation in the reading public, with fateful consequences for the history of American culture. For example, the opening wedge of the Enlightenment in America, the sermons of Archbishop John Tillot-

2. For Bayly, see Hodgson and Blagden, eds., *Notebook*, 83–84, 122. The other methods of obtaining copies of titles to which another stationer held copyright were "exchange" (barter) and pre-sale subscription. See ibid., 74–75; Cyprian Blagden, "The Memorandum Book of Henry Rhodes, 1695–1720," *The Book Collector*, III (1954), 108–113; John Dunton, *The Life and Errors of John Dunton, Citizen of London* . . . (London, 1818), 62. Comparison of the inventory of the stock of the New England bookseller Michael Perry in 1700 with those of a few of his counterparts in provincial English cities indicates the fundamental similarity of their operations. In each instance most of the entries are for one or two copies of a moderately expensive title intended for the bibliophiles, while severely practical titles (especially school texts and catechisms) and religious best sellers occur in somewhat larger quantities. There is, however, a single, highly significant difference: Perry alone did carry a few items in lots of a hundred or even more, all of them printed in New England. Like his London suppliers, and in this one respect unlike his English provincial equivalents, he was also a significant publisher and (judging from some of the domestic titles bearing the imprint of other Boston booksellers) a wholesaler. Cf., *The Boston Book Market*, 163–182; Robert Davies, *A Memoir of the York Press* (London, 1868), 342–371; W. Harry Rylands, "Booksellers and Stationers in Warrington, 1639 to 1657, with a Full List of a Stationer's Shop there in 1647," Historical Society of Lancashire and Cheshire, *Transactions*, XXXVII (Liverpool, 1888), 67–115; C. W. Chilton, "The Inventory of a Provincial Bookseller's Stock of 1644," *The Library*, 6th Ser., I (1979), 126–143.

son, was a classic instance of a conger publication. Undertaken by Chiswell and printed in large numbers, Tillotson's works were nonetheless financed as a sharebook venture and therefore distributed to every one of the twenty or so members of the conger in dribbles and drabbles of fewer than thirty copies at a time. The fraction of these fractions that regularly crossed the Atlantic managed to turn the work into the *sine qua non* for every colonial of intellectual pretension sufficient to maintain a library of any size—but without making a dent in the tastes of the general reading public. While New England audiences continued to consume American reprints of standard titles by the archbishop's Dissenting contemporaries, his work did not arouse sufficient interest to merit a single colonial edition until George Whitefield's denunciation of his alleged heterodoxy conferred upon Tillotson's corpus a retroactive *succés de scandale*.[3]

After 1700, a very different mental universe began to reach New England cognoscenti from the one still reiterated regularly by the domestic press, and for the first time the unity of the Puritan enterprise came into danger of dissolution. For the seventeenth century, however, when the colonies were hardly large enough to sustain multiple publics, the most dramatic effect of the book trade to America was quite simply its inability to contribute more than a small supplement to the sum total of available reading material. It is scarcely

3. For the conger publication of Tillotson, see Hodgson and Blagden, eds., *Notebook*, 85, 186–187; for Tillotson in America, Norman Fiering, "The First American Enlightenment: Tillotson, Leverett, and Philosophical Anglicanism," *New England Quarterly*, LIV (1981), 307–344. A mid-eighteenth century "network" of readers of imported titles on liberal religion is uncovered and described in Elizabeth Carroll Reilly, "The Wages of Piety: The Boston Book Trade of Jeremy Condy," in Joyce, *et al.*, eds. *Printing and Society in Early America*, 83–125. On the other hand, one has only to examine Clifford K. Shipton and James E. Mooney, comp., *National Index of American Imprints through 1800: The Short-Title Evans*, 2 vols. ([Worcester, Mass.], 1969), *s.v.* "Doolittle, Thomas," "Flavell, John," "Janeway, James," "Keach, Benjamin," and "Wilcox, Thomas," to note the sustained popularity of works by Dissenting Restoration divines in eighteenth-century New England reprints. For some of this literature, see C. John Sommerville, *Popular Religion in Restoration England*, Univ. of Fla. Social Science Monographs, LIX (Gainesville, Fla., 1977), 33–60; Hambrick-Stowe, *The Practice of Piety*, 266–268. See also David D. Hall, "The World of Print and Collective Mentality in Seventeenth-Century New England," in John Higham and Paul K. Conkin, eds., *New Directions in American Intellectual History* (Baltimore, 1979), 166–180; and his "The Uses of Literacy in New England, 1600–1850," in Joyce, *et al.*, eds., *Printing and Society in Early America*, 28–36.

surprising that over fifty English titles were reprinted in America between 1664 and 1700, even though in a large number of instances they were in the course of frequent reprint in England itself, and that the most frequently imported English titles all sooner or later required American editions to satisfy the demonstrated interest the imports had merely aroused.[4]

If the domestic press is recognized as the preponderant source of New England reading, then we must confront a remarkable situation. Most seventeenth-century New Englanders never read a line by the leading ministers of the first generation unless they happened to have acquired copies of their works in England before leaving or obtained them in America from other immigrants who had brought them over in their personal libraries. There was no American edition of any Thomas Hooker title until 1743, and John Cotton, except for his catechism, would have been known only from a 1686 American edition of *God's Promise to his Plantations*. John Davenport and Thomas Shepard did have a few American titles in circulation, but they enjoyed this very limited literary success because the former lived to see the beginning of expanded domestic printing and the latter had enjoyed a Cambridge ministry where his successors were well located to arrange for posthumous publication of his works (though he really

4. Using the same sources as in n. 2, p. 220 above, with the same precautions against ghosts, yields 54 English titles reprinted in America between 1664 and 1700, and I have *not* counted catechisms, publications of an official nature, almanacs and prognostications, writing manuals, or extracts from newspapers. A handful of the 54 probably earned a quick American reprint because their topicality precluded waiting for imported copies, and some of the rest may have been out of print in England itself (though the well-known deficiencies in the *Wing Short Title Catalogue*, even in the revised volumes, preclude any very definite conclusions on this point). Nonetheless, English supplies should have been available for many, perhaps most. As of 1664, Thomas Shepard's *The Sincere Convert* had already gone through thirteen English editions in twenty-three years but still required an American reprinting in that year. Edward Reyner's *Precepts for Christian Practice*, first published in 1644, reached its thirteenth edition by 1668, yet enjoyed an American reprinting in 1667. And when William Dyer's *Christ's Famous Titles* appeared in Massachusetts in 1672, it had already had English editions in 1662 and 1668 and would have a third the next year, 1673, as well as eight further editions by the end of the century—a circumstance that did not preclude another Boston edition in 1704. Numerous other instances could be adduced without difficulty. Equally, I cannot find *any* English title in the sources in n. 5, p. 222 above that achieved any degree of volume import and that did not subsequently enjoy multiple New England editions.

came into vogue only in the eighteenth century). Richard Mather alone of the founding clergy seems to have discovered, or rather re-membered, the value of reading and to have made some use of the domestic press along familiar Puritan lines: he had six hundred copies of his *Farewell Exhortation* run off and "on a certain Lords Day, he did, by the Hands of his Deacons, put these little books into the Hands of his Congregation, that so whenever he should by Death take his Farewel of them, they might still remember how they had been exhorted."[5]

We are now in a position to appreciate in full some of the more extraordinary aspects of New England authorship after 1660. The immediate and (even for its author) surprising popularity of *The Day of Doom* can be attributed in part to a situation where at its appearance in 1662 New England readers were quite simply starved for anything like an imaginative rendering of doctrine: small wonder that eighteen hundred copies of a ballad version of the day of judgment could be sold over three years and that still another edition was called for later in the 1660's.[6] (*The Pilgrim's Progress* would also do well in its Amer-ican career, and it seems odd that some enterprising Boston printer did not bring out Bernard's *The Isle of Man* before James Franklin published an American edition in 1716.)[7] The same desperate yearn-

5. Cotton Mather, *Magnalia Christi Americana*, I, 454; Winship, *The Cambridge Press*, 179–180. After eliminating known and probable ghosts, Richard Mather is still left with more titles in English bearing a pre-1700 New England imprint than any other minister of the founding generation.

6. The early editions of *The Day of Doom* present a bibliographical tangle. Cf., Matt B. Jones, "Notes for a Bibliography of Michael Wigglesworth's 'Day of Doom' and 'Meat Out of the Eater,'" American Antiquarian Society, *Proceedings*, N.S., XXXIX (1929), 77–80; O. M. Brack, Jr., "Michael Wigglesworth and the Attribution of 'I Walk'd and did a Little Molehill View,' " *Seventeenth-Century News*, XXVII (1970), 41–44; and Wigglesworth's own account, reprinted in full in John Langdon Sibley, *Biographical Sketches of Graduates of Harvard University . . .* , I (Cambridge, Mass., 1873), 271–272. My own hypothesis is that the figure of 1800 copies sold used by Wig-glesworth refers to *both* the first edition and a now lost 1663–1664 edition suggested by Brack, and that the latter was probably a reissue of the former with some sheets dropped and others added. (The "yeer's end" by which the 1800 copies were sold would then become 25 March 1664, and the date of the next American edition would be pushed back to 1668.)

7. The popularity of *The Day of Doom* has to be seen in context: Samuel Smith's *The Great Assize*, four sermons on the day of judgment, reached thirty-nine editions between 1615 and 1697; Bernard's *The Isle of Man*, an exposition of the nature of sin

ing for printed materials, only partly slaked even in the last decade of
the century, suggests one reason, a particularly prosaic one, for the
influence enjoyed by Increase and Cotton Mather in the religious life
of their time: they wrote a gigantic proportion of the devotional
works that the American wing of the Puritan movement had previously lacked so dramatically. In the 1690's, at high tide, the two
men together accounted for thirty percent of total titles *of all sorts*
printed in New England and of a much higher share of purely religious material. The sheer number, as much as the content of their
works, went a long way towards restoring the function of the printed
word as a main instrument of excitement and suspense.[8]

We do not today, to be sure, generally consider reading a Puritan
work exciting. The element of discovery in their literature is easy to
overlook because of a failure to distinguish among the leading titles
and especially between the two broad categories of English devotional works. The more immediately familiar comprised the very
long-lived and regularly reprinted compendia, such as the *Practice of
Piety*, the various exercises in the *ars moriendi* literature, and comprehensive descriptions of the morphology of conversion. They all served
as *vade mecums* spiritually and literally—their squat shape made them
perfect pocket books, and their low survival rate, for all the reprinting, suggests that they were routinely worn out being used in just this

---

in the form of an arraignment and trial of various allegorical vices, first published in
1626, ran to nineteen editions by 1683; and the Puritan classic *The Plain Man's Pathway
to Heaven* by Arthur Dent, a comprehensive doctrinal and practical guide in the form
of a dramatic dialogue, was at the very least in its twenty-ninth edition when Wigglesworth returned to New England in 1664. *The Day of Doom* was distinguished by
only two things: its ballad form and its near monopoly position in the imaginative life
of seventeenth-century New Englanders. (As a matter of fact, there are even English
precedents for the use of a ballad to inculcate Protestant dogma: cf. Spufford, *Small
Books and Pleasant Histories*, 10–11; John W. King, *English Reformation Literature: The
Tudor Origins of the Protestant Tradition* [Princeton, 1982], 209–231, 470–472.) In England, in competition with the titles just described and *The Pilgrim's Progress*, the work
enjoyed only the modest success of three editions in twenty-one years.

8. The 30% figure is taken from Morison, *The Puritan Pronaos*, 124. The count was
made without the benefit of the new material added to the total New England bibliography by the Bristol *Supplement* to Evans's *American Bibliography*, but the percentage
would not, in fact, change very much. See, in general, David Levin, *Cotton Mather:
The Young Life of the Lord's Remembrancer, 1663–1703* (Cambridge, Mass., 1978).

way. Popular as they were, they were reference books with all the dramatic structure of a cookbook or an abridged dictionary, and there are relatively few New England instances of this genre, reprint or native, until well after 1700. Given the nature of the colonial audience, the other main type of devotional work was really most needed, and at this form the Mathers, amongst others, excelled. They especially, in their absorption with an American style of practical divinity, turned to the printed word as a source of variety and novelty of experience.

Veteran sermon goers, after all, if they sometimes owned the standard manuals, probably found them old hat. Their excitement came from the rapid succession of new titles appearing regularly to weave some well-known lesson, devotional or casuistical, into a previously unsuspected pattern. Something like practiced theatregoers witnessing their tenth performance of *Othello*, they would lack the naive enthusiasm of a virgin audience but could still be surprised and moved by a fresh and powerful interpretation, provided it did not commit a palpable outrage on the received text. The curious publication history in England of most of the titles by prolific and avowedly popular preachers is almost certainly attributable to the habits of this seasoned readership. In a large number of instances the works of ministers of great repute went through one edition only or achieved a respectable number of editions in a short period and then, unlike the manuals, sank from sight. Many of these titles probably fell from favor because they were overtaken by the next entry from the same pen, but read at first blush a sermon such as *The Saint's Daily Exercise* of John Preston (nine editions between 1629 and 1634), or the Richard Sibbes collection published as *The Bruised Reed* (five editions, 1630–1637), or Jeremy Dyke's *The Mischiefe and Miserie of Scandall* (eight editions between 1630 and 1635), all gave a knowing, godly readership a source of stimulation that really does challenge comparison with the experience of a similarly initiated theater audience.[9]

9. Cf., a study of all English titles published in 1623 (the year of Shakespeare's first folio), which notes that of the fifty-seven sermons to appear that year, few were either reissued or reprinted. Their first press run, that is, was exhausted, but there was no market, except in twelve instances, for a second edition. Judith Simmons, "Publications of 1623," *The Library*, 5th Ser., XXI (1966), 211–212.

The bibliography of the Mathers follows the same pattern exactly, except that their titles rarely got beyond even a second edition because one or two thousand copies went a lot further in New England than in the much larger reading population of England.

The Mathers were never alone in their work. At fifty-two titles, Samuel Willard ran Increase Mather, at least, a pretty good race, and there were large numbers of other clerical entrants in the competition after 1670 with more modest contributions. Taking all their volume of print together, their revival of practical divinity in America parallels closely the history of fasting in replicating an English situation, by calling upon the long experience the English Puritans had gained in making popular Protestantism popular. There was, however, here too an adaptation to a specifically New England circumstance in the relative neglect of standard devotional materials for titles geared to a spiritually sophisticated audience. Bayly's *Practice of Piety* appeared in seventeenth-century New England only as an abridgment by John Eliot in the language of the Indians. English speaking believers had graduated to more advanced material a generation or two earlier.[1]

---

1. This is *not* to say that there were not *some* ultra-practical works of the manual variety available in New England, both by English and native authors (including the Mathers). See Hambrick-Stowe, *The Practice of Piety*, 272–277. I do think, however, Hambrick-Stowe concentrates a little too exclusively on this genre, given its minority position in the total number of religious titles printed in seventeenth-century New England, and is a little generous in his awarding of the description "manual" to works like *The Pilgrim's Progress*. Whatever its didactic quality, the experience of reading Bunyan's allegory was not the same as in consulting John Corbet's *Self-Imployment in Secret*. The denomination of Bayly's work as of "central importance" to Puritan piety (Hambrick-Stowe, *The Practice of Piety*, 269) is particularly unfortunate if one is talking about New England Puritans. The work had only one American edition in English (in 1718), and, as Eliot's choice of it for his Indian converts suggests, it was clearly regarded as a piece of spiritual juvenalia. Thus, in the only mentions of the book that I can find among New England spiritual autobiographies, Richard Eccles credits it (amongst other titles) with helping to open his eyes when he "was brought up in popery a good many years," and John Brock, unlike Eccles raised in a Puritan household, treats it as a godly child's first book of divine knowledge, which he read "through admonitions of [my] Parents" well before he was out of grammar school. See Selement and Woolley, eds., *Thomas Shepard's Confessions*, 175; Clifford K. Shipton, ed., "The Autobiographical Memoranda of John Brock, 1636–1659," American Antiquarian Society, *Proceedings*, N.S., LIII (1943), 97. Cf., the very similar role assigned to the book by Bayly's most famous English reader: John Bunyan, *Grace Abounding to the Chief of Sinners*, ed. Roger Sharrock (Oxford, 1962), 8.

Worship and doctrine by themselves never completed the more full-blown Puritan schemes, and would have been judged insufficient in the various formulations of the New England Way without the longstanding commitment to "discipline." Robert Cawdrey, a militant of the Elizabethan period, put the matter concisely (as was appropriate for a man then at work on the first English dictionary) when he wrote that "in the church where Discipline wanteth, although there be never sound & good preaching with catechising, against sin and wickednes, yet the edge therof is dulled, that is fruitlesse and of little force."[2] Cawdrey's words are worth dwelling on briefly for what they reveal about the original Puritan promise and the peculiar nature of its New England realization. By "discipline" he did *not* mean a pattern of behavior imposed by the drill sergeant at the officers' behest. Rather, discipline was the "edge" of doctrine, its "application" (as in the "application" or "use" section of a sermon) in a way that made unadorned doctrine operative knowledge. The Elizabethans had based much of their argument for reassigning church censures to the individual congregational consistory, with partial or full participation by the whole congregation, on the value of the exercise for those who joined in the censure: discipline, that is, was more a means of teaching the participants than of punishing sinners and deterring sin.[3] No English enthusiast for "the Discipline" really thought that a reformed polity would eradicate sin, any more than a totally godly magistracy would have been capable of so gargantuan a task. The more important job of the law, civil and ecclesiastical, was to complete the work of religious education by collective and symbolic affirmation.

The English Presbyterians never attained their hopes, and the American Congregationalists rapidly backed away from what they did achieve in their churches. The office of ruling elder (the discipline specialist) quickly atrophied, church censures in New England were on the whole administered sparingly, even hesitantly, and, it has been

---

2. *A Treasurie or Store-House of Similies* . . . , 2d ed. (London, 1609), 220–221.

3. John Field and Thomas Wilcox, *An Admonition to the Parliament*, in W. H. Frere and C. E. Douglas, eds., *Puritan Manifestoes: A Study of the Origin of the Puritan Revolt*, 2d ed. (London, 1954), 16. Cf., The Cambridge Platform in Williston Walker, *The Creeds and Platforms of Congregationalism* (New York, 1893), 211.

suggested, as society became more complex the county courts in developed localities took over the functions of resolving conflicts where once the churches had enjoyed original jurisdiction.[4] But in a Puritan culture, whose whole genius lay in making the adjective in that phrase inseparable from the noun, it would be a mistake of serious proportions to equate *civil* with *secular*. The county courts contained an institution at once very English and very Puritan: the grand jury.[5] Twice a year in some New England counties, once a year in the others, grand juries were impaneled for the purpose, in effect, of applying doctrine by presenting and indicting those who had notoriously crossed it: sabbath breakers, blasphemers, disturbers of the public peace, prenuptial fornicators and other moral offenders, scoffers at the ministry. Whether the county courts ever really suppressed vice and irreligion is hardly relevant. The Puritan commitment was most effectively spread in the law courts by the voluntary cooperation of a substantial and significant section of the population in enforcing the rules of the game, thereby coming to understand them with an operative faith rather than a mere intellectual assent.

In a sense, the New England courts inherited this role from their

4. David D. Hall, *The Faithful Shepherd: A History of the New England Ministry in the Seventeenth Century* (Chapel Hill, N. C., 1972), 95; Emil Oberholzer, Jr., *Delinquent Saints: Disciplinary Action in the Early Congregational Churches of Massachusetts* (New York, 1956), esp. Tables I–IX, 253–260; David Thomas Konig, *Law and Society in Puritan Massachusetts, Essex County, 1629–1692* (Chapel Hill, N. C., 1979), 90–107; David Grayson Allen, *In English Ways: The Movement of Societies and the Transferal of English Local Law and Custom to Massachusetts Bay in the Seventeenth Century* (Chapel Hill, N.C., 1981), 226–227. William E. Nelson in *Dispute and Conflict Resolution in Plymouth County, Massachusetts, 1725–1825* (Chapel Hill, N.C., 1981), 26–44, argues that in this jurisdiction the church remained the more important judicial agency prior to 1774. The *colony* of New Plymouth does seem to have been a standing exception to the generalizations made here about grand juries in the late 17th century (see below, nn 6, p. 234; 7, p. 235, and it is possible that the difference carried over into the eighteenth century in Plymouth County. But see also J. M. Bumsted, "The Pilgrims Progress: The Ecclesiastical History of the Old Colony, 1670–1775" (Ph.D. thesis, Brown University, 1965), 72–74, 86–94, who suggests that in discipline, as in church government generally, Plymouth tended towards anachronism, importing its institutions from the Bay just as they were going out of fashion there, so that the 18th-century practices were new, not survivals of an earlier era.

5. For the English grand jury in this period, see J. S. Morrill, *The Cheshire Grand Jury, 1625–1659: A Social and Administrative Study*, Leicester University Department of English Local History, *Occasional Papers*, 3d Ser., I (Leicester, 1976).

English originals, but in the different social and cultural circumstances of America the experience of grand jury service was necessarily also of a somewhat different order. The men on a New England grand jury were not simply so many local notables called on to assist his majesty's justices in the county of H. The English grand jurors may have had more autonomy of action in actual fact, but when it came to self-conception the New England bodies were called on to look upon themselves as doing far more than to "diligently enquire, and a true presentment make of all such matters and things as shall be given you in charge." Instead, the New Englanders were (in the words of the Bay colony oath) to "swear by the Living God, that you will diligently inquire & faithfully present to this court, whatsoever you know to be a breach of any law established in this Jurisdiction according the minde of God."[6] The element of joining in a common cause, rather than taking on an assignment, is much more obvious in the American oath, just as the portion of society recruited into running the experiment (and thereby indoctrinated in its terms) was very much larger than in England.

The reason, once more, was English practice in a New England setting. The New England grand jury was English in size (sixteen or seventeen men, for example, served on the Suffolk County panels in the 1670's, fourteen or fifteen on those of Essex County in the same period) and, up to a point, followed the English habit of making frequent use of repeaters. A man who served once was likely to serve several times, and in any given decade a good half or more of the jurors on a panel would have had previous experience at their work. Even so, the reach of the institution was much broader in America because of the smaller population of the individual counties: in an adult male population numbering only in the thousands, hundreds at any time would have had recent and sustained experience presenting

6. Cf. the English oath in ibid., 21–22, with the Bay Colony oath, *The Book of the General Lawes and Libertyes Concerning the Inhabitants of the Massachusetts . . .* (Cambridge, Mass., 1648), 58. The Connecticut oath is very similar to that of the Bay, but New Plymouth's is a pale copy of the English original. J. Hammond Trumbull, ed., *The Public Records of the Colony of Connecticut . . .* , I (Hartford, Conn., 1850), 546; Nathaniel B. Shurtleff, ed., *Records of the Colony of New Plymouth in New England*, XI (Boston, 1861), 85, 169.

offenders against the Puritan virtues. Whether the ratio was one man in five or one in fifteen, the segment of the population involved was substantial in itself and also significant beyond its considerable numbers. In social standing New England grand jurors mostly ranked among what might be termed the upper middle ordinary, the kind of person likely to end up as tithingman, town constable, selectman, and, in the country towns, perhaps as deputy now and again to the colony's general court. It would be absurd to label these town somebodies after their English counterparts as an "elite," the "county governors," or "minor gentry"; not all of them would have ranked as so much as "substantial yeomen." The New England grand jurors were simply the individuals of modest local influence who might have been expected to have become bastions of particularist sentiment. Instead, they were incorporated almost whole into field grade positions in the Christian warfare.[7]

Cotton Mather in a popular tract of 1705 had asked rhetorically, "will not a Form of Godliness, often by the Grace of God prove a vehicle for the Power of Godliness?" By "form" he meant a combination of household religious duties carried on so regularly that they became "as it were Entailed upon Posterity."[8] The resulting power, as Mather

7. For the English pattern of repetition and the status of the jurors, see Morrill, *The Cheshire Grand Jury*, 9–20. The generalizations presented here are derived from an analysis of the Suffolk and Essex County grand juries for the 1670s, taken from Samuel Eliot Morison, ed., *Records of the Suffolk County Court, 1671–1680* (Colonial Society of Massachusetts, *Publications*, XXIX–XXX [Boston, 1933]); George F. Dow and Mary G. Thresher, eds., *Records and Files of the Quarterly Courts of Essex County, Massachusetts*, IV–IX (Salem and Worcester, 1914–1975). The observation applies, however, with equal if not greater force to the Connecticut county courts after their creation in 1666 and to other small jurisdictions, such as York and Norfolk counties, because the number of jury positions, grand and petit, was so large, and the size of the eligible population so limited, that even with frequent repetition and (in the case of Connecticut and York County) annual terms, a sizable chunk of the adult male inhabitants had to be recruited as jurors just to keep the courts in operation. (The split jurisdictions in Essex and Norfolk counties had a similar effect.) Plymouth, as ever, did things differently, failing to establish county government until 1685, the year before the colony was absorbed into the Dominion of New England. See George D. Langdon, Jr., *Pilgrim Colony: A History of New Plymouth, 1620–1691* (New Haven, Conn., 1966), 204–206.

8. *Family-Religion Excited and Assisted*, 4th impression (Boston, 1720), 9. For the bibliography of this piece, see Thomas James Holmes, *Cotton Mather, A Bibliography of His Works* (Cambridge, Mass., 1940), I, 368–375.

undoubtedly knew, may have come by the grace of God, but it came through the ability of a pervasive routine to clothe the mundane in scripture. Seduced or coerced, the believer sooner or later would enter imaginatively into the truths of the Gospel because he met them at every turn and because he did not have an alternative way of making sense of his world that was anywhere near so coherent.

Here at last is the culture trap again, this time domesticated. No end in itself, household religion was simply another of the many threads in the loosely textured fabric of means by which the Puritan ministry had always hoped to blanket its converts. The household was supposed to be the "lowest place in the church," in the words of the Elizabethan radical Josias Nichols—he did not term it a refuge and a hiding place, though it could end up as such under unpropitious circumstances.[9] This comprehensive Puritan ideal was unrealized in England before 1640, unattainable there in the upheaval of the Interregnum, and unthinkable after 1660, when the levers of power in church and state clearly belonged, then and for the future, to somebody else. The achievement of the English ideal devolved exclusively on the second and third generations of New Englanders, lay and clerical, who found the obligation burdensome enough but hardly insupportable. Their common creation in America was never watertight and always underfinanced, and it was far more asymmetrical than any neat English plan would have allowed of, but it did credit of a sort to the *modus vivendi* eventually worked out between an aroused laity and a resurgent clergy.

For all the tensions that necessarily characterized Puritanism, at the last, in New England, *popular* and *clerical* turn out to be false antinomies. If the history of the Interregnum suggests an apparently irrepressible opposition between layman and minister, individual believer and prescriptive church, the experience of New England after 1660 establishes exactly the contrary judgment. This most lasting settlement in the history of a volatile movement was the one in which

9. *An Order of Household Instruction . . .* , Sig. A8v. Cf. Dudley Fenner, *The Artes of Logicke and Rhetorike* ([Middleburgh], 1584), Sig. A4r. (2nd set of signatures). For Nichols, see Peter Clarke, "Josias Nichols and Religious Radicalism, 1553–1639," *Journal of Ecclesiastical History*, XXVIII (1977), 133–150.

personal piety was nourished through a collective public commitment presided over by a standing clerical order. The laity did not in
any meaningful sense lose ground in New England in the later seventeenth century, even though the clergy rather clearly gained some,
and the spates of anticlericalism that erupted after 1660 meant little
more than that the relationship between the component elements of
the Puritan movement was as dynamic and as passionate as ever. To
vary a favorite Puritan metaphor, the noise of the quarreling was no
sure guide to the solidity of the marriage. It was quieter, more sullen
griefs that would one day, well into the eighteenth century, lead to
disillusion and then dissolution.

In the course of the transformation of popular Protestantism into a
genuinely Puritan establishment the clergy gained power neither
over bodies nor even over minds, but only and especially over words.
What we sometimes see as the decline in the stature and immediate
influence of the ministry after the passing of the first colonial generation was really the metamorphosis of the clergy into a clerisy: they
gave the ceremonial addresses on public days, wrote the tracts the
presses turned off, came to be identified as the source of all schooling
above the most rudimentary. Whatever the emotional temperature
of this emerging relationship between "a minister and his people,"
the clergy's involvement with the mental energies of the laity was as
intense as ever after 1660 and, it could be argued, growing.[1] Perhaps
there was more corporatism and less individual charisma in the progressive stranglehold on the most basic categories of thought and
imagination, but it would be a serious mistake to underrate its enduring influence. By a clever enlargement of their field of action the
clergy of the later seventeenth century managed to enhance their
influence without having to challenge the recently certified prerogatives of the godly. Then they covered up their achievement (in order
to fool themselves and posterity as much as the laity) by finding in
the sources of mastery the essence of corruption. The commerce that
carried their message was the font of worldliness, the fasts that rammed
the point home with all the power of mass ceremony were losing

1. For the second and third generations of the New England clergy, see Hall, *The
Faithful Shepherd*, 176–278.

battles against the invisible (and therefore irrefutable) inner decay, the court sessions that turned town Dogberrys into grave elders were so many witnesses to the sins of the land. It would all be very amusing if only we did not believe it still.

Alas, the measure of just how well the clergy did their work is provided by their unwilling heirs, the scholarly community. Contemplating their New England, we cannot quite seem to rid ourselves of the labels they chose for describing it. Even when we drop their sermons and diaries from the story entirely to study births, deaths, town meetings, and lawsuits in the vain hope of exorcising their presence, the narrative always seems to have a suspiciously clerical moral at its end. The position of the argument of this essay in the historical literature is itself an ironic testimony to just how durable the ministerial vision was and is. Surely, in any other historiographic context the claim that material progress strengthened the ability of a society to transmit and reiterate its official messages would not be an exercise in revisionism. The idea is so obvious, so very whiggish, that it must seem remarkable that it did not come first in the literature, to be challenged in turn by later and more subtle interpretations. Yet, curiously, the telling of New England history always seems to begin at the second stage, and one cannot forbear the suspicion that *all* the ranking interpretations of this century in one way or another betray the stamp of Puritan New England's very first authorized interpreters. To write of "declension," or "individualism," or "modernization," when we mean simply growth and adaptation, to assume without hesitation that the process of commercial expansion must be secularization and that institutionalization is antithetical to the spirit of religious life, is really to provide a new gloss on a very old text. It is to say once again, as we have been all too well taught to say, "For what is a man profited, if he shall gain the whole world, and lose his own soul?"

◄ DAVID D. HALL ►

# A World of Wonders:
## The Mentality of the Supernatural in
## Seventeenth-Century New England

THE people of seventeenth-century New England lived in an enchanted universe. Theirs was a world of wonders. Ghosts came to people in the night, and trumpets blared, though no one saw from where the sound emerged. Nor could people see the lines of force that made a "long staff dance up and down in the chimney" of William Morse's house. In this enchanted world, the sky on a "clear day" could fill with "many companies of armed men in the air, clothed in light-colored garments, and the commander in sad [somber]." Many of the townsfolk of New Haven had seen a phantom ship sail regally into the harbor. An old man in Lynn had espied

a strange black cloud in which after some space he saw a man in arms complete standing with his legs straddling and having a pike in his hands which he held across his breast . . . ; after a while the man vanished in whose room appeared a spacious ship seeming under sail though she kept the same station.

Voices spoke from heaven, and little children uttered warnings. Bend-

David D. Hall is Professor of History at Boston University.

The research that led to this essay was supported by the John Simon Guggenheim Memorial Foundation, the American Council of Learned Societies, the National Endowment for the Humanities (via the American Antiquarian Society), and Boston University. I am very grateful to these agencies for their support. I want also to thank Richard L. Bushman, Barbara Diefendorf, James Henretta, Keith Thomas, D. P. Walker, and Sam Bass Warner, Jr., for their comments on a previous version of the essay.

ing over his son Joseph's cradle one evening, an astonished Samuel Sewall heard him say, "The French are coming."[1]

All of these events were "wonders" to the colonists, events betokening the presence of superhuman or supernatural forces. In seventeenth-century New England it was common to speak of the providence of God as "wonder-working."[2] Some wonders were like miracles in being demonstrations of God's power to suspend or interrupt the laws of nature. Others were natural events that God employed as portents or signals of impending change. The events that Cotton Mather described in *Wonders of the Invisible World* were the handiwork of Satan and his minions. A wonder could also be something unexpected or extraordinary, like a sudden death or freak coincidence.[3]

In the course of the seventeenth century, many of the colonists would experience a wonder and many others tell stories of them. Either way, these events aroused strong feelings. An earthquake in New England in 1638 had caused

divers men (that had never known an Earthquake before) being at work in the fields, to cast down their working tools, and run with ghastly terrified looks, to the next company they could meet withall.[4]

Almost a century later, as an earthquake rocked Boston, the "young people" in Samuel Sewall's house "were quickly frighted out of the

1. See footnote 6, p. 267, below; George Lincoln Burr, ed., *Narratives of the Witchcraft Cases* (New York, 1914), 175; Increase Mather, *Remarkable Providences, illustrative of the earlier days of American colonisation* (London, 1856), 101, cited hereafter as *Essay*; "The Diaries of John Hull," American Antiquarian Society, *Transactions and Collections*, III (1897), 218; Cotton Mather, *Magnalia Christi Americana*, 2 vols. (Hartford, Conn., 1853–1854), I, 84; "The Diary of Noahdiah Russell," *New England Historical and Genealogical Register*, VII (1853), 53–54; Nathaniel Morton, *New-Englands Memoriall* (Cambridge, Mass., 1670), 52; *The Diary of Samuel Sewall*, M. Halsey Thomas, ed., 2 vols., (New York, 1973), I, 281.

2. Edward Johnson, *The Wonder-Working Providence of Sions Saviour*, ed. J. Franklin Jameson, Original Narratives of Early American History (New York, 1910); John Sherman, "To the Reader," in Cotton Mather, *Wonders of the Invisible World* (Boston, 1692).

3. Kitty Scoular, *Natural Magic: Studies in the Presentation of Nature in English Poetry from Spenser to Marvell* (Oxford, 1965), 5; Increase Mather, *The Latter Sign Discoursed of*, bound with *Kometographia* (Boston, 1682), second pagination, 7–11; Michael McKeon, *Politics and Poetry in Restoration England: The Case of Dryden's Annus Mirabilis* (Cambridge, Mass., 1975), 155–161.

4. Johnson, *Wonder-Working Providence*, ed. Jameson, 185.

shaking clattering kitchen, and fled with weeping cries into" their father's bedroom, "where they made a fire, and abode there till morning." In responding to such "marvellous" events, people used words like "awful," "terrible" and "amazing" to describe what had happened.[5] Every wonder made visible and real the immense forces that impinged upon the order of the world. A wonder reaffirmed the insecurity of existence and the majesty of a supreme God.

This essay is about the wonder as the colonists would know and tell of it. At the outset, we may dispose of one false issue: the people in New England who heard voices and saw apparitions were not deluded fanatics or "primitive" in their mentality. The possibility of these experiences was widely affirmed as credible in the best science and religion of the early seventeenth century. We can never answer with complete satisfaction the question as to why some persons do see ghosts or witness apparitions. But for the people of seventeenth-century Europe and America, these were ordinary events that many persons encountered, and many more believed in.

This is an essay, therefore, about phenomena that occurred on both sides of the Atlantic, and among both Protestants and Catholics. We may speak of a lore of wonders, an accumulation of stock references and literary conventions that descended to the colonists from Scripture, antiquity, the early Church and the Middle Ages. People in the seventeenth century inherited a lore that stretched back to the Greeks and Romans. Chaucer had told of portents and prodigies in *The Canterbury Tales*, as had the author of *The Golden Legend*, a medieval collection of saints' lives. Whenever the colonists spoke or wrote of wonders, they drew freely on this lore; theirs was a borrowed language.

To speak of continuity is to raise two other questions: how did this lore pass to the colonists, and how did it consort with their doctrinal understanding of the universe? The key intermediaries in transmitting an old language to the colonists were the English printer-

---

5. *Letter-Book of Samuel Sewall*, 2 vols., Massachusetts Historical Society, *Collections*, 6th Ser., I–II (1886–1888), II, 229; *Diary of Samuel Sewall*, Thomas, ed., I, 369; II, 796.

booksellers who published great quantities of wonder tales in the sixteenth and seventeenth centuries. They had allies in certain writers who put together collections of this lore to suit new purposes, like the emergence of Protestantism. Protestants drew freely on the lore of wonders, adapting it to indicate the merits of their cause. To this end Luther had retold the story of a "monster" fish found in the River Tiber, interpreting it as a portent of Rome's mistakes. And the wonder could serve to reinforce the concept of God's providence, a doctrine of importance to the early Reformers.

But what of all the "superstitions" that this lore reiterated? The language of the wonder was rich in motifs and assumptions that seem at odds with the mentality of the Puritans who colonized New England. In breaking with the past, and especially with Catholicism, the Puritan movement had turned against the "magic" of the sacraments and holy relics, of sacred places and saints' days. The religion of the colonists seems, in retrospect, to have forecast and initiated a "disenchantment" of the world.[6] The Puritan God was a God of order and reason, interpreted by learned men in the form of systematic theology. In such statements, Puritanism assumed the shape of a coherent world view, intellectually neat and tidy and swept clean of superstition.

Such, at least, is how we characteristically understand the religion of the colonists. But the lore of wonders as repeated and developed by the colonists cannot be reconciled with so static or so modernist an understanding. We may come instead to recognize that contradiction, or a kind of intellectual pluralism, was truer of the colonists than a uniform and systematic mode of thought. So too, we may come to recognize that these people were not hostile to a folklore that had roots in paganism. Indeed, the wonder tale would introduce them to a popular culture that drew on many sources and traditions.

6. Keith Thomas, *Religion and the Decline of Magic* (London, 1971). This complex, subtle book depicts seventeenth-century Protestants, and especially the more radical of the Puritans, as hostile to "magic"; and argues that the rural poor preferred the older beliefs that Puritans were opposing. But Thomas also provides much evidence of beliefs, e.g., astrology, that were not limited to the rural poor, and he is quite aware that Protestantism remained in touch with prophecy, exorcism, and even certain folk beliefs. My argument inevitably runs counter to the main emphasis of his book, but much of what I have to say is also present in his pages, and I am deeply indebted to the references he provides to sixteenth- and seventeenth-century sources.

In reiterating these tales, the colonists would affirm their own participation in this wider, older culture.

The lore of wonders was popular culture in the sense of being accessible to everyone; it was a language that all groups in society shared, known not only to the "learned" but to ordinary folk as well. It was popular in being so pervasive, and in being tolerant of contradictions. A full history of this culture and its absorption into Protestantism would lead in several directions, including that of witchcraft. My purpose is more limited, to begin upon a history of this lore as it was received by the colonists, and to trace how it provided them with a mentality of the supernatural.

Portents and prodigies were routine events in English printed broadsides of the seventeenth century. "Strange news from Brotherton," announced a broadside ballad of 1648 that told of wheat that rained down from the sky. "A wonder of wonders" of 1663 concerned a drummer boy who moved invisibly about the town of Tidworth. In "Strange and true news from Westmoreland," a murder story ends with the devil pointing out the guilty person. Hundreds of such broadside ballads, stories told in verse and printed on a single sheet of paper, circulated in the England of Cromwell and the Stuarts. Newsheets, which began appearing with some regularity in the 1640's, carried tales of other marvels. Pamphlets of no more than eight or sixteen pages contained reports of children speaking preternaturally and offered *Strange and wonderful News . . . of certain dreadfull Apparitions*. The yearly almanacs weighed in with their accounts of mystic forces emanating from the stars and planets.[7]

The same prodigies and portents would recur again and again in broadside ballads, newsheets, chapbooks, and almanacs. Tales of witchcraft and the devil, of comets, hailstorms, monster births and apparitions—these were some of the most commonplace. "Murder will

7. Hyder Rollins, ed., *The Pack of Autolycus or Strange and Terrible News of Ghosts, Apparitions . . . as told in Broadside Ballads of the Years 1624–1693* (Cambridge, Mass., 1927), 36, 114, 162, and *passim*; Joseph Frank, *The Beginnings of the English Newspaper 1620–1660* (Cambridge, Mass., 1961), 17; Bernard Capp, *English Almanacs 1500–1800* (Ithaca, N.Y., 1979), chap. 6; *Strange and wonderful News from Chippingnorton . . . Of certain dreadful Apparitions* [London, 1679].

out," as supernatural forces intervened to indicate the guilty. The earth could open up and swallow persons who tell lies. "Many are the wonders which have lately happened," declared the anonymous author of *A miracle, of miracles,*

as of sodaine and strange death upon perjured persons, strange sights in the Ayre, strange births on the Earth, Earthquakes, Commets, and fierie Impressions, with the execution of God himselfe from his holy fire in heaven, on the wretched man and his wife, at Holnhurst. . . .

A single ballad spoke of blazing stars, monstrous births, a rainstorm of blood, lightning, rainbows, and the sound of great guns. Others told of dreams and prophecies that bore upon the future of kings and countries. Almanacs and other astrological compendia reported similar events: comets, eclipses, joined foetuses, infants speaking.[8]

All of these were cheap forms of print. Hawked by peddlars and hung up in stalls for everyone to see and gape at, they reached the barely literate and the lower orders as well as readers of more means and schooling. The stories they contained would also turn up in a very different kind of book that ran to several hundred pages. Big books—perhaps in the grand format of the folio—were too expensive to circulate in quantity and had authors who announced themselves as of the "learned." But these differences in form and audience did not extend into the contents. The lore of portents and prodigies appeared in books like Thomas Beard's *The Theatre of Gods Judgements* as well as in the cheapest pamphlet.

Thomas Beard was a learned man, a graduate of Cambridge who practiced schoolteaching and received ordination as a minister. Born in the early years of Elizabeth's reign, he published *The Theatre of Gods Judgements* in 1597. Three more editions followed, the last of these in 1648. That same year, Samuel Clarke, like Beard a graduate of Cambridge and a minister, brought out a rival collection: *A Mirrour or Looking-Glasse both for Saints and Sinners, Held forth in about two thousand Examples: Wherein is presented, as Gods Wonderful Mercies to the one, so his severe Judgments against the other.* Clarke's *Examples* (to

---

8. Rollins, ed., *Pack of Autolycus*, 37, 62, 139, 82, 23; *A miracle, of miracles* [London, n.d.], 5; John Gadbury, *Natura Prodigiorum or, A discourse touching the nature of Prodigies* (London, 1660).

call it by the title the colonists would use) went through five editions, the final one appearing in 1671. Clarke was a non-conformist after 1662, ejected from the Church of England because he would not recant his presbyterianism. The sequel to his book was William Turner's folio *Compleat History of the Most Remarkable Providences, Both of Judgement and Mercy, which have hapned in this Present Age* (1697). To this series should be added another Elizabethan work, Stephen Batman's *The Doome warning all men to Judgmente: Wherein are contayned for the most parte all the straunge Prodigies hapned in the Worlde* (1581). Ministers all, Batman, Beard, Clarke, and Turner had a secular competitor in the hack writer Nathaniel Crouch. His *Wonderful Prodigies of Judgment and Mercy, discovered in above Three Hundred Memorable Histories* (1682) was one of a string of works on prodigies and strange wonders that Crouch would publish in the 1680's under his pen name of Robert Burton.

As in the ballads and chapbooks, so in these books nature offered up innumerable signs of supernatural intervention:

Now according to the variety and diversity of mens offences, the Lord in his most just and admirable judgment, useth diversity of punishments: . . . sometimes correcting them by storms and tempests, both by sea and land; other times by lightning, haile, and deluge of waters . . . and not seldome by remedilesse and sudden fires, heaven and earth, and all the elements being armed with an invincible force, to take vengeance upon such as traytors and rebels against God.

Earthquakes, multiple suns, strange lights in the sky, rainbows, sudden deaths, monstrous births—these were other frequent signs or signals.[9]

Like the ballad writers, Beard and Batman reported esoteric, even violent, events: rats that ate a man, a crow whose dung struck someone dead, the agonies of martyrs. In one or another of these books, we hear of dreams and prophecies, of crimes detected by some form of sympathetic magic, of thieves who rot away, and of armed men in

---

9. *The Theatre of Gods Judgements* (London, 1648), 409; Stephen Batman, *The Doome warning all men to the Iudgemente* (London, 1581), 317, 379, 390, 397.

the sky.[1] Much too was made of Satan. He offered compacts to young men in need of money, while sometimes serving as God's agent for inflicting vengeance. Many tales revolved around the curse, "the devil take you," and its surprising consequences:

Not long since a Cavalier in Salisbury in the middest of his health-drinking and carrousing in a Tavern, drank a health to the Devil, saying, That if the devil would not come, and pledge him, he would not believe that there was either God or devil: whereupon his companions strucken with horror, hastened out of the room, and presently after hearing a hideous noise, and smelling a stinking savour, the Vintner ran up into the Chamber: and coming in, he missed his guest, and found the window broken, the Iron barre in it bowed, and all bloody, but the man was never heard of afterwards.

The devil might appear in several guises. Black bears, a favorite of the ballad writers, turned up again in stories told by Beard and Batman, as did black dogs.[2]

In telling of these wonders, the men who organized the great collections borrowed from the broadside and the chapbook; a ballad tale of a woman who sank into the ground was reported in Clarke's *Examples*, in Crouch's *Wonderful Prodigies*, and again in Turner's *Compleat History*.[3] This flow of stories meant that "learned" men accorded credibility to wonders as readily as any ballad writer. In this regard, the great folios were no more critical or selective than the cheapest forms of print. The one format was the work of learned men, the other of printers and their literary hacks. But the two shared a popular culture of portents and prodigies, a common lore that linked small books and great, the reader of the ballad and the reader of the folio.

This was a lore that other Europeans were collecting and reporting

1. Beard, *Theatre of Gods Judgements*, 37, 48, 195; Batman, *Doome warning all men to the Iudgemente*, 403; [Nathaniel Crouch], *Admirable Curiosities, Rarities, & Wonders in England* (London, 1682), *passim*; Rollins, ed., *Pack of Autolycus*, 219. Here as elsewhere in this essay, the references could run into the hundreds in imitation of the dense texture of the great collections.

2. Samuel Clarke, *A Mirrour or Looking-Glasse both For Saints, and Sinners*, 2nd. ed., (London, 1654), 92–93; Beard, *Theatre of Gods Judgements*, Bk I, chapter 30; Rollins, ed., *Pack of Autolycus*, 75.

3. Rollins, ed., *Pack of Autolycus*, 62.

in the sixteenth and seventeenth centuries. Sixteenth-century German broadsides told of comets, multiple suns, monster births and armies in the air. A Lutheran who wrote an introduction to an encyclopedia of portents "attempted to define the spectrum of such 'wonder works,'" listing "signs, miracles, visions, prophecies, dreams, oracles, predictions, prodigies, divinations, omens, wonders, portents, presages, presentiments, monsters, impressions, marvels, spells, charms and incantations."[4] In Catholic France the *livrets bleus*, those inexpensive books that circulated widely in the seventeenth century, were dominated by accounts of apparitions, miracles, witchcraft, and possession. Some of these continental stories would reappear in England. Certain ballads were translated or adapted from a foreign source.[5] Thomas Beard described *The Theatre* as "translated from the French," and though his source remains unspecified, his book was parallelled by Simon Goulart's *Histoires admirables et memorables de nostre temps*, of which there was an English translation in 1607.[6] On the Continent, as in the England of Beard and Clarke, the distinction between reading matter that was "learned" and reading that was "popular" did not apply to tales of wonders. Nor was this lore of more appeal to Catholics than to Protestants. Indeed it seemed to cut across the line between the pagan and the Christian worlds.

No better demonstration of this blending exists than the eclectic sources on which Beard, Clarke and their contemporaries drew. Aside from newsheets and ballads, whether English or imported, most of their material was culled from printed books that subsumed the sweep of western culture. The classical and early Christian sources included Vergil, Pliny, Plutarch, Seneca, Cicero, Josephus (a favorite), Gildas, Eusebius, and Bede. Then came the historians and chroniclers of the Middle Ages: Geoffrey of Monmouth, Voragine's *The*

4. Miriam Chrisman, *Lay Culture, Learned Culture: Books and Social Change in Strasbourg 1480–1599* (New Haven, Conn., 1982), 257, 369ff; R. W. Scribner, *For the Sake of Simple Folk: Popular Propaganda for the German Reformation* (Cambridge, 1981), 125–127, 131, 184.

5. Rollins, ed., *Pack of Autolycus*, 81.

6. Simon Goulart, *Admirable and Memorable Histories containing the wonders of our time* (London, 1607). The original French edition appeared in 1547. Batman's *Doome* was largely a translation of Lycosthenes' *De prodigiis liber*.

*Golden Legend.* The sixteenth and seventeenth centuries supplied a host of chronicles and encyclopedias: *The Mirrour of Magistrates*, the *Magdeburg Centuries*, and others by such writers as Hollingshead, Polydore Vergil, Conrad Lycosthenes, Sleiden, Camden, and Heylin. No source was more important to the English writers than John Foxe's *Acts and Monuments*, itself a résumé of narratives and chronicles extending back to Eusebius. A final source was that great wonder book, the Bible. Its narratives of visions, voices, strange deaths, and witches lent credence to such stories of a later date.[7]

In plundering this great mass of materials, Beard, Batman, and their successors made modest efforts to be critical. As Protestants, they followed Foxe's lead in dropping from their histories most of the visions, cures, and other miracles associated with the legends of the saints. But otherwise the English writers were willing to reprint the stories that descended to them from the Middle Ages and antiquity. No one questioned the legitimacy of Pliny's *Natural History* and its kin, to which, indeed, these writers conceded an unusual authority. The parting of the ways between the "ancients" and the "moderns" lay in the future. In conceding so much to their sources, whether

7. The best guides (in English) to the lore of wonders are the literary historians whom I came to refer to as "the Shakespeareans," the men and women who have patrolled the sweep of English literary culture from Chaucer to Shakespeare and Milton, and who were very conscious of Shakespeare's roots in medieval and classical culture. A book of great practical utility, as my citations from it indicate, is S. K. Heninger, Jr., *A Handbook of Renaissance Meteorology* (Durham, N.C., 1960), which opens with an important survey of the encyclopedias that codified and transmitted so much of the wonder lore. No less important is Kester Svendsen, *Milton and Science* (New York, 1969), with its superb discussion in Chapter 1 of "The Compendious Method of Natural Philosophy: Milton and the Encyclopedic Tradition." The notes and cross references in Hyder Rollins's *Pack of Autolycus* remain the best guide to the print culture I describe briefly. Other studies of importance include: Don Cameron Allen, *The Star-Crossed Renaissance: The Quarrel about Astrology and Its Influence in England* (New York, 1966); Willard Farnham, *The Medieval Heritage of Elizabethan Tragedy* (Berkeley, 1936); J. S. P. Tatlock, *The Scene of the Franklin's Tale Revisited* (London, 1914), and his *The Legendary History of Britain* (Berkeley and Los Angeles, 1950); Robert W. Hanning, *The Vision of History in Early Britain from Gildas to Geoffrey of Monmouth* (New York, 1966); Paul H. Kocher, *Science and Religion in Elizabethan England* (New York, 1969); George Lyman Kittredge, *The Old Farmer and His Almanac* (Boston, 1904); and Henry A. Kelly, *Divine Providence in the England of Shakespeare's Histories* (Cambridge, Mass., 1970). An exhaustive survey is Lynn Thorndike, *A History of Magic and Experimental Science*, 8 vols. (New York, 1923–1958), esp. vols. IV–VII.

classical or of the early Church or even of the Middle Ages, Beard and Clarke admitted to their pages a strange mixture of ideas and themes. This was a mixture that requires closer scrutiny, for the stories in these books were charged with several meanings.

Wonder stories were interesting in and of themselves; even now, events that seem to defy nature attract our curiosity. But in the seventeenth century, each portent carried a large burden of meaning. Much of this burden was compounded out of three main systems or traditions of ideas—apocalypticism, astrology, and the meteorology of the Greeks. Each of these systems was in decay or disrepute by the middle of the century, under challenge either from an alternative, more up-to-date science or from a growing disenchantment with prophetic visionaries. But even in decay these systems continued to give meaning to the wonder tales.

The most widely used of these traditions was the meteorology of the Greeks and Romans. In Aristotle's physics, meteorology referred to everything occurring in the region of the universe between the earth and moon. As a science it encompassed blazing stars, comets (deemed to circle earth below the moon), rainbows, lightning, and thunder as well as fanciful or misinterpreted phenomena like apparitions in the sky. After Aristotle, the key commentator on meteorology was Pliny, whose *Natural History* "embellished Aristotle's rational theory with many elements of wonder and even superstition." Pliny had become available in translation by the 1560's, and most other major Roman writers who spoke of meteors—Seneca, Plutarch, Vergil—had been made available in English by the early seventeenth century. But English readers learned of blazing stars and comets chiefly from translated versions of a dozen medieval and Renaissance encyclopedias, or from poetic versions such as *La Sepmaine* (1578), the work of a French Huguenot and poet du Bartas. His long poem, which proved immensely popular in English translation, melded Protestant didacticism with the lore of meteors as "prodigious signs."[8]

No less commonplace to most Elizabethans was astrology, the

---

8. Heninger, *Handbook of Renaissance Meteorology*, 12, and chaps. 2–3.

science of celestial bodies. Elizabethans learned their astrology from a medley of medieval and renaissance handbooks. These books taught a Christian version of the science, affirming, for example, that the stars and planets had no independent power but depended on the will of God. Astrology reached a wide audience via almanacs and their "prognostications" as keyed to planetary oppositions and conjunctions. Weather lore was another common vehicle of astrological ideas and images.[9]

A third intellectual tradition was apocalypticism. Several different strands converged to form this one tradition. The Scripture offered up a vision of the end in the Apocalypse. The Old and New Testaments told of persons who could prophesy the future on the basis of some vision, or perhaps by hearing voices: "If there be a prophet among you, I the Lord will make myself known unto him in a vision, and will speak to him in a dream" (Numbers 12:6). The legends of the saints were rich in visions, as were the lives of martyrs in Eusebius.[1] Geoffrey of Monmouth, a thirteenth-century English writer, invented prophecies that he ascribed to Merlin. These would survive into the seventeenth century in the company of other legendary sayings—of "Mother Shipton," of the Sybilline oracles, or of obscure Germans whose manuscript predictions were always being rediscovered.[2] With the coming of the Reformation, apocalypticism gained new vigor as Protestants connected their own movement to the cryptic references in Revelation. The feeling was pervasive that contemporary history manifested the great struggle between Christ and Antichrist, and that some cataclysmic alternation was impending. In his influential explication of the Book of Revelation, Joseph Mede reaffirmed the prophetic significance of voices, thunder, lightning, hail, eclipses, blazing stars, and the rise and fall of kings. Mede re-

9. Ibid., 30–32; Allen, *Star-Crossed Renaissance*, chap. 5; Capp, *English Almanacs*, chap. 5.

1. Eusebius, *The Ancient ecclesiastical histories* (London, 1619), 64, 80; *Bede's Ecclesiastical History of the English People*, Bertram Colgrave and R. A. B. Mynors, eds. (Oxford, 1969), 141, 361–363; G. R. Owst, *Literature and Pulpit in Medieval England* (Cambridge, 1937), 129–130.

2. Tatlock, *Legendary History of Britain*, chap. 17; Rupert Taylor, *The Political Prophecy in England* (New York, 1911); Thomas, *Religion and the Decline of Magic*, chap. 13.

garded all the seals and trumpets in Revelation as forecasting real historical events, and in working out the parallels he made it seem that the Apocalypse would not be long postponed.[3]

But the more crucial contribution of the Reformation was the doctrine of God's providence. The doctrine antedated Luther and Calvin. Chaucer's Knight had spoken of "Destiny, that Minister-General / Who executed on earth and over all / That providence which God has long foreseen," and the Psalmist sang of a God who stretched out his protection to the ends of the earth. Nonetheless, the doctrine had a fresh importance in the sixteenth century. In reaffirming the sovereignty of God, the Reformers also wished to understand their own emergence as prefigured in God's grand providential design. John Foxe, the martyrologist, made providence the animating principle of his great book. In its wake, Thomas Beard would reassure his readers that God was immediately and actively present in the world, the ultimate force behind everything that happened: "Is there any substance in this world that hath no cause of his subsisting? . . . Doth not every thunderclap constraine you to tremble at the blast of his voyce?" Nothing in this world occurred according to contingency or "blind chance." All of nature, all of history, displayed a regularity that men must marvel at, a regularity that witnessed to the "all-surpassing power of God's will." From time to time this "marvellous" order was interrupted by other acts of providence, for God had the power to suspend the laws of nature and work wonders that were even more impressive than the routine harmony of things. The providence of God was as manifest in the swift and unexpected as in the "constant" order of the world.[4]

Beard, Clarke, and Turner were aggressively Protestant in pointing out the significance of God's providence, especially as it affected

---

3. Scribner, *For the Sake of Simple Folk*, 116–117, 140–147, 184; Katharine R. Firth, *The Apocalyptic Tradition in Reformation Britain, 1530–1645* (Oxford, 1979); Joseph Mede, *The Key of the Revelation, searched and demonstrated out of the Naturall and proper characters of the Visions* (London, 1643), Pt. 1, 88, 94.

4. Chaucer, *The Canterbury Tales*, trans. Nevill Coghill (Baltimore, 1952), 70; Peter Lake, *Moderate Puritans and the Elizabethan Church* (Cambridge, 1982), 119–120; Beard, *Theatre of Gods Judgements*, 88; Thomas, *Religion and the Decline of Magic*, chap. 4.

evil-doers, papists, and persecutors of the Church. In doing so, they continued to rely on astrology, apocalypticism, and meteorology for motifs and evidence. No one viewed these systems as in contradiction with each other. Indeed they seemed to reinforce the patterns of a providential universe. Astrology taught men to regard the heavens as infused with law and order. The meteorology of the ancients rested on assumptions about natural law. Science, whether old or new, was still allied with religion,[5] and the synthesis of Christianity and classical culture remained intact. Then too, the sciences of Greece and Rome were rich in possibilities for disruption and disorder. The conjunction of two planets could send shock waves through the universe. Stars could wander out of their ordained paths, and storms arise as nature fell into imbalance. The world as pictured by astrologers and scientists was prone to violent eruptions. This sense of things was echoed in apocalypticism, and writers on the Apocalypse would cite comets and eclipses as signs of the portending end. Meanwhile Satan raged incessantly against God's kingdom, leading many into sin and tormenting seekers after truth. Sin, injustice, persecution—these disorders of the moral universe were mirrored in the conflict and disorder of the heavens. An angry God was the supreme agent of disruption. Astrologers, the Hebrew prophets, the oracles of Greece and Rome, all spoke alike of doom portended in the turmoil of the heavens and the earth. A teleological universe yielded incessant signals of God's providential plan and his impending judgments.

As emblem of God's providence in all of its variety, the wonder had a rich significance. Still more possibilities for meaning were provided by a set of themes that circulated widely in Elizabethan England. One of these was the theme of decay or dissolution. It was a commonplace assumption among Elizabethans that the world was running down and soon would be exhausted. Portents never seemed

5. As Kocher proves at length in *Science and Religion in Elizabethan England*. The close ties between science and religion are evident in the letters that Cotton Mather sent to the Royal Society; many of them report events that previously had been described as "wonders" in his father's *Essay for the Recording of Illustrious Providences*. Cf. George L. Kittredge, "Cotton Mather's Scientific Communications to the Royal Society," American Antiquarian Society, *Proceedings*, N.S. XXVI (1916), 18–57.

to hint at progress or improvement but at impending chaos.[6] Another theme was *De Causibus*, or the rise and fall of great men. In Beard as in books like the *Mirrour of Magistrates*, Elizabethans read of kings and princes, of men of greed and overreaching ambition, who seemed propelled by some inevitable force to fall from their high rank.[7] A third theme concerned evil as a power operating almost on its own. Evil was not distant or abstract but something always present in the flow of daily life. A book like Beard's, with its grand metaphor of "theatre," made good and evil the main actors in the drama of existence.[8] Yet another motif was fortune, its symbol a great wheel that swept some people up and others down.[9] A final theme was the interpenetration of the moral and the natural orders. Disruptions of the moral order had their echo in nature, and vice versa. This sympathy or correspondence was why Elizabethans assumed that corpses bled when touched by guilty persons. Hence too this correspondence meant that ills of the body, like sickness and death, betokened spiritual corruption. All of the natural world was permeated by forces of the spirit, be they forces working for good or for evil.[1]

The wonder books incorporated all these themes without concern for how they might seem contradictory. Fortune and providence were, after all, competing if not antithetical interpretations. But the wonder books were remarkably tolerant. They made room for decayed systems of belief; in their pages the pagan coexisted with the Christian, the old science of the Greeks with the new Protestant emphasis on providence. The "learned" may have preferred more

6. Capp, *English Almanacs*, 165; Hershel Baker, *The Race of Time* (Toronto, 1967) 57–63; Joseph J. Morgan, Jr., *Chaucer and the Theme of Mutability* (The Hague, 1961); Victor Harris, *All Coherence Gone* (Chicago, 1949), chaps. 4–5.

7. Farnham, *Medieval Heritage of Elizabethan Tragedy*, chap. 7; Scribner, *For the Sake of Simple Folk*, 117; Beard, *Theatre of Gods Judgements*, 80.

8. Michael MacDonald, *Mystical Bedlam: Madness, Anxiety, and Healing in Seventeenth-Century England* (Cambridge, 1981), 175, 202. "There hath ever been from the beginning an inveterate antipathy between Satan and his instruments, and the children of God." (Clarke, *Examples*, 35.)

9. Howard R. Patch, *The Goddess Fortuna in Medieval Literature* (Cambridge, Mass., 1927); J. G. A. Pocock, *The Machiavellian Moment: Florentine Political Thought and the Atlantic Republican Tradition* (Princeton, 1975), 349–350.

1. E. M. W. Tillyard, *The Elizabethan World Picture* (New York, n.d.), chap. 7.

distinctions, and a man like Thomas Hobbes found the whole body of this lore distasteful.[2] But in the first half of the seventeenth century, the lore of wonders remained generously eclectic both in its themes and in its audience. Everyone in Elizabethan England had some access to this lore. Writers such as Shakespeare and Milton availed themselves of references and motifs that also were the stock of ballad writers. Conventional, familiar, tolerant and open-ended, the lore of wonders was a language that everyone could speak and understand.

To trace the uses of this language for two or three examples is to trace them for the whole repertory of signs and signals. For Beard and his contemporaries, comets were perhaps the most widely publicized of all the meteors described in ancient science. It was a commonplace of Renaissance discussions to view comets as portending drastic change if not disaster—"drought, the pestilence, hunger, battels, the alteration of kingdomes, and common weales, and the traditions of men. Also windes, earthquakes, dearth, landflouds, and great heate to follow." Du Bartas summed up this wisdom in his *La Sepmaine*:

> There, with long bloody Hair, a Blazing Star
> Threatens the World with Famine, Plague & War:
> To Princes, death; to Kingdomes many crosses:
> To all Estates, Inevitable Losses. . . .[3]

2. Thomas Hobbes, *Leviathan*, ed. Michael Oakeshott (Oxford, 1957), Pt. IV. Hobbes was almost *sui generis*; but there was widespread criticism in seventeenth-century England of astrology and apocalypticism, as well as an awareness that portents and prodigies were often manipulated for political benefit. This politicizing is evident in the flood of publications in 1679 and 1680, most of them anti-Catholic, anti-Stuart tracts in disguise, and in books like *Mirabilis Annus Secundus; Or, The Second Year of Prodigies. Being A true and impartial Collection of many strange Signes and Apparitions, which have this last Year been seen in the Heavens, and in the Earth, and in the Waters* (London, 1662), which, despite its title, is a radical Puritan onslaught against the restored monarchy. We are dealing with a series of contradictions, or better, of paradoxes: belief in portents, joined with skepticism about them; a conviction that some portents were not really significant, and that others were. For examples of this selectivity at work in the late sixteenth century, cf. L. H. Buell, "Elizabethan Portents: Superstition or Doctrine," in *Essays Critical and Historical Dedicated to Lily B. Campbell* (Berkeley and Los Angeles, 1950), 27–41.

3. Heninger, *Handbook of Renaissance Meterology*, 87–91; du Bartas, *La Sepmaine*, quoted on the reverse of the title page of Samuel Danforth, *An Astronomical Description of the late Comet or Blazing Star* (Cambridge, Mass., 1665).

His idiom came straight from Pliny, who, in viewing comets as "a very terrible portent," had noted their appearance "during the civil disorder in the consulship of Octavius, and again during the war between Pompey and Caesar."[4]

Thunder and lightning were other portents that drew on ancient sources for their meaning. In Scripture, they were repeatedly the instruments of an avenging God: "Cast forth lightning, and scatter them: Shoot out thine arrows, and destroy them" (Psalm 144:6). The prophecies of St. John in Revelation evoked the "voice" of thunder, lightning, and earthquakes (8:5; 10:4). Pliny had viewed thunder bolts as "direful and accursed," associating them with many kinds of wonders such as prophecy. To writers of the Renaissance, lightning seemed especially to betoken destructive violence. But the prophetic context could be invoked in plays like Marlowe's *Tamburlaine*, where the hero saw himself as the scourge of "a God full of revenging wrath, From whom the thunder and the lightning breaks."[5]

As for apparitions in the sky, the would-be scientific description in writers such as Pliny yielded to interpretation of such sights as portents of impending conflict or defeat. Among Beard, Clarke, and their contemporaries, a much repeated apparition story concerned the fall of Jerusalem. Recounting the destruction of Jerusalem, Josephus had described at length "the strange signes and tokens that appeared" before the city's fall. "One while there was a comet in form of a fiery sword, which for a year together did hang over the city." There were voices, and a man who cried out, "Wo, wo unto Jerusalem." Iron chariots flew through the air, and an army became visible in the clouds. All of this seemed credible to Elizabethans, and no less so, as we shall see, to the people of New England.[6]

Apparitions were credible on the authority of Josephus and Pliny, but they also figured in the folk belief of the English people. Folk belief is not easily distinguished from popular culture in an age when

4. Pliny, *Natural History*, trans. H. Rackham (Cambridge, Mass., 1949), I, 235 (Bk II.xxiii).

5. Ibid., I, 275 (Bk II.liii); Heninger, *Handbook of Renaissance Meteorology*, 72–87.

6. *The Famous and Memorable Workes of Josephus . . . Faithfully Translated . . . by Thomas Lodge* (London, 1620), 738; Heninger, *Handbook of Renaissance Meteorology*, 91–94; Rollins, ed., *Pack of Autolycus*, 38.

both could circulate by word-of-mouth. Where such beliefs arose and how they were transmitted—and whether they were fragments of some "primitive" mentality—are questions that are difficult to answer. What remains clear is that the wonder books made room for folklore also: stories of the devil as black dog or bear, the legends of the saints and their "white magic," tales of fairies, ghosts, and apparitions, of "murder will out," of curses and their consequences.[7]

So many sources; so many possibilities for meaning! In their tolerance, the great collections ended up without a unifying order of their own. Clarke verged off into sensationalism. Ballads recounted fables of serpents and dragons. Writers such as Crouch felt free to invent stories—as if most ballads were not fiction to begin with.[8] This playfulness was nowhere more amusingly revealed than in a chapbook of the 1640's that mated the predictions of the legendary "Mother Shipton" with the prophecies of a radical Puritan. The new and the old lay side-by-side without apparent contradiction.[9]

But were the colonists this tolerant, or did they order and discriminate in keeping with their Puritanism?

The same wonder tales that Englishmen were buying circulated in the colonies, often via books imported from the London book trade. As a student at Harvard in the 1670's, Edward Taylor had access to a copy of Samuel Clarke's *Examples*, out of which he copied "An Account of ante-mortem visions of Mr. John Holland."[1] In sermons of the 1670's, Increase Mather quoted frequently from Clarke and Beard.[2] Imported broadsides made some of Beard's stories familiar to New England readers; the Boston printer, John Foster, published in

7. Katharine M. Briggs, *The Anatomy of Puck: An Examination of Fairy Beliefs among Shakespeare's Contemporaries and Successors* (London, 1959); C. Grant Loomis, *White Magic: An Introduction to the Folklore of Christian Legend* (Cambridge, Mass., 1948); Kittredge, *Old Farmer and His Almanac*, chap. 6; T. F. Thiselton Dyer, *Folk Lore of Shakespeare* (London, 1884).

8. As Rollins, ed., *Pack of Autolycus*, points out repeatedly.

9. *Twelve Strange Prophesies, besides Mother Shiptons. With the Predictions of John Saltmarsh* (London, 1648).

1. William P. Upham, "Remarks," Massachusetts Historical Society, *Proceedings*, 2d Ser., XIII (1899–1900), 126–127.

2. Increase Mather, *Wo to Drunkards* (Cambridge, Mass., 1673), 28; "The Diary of Increase Mather," Massachusetts Historical Society, *Proceedings*, 2d Ser., XIII (1899–1900), 345.

1679 a facsimile of a London broadside, *Divine Examples of Gods Severe Judgments against Sabbath-Breakers*, a set of warning tales drawn mostly from *A Theatre of Gods Judgements*. Hezekiah Usher, a Boston bookseller, was importing copies of Nathaniel Crouch's *Wonderful Prodigies of Judgment and Mercy* in the 1680's,[3] and another of Crouch's books, *Delights for the Ingenious*, came into the hands of the children of the Goodwin family.[4] Many more such books and broadsides must have crossed the Atlantic in the seventeenth century, though leaving no specific trace of their presence.

In the absence of such evidence we may turn to books and pamphlets that the colonists were writing. Almanacs appeared each year as soon as the colonists had established a printing press. As in England, these local products included references to portents and wonders. The almanac for 1649 offered its readers a lengthy "prognostication" that played on the theme of earthquakes as a portent of impending catastrophe:

> Great Earthquakes frequently (as one relates)
> Forerun strange plagues, dearths, wars and change of states,
> Earths shaking fits by venemous vapours here,
> How is it that they hurt not, as elsewhere!

Like its European counterpart, the New England almanac contained cryptic clues to what the future held:

> The morning Kings may next ensuing year,
> With mighty Armies in the aire appear,
> By one mans means there shall be hither sent
> The Army, Citty, King and Parliament . . .
> A Child but newly born, shall then foretell
> Great changes in a winding-sheet; Farewell.[5]

The almanac for 1648 tucked portents and prodigies into a "Chronologicall Table" that later almanacs would update:

---

3. Worthington C. Ford, *The Boston Book Market, 1679–1700* (Boston, 1917), 149.

4. Mather, *Magnalia Christi Americana*, I, 205.

5. Kenneth B. Murdock, ed., *Handkerchiefs from Paul being Pious and Consolatory Verses of Puritan Massachusetts* (Cambridge, Mass., 1927), 109–111.

Mr. Stoughton and all the souldiers returned home, none being slain.
Mrs. Dier brought forth her horned-foure-talented monster.
The great and generall Earth-quake.[6]

Soon enough, moreover, the colonists were writing commentaries on meteors. The first to appear was Samuel Danforth's *An Astronomical Description of the late Comet or Blazing Star . . . Together with a brief Theological Application thereof* (1665). The comets of 1680 and 1682 stirred the Reverend Increase Mather to publish *Heavens Alarm to the World . . . Wherein Is Shewed, That fearful Sights and Signs in Heaven are the Presages of great Calamities at hand* and *Kometographia or A Discourse Concerning Comets*. In 1684, Mather undertook a more ambitious project, a compendium that resembled Clarke's *Examples*. *An Essay for the Recording of Illustrious Providences* was at once a collection of wonder tales and a plea for greater efforts among the colonists to preserve such stories.

Reiterating the commonplaces of a literary tradition, these books— the almanacs, the works of meteorology—are proof of the transfer of culture. It should be noted that Danforth and Mather were learned men who had become aware of scientific challenges to Aristotle's meteorology, challenges that jeopardized some aspects of the portent lore. Yet the two men put aside these alternatives to address a general audience, using an old language and familiar references, and insisting that "blazing stars" remained portents of God's providence.[7]

This message had wide credibility in seventeenth-century New England. We have some measure of its popularity in the record-keeping that went on. Certain public bodies, like the churches in Dorchester and Roxbury, incorporated references to "remarkable providences"—fires, storms, eclipses, victories, sudden deaths—into

6. [Samuel Danforth], *An Almanack for the Year of Our Lord 1648* (Cambridge, Mass., 1648). Mary Dyer's monstrous birth was perhaps the first New England wonder to receive international attention. Cf. *Newes from New-England of A most strange and prodigious Birth* [London, 1642].

7. "My chief design, is to inform and edifie the ordinary sort of Readers. Yet considering that God hath made me a debter to the wise as well as to the weak, I have added some things of the nature, place, motion of Comets, which only such as have some skill in Astronomy can understand" ("To the Reader," in *Kometographia*).

their records.[8] Each of the Puritan colonies summoned their people repeatedly to days of fasting and thanksgiving, and the calling of these days was cued to the perception of God's providence.[9] Early on, William Bradford, Edward Johnson, and John Winthrop wrote works of history that were richly providential in their narratives of how the colonists had overcome adversity and conflict. These books noted the usual array of signs and portents—eclipses, monster births, strange deaths and storms, miraculous deliverances and reversals—while telling also of more puzzling events, like the lights in the form of a man that were seen in Boston harbor, followed by a voice "calling out in a most dreadful manner, boy, boy, come away, come away."[1] Second- and third-generation historians would reiterate many of these stories, notably in Cotton Mather's *Magnalia Christi Americana* (1702).

All of this public record-keeping or public history was paralleled in private journals that functioned as individual "memorials" of "remarkable providences."[2] The most extensive of these diaries were kept by John Hull, a Boston merchant and the mint master for Massachusetts Bay, and the magistrate Samuel Sewall, who was Hull's son-in-law. Hull seemed almost overwhelmed at times by the flow of prophetic signals, as in his entry for a year—1666—itself accorded apocalyptic significance because 666 was the mark of the beast (Revelation 13:18).

At New Haven was distinctly and plainly heard the noise of guns, two, three, five at a time, a great part of the day, being only such noises in the

8. *Records of the First Church at Dorchester in New England 1636–1734* (Boston, 1891); *Roxbury Land and Church Records*, Boston Record Commissioners, *Reports*, VI (Boston, 1881), 187–212.

9. William DeLoss Love, Jr., *The Fast and Thanksgiving Days of New England* (Boston, 1895).

1. James Kendall Hosmer, ed., *Winthrop's Journal "History of New England," 1630–1649*, 2 vols. (New York, 1953 [orig. publ. New York, 1908]), II, 156.

2. A very large number of such journals or brief autobiographical sketches survive, and their authors include artisans and farmers as well as ministers and merchants. Two diaries kept by ordinary people are John Dane, "A Declaration of Remarkable Proudenses in the Corse of My Life," *New England Historical and Genealogical Register*, VIII (1854), 147–156; and Charles F. Adams, Jr., "Abstract of [John] Marshall's Diary," Massachusetts Historical Society, *Proceedings*, 2d Ser., I (1884–1885), 148–164, and its continuation, Samuel A. Green, "Remarks," ibid., 2d. Ser., XIV (1900–1901), 13–34.

air. The same day, at evening, a house at Northampton [was] fired by light-ning; a part of the timber split; a man in it killed . . . At Narriganset, in Mr. Edward Hutchinson's flock of sheep, were several monsters. In July were very many noises heard by several towns on Long Island, from the sea, distinctly, of great guns and small, and drums.

Early on in Samuel Sewall's record-keeping, he responded strongly to an eclipse: "Morning proper fair, the weather exceedingly benign, but (to me) metaphoric, dismal, dark and portentous, some prodigie appearing in every corner of the skies." For more than fifty years he kept track of many kinds of portents, from thunder storms and rain-bows to sudden deaths and disturbing sounds. A faithful buyer of each year's almanac, he inserted notes on deaths and weather portents in each monthly calendar.[3]

Hull and Sewall had witnessed many of the portents they took note of in their diaries; news of many others reached them second-hand. Travellers dropped by to tell of strange events, and Sewall heard of more from correspondents. A fierce hail storm that struck while he was having dinner with Cotton Mather led to an exchange of stories; Sewall remembered that a hail storm coincided with the Duke of Monmouth's ill-fated invasion of England in 1685, and Mather knew of other houses that had been struck by hail or light-ning. The stories that reached Hull and Sewall were being told and listened to all over New England.[4]

This trade in stories is revealed with unique vividness in two places, a notebook Edward Taylor kept at Harvard and the correspondence passing in and out of Increase Mather's household. In his notebook Taylor recorded the story of "magical performances by a juggler." He had heard the story from Jonathan Mitchel, the minister in Cam-bridge, who in turn had learned it from Henry Dunster, the president of Harvard, "during recitation." Dunster had it from the Reverend John Wilson—and here the chain is interrupted. In his notebook Taylor wrote down the essence of another story passed along by

3. "The Diaries of John Hull," 217–218; *Diary of Samuel Sewall*, Thomas, ed. I, 12. I have analyzed this diary at greater length in "The Mental World of Samuel Sewall," Massachusetts Historical Society, *Proceedings*, XCII (1980), 21–44.
    4. *Diary of Samuel Sewall*, Thomas, ed., I, 330–331.

word of mouth. A minister and Harvard president, Urian Oakes, had done the telling:

A child that was born at Norwich last Bartholomew-Day . . . being in the nurses arms last Easterday . . . being about 30 weeks old spake these words (This is an hard world): the nurse when she had recovered herselfe a little from her trembling, & amazement at the Extraordinariness of the thing, said Why dear child! thou hast not known it: the child after a pause, replied, But it will be an hard world & you shall know it.

To this same notebook Taylor added his extracts out of Clarke's *Examples* and, from some other printed source, the prophetic scaffold speech of an Englishman executed in 1651.[5]

The traffic in wonder stories was crucial to the making of Increase Mather's *Essay for the Recording of Illustrious Providences*. In the early 1680's Mather was soliciting his fellow ministers for contributions to his impending book. John Higginson of Salem, an older man who came to Boston as a student in the 1630's, responded to this call for stories by sending him word of the Reverend Joshua Moodey's collection of annotated almanacs, "so that I doubt not but besides those [stories] he hath sent you, you may have many more from him. For instance,—he speaks of 26 men thereabouts, dying or cast away in their drunkennes which calls to mind some such case here."

The following year, having learned from Mather that he did not "confine" himself "to things done in N.E.," Higginson wrote out and dispatched two wonder stories attributed to "persons credible," and of events "I believe . . . to be certain." Both concerned the devil, the one a story of a book that acted strangely on its readers, the other of a man who covenanted with the devil to insinuate "that there was neither God nor Devil, no Heaven nor Hell." The informant who told Higginson of the magical book, a man no longer living, had been a ruling elder of the church in Salem. Long after the experience—it happened back in England—he could still remember that,

as he read in [the book], he was seized on by a strange kind [of] Horror, both of Body & minde, the hair of his head standing up, &c. Finding these

---

5. Upham, "Remarks," 127–128. Taylor had access to one of the several versions of Christopher Love's scaffold speech; e.g., *The true and perfect Speech of Mr. Christopher Love* (London, 1651).

effects severall times, he acquainted his master with it, who observing the same effects, they concluding it was a Conjuring Book, resolved to burn it, which they did. He that brought it, in the shape of a man, never coming to call for it, they concluded it was the Devil.

The other story Higginson had collected in his days as minister at Guilford "from a godly old man yet living."[6]

As Higginson predicted, Joshua Moodey had stories to pass on. One was of a house inhabited by evil spirits, as told by the man who lived there. All was relatively quiet now; "the last sight I have heard of," Moodey added, "was the carrying away of severall Axes in the night, notwithstanding they were layed up, yea, lockt up very safe." From a "sober woman" Moodey also had a story of a "monstrous birth" that he described at length, concluding with an offer to "goe up and discourse with the midwife" if Mather wanted more details.[7]

Meanwhile Mather had heard from several informants in Connecticut. The minister in Stamford, John Bishop, had written him some years earlier to answer his inquiries about "the noise of a great gun in the air." In his new letter, Bishop poured out a flood of stories:

We have had of late, great stormes of rain & wind, & somtimes of thunder & lightning, whereby some execution hath been done by the Lord's holy Hand, though with sparing mercy to mankind. Mr. Jones his house at N[ew] H[aven] broken into, & strange work made in one room thereof especially, wherein one of his daughters had been a little before; & no hurt to any of the family, but the house only . . . A little after which, at Norwalk, there were nine working oxen smitten dead in the woods, in a few rods space of ground, & after that, at Greenwich (a small town neer us, on the west side) on the 5 mo. 13, (when we had great thunder & lightning), there were seven swine & a dog smitten all dead, & so found the next morning, very near the dwelling house, where a family of children were alone (their parents not then at home) & no hurt to any of them, more then amazing fear.[8]

More such stories came to Mather from other hands—a narrative of Ann Cole's bewitchment, together with the story of a man who drank too much and died, accounts of providential rainstorms and

6. *Mather Papers*, 282–287.
7. Ibid., 360–362.
8. Ibid., 306–310.

remarkable deliverances, and of "two terrible strokes by thunder and lightning" that struck Marshfield in Plymouth Colony.[9]

From his brother, finally, came a letter of encouragement. Nathaniel Mather had moved to England in the early 1650's and remained there. But he remembered many of the stories he had listened to while growing up in Dorchester, or as a Harvard student:

> Mrs. Hibbons witchcrafts, & the discovery thereof, as also of H. Lake's wife, of Dorchester, whom, as I have heard, the devil drew in by appearing to her in the likeness, & acting the part of a child of hers then lately dead, on whom her heart was much set: as also another of a girl in Connecticut who was judged to dye a reall convert, tho she dyed for the same crime: Stories, as I heard them, as remarkable for some circumstances as most I have read. Mrs. Dyer's and Mrs. Hutchinson's monstrous births, & the remarkable death of the latter, with Mr. Wilson's prediction or threatning thereof, which, I remember, I heard of in New England.

Flowing from the memories of a man long since departed from New England, these stories reveal how much was passed along in conversation, and how rapidly a stock of native wonder tales had been accumulated.[1]

Most of these local stories had counterparts in stories told by Clarke and Beard or by the ballad writers. Many of these older stories passed among the colonists as well, enriching and legitimizing their own testimonies of the supernatural. We may speak again of all this lore as constituting a form of popular culture. Everyone knew this lore. Its circulation was not limited to print, as the Mather correspondence indicates so clearly. Nor was it something the rude multitude but not the learned could appreciate. When presidents of Harvard told wonder tales in class, when ministers retold stories of "magical" books and freakish bolts of lightning, we can be sure that we are dealing with a culture shared, with few exceptions, by all of the colonists. One other aspect of this culture deserves emphasis. Its cast was thoroughly traditional, employing the same mix of intellec-

---

9. Ibid., 466–481. The Marshfield episode, told in a letter from the Rev. Samuel Arnold, was later published by N. B. Shurtleff as *Thunder & Lightning; and Deaths at Marshfield in 1658 & 1666* (Boston, 1850).

1. *Mather Papers*, 58–59. The Mary Dyer story had long since passed into print in several places; cf. note 6, p. 258 above.

tual traditions, the same references and conventions, as the lore in Beard, Clarke, and the ballad writers.

Consider Danforth and Mather's descriptions of the comets they had witnessed. Like so many other commentators before them, Danforth and Mather relied on the meteorology of the ancients, as mediated via medieval and Renaissance encyclopedias. In proving that comets were "Portentous and Signal of great and notable Changes," Danforth drew upon du Bartas while citing, as parallels, events such as the death of Julius Caesar, which, according to tradition, had been prefigured by a comet.[2] Mather cited Josephus, Cicero, du Bartas, Mede, and Scripture as authorities when preaching on the comet of 1680. The description he gave of a comet that appeared in 1527 was entirely derivative:

On the eleventh day of August, a most terrifying Comet was seen, of an immense longitude, and bloody colour. The form of it, was like a mans arm holding an huge Sword in his hand with which he was ready to strike. Such terrour and horrour surprized the Spectators of this Prodigy, as that some died away with dread & amazement.[3]

So, too, the references in diaries and in histories to lightning and the phenomenon of three suns repeated elements of an old code of reference. All of the traditional associations between lightning, disorder and prophecy lay in the background of Sewall's frequent diary entries on thunder and lightning, Cotton Mather's *Brontologia Sacra: The Voice of the Glorious God in the Thunder*, and Samuel Arnold's description of a storm that struck the town of Marshfield, in which "the most dismal black cloud . . . that ever" anyone had seen had passed overhead, shooting forth its "arrows."[4] The phenomenon of three suns, remarked on in Shakespeare's works and by medieval chronicles as signalling the overthrow of kings, remained a "wonder" to Edward Johnson, who linked the "unwonted sights" of "two

2. Danforth, *An Astronomical Description*, 16–21.

3. Mather, *Kometographia*, 96. Quoting again the familiar lines from du Bartas, *La Sepmaine*, Mather also spoke approvingly of apparitions in the air. In keeping with tradition, the colonists were sensitive to the shape and direction of comets; cf. Johnson, *Wonder-Working Providence*, ed. Jameson, 40; *Mather Papers*, 312.

4. Mather, *Magnalia Christi Americana*, II, 363–372; Shurtleff, *Thunder & Lightning*, 13–15.

Parlii, or images of the Sun, and some other strange apparitions," with the "desperate opinion" of persons who in New England "would overthrow all the Ordinances of Christ."[5]

From medieval handbooks the colonists also borrowed the language of astrology. For them it was a Christian science; the stars were signs not causes. New England almanacs retained the old combination of weather lore and astrological prediction, as in an essay Israel Chauncey inserted in his almanac for 1663 on "The Natural Portents of Eclipses, according to Approved Authors."[6] Just as commonplace were the allusions to the consequences of certain planetary motions: "On October the third will be celebrated a famous conjunction of Saturn and Mars, and wherein they are deemed the two Malevolent and Infortunate Planets, the conjunction thereof (say Astrologers) Imports no good."[7] The mixture of astrology and political prediction that had flourished amid civil war in England also reached the colonies in 1690, when a printer newly disembarked from London published an abridged edition of John Holwell's fiercely anti-Tory, anti-Catholic *Catastrophe Mundi: or, Europe's Many Mutations Until the Year 1701.*[8]

Even more appealing to the colonists was the apocalyptic tradition. Visions, dreams, unseen voices—all these were almost everyday experiences, talked about in private and, remarkably, in books. Little children who spoke preternaturally were, as in the ballad literature, accorded special notice, as Taylor indicated by preserving the story of the child who told his nurse it was "an hard world." Nathaniel Morton reported an unseen "voice" that had alerted the beleaguered colonists at Plymouth to arson in their storehouse.[9] The Reverend Noadiah Russell

5. Johnson, *Wonder-Working Providence*, ed. Jameson, 243. Cf. "The Diaries of John Hull," 208; *Mather Papers*, 349; and for the tradition, Rollins, ed., *Pack of Autolycus*, 38; Batman, *Doome warning to Iudgemente*, 304.

6. Israel Chauncy, *An Almanack of the coelestial motions for . . . 1663* (Cambridge, Mass., 1663).

7. Noadiah Russell, *Cambridge Ephemeris. An Almanac . . . for . . . 1684* (Cambridge, Mass., 1684).

8. *Holwell's Predictions: of many remarkable things, which may probably come to pass* (Cambridge, Mass., [1690]).

9. Morton, *New-Englands Memoriall*, 52.

heard of a man in Connecticut . . . who was taken with a sudden shivering after which he heard a voice saying that four dreadful judgments should come speedily upon the whole world viz: sword, famine, fire and sickness which should, without speedy reformation prevented, begin at New England.[1]

To interpret dreams as prophecy was to participate in a long-established tradition. John Winthrop, to whom a minister had told a dream of his, responded with another of his own:

coming into his chamber, he found his wife . . . in bed, and three or four of their children lying by her, with most sweet and smiling countenances, with crowns upon their heads, and blue ribbons about their eyes. When he awaked, he told his wife his dream, and made this interpretation of it, that God would take of her children to make them fellow heirs with Christ in his kingdom.[2]

The *Magnalia Christi Americana*, a veritable encyclopedia of New England wonder tales, included many dreams and other acts of prophecying. The Reverend John Wilson had prophetic dreams as well as a "certain prophetical afflatus" that made his prayers affect or forecast the future. Another minister, John Eliot, was gifted with "forebodings of things that were to come," and a third, John Brock of Marblehead, could predict success for fishermen and locate missing boats![3]

Here we sense ourselves approaching folk belief. The wonder tales that passed among the colonists were openly folkloric in certain of their themes and motifs. Stephen Batman had incorporated the folk tradition of spectral, shape-shifting black dogs into *The Doome warning to Iudgemente*.[4] A century later, people in New England testified

1. "The Diary of Noahdiah Russell," 54. The references to such experiences were many; and I mean to write about them elsewhere, as the discussions of millennium and eschatology in New England Puritanism do not pay adequate (if any) attention to the everyday experience of prophecying. Anne Hutchinson was gifted with prophetic sight and visions; cf. David D. Hall, ed., *The Antinomian Controversy, 1636–1638: A Documentary History* (Middletown, Conn., 1968), 271–273.

2. Winthrop, *Journal*, I, 84, 121.

3. Mather, *Magnalia Christi Americana*, I, 314–316, 544; II, 37–38. As with visionary prophecying, I must pass by many other instances, as well as avoiding the stories provided by Beard, Clarke, and Turner.

4. The folklore of black dogs is summarized in Katharine M. Briggs, *British Folk Tales and Legends: A Sampler* (London, 1977), 115–120.

that they had seen the devil in the shape of a black dog. William Barker, Jr., a confessing witch at Salem in 1692, had seen "the Shape of a black dog which looked Verry fercly Upon him" as "he was Goeing into the Woods one Evening" in search of cows. Sarah Carrier, enticed into witchcraft by members of her family, was promised "a black dog."[5] Many of the witnesses at Salem had been visited at night by apparitions of persons crying out for vengeance on their murderers. Such stories were a staple of folk legend and also of the ballad literature.[6] Another folk belief expressed at Salem was the power of white—or in this case, black—magic to keep persons dry in rainstorms. A witness had become suspicious of a visitor whose clothes showed no signs of passing through a storm on muddy roads. Many centuries before Salem witchcraft, the legend had grown up of a saint who remained dry in spite of rain. His was the power of white magic. In some fashion that defies analysis, the colonists were able to repeat this story, though modifying its details and making it a devil story.[7]

Where many of these strands converge—folklore, apocalypticism, white magic, the meteorology of Pliny and Aristotle—is in Increase Mather's *Essay for the Recording of Illustrious Providences*. Because it built upon the wonder tales that people told as stories, the *Essay* has something of the quality of a folk narrative. Yet it is also a "learned" book. Between his own books—he owned the largest private library in New England—and those he found at Harvard, Mather could pillage most of western culture for his lore of portents. In keeping with its bookish sources, the *Essay* borrowed widely from the ancients and their mediators of the Renaissance. It borrowed also from the English collectors, especially Samuel Clarke and his *Examples*. And since Mather was committed to the mystery of the supernatural, he spent portions of the *Essay* arguing the validity of wonders against contemporary Europeans who were growing skeptical. As proof of the reality of witchcraft, he would repeat

5. Paul Boyer and Stephen Nissenbaum, eds., *The Salem Witchcraft Papers*, 3 vols. (New York, 1977), I, 74, 202–203; III, 742; II, 568.
6. Ibid., I, 166, 246–247.
7. Ibid., II, 578. Cf. Loomis, *White Magic*, 39.

the story of the invisible drummer boy of Tidworth, taking it as true on the authority of the English minister and proto-scientist Joseph Glanville, though knowing that the story was denounced by others as a fable.[8]

The man on the receiving end of stories from his fellow clergy made use of some of them but not of others. The book bears signs of haste, as though his printer were impatient and his own control of what he wished to do imperfect. Chapter one told of "sea-deliverances," some of them native, others taken from an English book. In chapter two, a potpourri of stories, Mather reached back to King Philip's War for a captivity narrative and two related episodes; after telling of another "sea-deliverance," he opened up his Clarke's *Examples* and began to copy from it. In chapter three, on "Thunder and Lightning," he quoted from John Bishop's letter and added several other stories of lightning in New England. But the chapter ended with two German stories, some references to Scripture and several bits of pedantry. Chapters four, six, seven, and eight were meditations and general arguments on providence, using European sources. Chapter nine demonstrated how thin the line was between the wonder and the curiosity, for here he told of persons who were deaf and dumb but learned to speak.[9] Chapter ten, "Of remarkable tempests," covered hurricanes, whirlwinds, earthquakes, and floods; chapter eleven, "concerning remarkable judgements," related how the enemies of God—Quakers, drunkards, and other enemies of New England—had been punished. Mather added a letter from Connecticut as chapter twelve, and in chapter five drew together several stories of "things preternatural"—demons, apparitions, and evil spirits.

The many layers of the *Essay* included the esoteric. Like Beard and Clarke before him, Mather had an eye for the unusual event. Some of his stranger stories were borrowed from a manuscript, presumably of English origin, that he had inherited from John Davenport, the long-time minister of New Haven. From it he drew a

8. Joseph Glanville, *A Blow at Modern Sadducism in some Philosophical Considerations about Witchcraft*, 4th ed. (London, 1668); Rollins, ed., *Pack of Autolycus*, 115.

9. The same generosity is characteristic of Beard and Clarke, and has medieval precedents; Tatlock, *Legendary History of Britain*, 276–277.

Faust-type story of a young student who contracted with the devil for money. But the black magic of the devil yielded to the higher powers of a group of faithful ministers, whose prayers forced Satan

to give up that contract; after some hours continuance in prayer, a cloud was seen to spread itself over them, and out of it the very contract signed with the poor creatures blood was dropped down amongst them.

From this manuscript Mather drew an even more sensational story of a minister who drank too much, went to a cockfight on the Lord's Day, and who, while "curses . . . were between his lips, God smote him dead in the twinkle of an eye. And though Juxon were but young . . . his carcase was immediately so corrupted as that the stench of it was insufferable."

From the same collection, finally, Mather copied out a "strange passage" concerning a man suspected of stealing sheep who swore his innocence and

wished, that if he had stollen it, God would cause the horns of the sheep to grow upon him. This man was seen within these few days by a minister of great repute for piety, who saith, that the man has a horn growing out of one corner of his mouth, just like that of a sheep; from which he hath cut seventeen inches, and is forced to keep it tyed by a string to his ear, to prevent its growing up to his eye.

Here again we sense ourselves confronting folk belief. This story of the sheep's horn had its parallel or antecedent in a medieval legend of a man who stole and ate a sheep, and then found a sheep's ear growing out of his mouth. The story of a student who compacted with the devil had roots in legends of the saints and, more remotely, in lore of eastern cultures.[1]

How like it was for wonder tales to build on folk or pagan legends! With its mixture of motifs and sources, *An Essay for the Recording of Illustrious Providences* reaffirmed the traditional tolerance of the genre. The tolerance of the *Essay* was mirrored in broader patterns of response. As readers and book buyers, the colonists were caught up in

1. Mather, *Essay*, "Introduction"; H. L. D. Ward, *Catalogue of Romances in the Department of Manuscripts in the British Museum*, 3 vols. (London, 1883–1910), I, 257, II, 595.

the wonder tale as it appeared in Beard and Clarke. As storytellers, they repeated to each other a growing stock of local wonders. And in their almanacs and diaries they recorded the prodigies and portents that were the stuff of everyday experience—the voices and strange sounds, monster births and lightning bolts, apparitions in the sky and doings of the devil. In confirming the validity and significance of all of these phenomena, Mather's *Essay* summed up a popular culture that the colonists shared in common with most other Europeans. His book epitomized the transfer of old ways of thinking to the New World.

But still we need to ask what kind of world view was it that accepted the reality of evil spirits and of sheep's horns growing out of some-one's mouth? The answer to this question lies elsewhere than in the theology of John Calvin or William Perkins. We are so accustomed to inflating the significance of Puritanism that we easily forget how much else impinged upon the making of beliefs among the colonists. Indeed, the historians who have commented on Mather's *Essay* have actively resisted its complexity. A century ago, the rational-minded Moses Coit Tyler was irritated by Mather's "palpable eagerness . . . to welcome, from any quarter of the earth or sea or sky, any mes-senger whatever, who may be seen hurrying toward Boston with his mouth full of marvels." Tyler deemed the stories in the book vari-ously "tragic, or amusing, or disgusting, now and then merely stu-pid," and in one sweeping statement he condemned the book as "at once a laughable and an instructive memorial of the mental habits" of the colonists. Fifty years later, Kenneth Murdock tried to rescue the *Essay*, and by, implication, Puritanism, by insisting that Mather was up-to-date in his science and in his efforts to weigh and judge the evidence for marvels. Dismissing this interpretation, Perry Miller politicized the book, while admitting that it "seems a collection of old-wives tales and atrocity stories, at best hilariously funny and at worse a parade of gullibility." This indifference to the texture of the *Essay*—Miller did acknowledge that its roots lay "in a venerable tra-dition, stretching back to the medieval exempla"—was symptomatic of a larger indifference to traditional belief and popular culture in

early New England.[2] Center stage was wholly occupied by the com-
plexities of Puritanism as an intellectual system, and if certain other
beliefs, like witchcraft, lingered in the wings, they could safely be
ignored since they were headed for extinction.

But the mental world of the colonists was not really fashioned in
this manner. High or low, learned or unlearned, these people had
absorbed a host of older beliefs. A modern critic who has written on
Milton and science remarks that everyone in the early seventeenth
century relied on a body of common knowledge that stemmed from
Pliny, Aristotle, and the encyclopedists. This old lore was being
challenged by new theories of the planets; yet like Mather and the
colonists, Milton "was not ever seriously interested in a contest of
cosmological theories." As a Christian and a Puritan, Milton believed
that the universe was theocentric and teleological. He was also quite
at home with a "popular science" that included astrology, finding
"no incompatibility between" this science and the doctrines of free
will and providence. This eclectic synthesis supported a view of the
everyday world as hovering between anarchy and order. Decay and
corruption were constant, and disorder in the moral sphere of things
was echoed in the disorder of nature. Such a mixture of science and
religion in Milton was formed out of intellectual, or popular, traditions that long antedated Puritanism.[3] It is not important to give
dates or exact boundaries to these traditions. The point is rather that
certain deeper layers of belief—call them folklore, call them "popular"—flowed into Milton's world view as into Increase Mather's.[4]

2. Moses Coit Tyler, *A History of American Literature during the Colonial Time*, rev.
ed., 2 vols. (New York, 1897), II, 73; Kenneth B. Murdock, *Increase Mather: The Fore-
most American Puritan* (Cambridge, Mass., 1925), 170–174; Perry Miller, *The New
England Mind: From Colony to Province* (Cambridge, Mass., 1953), 143; but for apparent approval of Murdock's arguments, cf. 180.

3. Svendsen, *Milton and Science*, 5, 44, 84.

4. In trying to account for attitudes toward the Negro in early America, Winthrop
Jordan was driven to speaking of "deeper" attitudes that somehow formed and were
perpetuated in Elizabethan culture: Jordan, *White over Black: American Attitudes Toward the Negro, 1550–1812* (Baltimore, 1969), viii–ix, and chap. 1. My problem is akin
to his, in that the popular culture I am describing was remarkably tenacious and
encompassing, even though its exact sources and lines of influence cannot readily be
specified. Robert St. George's essay in this volume deals with similar attitudes in
terms of their deeprootedness.

Armed with this insight, we come finally to understand that the mentality of the supernatural in seventeenth-century New England encompassed themes and motifs that owed little to formal theology or to Puritanism. The people of New England viewed the world about them as demonstrating pattern and order. This was the order of God's providence; their world, like Milton's, was theocentric. It was also teleological, its structure the grand scheme laid out in the Apocalypse, the war of Antichrist against the godly. The forces of evil were immensely strong and cunning, in such sort that the providential order could seem to be "overthrown and turned upside down, men speak[ing] evill of good, and good of evill, accounting darknesse light, and light darknesse."[5] Disorder was profound in other ways. The world was rife with violence—with wars and persecution, pestilence and famine, pride, greed and envy. A righteous God could strike with terrible swiftness, disrupting natural law to punish evildoers or afflict the godly. The devil too had powers to wreak havoc. Each kind of violence was attuned to every other, as were the forms of order. This correspondence enriched the meaning of portents and prodigies, making them more terrifying. The plan and order of the universe was, after all, not always visible or readily deciphered. If there were purpose and plan, there were also the marvellous, the inexplicable, and the wonderful:

One providence seems to look this way, another providence seems to look that way, quite contrary one to another. Hence these works are marveilous. Yea, and that which does add to the wonderment, is, in that the works of God sometimes seem to run counter with his word: so that there is dark and amazing intricacie in the ways of providence.[6]

There was mystery at the heart of things. Death could strike at any moment, the devil could mislead, the earth begin to tremble. In dramatizing all these possibilities, the wonder tale evoked the radical contingency of a world so thoroughly infused with invisible forces.

This mentality of the supernatural reflects the syncreticism of the

5. Beard, *Theatre of Gods Judgements*, 2.
6. Increase Mather, *The Doctrine of Divine Providence Opened and Applyed* (Boston, 1684), 43, 30–32, 34, 81, 133; and for the figure of the wheel and the rise and fall of kings, cf. pp. 9, 16–17. The image of the wheel derives from Ezekiel 1:15–16, et seq.

Christian tradition. Early in its history Christianity had come to terms with the pagan notion of the prodigy and with such systems as astrology. The mixture that resulted cannot arbitrarily be separated into distinct spheres, one "magical" or pagan, the other orthodox or Christian.[7] As one modern historian has noted, the early modern European was receptive to the wonder tale because he "believed that every body, living or inanimate, was composed of matter and a spirit. This idea was shared by eminent minds right up to the scientific revolution in the seventeenth century; it underlay the neo-Platonic belief of the Renaissance in the souls of stars and justified the persistence of astrology." In this same period no one could "make a clear distinction between nature and supernature" or view the world as simply "ruled . . . by laws" and not "caprice."[8] This way of thinking made its way across the Atlantic with the colonists. Theirs too was a syncretic Christianity. In tolerating the wonder tale and all its underlying themes, the colonists demonstrated the capacity to abide contradiction and ambiguity. So too they demonstrated their attachment to an old mentality, a popular culture transmitted through the lore of wonders.

7. As is suggested by Jon Butler, "Magic, Astrology, and the Early American Religious Heritage, 1600–1760," *American Historical Review*, LXXXIV (1979), 317–346, an essay that seems almost perverse in its refusal to acknowledge the syncreticism of seventeenth-century religion and the common interest of both clergy and laity in such "superstitions." The most important description of intellectual tolerance and syncreticism in seventeenth-century England is MacDonald, *Mystical Bedlam*, which in this regard serves to correct the impression that arises from Thomas, *Religion and the Decline of Magic*, of a clear line between the two. Anthropologists struggle to define the difference between magic and religion; literary and cultural historians by and large agree in de-emphasizing the distinction. "Our hard and fast distinction between the natural and the supernatural was unknown in the middle ages; there was no line between jugglery . . . and magic, most people not knowing how either was performed; indeed any remarkable performance with a secular background . . . might be called a miracle." Tatlock, *Legendary History*, 362–363. "It is of course notoriously difficult . . . to say where religion becomes magic: the genuine Middle English charms (like many of their predecessors in Old English) use much religious imagery." Douglas Gray, *Themes and Images in the Medieval English Religious Lyric* (London, 1972), 34. See also Jean-Claude Schmitt, "Les Traditions Folkloriques dans la Culture Médiévale," *Archives de Sciences Sociales des Religions*, LII (1981), 5–20, a reference I owe to Keith Thomas.

8. Jean Delumeau, *Catholicism between Luther and Voltaire: A New View of the Counter-Reformation* (London, 1977), 63.

Before the century ended, this mentality began to fall apart. Witch-craft, prophecy, and portents came under attack from a coalition of scientists, freethinkers, and clergy (especially Anglicans) who wanted to discredit them as "superstitions." The world lost its enchantment as the realm of nature became separate from the realm of spirit. Comets lost their role as portents; a Harvard graduate of another generation spurned this old belief in an essay published in 1719. Wonder tales, and the mentality embedded in them, lived on but now more clearly in the form of fringe or lower-class beliefs.[9] No learned man dared take the point of view that Increase Mather had assumed in 1684. In its own day, the wonder tale united what became sundered in the eighteenth century. Living as we do on the further side of disenchantment, it is not easy to reenter a world where matter and spirit were interlinked, where "superstitions" remained credible. But therein lies the challenge of the wonder.

9. [Thomas Robie], *A Letter to a Certain Gentleman, &c.* (Boston, 1719), 8; J. F. C. Harrison, *The Second Coming: Popular Millenarianism, 1780–1850* (London, 1979), chap. 3.

**⊸⊷ ROBERT ST. GEORGE ⊷⊶**

# "Heated" Speech and Literacy in Seventeenth-Century New England

Is the Tongue a Linguist? Many times it speaketh
more Languages than is fit.[1]

AS historians gradually recognize the complexity of everyday life
in the past, their attention to the study of communication as
a formative basis of social structure increases. Within the
past decade the study of communication from an historical viewpoint
has centered on literacy. Studies of the distribution and consequences
of literacy skills, in particular, have demonstrated the implications of
reading and writing for the diffusion of popular religious beliefs and
political ideologies, debated whether or not reformed Protestantism
was a "cause" of widespread education in the early modern West,
correlated the presence of basic skills and the order in which they
are learned to occupational success and emergent social class distinctions, and even shown that the ability to write may have affected
the way a person remembered his or her own upbringing.[2] In dif-

1. George Web, *The Araignment of an unruly Tongue* (London, 1619), 72. I am indebted to David Grayson Allen and David D. Hall for reading an earlier draft of this
essay, and to John Murrin, Stephen Foster, John Demos, Susan Amussen, and John
Brooke for their comments when the paper was presented. I am also grateful to the
American Antiquarian Society for supporting me while researching this paper with
an Albert Boni Fellowship.
2. See, for example, David D. Hall, "The World of Print and Collective Mentality
in Seventeenth-Century New England," in John Higham and Paul Conkin, eds., *New
Directions in American Intellectual History* (Baltimore, 1979), 166–180; Hall, "Literacy,
Religion, and the Plain Style," in Jonathan L. Fairbanks and Robert F. Trent, eds.,
*New England Begins: The Seventeenth Century*, 3 vols. (Boston, 1982), II, 102–112;

Robert Blair St. George is Assistant Professor of American Studies at Boston University.

ferent ways, this new body of work focuses critical attention on the difficulties of equating literacy, per se, with an abstract process of "modernization" that plagued much of the writings completed during the 1950's and 1960's on the advancement of "peasant" cultures to "civilization."[3] But what remains surprising in much historical work is that, in exploring the meaning of transitions from "oral culture" to "written culture," the meaning and function of speech either has been taken for granted as an historical constant or else has been overlooked.

After all, we are taught in school that speech constitutes a "premodern" form beyond which we have progressed in our concern for written words that have the power to decontextualize and decentralize knowledge itself. Yet even in literate societies, speech continues to be a fundamental component in the routine shaping of social reality. And in some historical communities—like seventeenth-century New England—speech remained the principal means of discourse simply because large segments of the population, especially women, were illiterate. Indeed, the study of speech is so crucial to the study of reading and writing that these processes should be approached as an ethnographic totality; since the acquisition of speech typically occurs prior to either reading or writing, part of the context of the latter skills is speech itself. Although educators, anthropologists, and linguists have long recognized the interdependency of speaking, reading, and writing, historians have been reluctant to see it as central to the questions they have in mind.[4]

---

Kenneth A. Lockridge, *Literacy in Colonial New England* (New York, 1974), 43–71; Egil Johansson, "The History of Literacy in Sweden," in Harvey J. Graff, ed., *Literacy and Social Development in the West* (Cambridge, 1981), 151–182; Graff, *The Literacy Myth: Literacy and Social Structure in the Nineteenth-Century City* (New York, 1979); and Margaret Spufford, "First Steps in Literacy: The Reading and Writing Experiences of the Humblest Seventeenth-Century Spiritual Autobiographers," *Social History* IV (1979), 407–435.

3. See the sections on literacy in Everett M. Rogers and Lynne Svenning, *Modernization Among Peasants: The Impact of Communication* (New York, 1963), 51–95, esp. 94: "most important was a general motivation for modernization, perhaps typified by one peasant who said he enrolled 'to come from darkness into light'"; Alex Inkeles and David H. Smith, *Becoming Modern* (Cambridge, Mass., 1974); and Charles Tilly, "Talking Modern," *Peasant Studies* VI (1977), 66–68.

4. Historians should read: Michael Stubbs, *Language and Literacy: The Sociolinguistics*

Their hesitancy surely is related in part to a perceived lack in precise documentation. Unlike written or material artifacts, speech is by definition ephemeral. Once uttered, the word totally disappears. Or does it?

On 25 June 1661, Beatrice Canterbury of Salem, Massachusetts, stood before the local magistrates to answer a charge "for wicked and reviling speeches toward her son-in-law," one Benjamin Woodrow. By slandering and cursing him, she had hoped to convince her daughter Rebecca that her choice of a husband was unacceptable. Over the next few weeks, some of Canterbury's neighbors submitted depositions, essentially their own stories of what had happened early that June. One of them, written by Elizabeth Buxton, herself an exceptional Salem goodwife for her ability to write a clear hand, explained how

she heard her say to her daughter that [']her husband was both a rogue and a thiefe,['] her daughter sayd [']she must prove it['] she sayd [']he was a thiefe for that he had stolen the best flower in her garden, & a rogue because he had brought her body to shame['] saying she [']did thinke the divel would picke his bones['] this deponent sayd unto her [']she did not wel to speak so to her daughter agaynst her husband. but you should doe him the best good you can & give him good counsel for now he is your

---

of *Reading and Writing* (London, 1980); John Oxenham, *Literacy: Writing, Reading and Social Organization* (London, 1980); David Silverman and Brian Torode, *The Material Word: Some Theories of Language and its Limits* (London, 1980); John F. Szwed, "The Ethnography of Literacy," in Marcia Farr Whiteman, ed., *Writing: Functional and Linguistic-Cultural Differences* (New York, 1982), I, 13–23; Dell Hymes, *Foundations in Sociolinguistics: An Ethnographic Approach* (Philadelphia, 1974), 1–66, 125–142; and Keith Basso, "The Ethnography of Writing," in Richard Bauman and Joel Sherzer, eds., *Explorations in the Ethnography of Speaking* (Cambridge, 1974), 425–432. Two excellent works by historians draw upon this literature: Richard Bauman, "Speaking in the Light: The Role of the Quaker Minister," in Bauman and Sherzer, *Explorations in the Ethnography of Speaking*, 144–162; and Peter Burke, "Language and Anti-Language in Early Modern Italy," *History Workshop*, XI (1981), 24–32. Hall, "The World of Print and Collective Mentality in Seventeenth-Century New England" envisions the historian's task as describing the totalizing nature of communication in the past; he urges systematic investigation "to describe the formulas, the assumptions, that comprise collective mentality in seventeenth-century New England" (p. 176). The political implications of describing any really *collective* mentality in colonial America have yet to be discussed fully; see the comments in Carlo Ginzburg, *The Cheese and the Worms: The Cosmos of a Sixteenth-Century Miller*, trans. John Tedeschi and Anne Tedeschi (New York, 1982), xiii–xxvi.

son[']: she the sayd Cantlebery's wife answered that [']the divel should picke his bones before she would owne him to be her son.[']⁵

Like all court documents, this one is written. Yet, as indicated by the inserted quotation marks, it contains six passages from a completed and *spoken* conversation. Although writing invariably imposed a filter of memory and form on the original spoken text and probably transformed its exact syntax and presentational style, what remains is at least the "said" of speech—the actual words that qualified in seventeenth-century New England as sufficiently offensive to warrant legal action. And because Elizabeth Buxton made it very clear that such words occurred in spoken conversation, itself the principal genre in which seventeenth-century individuals constructed and maintained social reality, we can assume that such words conveyed specific social meanings they understood immediately.

Because court records provide the most detailed insight into seventeenth-century speech, this essay on the nature and meaning of speech in seventeenth-century New England naturally relies on the kinds of words that landed their speakers in court. Illegal speech acts were as base as sermons and prayers were eloquent, but, by defining the inverse of appropriate action, they reveal just as powerfully the underlying values of early New England culture. More specifically, the detailed analysis of the court records of Essex County, Massachusetts, between 1640 and 1680 suggests that offensive speech was crucial in defining the respective gender domains of men and women; recognition of the rules underlying these expressive domains in turn helps lead to a systematic and unified conception of literacy in past life by suggesting connections between the social meanings of spoken and written communication. Yet before addressing these issues, we must realize that attitudes toward speaking are not historically constant. Seventeenth-century people in both old and New England had a conception of speech very different from our own. To them, speech

5. Records and files of the Quarterly Courts of Essex County, Massachusetts, typescript copy made by Archie N. Frost, 1930–1934, on deposit at the Essex Institute, Salem, Massachusetts, VII, 40, dated 13 November 1661. See also George Francis Dow, ed., *Records and Files of the Quarterly Courts of Essex County, Massachusetts*, 8 vols. (Salem, 1911–1921), II, 340.

seemed inherently more mysterious, dangerous, and "real" than it does today.

In his lengthy book, *The Araignment of an unruly Tongue* (1619), George Web offered his readers a description of the human tongue, the organ responsible for speech. Like other seventeenth-century ministers who addressed the subject, he admitted the contradictory properties of the tongue—and of speech by implication—when he warned:

It is a *Fountaine*, whence *waters flow both sweet and bitter*, It is a *Forge* both of *Blessing* and *Cursing*, It is a *Shop* both of *precious Balme* and *deadly Poyson*, It is the *Trouchman* both of *Truth* and *Error: Fire* and *Water* are enclosed in it, *Life* and *Death* are in the power of it; It is a necessarie good, but an *Unruly* evill, very profitable, but exceeding hurtfull.[6]

The repeated image of unresolved opposition is a dominant theme in seventeenth-century treatises on speech and its attendant evils: fire and water, forge and fountain, sweet and bitter, life and death, good and evil. On the one hand, speech was the single human faculty that contemporary authors seized upon as the touchstone of man's superior intellect and ordained dominance over lesser creatures of the earth. In cataloging the properties of the tongue, seventeenth-century ministers praised it as the interpreter and controller of worldly affairs. The ability to speak, they argued, proclaimed man's rationality and mastery of his environment. On the other hand, speech was the source of misrule and social conflict most difficult to control. Indeed, seventeenth-century individuals thought it a supreme irony that so small an organ as the tongue could prove to be so dangerous. "It is easier to tame a wild *horse*, than a wild *Tongue*," wrote Web. "We put bits . . . in horses mouthes [so] that they may obey us; and *wee turne about their whole body: but the Tongue can no man tame*." He went on to quote one authority who claimed that "Halfe the sinnes of our life . . . are committed by the tongue," and another whose verdict was grimmer still: "there is no wrong or injurie done in the world, but first or last the tongue hath a share in the same."[7]

---

6. Web, *The Araignment of an unruly Tongue*, 2–3, paraphrasing liberally from Proverbs 18:21.
7. Web, *The Araignment of an unruly Tongue*, 87.

Of immediate concern to communities in seventeenth-century New England was the subversive threat that speech posed to social order. Fully cognizant of such danger, the leaders of Massachusetts Bay took prompt action to insure that the General Laws of 1641 included punishments specific to lying, blasphemy, cursing, slander, and swearing. After all, as one author had warned, "It is the tongue which breaketh the peace between neighbours," and peaceful cooperation was vital to the establishment of permanent English settlement.[8] Speech was particularly dangerous because it seemed to defy predictable categorization according to the social class of the speaker. It affected all men. "Lamentable and fearful is the abuse of the tongue among *all sorts and degrees of men* everywhere," observed William Perkins in 1615.[9] And how could one logically expect any man to keep a constant watch over his speech? "Hee is a perfect man that can rule his Tongue,"[1] and all men were imperfect by nature.

Because illicit speech fell outside their hierarchic view of social character, seventeenth-century people thought it anomalous and fundamentally indeterminate. The metaphors used by contemporary authors to describe the tongue dramatize the belief they and their audience shared in its likelihood to lead to spiritual downfall and social heresy. The tongue was considered a "witch," a "practiser of poysonings," a "box of poison," a murderer that cuts "like a *Rasor*," "the first corrupting Instrument," the "unruliest member" that "defiles the whole body," an arrow, a hammer, a sword, a traitor, a "common pickpurse," and a "notorious Robber." Speech itself was thought "*harder to be tamed . . . than a strong City is to be conquered.*"[2] All of these images refer to destruction; weapons, poison, pollution, and,

---

8. See *The Book of the General Lawes and Libertyes Concerning the Inhabitants of the Massachusetts*, ed. Thomas G. Barnes (San Marino, Cal., 1975 [orig. publ. Cambridge, Mass., 1648]), 1, 5, 6, 35–36, 45; Web, *The Araignment of an unruly Tongue*, 28.

9. William Perkins, *A Direction for the government of the Tonge according to Gods word* (London, 1615), sig. A2. Emphasis added.

1. Web, *The Araignment of an unruly Tongue*, 144–145.

2. These metaphors are drawn from: Web, *The Araignment of an unruly Tongue*; William Ward, *Gods Arrowes, or, Two Sermons, concerning the visitation of God by the Pestilence* (London, 1607); and from Robert Boyle, *A free discourse against Customary Swearing* (London, 1695).

finally, socially liminal creatures who were believed to destroy society itself.

Beneath the circulation of ministerial tracts warning people to mind their words, a few unanswered questions compounded the mystery of speech in the minds of seventeenth-century New Englanders. What "caused" such verbal outbreaks? Was it Satan acting through man's body? Or did words come from man's own mind? Indeed, what part of the human body controlled what was said? Although it remains difficult to know the perceived causes in every case, one general fact does seem clear—all of the words to which people reacted in an adverse way were spoken in the context of anger and hostility, and such aggression seems to have been a constant and almost inescapable presence in early New England communities.[3]

Seventeenth-century people viewed being angry or "in a passion," as it was often called, as a temporary condition in which an individual's rational understanding and will gave way to the momentary influence of his senses, believed to be the source of emotion. Under normal conditions, reason held the senses in check. But when the latter gained control because of an imbalance of bodily humors, people were prone to utter words which they had not sufficiently pre-meditated and controlled for situational propriety. Passion, like anger, seventeenth-century people believed,

is no other thing, but a motion of the sensitive appetite, caused by the apprehension or imagination of good or evill, the which is followed with a change or alteration in the body, contrary to the Lawes of Nature. Whereby it appeares, that passions, to speak properly, reside onely in the sensitive appetite, and that they are not fashioned [except] in the irrationall part of the soule.[4]

If "passion" was a state that witnessed the emergent dominance of irrationality, it also admitted momentary flashes of *uncontrolled* speech as part of the "change or alteration in the body" it produced. In

---

3. On aggression in seventeenth-century New England life, see John Demos, *A Little Commonwealth: Family Life in the Plymouth Colony* (New York, 1970), 49, 135–138.

4. Nicholas Coeffeteau, *A table of humane passions* (London, 1621), 2–3.

Newbury, Massachusetts, in August 1679, Caleb Moody complained that William Fanning and his wife swore they would knock out his brains and cripple his wife. Two maidservants also heard Fanning curse. When brought to court, Fanning realized he had no defense and admitted "that in his passion he might have done these things,"[5] the implication being that curses and threats accompanied a loss of memory when a person's awareness of social restraints fell victim to his senses.

If hostile words and deeds resulted from being in a passion, which in turn was associated with the "sensitive appetite" and by extension the "irrationall part of the soule," where in the body was the source of the actual aggressive words? In diagnosing disorderly speech, some seventeenth-century physicians relied exclusively on the findings of Galen, whose explanations of speech control and impairment in the second century A.D. were among the first to derive from anatomical experimentation and exploration. Galenic tradition maintained that speech was the messenger of the soul, and since both the rational and irrational parts of the soul were believed located in the ventricles of the brain, speech of any kind was thought to originate in the head. From this point of view, aggressive speech uttered in an impassioned state came as well from the head, since it sprang from the irrational segment of the soul. Galen asserted this theory against his colleagues who believed in the cardiac location of the soul. In addition, a long-standing tradition of medical investigation prior to the seventeenth century demonstrated that both anger and offensive speech could be traced to a temporary physiological imbalance in which the choleric or sanguine humors were dominant. From this perspective, seventeenth-century individuals believed that angry speech was intrinsically hot and dry and that defective or impaired speech (e.g., stammering or aphonia), was by definition hot and

5. *Essex County Court Records*, VII, 381. The relationship between anger and aggressive speech is also discussed in *The Testaments of the twelve Patriarchs, the Sonnes of Jacob*, trans. Robert Grosthead (London, 1601), sig. Gvi, in "The Testamente of Dan . . . concerning anger & lying": "Wherefore consider the power of wrath how vaine it is, For he is bitter in speech, and walketh at sathans right hande, that his deedes may be wrought in untrustinesse and lying, so sathan dooeth first of all sting him by speech."

moist.[6] In both cases, the presence of heat was universally recognized and accepted. Aggressive speech was "heated" speech.

To this explanation of "heated" speech seventeenth-century Puritans grafted beliefs derived from biblical exegesis that connected speech with emotion and located both the emotions and the "irrationall part of the soule" in the heart, in direct contradiction to Galenic theory. William Perkins, an English clergyman whose works circulated widely in seventeenth-century New England, urged members of his congregation to contrition by reminding them "the pure heart is most necessary becausest *it is the fountain of speech*"; his colleague William Ward agreed, stating that "a man (because of *the aboundance of the heart the mouth speaketh*) may know . . . the Children of the Divell by their Speech."[7] Seventeenth-century residents of Essex County shared the belief that the "Children of the Divell" used heated speech, a conviction which lay beneath the frequent analogy they made between the heat of speech, the fires of hell, and Satan himself. In 1660, Samuel Graves of Ipswich said he heard John Pindar "use the devil in his mouth often times . . . in such words as were not fit to be spoken"; the wife of William Ellet told another Lynn woman that she "was a fire brand of hell for her lying tongue"; and two Essex County women were described by a neighbor in 1657 as being "in combustion" when, in the course of arguing, one had called the other a "lousie slutt."[8] Speaking of cursers, another English divine said it seemed "as if their throats were Hell it selfe."[9]

Finally, seventeenth-century people thought any tongue that spoke heated words was filled with poison, and a distant cousin to the venomous mouth of that Edenic serpent whose wicked words had led men astray for eternity. "The tongue is a fire," wrote St. James,

6. Ynez Violé O'Neill, *Speech and Speech Disorders in Western Thought Before 1600* (Westport, Conn., 1980), 59–60, 109–110.

7. Perkins, *A Direction for the government of the Tonge*, sig. A3v; Ward, *Gods Arrowes*, 6. See also Thomas Adams, "The Taming of the Tongue" in *The Works of Thomas Adams*, ed. Joseph Angus, 3 vols. (Edinburgh, 1861–1862), III, 20: "Swearers, railers, scoldes have hell-fire in their tongues."

8. *Essex County Court Records*, I, 133; II, 166, 248.

9. Thomas Beard, *The Theatre of Gods Iudgments* (London, 1631), 179. I am indebted to David D. Hall for this reference.

"and setteth on fire the course of nature; and it is set on fire of hell
. . . *it is an unruly evil, full of deadly poison.*"[1] Selectively fusing some
parts of Galenic tradition with biblical mandate, seventeenth-century New Englanders conceived of emotion, the devil, fire, and the
heart as interrelated, immanent in passion, and concretely enacted in
heated speech. From Galen they took the idea of impassioned speech
being caused by the elemental heat of humoral imbalance. And while
they followed his suggestion that the rational soul was located in the
head, they clung to biblical teachings claiming the heart as the source
of emotion and hence of irrationality. While a lack of documentation makes it difficult to trace out these beliefs in detail, there is no
doubt that people in seventeenth-century Essex County believed
that the tongue spoke what the heart commanded; in Ipswich in
1668, Robert Cross and his wife Anna reported how one night they
heard Thomas Wells call another man "a common liar" and say
"that it cannot enter in to the heart of a man to conseve[,] neather
in the Tongue of man to expresse the wickednesse yt is in him."[2]

The mystery of heated speech—its apparently universal usage and
the rich overlay of classical and Christian explanations for its etiol-
ogy—contributed to its being thought extremely unpredictable and
dangerous in seventeenth-century New England. For the same reasons, the colonists thought of the human mouth as richly symbolic.
When nineteen-year-old Mary Langley of Lynn described Richard
Haven's verbal attack on her father for having lamed his hogs in
March 1663, she noted that after the assailant yelled "thou rogue I
could find [it] in my heart to spill thy heart blood upon the ground
thou rogue thou," he "foomed at the mouth,"[3] a sure sign of his
being out of control and markedly "animal" or irrational in his behavior. The angry man, wrote the Puritan divine John Robinson,

1. Quoted in John Webster Spargo, *Juridical Folklore in England, Illustrated by the
Cucking-Stool* (Durham, N.C., 1944), 106. I am indebted to David D. Hall for this
reference. See also the ballad quoted on p. 312, n. 8.

2. *Essex County Court Records*, IV, 49. Perkins, *A Direction for the government of the
Tonge*, sig. A2, adds that it would make "a mans heart to bleed to heare and consider
how Swearing, Blaspheming, Cursed speaking, Railing, Slandering, chiding, Quarreling, Contending, Iesting, Mocking, Flattering, Lying, Dissembling, [and] Vaine
and Idle talking overflow in al places."

3. *Essex County Court Records*, III, 33.

appears with *"his lips fumbling*, his face pale, *his teeth gnashing, his mouth foaming*, and other parts of his body trembling and shaking."[4] In addition, frequent references to biting, sucking, and eating in witchcraft narratives make explicit the crucial relationship that seventeenth-century Essex County residents saw between evil and the mouth, an association made more perplexing because, paradoxically, it was also through the mouth of man that God made His Word known in a region that remained only about sixty-percent literate until the second decade of the eighteenth century.[5]

The tension in all speech—that it could, depending on circumstances largely unseen and wholly unknowable to man, burst forth as either blessed or sinful, reasoned or irrational, from the head or from the heart—led seventeenth-century people to pay extremely close attention to all utterances. Speech was a principal sign of the progress in the ongoing battle between God and Satan in which all men were soldiers. It both conveyed the Word of God and belched forth the flames of hell. When speech itself stopped, the silence that intervened was no less studied. God's order resulted in peace among men, and "peace in effect," wrote one English legal authority, "is the amitie, confidence, and *quiet* that is between men, And he that breaketh this amitie or *quiet* breaketh the peace."[6] At the same time, the loss of speech could also result from drunkenness, traumatic response to physical violence, or insanity. One Salem woman was discovered in 1680 "in a senceless stupifyed condition not able to speak one word."[7] Instances of dramatic and sudden aphonia were all the

4. Quoted in Demos, "Demography and Psychology in the Historical Study of Family Life: A Personal Report," in Peter Laslett and Richard Wall, eds., *Household and Family in Past Time* (Cambridge, 1972), 568.

5. On seventeenth-century orality, see Demos, "Underlying Themes in the Witchcraft of Seventeenth-Century New England," *American Historical Review*, LXXV (1970), 1323–1324. The literacy level of Essex County is estimated on the basis of signatures in Lockridge, *Literacy in Colonial New England*, 20, 47–48. Literacy remained at 60% until circa 1715 and then increased dramatically to near universal literacy; see also pp. 316–317, below.

6. Michael Dalton, *The Countrey Justice* (New York, 1972 [orig. publ. London, 1622]), 7.

7. *Essex County Court Records*, VIII, 59; see also O'Neill, *Speech and Speech Disorders*, 62. Other causes of aphonia cited in Essex County records included fear and apparitions of supernatural creatures (*Essex County Court Records*, VII, 421; II, 159; V, 221,

more worrisome because of popular beliefs that the loss of speech was a sign that God was punishing man for a specific speech offense. Consider the case of the widow Anne Averies, an unfortunate London woman,

who *foreswore* [perjured] herselfe for a little money that she should have paid for six pounds of tow at a shop in Woodstreet: for which cause being suddenly surprised with the justice of God, she *fel down speechlesse forthwith*, and cast up at her mouth in great aboundance, and with horrible stinke, that matter which by natures course should have been voided downewards, and so died, to the terrour of all perjured and foresworne wretches.[8]

Because speech defied prior categorization as either blessed or sinful, it framed and helped mark aggressive social encounters as essentially unpredictable. As soon as someone opened his mouth, no one could guarantee whether God or Satan stood behind what might issue forth. Because the act of speaking itself was endowed at every word with cosmic significance that fell outside man's ability and logic to control, it momentarily suspended the determinacy of existing social reality, leaving an opportunity for personal relations among friends, neighbors, and enemies not only to be redefined, but also actively destroyed.

Within this view of speech, the actual words exchanged in seventeenth-century Essex County warrant attention in three principal ways. First, we must examine how seventeenth-century people classified acts of heated speech. Here the records offer many clues; they specify twelve different kinds of "heated" language, sixty-nine dis-

---

266). For additional thoughts on the cultural function of silence—an understudied topic—see Keith Basso, "To Give Up on Words: Silence in the Western Apache Culture," *Southwestern Journal of Anthropology*, XXVI (1970), 213–230, and Susan U. Phillips, "Participant Structures and Communication Competence: Warm Springs Children in Community and Classroom," in Courtney B. Cazden, Vera P. John, and Dell Hymes, eds., *Functions of Language in the Classroom* (New York, 1972), 370–394.

8. Beard, *Theatre of Gods Iudgments*, 178. Compare this to the story of Thomas Arundel in Web, *The Araignment of an unruly Tongue*, 122, "who having abused his Toung to an uniust sentence against the Lord *Cobham*, was stricken with soe sore a paine and swelling in his Tongue, that he could *neither swallow nor speake*." O'Neill, *Speech and Speech Disorders*, 182, cites another story about an Italian nobleman who lost both his memory and speech after being hit on the head. The seventeenth-century belief that memory and speech were controlled by the same part of the brain underlies their preference to read and write aloud.

tinct types of "heated" speech or ways of speaking, and twenty-seven
additional kinds of words considered sufficiently vicious to warrant
legal action by their listeners (see Appendix 1). Yet the actual structures of heated speech also fit into prevailing legal definitions, and
we must describe in detail their intersection. Second, we need to
chart the overall pattern of speech transgressions. Did, for example,
one kind of offense increase steadily as another declined, and if so,
what might this suggest about the changing social basis of litigation?
Finally, we need to explore the meanings of the offensive words
themselves, what kinds of punishment they received, and how they
functioned to establish the respective speech domains of men and
women.

County courts in seventeenth-century New England considered
presentments for heated speech either as criminal offenses or as civil
offenses (Figure 24). A criminal case resulted when an individual
spoke out in one of two ways. On the one hand, swearing or cursing
constituted *blasphemy* because the speaker was presuming to control
the will of God in attempting to execute against other men judgments reserved in the Old Testament (Deuteronomy 28:15–20) for
His wisdom alone.[9] On the other hand, *sedition* included any speeches
that protested or rebuked institutional authority and, by implication,
the implicit authority of God's patriarchal prerogative as embodied
in the secular affairs of men. Civil cases involved speech offenses in
which one individual took another to court seeking satisfaction for
one of two kinds of "damage" or destruction that resulted from
verbal assault. *Immanent destruction*, or damage that one person would
invoke or promise to another, consisted of *threats*. Similar in some
respects to curses in their wish that harm would indeed occur, threats
were less serious because they suggested only that disaster would
come at the hands of man. Opposed to immanent destruction was
*enacted destruction*, which in turn involved specific words that *de-*

9. On the role of blasphemy in reformed Protestant culture, see Leonard W. Levy,
*Treason Against God: A History of the Offense of Blasphemy* (New York, 1981), 122–
330. Blasphemy was a capital offense in Massachusetts Bay; see *Lawes and Libertyes*,
ed. Barnes, 5, and the Old Testament text upon which the colonial law was based,
Leviticus 24:15–16.

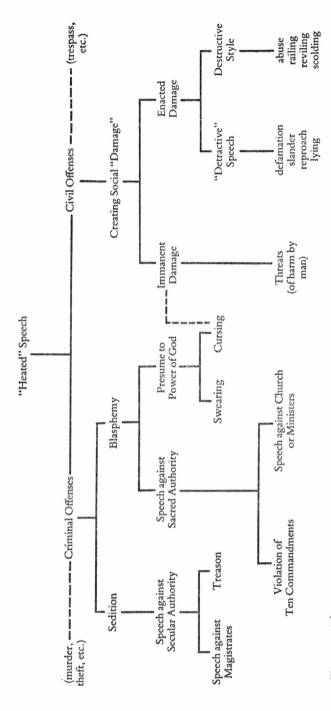

Figure 24. The Structure of "Heated" Speech in Seventeenth-century New England and its Location in Contemporary Law (use with Tables 1 and 2).

## TABLE 1

Presentments for "Heated" Speech in Essex County, Massachusetts, 1640–1680.*

| Offense | 1640–1650 | | 1651–1660 | | 1661–1670 | | 1671–1680 | | Total | |
|---|---|---|---|---|---|---|---|---|---|---|
| | No. | ( %) | No. | ( %) | No. | ( %) | No. | ( %) | No. | ( %) |
| Criminal | 161 | ( 62.2) | 69 | ( 41.8) | 112 | ( 56.9) | 151 | ( 64.3) | 493 | ( 57.6) |
| Civil | 98 | ( 37.8) | 96 | ( 58.2) | 85 | ( 43.1) | 84 | ( 35.7) | 363 | ( 42.4) |
| Total | 259 | (100.0) | 165 | (100.0) | 197 | (100.0) | 235 | (100.0) | 856 | (100.0) |

* For explanations of what the respective categories of criminal and civil offenses included, see Figure 24 and pp. 287–290, above.

## TABLE 2

Presentments for "Heated" Speech in Essex County, Massachusetts, 1640–1680: Civil Offenses.†

| Offense | 1640–1650 | | 1651–1660 | | 1661–1670 | | 1671–1680 | | Total | |
|---|---|---|---|---|---|---|---|---|---|---|
| | No. | ( %) | No. | ( %) | No. | ( %) | No. | ( %) | No. | ( %) |
| Threats | 7 | ( 7.1) | 8 | ( 8.3) | 9 | ( 10.6) | 14 | ( 16.7) | 38 | ( 10.5) |
| "Detractive" Speech | 84 | ( 85.8) | 76 | ( 79.2) | 62 | ( 72.9) | 49 | ( 58.3) | 271 | ( 74.6) |
| Destructive style | 7 | ( 7.1) | 12 | ( 12.5) | 14 | ( 16.5) | 21 | ( 25.0) | 54 | ( 14.9) |
| Total | 98 | (100.0) | 96 | (100.0) | 85 | (100.0) | 84 | (100.0) | 363 | (100.0) |

†George Francis Dow, ed., *Records and Files of the Quarterly Courts of Essex County, Massachusetts*, 8 vols. (Salem, 1911–1921).

*tracted* from an individual's livelihood, and *destructive styles* of verbal assault that qualified as damaging in their own right.

Under seventeenth-century English law, the words defined as "actionable" in cases of defamation, slander, or reproach had to fulfill stringent criteria. According to one treatise of the 1640's, legal arguments could only cite as actionable

> scandalous words which touch or concern a man in his life, liberty or member, or any corporall punishment; or which scandal a man in his office or place of trust; or in his calling or function by which he gains his living; or which tend to the slandering of his title or any other particular damage; or lastly which charge a man to have any dangerous infectious disease by reason of which he ought to separate himselfe, or to be separated by the law, from the society of men.[1]

"Damage," in other words, resulted from any malicious speech that led the plaintiff to a position of social stigma because of an enforced moral distance, economic hardship, or physical exclusion. Since any one of these charges could result in real *temporal* damage to the defendant, they were heard and acted upon by the court of common law.

Beginning early in the seventeenth century some English magistrates began hearing arguments maintaining that a damaged reputation warranted legal action in that it, too, could directly affect one's social position. "Where the words spoken do tend to the infamy, discredit, or disgrace of the party, there the words shall be actionable," wrote one judge in a decision of 1611, while another pronounced that "whenever words tended to take away a man's reputation he would encourage actions for them, because so doing would contribute much to the preservation of the peace."[2] The resulting liberal extension of defamation under the common law was the norm in seventeenth-century New England, and most of the civil cases brought before the quarterly courts of Essex County sought damages from

---

1. Quoted in William S. Hollingsworth, *A History of English Law*, 12 vols. (Boston, 1908–1938), VIII, 347. "Scandal" is related etymologically to "slander" (O.E.D.). The movement of defamation cases from ecclesiastical to common law courts is outlined in Ronald A. Marchant, *The Church Under the Law: Justice, Administration and Discipline in The Diocese of York 1560–1640* (Cambridge, 1969), 12–85; I am indebted to Stephen Foster for this reference.

2. Quoted in Hollingsworth, *A History of English Law*, VIII, 352, n. 6.

the "theft" of reputation, itself an intangible form of property, by a townsman with a heated tongue. The idea that defamation, slander, and reproach were united conceptually by the "theft" each implied was recognized during the period. "The Tongue is a common *pick-purse*," wrote one author, who went on to explain that such robbery took three principal forms—taking a man's name, his goods, and, in dire instances, his life. And, like defamation, slander, and reproach, lying was also a kind of theft because it robbed a situation of its truth.[3]

A less complicated category, comprised of how such thefts were actually said, involved transgressions against appropriate verbal *style*: abuse, railing, reviling, and scolding. All of these seem to have combined a harshly negative tone with loud yelling and screaming. Such rude and sharp remarks offered corrective discipline and conveyed the intensity of outright anger itself.

These three types of civil offenses did not always appear as singular phenomena. In many instances they erupted simultaneously. In 1647 Robert Blood of Lynn answered charges for "abusing Henry Rodes" in "threatening him"; twenty years later a servant "was convicted . . . of railing and threatening speeches against the country and his master, threatening to kill him ['I will have the hart blood of thee or thine . . .'], and other gross abuses offered to his dame."[4]

If we compare the relative rates of presentment for criminal and civil offenses, the former remained statistically dominant in Essex County between 1640 and 1680, except for a slight reversal in the 1650's (Table 1). Within the range of civil presentments alone (Table 2), offenses for detractive speech consistently comprised almost seventy-five percent of all cases, although its relative dominance slipped steadily from over eighty-five percent in the 1640's to just over fifty-five percent in the 1670's. And while it declined, presentments for threats and destructive style steadily increased. Taken together, the rates of presentment for heated speech suggest there may have existed subtle shifts of emphasis within specific genres of crime that offer

---

3. Web, *The Araignment of an unruly Tongue*, 23–24; Demos, *Entertaining Satan: Witchcraft and the Culture of Early New England* (New York, 1982), 79.

4. *Essex County Court Records*, I, 285; III, 376.

clues to underlying social change. For example, when the shifting rates of presentment for speech offenses in seventeenth-century Essex County are correlated with the rapid rise in the area's population beginning in the late 1650's,[5] the real drop in the rate of presentments as a whole appears dramatic. And within the overall drop in the frequency of civil presentments, the emphasis shifts from the extremely high rate of "detractive" speech in the 1640's to the comparatively high rates of threats and destructive style in the 1670's. Against the steady backdrop of criminal cases, civil complaints shift from the very direct assault on reputation explicit in defamations to an increasingly indirect or less engaged type of damage suggested by threats and verbal abuse.

These patterns suggest that the particular way people chose to channel interpersonal aggression may have changed during the seventeenth century. Due to the mechanics of settlement, the adjustment of English regional models for daily life, and the pressures of establishing new reputations among total strangers, people in the 1640's were more likely to use defamation as a means of claiming social turf. As society became more firmly established, the pattern quickly reversed. Increasingly competitive for status within the context of more densely overlapping kinship and economic networks, people in the 1670's chose to tread more lightly on reputation *per se*, since words uttered in a moment of anger were ever more likely to land unintentionally on the ears of a distant cousin who would take immediate offense with family cohesion hanging precariously in the balance. Indeed, the presentments suggest that aggressive style and veiled threats were viewed as an increasingly effective form of reprimand in the more complex social web of the late 1670's, because these forms could openly express their speaker's displeasure without risking so great a potential change in his social identity.

5. On rising population density in the late seventeenth-century, see the summary offered in David Grayson Allen, "'*Vacuum Domicilium*': The Social and Cultural Landscape of Seventeenth-Century New England," in Fairbanks and Trent, eds., *New England Begins*, I, 7; data for specific towns appear in Susan L. Norton, "Population Growth in Colonial America: A Study of Ipswich, Massachusetts," *Population Studies*, XXV (1972), 433–452; and Lockridge, "The Population of Dedham, Massachusetts, 1636–1736," *Economic History Review*, 2nd Ser., XIX (1966), 319–344.

If the "said" of speech led to social strife, what were the words recognized as sufficiently powerful to provoke a legal contest? The words hurled in anger over hedgerows and fences were extremely redundant and elaborate, with extended lists suitable for men and women, respectively. Of a total of ninety principal words used in Essex County during the middle of the seventeenth century, fifty-eight were appropriate to men, thirty-two to women, while an additional six landed on the innocent ears of children. (See Table 3 and Appendix 2). Those used most frequently could be modified with additional pejoratives. "Dog" had five modifiers, including base, black, foresworn, and French, as well as close equivalents in five variants of "curr." Slut, pig, bawd, knave, and liar had three variants, witch had four, and devil had seven variants. Rogue occurred by itself and with any one or more of thirteen modifiers, including base, cheating, cowardly, long-shanked, thievish, old, and white-livered. The presence alone of such intensive descriptive attention to these key words suggests they may have been viewed as more dangerous in a cultural sense than other words. If we examine some of them in detail, we discover that they were so powerful and believed harmful in a very "real" sense because they made areas of cultural indeterminacy socially explicit.

TABLE 3

Damaging Words and Gender in Essex County,
Massachusetts, 1640–1680

| Type of word | Damage to: | | | |
| --- | --- | --- | --- | --- |
| | Man | Woman | Child | Total |
| Principal | 58 | 32 | 6 | 96 |
| Modifier | 63 | 25 | 1 | 89 |
| Total | 121 | 57 | 7 | 185* |

* N=185 (96.9%) of 191 known presentments (use with Appendix 2).

Take, for example, animal names. Two animals dominate the records: dogs (by variants of dog and cur) and pigs (by pig, sow, and hog). Animals in general and these two animals in particular derived their impact as pejoratives in part from the seventeenth-century belief that animals had no souls and therefore no chance for salvation. In a moment of spiritual despondence, John Bunyan admitted, "I blessed the condition of the Dogge and Toad . . . for I knew they had no Soul to perish under the everlasting weights of Hell for sin, as mine was like to do."[6] And seventeenth-century people who could read knew that the word "dog," God spelled backwards, itself was the Devil's handiwork. Animal terms also played on the deep ambivalence with which seventeenth-century Englishmen viewed domesticated creatures. Raising dogs for a purpose other than food or work, they allowed dogs into their homes and named them with affection. Dogs, at times, *seemed* almost human, but they lived off scraps thrown at random from their master's table. And both dogs and toads were classed as inedible. Dogs were subject to someone else's will for survival. They were both servile and dependent. "Curr" carried overt meanings of "low-class" or "ill-bred." For a man in seventeenth-century Essex County to be called a dog—and men alone were so named—implied that he was not economically self-sufficient, that he contributed nothing to his family's livelihood, that he had no hope for redemption, and that he might be working with Satan.

Women in Essex County took equal offense at being called a pig, sow, or hog. Pigs were raised for no reason other than to be slaughtered, unlike chickens, cows, goats, or sheep, which while alive could at least provide eggs, milk, cheese, butter, and fleece before being killed for meat. This alone made raising pigs a moral issue and put them in a strange ethical category within seventeenth-century thought. In addition, pigs in some parts of England were allowed into the farmer's house and fed from the table like dogs.[7] They were also among the beasts declared by God to be an abomination to his chosen people (Leviticus 11:7). Along with other prohibited animals, the pig was believed an incarnation of the Devil. When William Morse's house in Newbury was visited by spirits in late 1679, for example, he noted the recurrent appearance of hogs running in and out of his

6. John Bunyan, *Grace Abounding to the Chief of Sinners*, ed. Roger Sharrock (Oxford, 1962), 33.

7. Edmund Leach, "Language and Anthropology," in Noel Minnis, ed., *Linguistics at Large* (New York, 1971), 153–154. See also the discussion of animals and abomination in Mary Douglas, *Purity and Danger: An Analysis of the Concept of Pollution and Taboo* (London, 1966), 41–57.

house during day and night, despite the presence of locked doors in their path.[8] Pigs were unclean, dependent, exploited by men for their own benefit, and controlled by Satan. With these multiple meanings, the word "pig" was harmful to women not only as an immediate social pejorative, but also because it reminded them of their descent from Eve, the first woman to act out the will of the Devil to the detriment of all men.

Other words, used with a specific gender in mind, suggest a fundamental difference in the appropriate social roles of men and women. Men in particular found damaging any words which, like dog, pointed to economic weakness or pushed too far an unethical dependence on the good will of their neighbors. The word thief, while aimed on occasion at women, was used most frequently to damage a man; it implied a lack of willingness to provide for oneself the necessities of life. The thief or robber had a sinful heart. "The principal cause" of theft, claimed one minister,

is covetousnesse; which is so unruly an evill, and so deeply rooted in the heart of man, that ever yet it hath used to encroach upon the goods of others, & to keepe possession of that which was none of its owne; breaking all the bonds of humanitie, equitie, and right, without being contained in any measure or mean.[9]

Like dogs, thieves were economic parasites on other men, a fault viewed during the period as an admission of failure as an householder.

The moral implications of economic parasitism lay at the root of other words against men, of which rogue seems to have been the most often used in seventeenth-century Essex County. In order to understand the peculiar grip that a term like rogue had on early New Englanders, we need look no further than the writings of popular authors like Thomas Harman, John Awdely, or Robert Greene, whose books describing the habits and speech of vagabonds and other marginal characters in Elizabethan England portray their immoral and anti-social qualities in detail. Harman, for example, offers a definition of rogues as men who, merging mendicancy with transvestism,

8. *Essex County Court Records*, VII, 355–359. See the insightful analysis of the Morse witchcraft case in Demos, *Entertaining Satan*, 132–152.

9. Beard, *Theatre of Gods Iudgments*, 442.

will go fayntly and looke piteously, when they see, either meete any person, having a kercher . . . tyed aboute their heade, with a short staffe in their hand, halting, although they neede not, requiri[n]g almes of such as they meete, or to what house they shall come. But you may easely perceive by their colour, that they cary both health and hipocrisie about them, whereby they gette gain, when others want that cannot fayne and dissemble.[1]

For the majority of yeomen in Essex County, these creatures epitomized the social problems that over-crowding and emergent social class conflict had created in their home counties before emigration and which, they believed, the Devil was now using to stain the purity of their New Israel. Rogues, fellows, and knaves were suspicious men who did not own land, did not work, and survived off the labor (and Christian naïvete) of their neighbors. In *The Countrey Justice*, a legal treatise used in New England by local magistrates, Michael Dalton devoted several pages to the rogue, defining him in great detail as any person "offending as hereunder is mentioned":

All persons above the age of seven yeares, going about begging, upon any pretence or colour whatsoever.

All idle persons going about the countrie, either using any subtil craft, or unlawfull games, or being fortune tellers, or juglers, or using any other like crafty science.

All Pedlers, petie Chapmen, Tinkers, and Glasse men wandring about.

All wandring persons and common labourers, being able to [labor] in body, using loitering, and refusing to worke for reasonable wages, not having living otherwise than by labour to maintain themselves.

Poore persons.

Souldiors or mariners.

Poore diseased or impotent persons.

Persons infected, or dwelling in houses infected with the plague.

[And] all persons being able to labour, and thereby to relieve themselves and their families, that shall run away, or threaten to run away and leave their charge to the parish, &c.[2]

In short, the word "rogue" carried with it connotations of membership in all the injured classes of seventeenth-century society that the bourgeois yeoman resented having to support in a world of values

1. Thomas Harman, *A Caveat for Commen Cursetors* (London, 1567), sig. Ci.
2. Dalton, *The Countrey Justice*, 109–110.

that he had helped to make rigid and highly stratified. The rogue was a burden on others. He did not participate in an economy structured by the scarcity of land. He actively sought to avoid work. He wandered. He was poor, diseased, and with little or no guilt would desert his family if something better came along. He was a social failure, a puppet of Satan challenging the courage of the Christian soldier.

In contrast to the pejoratives aimed at economic self-sufficiency, occupational status, or physical strength as the basis of a man's reputation,[3] most slurs against women stressed bodily filth, sexual incontinency, and moral degeneracy. Typical words included "slut," "Jezabel," and "unchaste filthy creature." In addition, women were more often called "adultress," "bawd," "whore," and "hypocrite" than were men. All of these terms refer to moral infractions that contemporary authors—all of whom were men—cautioned women not to commit. "Adultery is forbidden," warned one writer, "and grievous threatnings denounced against all those that defile their bodies with filthie and unpure actions, estrange themselves from God."[4] A direct violation of the Seventh Commandment, adultery was socially dangerous because it sought to subvert the sexual prohibitions that insured the structure of kinship.

Closely related to adultery was prostitution, and anyone who acted as a procurer for that purpose was a bawd, and just as guilty in the eyes of God as the whores or "queanes" themselves. By calling a woman a "brazen-faced bawd" or a whore, one was by implication calling her house—her domain of work, child-rearing, and moral guidance—a place of prostitution. By further implication, her children born in that house were bastards; one seventeenth-century woman said that her neighbor "was a whore and that she had severall children by other men, and that Cuckoldlay old Rogue her husband owned them."[5] Bawds, whores, and adulterers engaged in duplici-

---

3. On the importance of physical strength to men's reputations, see the case in Marblehead in 1670 when William Hollingswood tried to draw Hezekiah Dutch into hand-to-hand combat by saying "if he would not fight him he would proclaim him a coward throughout the town"; *Essex County Court Records*, VII, 253.

4. Beard, *Theatre of Gods Iudgments*, 357.

5. Quoted in Roger Thompson, *Women in Stuart England and America: A Comparative Study* (Boston, 1974), 244.

tous social relations. They were distrusted and scorned as sinners. The same was true of hypocrites, who, being inauthentic in their worship, failed to live up to God's covenant with man.[6]

One of the most frequent modifiers that insulted men and women alike was "old." While being elderly in seventeenth-century New England commanded respect from some as a sign of being closer to death, salvation, and God, it was also a badge of weakness, vulnerability, a lack of sexual identity, and a dependency on grown children who often resented the strain an aged parent put on their own family life. Some children were able to articulate their resentment; John Paine, a carpenter in the Plymouth Colony, confided to his diary his disdain for "some older infirm person whose life is Even a burden to them Selves and they them Selves a burden & a trouble to all about them."[7] Perhaps Paine and others faced with caring for the elderly had encountered the anguish of watching a loved one lapse into senility. "A man in his old age, doe become a very childe again in his understanding," wrote Henry Swinburne late in the sixteenth century.[8] The dependency of old age and its accompanying physical decline reduced men to children and lay behind the occasional use of

6. Beard, *Theatre of Gods Iudgments*, 107, defines hypocrites as individuals who "have nothing in them but a vaine shew of coyned religion, and so by that meanes breake the first commandement; thinking to bleare Gods eyes with their outward shewes and ceremonies, as if he were like men, to see nothing but that which is without, and offereth it selfe to the view." For definitions of other seventeenth-century pejoratives, see: Joseph T. Shipley, *Dictionary of Early English* (New York, 1955); Walter W. Skeat, *A Glossary of Tudor and Stuart Words*, ed. A. L. Mayhew (Oxford, 1914); and James Orchard Halliwell-Phillips, *A Dictionary of Archaic and Provincial Words . . .*, 2 vols. (London, 1865). See also Roger Thompson, *Unfit For Modest Ears: A Study of Pornographic, Obscene, and Bawdy Works Written or Published in England in the Second Half of the Seventeenth Century* (London, 1979); and G. R. Quaife, *Wanton Wenches and Wayward Wives: Peasants and Illicit Sex in Early Seventeenth-Century England* (New Brunswick, N.J., 1979), 124–185.

7. "Deacon John Paine's Journal," *The Mayflower Descendant* IX, (1908–1909), 99. On the ambivalent and often conflicting views toward old age in seventeenth-century New England, see Demos, "Old Age in Early New England," in Demos and Sarane Spence Boocock, eds., *Turning Points: Historical and Sociological Essays on the Family*, supplement to the *American Journal of Sociology*, LXXXIV (1978), S248–287; and Gene W. Boyett, "Aging in Seventeenth-Century New England," *New England Historical and Genealogical Register*, CXXXIV (1980), 181–193.

8. Henry Swinburne, *A Treatise of Wills and Testaments* (London, 1635), I, 73, book 2.

"boy" as a pejorative. For women, old age brought with it de-
sexualization, physical decay, and a greater chance of being called
a witch.[9]

A final group of pejoratives emerged with the appearance of ethnic minorities other than the English in Essex County. From the
beginning of settlement individuals from Wales, Ireland, and Scotland served as the butt of insults, and phrases like "Welsh curr" and
"Scotch rogue" pepper the records of civil cases throughout the century. Starting in the 1670's, the presence of immigrants from the
Channel Islands of Jersey and Guernsey introduced a new linguistic
minority which, while initially confined to the servants and fishermen that Philip English and Zachary White imported, soon grew in
number and contributed to the complexity of speech communities
in seaport towns like Salem and Marblehead. In short order, slurs
like "Jerse cheater" and "French dog" appeared in the insult reper-
toire of men like constable John Waldron of Marblehead.[1]

In their quantity and diversity, curses, swear-words, and threats
were far less elaborate than "detractive" words. Curses could be
made against people or animals and took similar forms in either
case. They usually requested that God visit pestilence on the victim,
or that he be taken by the Devil, and sometimes both. Francis Us-
selton of Salem cursed one of his neighbor's swine in 1657 by saying
"A pox of god upon her & the divill take her"; in 1652 William
Snelling, a Newbury resident, inadvertently used a local proverb
from his home town of Plympton St. Mary, Devon, in front of his
East Anglian Ipswich neighbors—"as for our foes, a plage on theire

9. On the relationship of aging and witchcraft in women, see Demos, *Entertaining
Satan*, 64–70.

1. *Essex County Court Records*, IV, 92 (1672). Similar slurs against French new-
comers to both Newport and East Greenwich, Rhode Island, in the early 1670's are
recorded: Henry Palmer of Newport called Stephen Sabeere of East Greenwich a
"French dog," and "French rogue," in 1672; John Osborne Austin, *The Genealogical
Dictionary of Rhode Island* (Baltimore, 1978 [orig. publ. Providence, 1887]), 143. On
the conflicts between Channel Islanders and Englishmen in Essex County, see David
Thomas Konig, *Law and Society in Puritan Massachusetts: Essex County, 1629–1692*
(Chapel Hill, N.C., 1979), 70–74; and Konig, "A New Look at the Essex 'French':
Ethnic Friction and Community Tensions in Seventeenth-Century Essex County,
Massachusetts," Essex Institute, *Historical Collections*, CX (1974), 167–180.

heeles and a pox on theare toes"—and they took him to court.[2] Most cases of swearing involved some mention of "the blood and wounds of Christ." The common threat in Essex County consisted of "I will knock out your brains," "I will have your heart's blood on the ground," or some variation of the two.

All of these heated exchanges, whether they involved a curse, a threat, or a slander, could lead quickly to genuine hostility that intensified as rapidly as it had erupted. Consider the fierce escalation of a "combustion" between Thomas Wells and William Nelson of Rowley in 1669. Nelson told the court how he and John Bare, a neighbor, began splashing water on one another as they were walking along the road with Wells on a summer day. Some of the water fell on Wells, who was carrying an axe on his shoulder. Feeling himself being splashed, he swore by "God's wounds that he would split them downe." Nelson then asked, "Whie will you bie in such a pashon for so smale a matter?" Wells replied that he "would not suffer such an affrount from no man no not from King Charles if he was here . . . [I] would trampell hem under my Foot."[3] The intensity of reaction and the instant transformation of reason into rage were part of the same passion that gave rise to heated speech itself.

The swift intensification of anger in this and other encounters demonstrates that seventeenth-century people were extremely sensitive to heated speech because they attributed to it a reality that we no longer acknowledge. Despite all the historical literature extolling the communal solidarity and the heirarchic permanence of seventeenth-century New England's "peasant" society, heated speech reminds us how fragile it could be at certain levels. A defamation or reproach was "real" because it pointed to a recognized shortcoming in the social personality of the victim—someone who, for example, was viewed as being wealthy but unable to make appropriate decisions, or someone who was powerful but self-serving—and the implicit warning that if the person tried to "complete" his or her personality at the expense of others, he would fail.[4] To be exposed in public as

---

2. *Essex County Court Records*, II, 50, 250.
3. *Essex County Court Records*, IV, 105.
4. Compare the functions of insults and accusation in West Africa in Marc Augé,

socially "incomplete" could have very real consequences, since a loss in the presentation of household authority could result in ridicule, weakness in town affairs, and possible economic loss. In addition, defamation was believed "real" since God promised punishment to both those who spread slanderous rumors as well as those who listened. Individuals who witnessed or heard a slander were warned to turn upon it a deaf ear, a frowning look, and a sharp reproof, for all such encounters were held as the work of the Devil. Their ministers claimed Satan was in the heart and the mouth of the curser, and that hell was in his throat. And although modern language theory maintains words to be arbitrary signs and merely referential, seventeenth-century speakers believed that the uttering of the word itself could result in actual physical destruction. With the Devil's power unleashing itself before their ears, Essex County yeomen believed in the power of a curse to ruin crops, burn a house, or kill a new lamb.[5]

Certainly part of the reality of heated speech was due to its being punishable by law. The degree of damage inflicted by heated words and their relative publicity bore directly on the kind of punishment the offender received. An offense and its punishment were symmetrical opposites; the inverse of stealing a neighbor's good name was having one's own taken away; the opposite of reputation was shame. Of course, on a cosmic level all offenses were subject in theory to divine judgment, and popular literature reiterated the warnings against evil speech given in the Bible. A typical story, similar in many respects to the sad tale of Anne Averies, recounted the tragic fate of a

---

"Sorciers Noirs et Diables Blancs: La Notion de personne, les croyances a la sorcellerie et leur évolution dans les sociétés lagunaires de basse Côte-d'Ivoire," in *La Notion de Personne en Afrique Noir*, Colloques Internationaux du C.N.R.S., no. 544 (Paris, 1973), 518–527, with those of seventeenth-century witchcraft in Demos, *Entertaining Satan*, 67–69. See also Robert M. Adams, *Bad Mouth: Fugitive Papers on the Dark Side* (Berkeley, Calif., 1977), 21–42.

5. Web, *The Araignment of an unruly Tongue*, 161–163. Elsewhere (pp. 158–160), Web details the rationale behind divine punishment for slanderers: "whether . . . a Talebearer or a Tale-receiver be more dangerous and damnable, it is hard to iudge: for the Talebearer hath the Divell in his tongue, and the Tale-receiver hath the Divel in his eare . . . It is iniurious to our own soules, to give any credite or countenance to an evill tongue: for he whose eare is open to loosetongu'd creatures, becommeth accessary to their sin, and guilty of the same offense with them." Keith Thomas, *Religion and the Decline of Magic* (New York, 1971), 502–511.

woman who, having renounced her profession of faith, "was so seised upon and possessed by an evill Spirit, that . . . she fell to lamenting, and tormenting her own flesh, and *Chopt in pieces with her daintie teeth her rebellious tongue*, wherewith she had spoken wicked words."[6] On a more local level, punishment focused on various forms of public censure designed to subject the convicted speaker to the public ridicule of his neighbors as a means both of breaking his will and of temporarily excommunicating him from the respectable members of his community.[7]

The least public type of censure was the payment of a fine, a literal payment of a debt to society demanded most often in cases of lying, defamation, swearing, and cursing. Fines in Essex County ranged from five shillings to six pounds, depending on the exact nature of the infraction and whether or not it was a first offense. Fines had the obvious advantage of relative privacy; an offender could satisfy the court and not parade his wounded pride so actively before his fellow townsmen. But only wealthy individuals could always pay a fine. Others had no choice but to endure public embarrassment, three distinct types of which prevailed in Essex County during the seventeenth century.

The first technique was the public confession, a ritual event in which the convicted would recite pleas for forgiveness in front of their local meetinghouse on a lecture day, thus ensuring that most of the community would be present to judge their fitness to participate anew in the moral economy of their town. These confessions followed a specific form in which the offender began by recounting the charge against him, asked for the forgiveness of his friends, and concluded by seeking a guarantee of their and God's assistance in the future. A confession by Thomas Wheeler of Lynn written in 1653, after he was convicted "for sinful speeches" against the town's minister, Thomas Cobbett, is typical of the genre:

6. Beard, *Theatre of Gods Iudgments*, 71–72. Emphasis added.

7. George Lee Haskins, *Law and Authority in Early Massachusetts: A Study in Tradition and Design* (New York, 1960), 210. Haskins adds that "A reputation for godliness was, of course, a principal criterion for the visible sainthood so prized by serious Puritans."

Whereas I Thomas Wheeler of Lin have bene convicted at the last Court at Salem for speakinge sinfull and reprochfull speechis ag[ai]nst Mr[.] Cobbett caluminatinge the doctrine by him delivered and for other evill speechis uttered ag[ai]nst som oth[e]r of the Inhabitants of Lin which though I doe not p[er]fectly rememb[e]r yet seeinge it is testified ag[ai]nst me I have noe reason but to beleeve it to be true and therefore doe acknowledge my greate sin and offence in soe speakinge humblie intreatinge those whom it doth concern to passe it by and receive sattisfaction by this mine humble acknowledgm[e]nt p[ro]misinge for the time to come god helping me to be more watchfull over my words and speeches.[8]

The crucial breaking of Wheeler's will and his submission to community judgment occur when he admits that despite his not recalling the words *per se*, so many people have accused him that "I have noe reason but to beleeve it to be true." Wheeler chose to submit and opt back into the structure of local values. The relative truth of the allegations, he realized, was secondary to his reacceptance by town and congregation.

The second type of punishment meted out in Essex County were papers upon which the offense was written. The papers were attached to the convicted person's body. The offender then had to display his crime by standing in a public place where all could read the paper. When Joseph Severans of Hampton was convicted in 1673, he was ordered to stand at the meetinghouse door for one-half hour before the lecture began with the following incriminating words in capital letters pinned to his breast. "THIS PERSON IS CONVICTED FOR SPEAKING WORDS IN A BOASTING MANNER OF HIS LAS-CIVIOUS & UNCLEAN PRACTICES."[9] He was also fined. In some instances, the use of papers was combined with other punishments that mocked the evil tongue even more. Bridget Oliver of Salem was gagged as well as put on public display with a paper for calling her husband "old devil" and "old rogue," and George Dill of Salem was ordered in late 1639 to "stand att the meeting hous doar next Lecture day with a Clefte sticke upon his Tong, & a pap[er] upon his hatt

---

8. *Essex County Court Records*, I, 286.

9. *Essex County Court Records*, V, 239–240. In Salem in 1649, Ralph Fogg had to "stand at the whipping post half an hour after lecture with a paper in his hat spelling out his crime" (*Essex County Court Records*, I, 185–186).

subscribed [']for gross pr[e]meditated Lying.[']"[1] Finally, the use of papers could be combined with more severe physical punishment. Elizabeth Hewlett of Salem, convicted of "slanderous speeches against Mr. Zerobabell Endicott in fathering her child with him," was to be whipped twenty stripes as well as having to wear upon her forehead the words "A SLANDERER OF MR. ZEROBABELL ENDICOTT."[2] In all instances, papers were attached to either the breast or the head, indicating again the fundamental confusion over where in the body heated words originated.

Corporal punishment was the third and most desperate means of humbling an offender into submission. In seventeenth-century Essex County, two techniques were common—the stocks and whipping. In most instances the stocks were an alternative to paying a fine; one-half hour or one full hour was normally the time specified for confinement. The stocks were always located in a public place. If New England stocks followed the design of their English precedents, they forced the prisoner to sit down with his or her feet held securely between two horizontal oak rails which were then locked in place. In some cases only one foot was secured. In others, both feet could be enclosed, resulting in greater discomfort for the prisoner and less agility in dodging anything that might be thrown at them in mockery or contempt.[3]

The most serious offenders felt the sting of the constable's whip. Most seventeenth-century towns had a whipping post in a central location. Generally a frame of two uprights supporting a crossbar to which the prisoner's wrists were tied, the "post" was high enough to prevent the prisoner from hunching over to protect his bared back and shoulders. Whips were made either of branches or rushes bound roughly together or leather thongs knotted and tied to a wooden handle. Individuals were whipped for lying, slandering, and cursing if their crimes were of a "high" nature or if the offender was a servant. In 1648, John Bond was presented for making "unclean speeches," having said that Alice Spooner, a married neighbor, had given birth

1. *Essex County Court Records*, I, 15; VI, 386.
2. *Essex County Court Records*, I, 361–362, 380.
3. *Essex County Court Records*, I, 185.

to his child. The court ordered him "severely whipped."[4] John Cooke, a Salem servant, was sentenced in 1640 "to be severly whipped and have a shackle put upon his leg for resisting his master's authority."[5] Iron shackles and manacles symbolized the servitude that Cooke tried to protest. Finally, whipping was used in combination with fines and the stocks to discipline repeat offenders. Lying was punished, for example, with different levels of social and corporal censure if it was a first, a second, or a third offense. In cases of total disobedience, like that of John Porter, Jr., a Salem mariner who repeatedly swore at and cursed his parents in the early 1660's, speech offenders could be sent to prison.[6]

Punishment, like the immediately understood meanings of heated words, intensified the reality of aggression in seventeenth-century society. Yet given the power of such words and their legal punishment, what can we say about the relative involvement of men and women in heated speech acts? Who accused whom? Did men accuse other men more than women, or vice versa? Were there types of accusation that rarely, or perhaps never, occurred?

Despite the overt bias toward male involvement that all seventeenth-century court records share, some patterns appear. First, men so overwhelmingly outnumber women in the Essex County records that one cannot avoid concluding their more frequent involvement in the public display of aggression. Yet the relative dominance of male over female participation was not uniform across all classes of

4. *Essex County Court Records*, I, 152.

5. *Essex County Court Records*, I, 20. Whipping was singled out by some Essex County residents as cruel and unfair punishment; see the 1656 complaint of William Young of Andover who wished "them all hanged who instituted whipping, and . . . thought they must have been a company of rude deboyst fellows" (*Essex County Court Records*, I, 424).

6. *Lawes and Libertyes*, ed. Barnes, 35: Lying "shall be fined for the first offence ten shillings, or if the partie be unable to pay the same then to be set in the stocks . . . not exceeding two hours. For the second offense in that kinde whereof any shall be legally convicted the sum of twenty shillings, or be whipped upon the naked body not exceeding ten stripes. And for the third offense that way forty shillings, or if the partie be unable to pay, then to be whipped with more stripes, not exceeding fifteen." For an extreme case of imprisonment, see the discussion of John Porter, Jr., of Salem in Konig, *Law and Society in Puritan Massachusetts*, 175–176.

heated speech. If we look at the gender of known defendants (Table 4), we see that a higher proportion of women to men (approximately 1:2) were involved in cases of destructive style than in any other category. By contrast, men outnumbered women almost five to one in cases of detractive speech, and in both threats and criminal cases the ratio of men to women was six to one. Of a total of 363 presentments for civil offenses, about seventy-two percent of the defendants were men, about seventeen percent were women, and an additional ten percent were a man and his wife acting jointly.[7]

Turning to the gender of plaintiffs (Table 5), the selective dominance of men is again unmistakable. Of the 363 civil presentments, men brought eighty percent to court, while women brought about sixteen percent; the remainder were brought by a husband and a wife acting together.[8] And within each type of offense patterns appear that are related, but not identical, to those for the defendants. For example, as either plaintiffs or defendants, men and women respectively had close to the same amount of participation in presentments for destructive style. As plaintiffs, women were almost as sensitive to this as they were to detractions, the two categories together making up thirty-four percent and forty-six percent, respectively, of all the crimes they complained against. Threats comprised only about nineteen percent of women's complaints, suggesting on the one hand that threats were not often made against women, or on the other, that they may not have reacted to them with great intensity. By contrast, men took other people to court most often for damage to their reputation—a total of 231 cases comprising eighty percent of all actions they filed. Presentments for threats and destruc-

7. This percentage is higher than that which prevailed for female defendants as reported in Peter Moogk, "'Thieving Buggers' and 'Stupid Sluts': Insults and Popular Culture in New France," *William and Mary Quarterly*, 3d Ser., XXXVI (1979), 533, and suggests that seventeenth-century New England culture tolerated greater female participation, i.e., greater accusation of women, than did the culture of New France. The participation of men was the same in both places—72%. The difference came in New England cases in which a man and his wife acted as joint plaintiffs and defendants; see also Thompson, *Women in Stuart England and America*, 165.

8. Moogk, "'Thieving Buggers' and 'Stupid Sluts,'" 534, indicates that in New France 28% of plaintiffs were women and in La Rochelle, France, 20% were women. In seventeenth-century Essex County, the figure was only 16%.

## TABLE 4

### Defendants and Gender in the "Heated" Speech of Essex County, Massachusetts, 1640–1680

| Gender of Defendant | Threats | | Civil Cases "Detractive" Speech | | Destructive Style | | Criminal Cases | | Total | |
|---|---|---|---|---|---|---|---|---|---|---|
| | No. | ( %) | No. | ( %) | No. | ( %) | No. | ( %) | No. | ( %) |
| Man(-en) | 32 | ( 84.2) | 197 | ( 72.7) | 35 | ( 64.8) | 151 | ( 84.4) | 415 | ( 76.6) |
| Woman(-en) | 5 | ( 13.2) | 39 | ( 14.4) | 18 | ( 33.3) | 26 | ( 14.5) | 88 | ( 16.2) |
| Both man & woman | 1 | ( 2.6) | 35 | ( 12.9) | 1 | ( 1.9) | 2 | ( 1.1) | 39 | ( 7.2) |
| Total | 38 | (100.0) | 271 | (100.0) | 54 | (100.0) | 179 | (100.0) | 542 | (100.0)* |

* N=542 (63.3%) of total of 856 presentments recorded in which gender of defendant can be determined. This number is low because only 179 (36.3%) of the 493 total criminal presentments recorded definitively give the gender of the accused (i.e., the remaining cases usually just mention a family surname).

## TABLE 5

### Plaintiffs and Gender in the "Heated" Speech of Essex County, Massachusetts, 1640–1680: Civil Offenses

| Gender Relation* | Threats | | "Detractive" Speech | | Destructive Style | | Total | |
|---|---|---|---|---|---|---|---|---|
| | No. | ( %) | No. | ( %) | No. | ( %) | No. | ( %) |
| M v. M | 23 | ( 60.5) | 159 | ( 58.9) | 18 | ( 33.3) | 200 | ( 36.9) |
| M v. M+M | 1 | ( 2.6) | 11 | ( 4.2) | 1 | ( 1.9) | 13 | ( 2.4) |
| M+M v. M | – | – | 4 | ( 1.6) | 2 | ( 3.7) | 6 | ( 1.1) |
| M v. W | 1 | ( 2.6) | 29 | ( 10.6) | 8 | ( 14.6) | 38 | ( 7.8) |
| M+M v. W | – | – | – | – | – | – | – | – |
| M v. W+W | – | – | – | – | 1 | ( 1.9) | – | –** |
| M v. M+W | 1 | ( 2.6) | 28 | ( 10.2) | – | – | 29 | ( 5.3) |
| W v. W | 4 | ( 10.5) | 8 | ( 3.1) | 9 | ( 16.7) | 21 | ( 3.9) |
| W v. W+W | – | – | 1 | –** | – | – | 1 | –** |
| W+W v. W | – | – | – | – | – | – | – | – |
| W v. M | 7 | ( 18.6) | 14 | ( 5.3) | 10 | ( 18.5) | 31 | ( 5.7) |
| W+W v. M | – | – | – | – | 1 | ( 1.9) | 1 | –** |
| W v. M+M | – | – | 1 | –** | – | – | 1 | –** |
| W v. W+M | – | – | 3 | ( 1.2) | – | – | 3 | ( 1.0) |
| M+W v. M | 1 | ( 2.6) | 8 | ( 3.1) | 3 | ( 5.6) | 12 | ( 2.2) |
| M+W v. W | – | – | 1 | –** | – | – | 1 | –** |
| M+W v. M+W | – | – | 4 | ( 1.6) | 1 | ( 1.9) | 12 | ( 2.2) |
| Total | 38 | (100.0) | 271 | (100.0) | 54 | (100.0) | 363 | (100.0) |

* M=man; W=woman
** Indicates percentage lower than .500.

tive style comprised ten and just over nine percent of their remaining complaints, respectively. Women appear to have been more prone to use destructive style and threats than did men, and less likely by far to use detractive speech. In fact, they were outnumbered by men as plaintiffs in cases of detractive speech by almost ten to one. The latter point suggests that women, when they wanted to inflict verbal damage, did so differently from men. Men would use defamation to damage another's reputation, while women would use a heated style more often as a means of moral rebuke. Women were not only involved much less often in defamation cases than were men; defamation seems not to have mattered to women in quite the same way.

Indeed, women seem to have taken the issue of reputation far less seriously than did men. Their vocabulary for defamation, slander, and reproach was far less elaborated, suggesting that for them it may not have been as developed and perfected a skill. In some instances, Essex County women directly questioned the male need to emphasize reputation at the expense of both people and property. In 1661, John Hathorne of Salem filed an action of slander against William Langley and Joan Langley of Salem. Hathorne exceeded the defendants' expectations when, instead of attaching a cow or sheep—the usual move in a slander case—he arrogantly attached all of their property, including house, land, and livestock. The day after the writ of attachment was executed, Joan Langley complained to her friend Mary Browne that the writ was far too severe and put their livelihood in peril. Browne ventured an explanation: "I suppose he esteemes his name more than all your estate," at which Langley in amazement replied, "Is his name so good?"[9] William Langley understood Hathorne's challenge and said nothing, fully aware that the relationship of one man to another was qualitatively different from that between women.

If we look at which gender relations *did not* lock horns, three distinct combinations appear that shed some light, however faintly, on men's and women's attitudes toward one another. First, two people of any gender(s) never complained against one woman acting on her own (M+M $v$. W, W+W $v$. W, M+W $v$. W). Second, with

9. *Essex County Court Records*, II, 286.

only one exception, one man and two women never engaged one
another, no matter who was plaintiff and who was defendant (M *v.*
W+W, W+W *v.* M). And third, again with only a single exception, one woman never complained against two defendants of the
same sex (W *v.* M+M, W *v.* W+W). The fact that people in these
gender relations never or only very rarely took one another to court
suggests that such relations were seen as asymmetrical oppositions
that were culturally unfair or inappropriate, and thus could not support a legal action for heated speech in seventeenth-century Essex
County. It suggests also that beneath the differing sensitivity of men
and women to actionable words ran a substratum of social conventions which could not be violated without bringing shame to the
parties involved.

Consider the rules that men acknowledged when complaining
against women. Two men did not seek justice under any circumstances from one woman; it must have been an embarrassment to
each of their senses of authority to appear publicly as if they could
not achieve legal satisfaction against a woman on their own. Conversely, one man did not complain against two women, for that implied he was being too sensitive in letting two women raise his ire or
"get his goat" at the same time for the same reason. And for a married
couple to prosecute one of their female neighbors was simply an
unfair social match, pitting a complete household against a fragment of another. One woman never complained against two men,
perhaps because that would constitute, even in the relatively progressive legal system of seventeenth-century New England, a challenge to male dominance that could not be tolerated. Finally, two
of these unworkable oppositions point to a gender relationship that
failed to occur no matter who was plaintiff or defendant: two women
and one woman (W. *v.* W+W, W+W *v.* W). The absence of this
relationship suggests that women, unlike men, would not enter into
an asymmetrical argument with members of their own sex that
would of necessity make one side weaker than the other. Women
would take on other women on a one-to-one basis, or join forces
against one man, but they would not risk public disequilibrium with
other women.

Given the public nature of speech offenses and the fact that many of them took place in areas outside the house that were marked in seventeenth-century New England as specifically male spatial domains,[1] it is not surprising that most of the recorded cases of detractive speech involved men alone. Women were denied access to these male domains on an everyday basis. Confined more often to private or "back" spaces—the house, the farmyard, or the garden—or else to the meetinghouse, which for doctrinal reasons extended them greater status, women cared little for the abstract world of verbal honor in which their men sparred for economic parity as they attacked and defended their chronically frail reputations. In this spatial sense, at least, Cotton Mather may have been accurate when he claimed that seventeenth-century women were "People who make no Noise at all in the World; People hardly Known to be in the World; persons of the *Female Sex* . . . buried with *Oblivion* in the World."[2]

What does seem unusual in the Essex County evidence is the remarkably low total percentages of female involvement in speech transgressions as either plaintiffs or defendants, averaging about sixteen percent throughout the period. In other words, no matter how we look at the records, for every one woman who appeared in court there were at least five or six men. Such low female participation hardly squares with the contemporary belief that women were more prone to offensive speech of all sorts than were men. "The Faculty

1. Aggressive speech acts involving men almost never occurred inside the house. Instead, they took place: *outside* a house in Marblehead (1680); "while ditching in the marsh" near Hampton (1669); while bringing "a cart through his meadow" in Salem (1669); at "William Nik's stage while talking" in Marblehead (1666); "at the smith's shop in Rowly" (1663); "in the stable or cowhouse" in Newbury (1662); "at his own door," but not *inside* a house at Marblehead (1680); and "at the warehouse of Capt. Whit[e]," in Ipswich (1674); see *Essex County Court Records*, VII, 420; IV, 184, 187; III, 343, 80, 54; VII, 425; V, 411. This behavior is consistent with that observed in other writings. Speaking of the evil tongue, Web (*The Araignment of an unruly Tongue*, 50–51) said "the most proper places of his residence, are *Ale-houses, Tavernes, Playhouses, Bake-houses, Wooll-lofts, and Gossip meetings*." For the rationale behind the house as both female domain and a sign of rationality, see Robert Blair St. George, "'Set Thine House in Order': The Domestication of the Yeomanry in Seventeenth-Century New England," in Fairbanks and Trent, eds., *New England Begins*, II, 165–170.

2. Cotton Mather, *Ornaments for the Daughters of Zion* (Delmar, N.Y., 1978 [orig. publ. Boston, 1741]), 34–36.

of *Speech* is of such noble & of such a signal Figure in the Constitution of Mankind," wrote Mather, "that it is a thousand Pities, it should be *abus'd*." He continued, deliberately reporting what his parishioners believed and not what he actually thought: "*Womankind is usually charged with a peculiar Share in the World's Abuses of it*."[3] Instead of all women being at fault, Mather maintained, only a few were blameworthy and those few had given their sex such a negative reputation that "it is indeed a Piece of great Injustice, that every Woman should be so far an *Eve*, as that *her* [Eve's] Depravation should be imputed unto all her Sex."[4] Another author added his belief that not only was the heart the frequent source of heated speech, but the heart itself could be found in an angry woman's mouth.[5]

With less self-consciousness Mather suggested that women in seventeenth-century New England may have been regarded as more talkative than men, which might explain why the words of women were frequently distrusted. "Be careful that you don't *speak too much*," he warned his young female readers, "because that when the Chest is always *open*, everyone count[s] there are no Treasures in it; and the Scripture tells us, 'tis the *Whore* that is *clamorous*, and the *Fool*, that is *full of Words*."[6] If women were viewed as naturally more talkative than men, their words may also have been tolerated longer and had less weight attributed to them. Part of the low percentage of female presentments may have been due to a husband's greater willingness to be constantly scolded than to admit to his neighbors how little control he had over his spouse. When women did appear

3. Ibid., 54. Thomas Adams, "The Taming of the Tongue," 17, adds: "Woman, for the most part, hath the glibbest tongue . . . She calls her tongue her defensive weapon . . . a firebrand in a frantic hand doth less mischief. The proverb came not from nothing, when we say of a brawling man, He hath a woman's tongue in his hand."

4. Mather, *Ornaments for the Daughters of Zion*, 54.

5. *The Testaments of the Twelve Patriarchs*, ed. Grosthead, cii.

6. Mather, *Ornaments for the Daughters of Zion*, 55. Mather also warned his female readers (p. 56) "O let there be no *Dross* in your whole *Communication*. The *Dross* of your own *Wrath*, vented in scolding, fury, vile Names; the *Dross* of your own *Worth*, vented in boasting, bragging, self-ostentation; the *Dross* of all *filthiness*, vented in baudy Talk about the Things which 'tis a *Shame* to *speak*; Let all this *Dross* be purged out of all your *Speech*."

in court, however, their sentences were usually severe. Perhaps talk-ativeness and the doubt cast by men on anyone who was "full of Words" contributed to women being portrayed as liars. When in 1658 William Deane of Ipswich shouted at Susanna Wade, "Fy upon thee woman, base lyar, o fy, upon thee woman, thou art a base lyar I will not regard a word you sayest . . . more than a straw," he was only stating what most people—including some women—freely ac-knowledged. Indeed, some seventeenth-century women were aware of being thus stereotyped and had to make a special appeal to be taken at their word.[7] Coupled with their perceived tendency to talk too much and to lie was a belief that when women cursed, they— like the poor and the diseased—did so with greater power. "No venemous Snake stings like a Woman's tongue,"[8] ran one English street ballad of the 1640's, reinforcing Mather's connection between women, words, Eve, the serpent, and their combined harm to mankind.

Without doubt much of the absence of women from the court records can also be attributed to their understood role in the home and their position subordinate to the rule of their husbands. At least one part of the Puritan conception of love in marriage, the idea of the wife's submission to her husband, relied on verbal deference in both directions. The husband was to remain mild at all costs. "Whether an husbands speech be *to his* wife before her face, or *of*

7. *Essex County Court Records*, II, 63. See also Demos, *A Little Commonwealth*, 165, where the mother of John Gorham of Yarmouth, Massachusetts, begged her son to remain at home, saying "if you would beleive a woman beleive mee that your father saith that you shall never be Molested."

8. Quoted in Spargo, *Juridical Folklore in England*, 114, n. 6. Susan Harding, "Women and Words in a Spanish Village," in Rayna Reiter, ed., *Toward an Anthropology of Women* (New York, 1975), 302n, cites one woman in the northeastern Spanish village of Oreol who believed that women by nature have "wicked tongues." Women, the poor, and the diseased relied on the power of speech in the absence of other resources for affective critique. As Ward, *Gods Arrowes*, 6, observed, "the poore man sweareth for necessity," and women were no different (see note 3, p. 311 above). Konig, *Law and Society in Puritan Massachusetts*, 149, is liberal in believing that the poor and women used cursing and magic to better themselves; I think they relied on it more often to deconstruct actively existing social relations. For the interrelationships of economic status and women, see Carol Frances Karlsen, "The Devil in the Shape of a Woman: The Witch in Seventeenth-Century New England" (Ph.D. diss., Yale University, 1980), 104–169. In England, poor men and women alike cursed landlords who were enclosing their lands, hoping their words would cause the death of the landlord and his heirs (Thomas, *Religion and the Decline of Magic*, 505).

*her* behinde her backe, it must be sweetned with mildness," wrote William Gouge in the early 1620's.[9] Like other early seventeenth-century social theorists, Gouge was able to prescribe such mildness knowing that its success in family government depended on the husband's ability to command respect, and this was in part why reputation was so important to men. He warned husbands who tended to abuse their wives with verbal cruelty that by their speech they would "make themselves contemptible, and so lose their authority."[1] In return for the mildness of their spouse, wives were expected to be deferential, protect their husband's name in public and in private, and not pry into their husband's personal affairs. Despite the latter dictum, seventeenth-century women must have devised linguistic strategies to ferret out all but the most secret of their beloved's plans, and the techniques they used probably contributed still more to their husbands' belief and distrust of women's verbal cunning.[2]

Closely related to a woman's dominance within the household was the existence of female speech genres that probably rivaled the theatre of male reputation-making for power: rumor and gossip. Yet unlike the transgressions that leap from the written record to document the importance of reputation for men, few instances appear that shed light on this darker, almost secret, side of female

9. William Gouge, *Of Domesticall Duties* (London, 1622), 371–372.

1. Gouge, *Of Domesticall Duties*, 355.

2. Susan Harding, "Women and Words in a Spanish Village," presents a speech community organized much like that of early New England. Especially suggestive is her summary (pp. 292–293) of how wives found out about their husbands' private lives: "To penetrate the privacy of their husbands, wives become skilled at asking them questions, tiny and discreet questions, about their actions and activities. A woman seems to assume that she cannot ask a straight question of her husband on some matters and expect a straight answer. So she breaks the question up into piecemeal questions with the aim that together their answers will unobtrusively answer, or give her grounds for inferring the answer, to the question she could not openly ask. Women also may learn to fragment their demands into tiny pieces—first ask for one piece, get it, then another, and so on, until the pieces add up to the whole demand. Another tactic is to make the whole demand at once, but not as such, not by directly or explicity asking for anything; instead, by talking about what is at issue, focusing on it in fine tuning, going on about details, and so avoid a wholesale, final, negative response. Husbands come to think of their wives as verbally cunning and manipulative, and collectively men imagine that these are the natural characteristics of women. But skills of verbal finesse and subterfuge are a function of, and an adaption to, women's subordinate and dependent position with regard to control over resources."

speech domains. In 1672, for example, Elizabeth Goodell of Salem charged John Smith with making several abusive carriages toward her. When the case came to trial, several of her neighbors came forward and betrayed her, saying that she did some of the "lascivious things" of her own free will. Goodell replied that such stories were greatly exaggerated. She had told her husband and her sister in private what had happened, she insisted, but the news had "come to the mouths of such talkers as have perverted the truth and made the matter appere far worse than ever it was"; undoubtedly, two women that Goodell recognized in Court as merely "pretended friends" had spread the story with additions of their own design.[3] Although little evidence survives, much of these interchanges probably took place at the "gossip meetings" mentioned by Web, which were probably one of the few all-female social forms of the period.

Overall, the few references to gossip and rumor work in concert with other forms to suggest that the heated speech of women centered on issues relating to personal morality, the subjective side of human relationships, and kinship ties—that is, to the seventeenth-century household as a female domain in its broadest sense. Men, on the other hand, were more often concerned with issues of social status, crops, livestock, and their ability as self-sufficient participants in the local economic community. In short, both the gender roles of speech and the functions of heated speech in damaging men and women with specific kinds of pejoratives, reinforced the separate but interdependent interests of men and women. Women seem to have regulated the community of morality, men the community of commodity exchange. In turn, this division of expressive acts was linked to the prevailing division of routine labor in everyday life. Men were farmers, artisans, and producers. Women were regulators of process and the individuals assigned to insure the morality of social relations. These separate roles were engaged as well on the level of

3. *Essex County Court Records*, V, 52–54. Two years later a woman, trying to help her brother avoid becoming the subject of a rumor that he had been cuckolded, asked her sister-in-law to keep the third party from frequenting her house, "if it were not to stop the mouthes of people, for their mouths were open." Her sister-in-law replied: "let them shut them againe, for here he should come in spite of your teeth or any body els." Ibid., V, 401–402 (1679).

popular protest, where women railed against ministers, figureheads of moral inspiration, and men derided magistrates, whose tasks included overseeing the litigation of property disputes.[4]

An awareness of the relationship between speech and gender domains is crucial in two ways to relating the cultural significance of heated speech to that of written language. First, on a general level, speech relates directly to both reading and writing simply because seventeenth-century people often spoke aloud the words they were reading or writing in graphic form. This basic fact has two correllates. Because reading and writing were often spoken and aural as well as graphic and visual activities, they must have been committed to memory according to rules for hearing sounds, which for a newly literate person may have been more developed than those for the recording of a printed image.[5] In addition, it suggests that in many instances the particular syntactic and rhythmic presentation of written words must have been fundamentally similar, even continuous, to that characteristic of speech. Elizabeth Buxton's deposition is a case in point; the repeated use of the pronoun "her" in the written text is confusing until the text is *spoken*, and then proper emphases appear to make sense of the action. Other texts show constant restatement, insertions, a lack of systematic punctuation, and a high degree

4. Among many examples, see the following: In 1652 in Salem a women was presented "for reproachful and unbecoming speeches" against Mr. Perkins, a church deacon, for saying "if it were not for the law, shee would never com to the meetings, the teacher was soe dead, and accordingly shee did seldom com and withall p[e]rsuaded goodwife Vincett to com to her house, on the Saboth day, and reade goode bookes, affirminge that the teacher was fitter to be a ladyes Chambermaid, then to be in the pulpitt" (*Essex County Court Records*, I, 275); and in 1654 Elizabeth Legg of Marblehead was presented for "Speaking Slitely and scornful[ly] of Mr. Walton," the town's unordained minister. She said "I could have a boy from the Colledg [Harvard] that would preach better than Mr. Walton for half ye wages" (Ibid., I, 378). Men's protests against magistrates include John Goit's 1641 pronouncement that "its better to goe to hell gate for mercy than to Mr. Endecott for instice" (Ibid., I, 35); John Burston's 1661 statement that the magistrates in Salem "were robbers and destroyers of the widows and the fatherless" (Ibid., II, 337); and Thomas Baker's 1679 admission that "he did not care for all the laws in the country." When Baker learned his case would be heard by Major John Hathorne in Salem, he replied that he "would not be tried by that white-hat, limping rogue" (Ibid., VII, 331).

5. On the relationship between oral memory and formulaic textual rules, see Albert B. Lord, *The Singer of Tales* (New York, 1978), 30–67, 124–140.

of orthographic variety in a single paragraph—all signs that rules for speech still retain their priority within the text over emergent written conventions.[6]

Second, the existence of gender domains within seventeenth-century speech may help us understand why literacy failed to rise above sixty percent in Essex County until the second quarter of the eighteenth century. We can begin by asking a simple question: Do people even *need* basic literacy skills if speech alone still succeeds in regulating social exchange and clarifying social relations? The answer is a firm "maybe not" that forces us to address an apparent contradiction in Puritanism that bears directly on the importance of literacy skills—especially writing—to seventeenth-century social theory. On the one hand, like all reformed Protestant sects, the Puritans stressed the importance of basic literacy skills as a means of confronting directly the Word of God. Yet on the other hand, Puritanism also stressed the enforced separation of gender labor as the basis of family government, and part of what kept the roles of men and women separated was speech. Indeed, the role of speech—heated or otherwise—in articulating different categories of cultural experience was a fundamental means of insuring social order itself. Speech organized life in a straightforward way that corresponded to the teachings of Christ; it was a foundation stone upon which "little Commonwealths" comfortably rested.

By comparison, writing represented a threat to such stability in that it could seem like *genderless* communication. Writing could exist apart from a specific social context. It could blur the distinctions that underlay social organization. Indeed, writing seems to have done to words in the early eighteenth century what wages would do to work one hundred years later.[7] With this in mind, Puritanism, *per se*, seems to have contributed to the diffusion of reading and writing skills up

6. Stubbs, *Language and Literacy*, 29–31; I. J. Gelb, *A Study of Writing: The Foundation of Grammatology* (Chicago, 1952), 223–228.

7. Ivan Illich, *Gender* (New York, 1982), 3–22. Illich, pp. 132–139, also discusses and cites relevant bibliography for divisions in male and female speech; what we still need are explorations in gender and writing. Illich's work is controversial and in many ways radically conservative; see Keith Thomas' review of *Gender*, "Back to Utopia," *New York Review of Books*, 12 May 1983.

to a point and no further. Universal male literacy was fully consistent with Puritan social theory, since it reinforced the authoritarian structures already in place. But full literacy for both men and women threatened to blurr the rigid division of labor that kept women actively in control of morals and men in control of commodities. For this reason, Essex County was the last county to move toward full literacy, and only did so as the Puritan orthodoxy lost its firm hold on local congregations.

If the Puritanism that dominated New England society in the seventeenth century was a religion of the Word, it was a religion that admitted the potential within all kinds of words. Certainly it valued the read Word of the Gospel, as illiterate people marvelled at stories read aloud by educated neighbors, and the written words of published ministerial tracts and zealously kept diaries. Perhaps more fundamentally it recognized the power of spoken words to shape not only the most eloquent of sermons but also the thorniest reprimands and scolds of household talk; these extremes mark the edges of the totality of an oral literature that has vanished except for small traces —a passage from a conversation here, a momentary flash of oral style there. Ultimately, the complex interweaving of all these kinds of verbal communication moved, at irregular rates and with differing associations of social class and gender domain, toward a single goal in the minds of seventeenth-century people. By clarifying both ideas and social boundaries, different kinds of words provided the preeminent genre of cultural reflexivity. And in such reflexivity lies the goal of studying literacy and speech together, as an ethnographic totality: to discover how people in the past and present structured, contemplated, and shared their own knowledge.

APPENDIX 1. CATEGORIES OF AGGRESSIVE VERBAL BEHAVIOR
IN ESSEX COUNTY, MASSACHUSETTS, 1640–1680

## I. *"Kinds"* of Language (*12*)

| | |
|---|---|
| abusive | ill |
| bad | lascivious |
| baudy | retorting |
| evil | saucy |
| foul | scurrilous |
| gross | untoward |

## II. *"Kinds"* of Speech or Speaking (*69*)

| | |
|---|---|
| absurd | lascivious |
| abusive | light |
| affronting | lying |
| arrogant | obstinate |
| bawdy | malignant |
| boasting | misinforming |
| calumnating | nasty |
| common | naughty |
| contemptuous | nicknaming |
| cursing | not positive [-ly] |
| profane | not sufferable |
| wicked | offensive |
| dangerous | of a high nature |
| derisive | peremptory |
| desperate | perverse |
| discouraging | presumptuous |
| disturbing | quarrelling |
| evil | railing |
| false | rebellious |
| faltering | reproachful |
| filthy | reviling |
| indecent (song) | ribald [-ry] |
| injurious | rude [-ly] |
| irreligious | scoffingly |
| insinuation | scornful |
| insulting | scurrilous |

sinful
slanderous
slighting
swearing
  falsely
  rashly
taunting
threatening
troublesome
unadvised [-ly]
unbecoming

unclean
unlawful
unmannerly
untrue
unworthy
uttering
vain
vile
violent
wanton
wicked

### III. *"Kinds" of Words* (27)

abusive
bad
base
blasphemous
clipped
common
disloyal
disparaging
foolish
frequent
harsh
high
idle
maliciously raised

miscarriage in
mutinous
opprobrious
provoking
railing
reviling
scolding
seditious
treasonable
unchaste
uncivil
unseemly
wild

### IV. *"Kinds" of Gestures* (1)

unseemly

APPENDIX 2. AGGRESSIVE WORDS AND GENDER DISTINCTION
IN ESSEX COUNTY, MASSACHUSETTS, 1640–1680

### I. *Words that "Damaged" Men*

ape
  simple
backbiter
bastard
bawd
beast
bloodymen
blood-thirsty men
boys
  jackanapes
  mallapart
  proud
  rascally
  saucy
cheat [-er]
  Jersey
Clan-backs
curr
  cockolly
  foresworn
  Indian
  shamble-hand
  Welsh
cuss
  cowardly
debased
devil
  black
  foresworn
  Gurley-gutted
  old
devil's packhorse
dog
  base
  base Welch
  black

foresworn
French
fellow
  base
  cursing
  deceitful
  false
  jealous
  lousy
  lying
  malicious
  picking
  pimping
  pitiful
  quarrelling
  swearing
  vile
flatterers
fools
  lying
  prating
hell-hound
Honey
hypocrite
imp
Ishmaelite
Jack
  lying
  saucy
Jack-a-napes
knave
  base
  cheating
  lying
leeringest hang dog that
  was in the world

liar
  common
like Laban
limb of the devil
loggerhead
murderer
not fit to live upon Godes earth
persecutor of God's people
pimp
rascal
  base
  saucy
robber
Robin Hood
rogue
  adultrous
  base
  cheating
  cowardly
  foresworn
  long-shanked thievish
  old
  Scotch
  thievish

Welch
white-hat limping
white-livered
wopper-jawed
rude
scoffer
shittabed
slave
  drunken
such as make a house desolate
theif
  highway
toad
  damned
verryest rascal in New England
whelp
witch
wizard
  old
wretch
  damned
  foresworn
  wicked

## II. *Words that "Damaged" Women*

adulteress
bawd
  base
  brasen-faced
  impudent
  old
blot and reproach to the Church
bold, badly spoken thing
captain
creature
  filthy
  unchaste
curr
  pitiful

dear
devil
  base
  little
  lying
fire brand of hell for
  her lying tongue
gamar pisse house
gamar Shite house
hag
  old
hogge
  old
hus[se]y

hypocrite
jade
  base
  lying
Jesable
liar
  base
  common
  verriest
lieutenant
mill-mare
pennycoinquick
rotten member and a scandal
  to the Gospel
roundhead
scandalous
slut
  base
  crooked-back
  lousy

sow
  base
  bobtail
  filthy
  lying
thief
toad
  base
  lying
witch
  black-mouthed
  old
  spiteful
  ugly
woman
  base
  devilish
  false
  foresworn
  lying

### III. *Words that "Damaged" Children*

bastard
dog
  base
puncke

stue
tallafast que[e]ne
Tinckers trull

### IV. *Words that "Damaged" Public Authorities*

Ministers: Catch-pole
          deceivers of the People
          ladyes Chambermayd
Magistrates: robbers and destroyers to the widows and fatherless
            logreded poopes

# New England and a Wider World: Notes on Some Central Themes of Modern Historiography

S CIENTISTS, it is said, learn in order to discover; humanists discover in order to learn. This suggests once again how anomalous a field of scholarship history is. For while discoveries in historical scholarship, as in science, create great personal satisfaction and bring substantial professional rewards, they can at best be only small adjustments in the immense and ever enlarging map of historical learning, the whole of which—the old information and the latest discoveries—must be absorbed anew by every historian. There are discoveries in these nine essays on seventeenth-century New England—a subject that every generation, apparently, is fated at first to believe is exhausted, only to discover that it is far from that, and to enrich it with yet another wave of fresh and innovative study. And they contribute incrementally to general shifts in perspective and understanding that are otherwise under way.

Karen Kupperman suggests, in her intriguing essay on the Puritans' perceptions of climate, a new approach to understanding the sense of disillusion and confusion and the desire for renewal that overwhelmed the Puritan leadership at the end of the century. Joan Thirsk relates the agricultural practices of New England farmers to a distinctive wave of agricultural innovation in the economically troubled British provinces in the seventeenth century and suggests that it was the New Englanders who carried forward the English experiments that fell away in the home country in the more prosperous eighteenth century. Vickers identifies for the first time a socio-economic subcul-

© Bernard Bailyn, 1984.
Bernard Bailyn is Adams University Professor of History, Harvard University.

ture of seventeenth-century New England whose origins can be traced back to the transient Basque, Norman, and West Country fishermen of the sixteenth century and whose absorption into the settled world of eighteenth-century New England can be traced in finely attentuated lines of the later century's social history. Hall discovers a more ordinary mental world for the Puritans than that of formal theology and its ancillary social and political theories—a world of superstition, magic, strange providences, marvels, and the occult, a world not peculiar to them but shared, as Keith Thomas has shown so vividly, by the whole of the early modern world. And Miller discovers that the Puritans, too, resorted to graphic art to satisfy "an internal world of necessity." They were eager to make use of the craft of portraiture, not only because it met political and social needs —celebrating the importance of the family, reinforcing the distinction of a ruling elite, and chastening human vanity by recalling the inevitability of death—but also and simply because it appealed to the universal delight in color and in visual form.

These are discoveries—and there are others, if less specific. Harris depicts, in the human geography of French Canada, the process by which a vernacular subculture emerged from the blending of major cultures in the peculiar environment of a remote province, and he suggests the way this kind of study may be used to understand a similar development in New England. And Allen, in contrast, identifies specific continuities between local cultures in Old England and New. But all of these discoveries are in a field of humanistic scholarship, and so their value, in the end, lies in their enrichment of a coherent and comprehensive understanding of the subject as a whole. Each paper stands alone but contributes to the general purpose of introducing a new phase in the ever-broadening and deepening study of New England's, and ultimately America's, origins. What general view do these essays together project, what new approach, or framework of understanding? Are there central themes that emerge from these diverse discoveries and explanations?

Two, it seems to me, are striking. The papers reveal, first, the degree to which latent circumstances, unknown and indeed largely unknowable by the people of the time, conditioned not only their physical and social lives but their mental worlds as well. Much of the struggle of the New Englanders' world was an effort to deal not directly with the latent sources of their difficulties—for the colonists had no means of grasping them—but with their palpable manifestations. So the Puritans knew with an absolute certainty that climate was a function of global location and therefore that similar positions of latitude would have similar climates. When New England's climate in the early seventeenth century failed to fit the expected picture, they could account for that by an ancillary belief, that human cultivation affected climate, and hence that in time, as cultivation expanded, climate would conform to expectation. When it did not, as the severity of the New England weather worsened at the end of the century, they were forced back to Providential—ultimately moral—explanations to fight off complete bewilderment and incomprehension and to bring the situation under intellectual control. There can be no finer, more succinct and vivid, example of the richness of explanation that emerges from the fusion of latent and manifest elements in complex historical situations. This fusion of the unknown and the known, the hidden and the visible, the buried circumstantial and the palpable evidential, is, I believe, one of the key developments in modern historical writing, and it produces, as in Kupperman's essay, a significant sophistication of understanding.

And not only in Kupperman's essay. Harris, too, focuses on a modern understanding of ecological phenomena not visible or graspable as such by people of the seventeenth century, and on the way they struggled to deal with these issues, not systematically but haltingly, pragmatically, partially, inconsistently. With their motivation pitched to what Harris nicely calls "a deductive overtone," the New Englanders approached life far differently than did the Newfoundland fishermen, the Acadian dike-building maritime farmers, and the Canadian fur traders, but they faced willy-nilly parallel problems shaped by the environment, and so like the settlers to the north reached selectively back into their original culture. Functionless memories faded, "the collective European heritage thinned," and a New England configuration emerged, emphasizing family, a craving for land, and above all the power of private property. At root was an altered physical environment, and above all a different ratio of land and people. This last is nothing Harris observes for the first time, but he uses it afresh to explain what otherwise is vague and barely perceived: how the original pockets of local, homogeneous New World culture transferred from the old—precisely the elements depicted by Allen—led in time to an increasingly "thin," blended, culture as settlement expanded westward, and to a simplification of cultural memories. And where settlement nodes exported but did not import people, the distinctive, inherited ways described by Allen could survive for generations while the leaner, disaggregated, more diffused culture, a "severe abstraction" from Europe, evolved out on the expanding borderland. All this was happening in the late seventeenth century, all this the scene of struggle, though no contemporary could have traced its roots to the processes of human geography and to an altered ratio of land and labor. It would have taken a mind of genius to have seen the cultural meaning of these latent ecological pressures —and in time, in the eighteenth century, one appeared. Dr. Johnson's mode of discourse is altogether different from Professor Harris's, but he saw it all with brilliant clarity when in 1773 he discovered with shock and dismay the depopulation of western Scotland by migration to North America. The thousands who leave for America, he wrote with an acute understanding of cultural power and diffusion, are lost to the nation, "for a nation scattered in the boundless regions of America resembles rays diverging from a focus. All the rays remain but the heat is gone. Their power consisted in their concentration: when they are dispersed, they have no effect."

In other papers besides Kupperman's and Harris's, analysis of latent forces gives new meaning to the manifest struggles of seventeenth-century New Englanders. Something of the same is hinted at in Thirsk's essay. New Englanders had no capacity to relate their innovations to short-lived agricultural experiments on marginal land in the English provinces. But the historian can make that connection and thereby enlarge the explanatory power of the account that can now be written. Similarly, too, the character of the fishermen's lives in Essex County was a product of the seasonality of the swarming of the cod, and so too were the problems the fishermen's unstable, impoverished, riotous, and individualized lives posed for the Puritan

magistrates. And the substratum of belief in magic, sorcery, astrology, and other occult sciences in general lay like a hidden reef beneath
the surface of the rational, articulated Protestant profession the Puritans formally acknowledged. Their inner lives were therefore strange
mixtures of formal theology, of rationalized belief, of structured
ritual and intellection on the one hand, and unacknowledged superstitions, irrational fears, and compulsions on the other. The reality of
their subjective existences was thus a fusion of the two—neither the
self-conscious apologetics of the "New England mind" nor the half-
submerged magic and superstition of ancient folklore, but the fusion
of the two in forms we only now begin to understand.

But there is an even broader consensus among these essays, a more
widely shared approach, which, too, reflects the dominant currents of
modern historiography. Though all of these papers deal with a restricted geographical region, none of them are simply exercises in local history. All of them draw their intellectual force from references
to a wider world, and it is a world in respect to which New England
civilization was an altogether marginal phenomenon. New England
appears only at the very end of Harris's and Thirsk's papers: the
substance of their discussion is French Canada and England, but developments in these larger worlds illuminate New England's history.
Reference to a general background of climatological belief is the
essential starting point for Kupperman's analysis. Allen's expressed
theme is the degree to which New England is a recreation of local
English variations. Vickers implies a double relation of the local to
the general: the relation of the New England fishing industry to
Atlantic commerce as a whole, and of the Essex fishermen to the
core culture of Puritan New England. And the others, too—Foster,
Hall, St. George, and Miller—all find the springs of their explanations
in the marginal relation of New England to a greater British world.

This common point of view is no accident. As I have elsewhere
noted, the force of current scholarship seems to be leading increasingly to the enlargement of spheres of analysis and to the perception
of filiations from central phenomena to their peripheral extensions.
American developments in the seventeenth century, to say nothing
of New England's regional developments, took place on the far
outer margins of the British-Atlantic world, and they gain their

meaning from that fact. They were phenomena on the outer periphery—I use that word and not "frontier." The word "frontier" does not appear in any of these essays. For "frontier" implies an advance toward a goal, a positive march forward, a leap ahead, as scientists advance by their discoveries toward new frontiers of knowledge and control. Hsitorians once saw the history of the New England settlements as a "frontier" phenomenon. Those who wrote in that tradition implied that everything that happened was a movement toward a goal—which, whether acknowledged or not, was an ultimate Americanization most fully realized in the self-sufficient frontiersman of the middle Western states. There is no such implication in the metaphor of "periphery." The image is not that of a *forward* edge, leading outward toward a final goal, but of an *outer* edge, the radial margin kept firm, coherent, and operative by spokes connecting it to an inner hub. It denotes a distance from, not a movement toward; its implications are regressive not progressive. The metaphor implies, as Dr. Johnson knew, a thinning out, an attenuation, a weakening filiation leading away from the heartland, away from coherence and relevance, toward an unknown world whose ultimate meaning could not be clearly discerned.

In this sense New England lay not on the frontier but on the outer periphery. This, it seems to me, is the dominant theme of these fresh and suggestive essays. They reveal aspects of, they turn up corners of, an emerging culture on the far outer margin of Britain's metropolitan civilization. They face inward, to the east, not outward, to the west. They are nostalgic, backward looking—and correctly so. For, consciously or unconsciously, that was the stance the people of the time took to the greater world. These are contextualist essays, in their approach the very opposite of that optimistic whiggism that refers events to eventualities and that therefore can never contain surprises. They are efforts to comprehend segments of the past within their own sockets of time and place, and those locations lie at the boundaries of a greater world. It is the substantial merit of these papers that they probe the contexts of the past, and that they depict the struggles of a peripheral society to master problems whose sources lie hidden from view.

# Index

## A

Acadia, 139 *ff.*, 147
Adams, John Quincy, 77
Adultery, 297
Afro-Americans, *see* Blacks
Agriculture: Acadia, 140; England, 39–54; French colonies, 142, 146 *ff.*; New England, 14–19, 63, 65 *ff.*, 71 *ff.*, 94, 95, 122, 123, 127, 132, 137, 150
Albany, 32
Alcohol, in fishing towns, 113
Allegory, in Elizabethan art, 182; in Puritan art, 178–181
Allen, Joseph, 162 *n.* 2
Allerton, Isaac, 88, 89
Almanacs, 243, 250, 257, 265
American Revolution, 149
Ames, William, 162 *n.* 2; *The Marrow of Theology*, 158–159
Andover, 61
Anglican Church, 56. *See also* Church of England
Animal names, as pejoratives, 293–294
Apocalypticism, 249–252, 254 *n.* 2
Appledore, 45
Apples, 66, 72
Aristotle, 249, 258, 267, 271
Arnold, Samuel, 264
Arts, 164 *n.* 7
Ashby de la Zouch, 208
Ashmole, Elias, 154
Astrology, 249, 252, 254 *n.* 2
Asia, climate, 4 *n.* 1
Avalon, 137
Averies, Anne, 286, 301
Awdely, John, 295

## B

Bailyn, Bernard, 178
Baker, Mrs., 155

Baker, Thomas, 315 *n.* 4
Baker family, 177
Baldwin, John, 71
Baldwin, Richard, 71
Baptists, 191
Bare, John, 300
Barker, William, Jr., 267
Barn Elms, 45
Barnard, John, 115–116
Bartoll family, 108
Basques, 135, 138–139
Batley, 192–193
Batman, Stephen, *The Doome*, 245, 246, 248, 266
Bay Psalm Book, 222
Bayly, Lewis, *Practice of Piety*, 212, 225, 229; Native American edition, 231
Baynes, Paul, 196
Beard, Thomas, 245–249, 251, 253, 255, 256, 263, 264, 268, 270; *Theatre of Gods Judgements*, 244
Becon, Thomas, *The Sick Mannes Salve*, 180
Bede, 247
Bedford, 62
Belcher, Jonathan, 165 *n.* 9, 174
Belle Isle, Strait of, 135
Bellomont, Earl of, 32
Benes, Peter, 181–182
Bennett, John, 112
Berkshire (England), 61
Bernard, Richard, *Isle of Man*, 197, 228
Bible, 219 *ff.*, 248, 250, 264
Biography, colonists' interest, 164–165
Bishop, John, 262, 268
Black Death, 119, 129
Blacks, 271 *n.* 4
Blagdon Park, 44
Blasphemy, 287 *ff.*
Blood, Robert, 291
Bolton, Charles Knowles, 175–176
Bond, John, 304–305
Books, 221 *ff.*